LESSONS
OF EMPIRE

The Social Science Research Council was founded in 1923 and remains an independent, nonprofit organization. With partners around the world, the SSRC mobilizes existing and new knowledge on important public issues, fosters innovation, links research to practice and policy, strengthens individual and institutional capacities for learning, and enhances public access to information.

This book is the fifth in a series jointly published by The New Press and the SSRC designed to investigate emerging policy trends in the wake of 9/11.

Other books in the series are:

Bombs and Bandwidth

Critical Views of September 11

The Maze of Fear

Understanding September 11

LESSONS OF EMPIRE

IMPERIAL HISTORIES AND AMERICAN POWER

EDITED BY CRAIG CALHOUN,
FREDERICK COOPER,
AND KEVIN W. MOORE

PROJECT COORDINATED BY THE
SOCIAL SCIENCE RESEARCH COUNCIL

THE NEW PRESS

NEW YORK
LONDON

Requests for permission to reproduce selections from this book should be mailed to:
Permissions Department, The New Press, 38 Greene Street, New York, NY 10013

Published in the United States by The New Press, New York, 2005
Distributed by W. W. Norton & Company, Inc., New York

LIBRARY OF CONGRESS CATALOGING-IN-PUBLICATION DATA
Lessons of empire: imperial histories and American power / edited by Craig Calhoun, Frederick
Cooper, and Kevin W. Moore; project coordinated by the Social Science Research Council.
p. cm.
Includes bibliographical references and index.
ISBN-13 978-1-59558-096-2 (hc) 978-1-59558-007-8 (pbk)
ISBN-10 1-59558-096-4 (hc) 1-59558-007-7 (pbk)
1. World politics. 2. Imperialism—History. 3. Colonization—History. I. Calhoun, Craig J., 1952-
II. Cooper, Frederick, 1947- III. Moore, Kevin W. IV. Social Science Research Council (U.S.)
D32.L47 2006
325'.32'09—dc22   2005053402

The New Press was established in 1990 as a not-for-profit alternative to the large, commercial
publishing houses currently dominating the book publishing industry. The New Press operates in the
public interest rather than for private gain, and is committed to publishing, in innovative ways, works
of educational, cultural, and community value that are often deemed insufficiently profitable.

www.thenewpress.com

Composition by NK Graphics

Printed in Canada

2   4   6   8   10   9   7   5   3   1

CONTENTS

IV. EMPIRES AS INTERNATIONAL ACTORS

ACKNOWLEDGMENTS

This book started with discussion in a Social Science Research Council board meeting. "Empire" was becoming a ubiquitous theme in considerations of global change and especially of U.S. actions abroad. Many spoke of "lessons" to be drawn from the experience of empires past. But just what historical references informed the use of the term was often unclear—and when the references were clear they often seemed arbitrary. So we set out to bring together a range of scholars who could relate serious scholarship on different historical cases of empires and comparative analyses of issues of imperial power to contemporary affairs. The result was first a conference in September of 2003, and then considerable labors of revision to produce this book.

Most of all, the editors are grateful to the contributors. The scholars involved not only took time from busy schedules to write their own papers, but offered critiques of each other's work and helped in formulating more clearly the larger questions the project posed. We are grateful also for the support of the Social Science Research Council. The SSRC has over the years done more than almost any other institution to make possible the integration of historical and comparative knowledge in the service of understanding public issues. It thus supported this project long before it was ever conceived, by supporting research into political institutions and practices in specific historical contexts that is indispensable for more careful and accurate grasp of new phenomena. And of course, the SSRC also supported this project in the narrower sense of funding the conference and providing staff support in producing this book.

The Council's support had very human faces: Paul Price, the Council's editor, was indispensable in this project as in much else. He was a source of clearer thinking as well as clearer prose and he greatly reduced the number of weeks by which we missed our deadlines. Liliana Potenza took charge of all manner of organizational matters in her marvelously helpful way.

We are also grateful to the NYU Department of History, which provided space for the initial conference. And we appreciate the continuing work of our colleagues at The New Press. This is the fifth in a series of books connecting the necessary knowledge of social science to key issues in contemporary public affairs.

We hope our efforts have brought a richer and more diverse historical knowledge to bear on the question of what lessons if any can be drawn from previous experience of empire.

—CC, FC, and KM
August, 2005

LESSONS
OF EMPIRE

INTRODUCTION

Empire for a time became a quaintly antiquated word, banished from the political spectrum with the collapse of European colonial rule in Africa and Asia. Now, the word has come back. Journalists, scholars, and politicians try to come to grips with the singular power of the United States and its apparent willingness to intervene in territories generally recognized as sovereign. For the most part, empire is evoked in two opposite ways. The first might be termed "empire as epithet": the mere use of the word underscores the illegitimacy of American interventionism. The other is "empire as model" and relies on a very different image of empire, not as the arrogant exercise of power over people who are somehow different, but as the benevolent exercise of authority by those who have achieved political responsibility over those incapable of it.

Curiously, most evocations of empire do little to probe the empires that have actually existed in the course of history.[1] They often draw a single "lesson" from a complex historical context. Yet the lessons of empire do not leap from the pages of history unambiguous and uncontested. Missing are the historical trajectories—often long and convoluted—of particular empires; the relationship of empires with each other; the ways in which interactions or rulers, agents, and colonized people shaped empires; and the economic and cultural processes in which imperial formations played a part, but not necessarily a determining part. This volume brings together scholars who have studied actual empires, along with scholars of international politics who can help link that historical knowledge to the current political conjuncture.

Most current historical scholarship on empire stresses the limits of imperial power, the compromises with local and regional systems of authority, and commercial networks upon which imperial stability depends, the contradictions at the heart of efforts to use colonial power as an agent of reform.[2] Popular political writing, however, more often stresses imperial power—whether in a celebratory mode combined with calls for the United States to assume imperial leadership or in a condemnation stressing the all but unchallengeable global power of empire.[3] This suggests a possible disconnect between the lessons that participants in public debate are drawing from the concept of empire and the implications of cutting-edge research on historical empires. We asked a group of scholars who have contributed to that research to reflect on the significance of their work both for the broad study of empires across time and space and for its implications for contemporary politics. In the months since the conference on which this book is based, the importance of thinking about limits of power has become tragically evident. As previous colonizing powers learned, conquest is easier than rule. The mightiest power on earth has found its military forces extended, its budget strained, and its public bitterly divided over the administration of a territory of modest size and minimal political resources.

We have drawn on case-based knowledge to expand and situate our understanding of the current organization of American power in the world. Analogies and contrasts from studies of empire and similar arrangements of global power are central to the volume, but we do not presume that any conception of empire—whether "formal" or "informal"—exhausts the relevant frame of comparative reference. We have invited the contributors to engage questions of hegemony, nationalism, and related organizations of power as they have played out in the United States and in other "imperial" projects. In what ways, for example, is the current global power of the United States similar to or different from earlier empires? Can the differences between power, force, and hegemony be sufficiently explained by the category of empire? Is the United States in fact pursuing a classically imperial project of rule over others, whether in pursuit of a "civilizing mission" or economic exploitation? If, in contrast, the United States today represents a new form of domination, what are the international and domestic implications of this? What kinds of relationships between "home" and "colony" are coming into being? Finally, if empire is not the best way to understand the current situation, what are the alternatives?

The tendency to use empire as a metaphor, either for unlimited state power or for projects of uplift and reform, tends to blur the categories we need in order to analyze specific forms of political power. The chapters of George Steinmetz and Jack Snyder bring out some distinctions in how a powerful polity intervenes in the affairs of weaker ones. Such distinctions in forms of power might include: imperial (intervening in a polity without actually governing it), hegemonic (setting the rules of the game that others must follow), and colonial (governing internal affairs of a subordinated polity). Even as iconic an empire as that of Great Britain in the nineteenth century acted "imperial" in regard to countries in Latin America and China at the same time as it acted "colonial" in Africa. But we need to be careful about thinking of empire as something one "society" did to another, for societies have themselves been constituted out of the interplay of empires.[4] Our contemporary tendency to think of societies as well-defined, bounded, self-conscious units is misleading when projected backward—and misses a great deal of twentieth-century history.[5] Building empire around a "core" people projecting power outwards is only one part of a range of possibilities; the Ottoman, Russian (including its twentieth-century, Soviet, variant), and Austro-Hungarian empires cannot be well understood as projections of Turkish, Russian, or Germanic societies (see the chapters of Caglar Keyder and Ronald Suny).

Arriving at a precise definition of empire and debating whether such and such a situation fits it is not the only question of importance. As Ann Stoler suggests, the conditions that make plausible the use of such a term is very revealing about the nature of political debate at a particular moment. Claims *not* to be an empire are also ideologically loaded, as are claims to being a different kind of empire from anybody else, something which several contributors point out are common to many empires. Stoler and Emmanuelle Saada emphasize that older European empires saw themselves as regimes of exception, setting up different sets of laws and rules for the "colonized," giving rise to debates and uncertainty over how such systems reflected back on the legitimacy and consistency of the empire as a whole. Such considerations lead us to give attention to the ways in which regimes of exception—whether in defining a "rogue" state whose sovereignty is unworthy of respect or an "enemy combatant" unworthy of protection under American law or Geneva conventions—are defined and defended today. Perhaps the invocation of empire is a way of breaking into a set of international norms that have achieved generalized support over the past decades on the universality of sovereignty and respect for rules of international conduct. Empire talk reframes issues on the basis of hierarchical distinctions between states and peoples who merit sovereignty and self-determination and those who do not.

At the same time, recognizing the importance of regimes of exception gives rise to concerns that they may not be so exceptional. Some contributors to this volume—Sanjay Subrahmanyam, Craig Murphy, and Stoler for instance—express concerns that the effects of imperious behavior abroad can come home, fostering intolerance and xenophobia.

But if the present use of the term is worth pondering, regardless of its accuracy in regard to contemporary politics, thinking about historical empires also helps us understand alternative forms of political power, their trajectories, and their consequences. We can set out a family description of "empire," if not a precise definition: a political unit that is large and expansionist (or with memories of an expansionist past), reproducing differentiation and inequality among people it incorporates. Empire could be a phase in a polity, for if incorporation ceased to entail differentiation, it could result in a relatively homogeneous polity that becomes more nation-like and less empire-like. Uniformity could reflect assimilation, imposed or otherwise, or extermination. The manner in which distinction is institutionalized is crucial to empire building, and the difficulties of presiding over a polity that was both incorporative and differentiating shaped the policy choices made by the rulers of empire.

While our contributors apply the analytic insights that arise from the study of particular empires, or particular political/historical situations, to the United States's role in the world today, we also wish to historicize the very idea of "American empire" and stress that questions of whether or not the United States is an empire have been with us for a very long time. Any exploration of America's alleged "new" empire, therefore, should recall that there truly was (and to a considerable extent still is) an "old" American empire. There is a reason the "Marine Hymn" rings out "from the Halls of Montezuma to the Shores of Tripoli." The United States did not join in the European "race for Africa" (though it did create a quasi-imperial dependency in Liberia). But, as Julian Go argues herein, the United States was active in acquiring overseas territories during the late nineteenth and early twentieth centuries and ran into—in the Philippines, the Pacific Islands, and Puerto Rico—the dilemmas of rule that other conquering powers at the time faced. The tutelary ideology on which the architects of American empire drew in the Philippines and elsewhere has much in common with mantras of "commerce, civilization, and Christianity" in the British empire or the "civilizing mission" in the French, as well as in claims to be spreading democracy and the free market today. During the same period as its overseas colonizations, the United States was also active in ways reminiscent of the "imperialism of free trade" that scholars have used to describe British policy before the late nineteenth century: efforts to open ports and secure free trade, and also to secure positions of power amid the empires of others.[6] The "opening" of Japan and the insistence on rights to trade in Hong Kong and China stood alongside the conquest of the Philippines; it would be misleading to think of the United States as always a "national," rather than an "imperial," power, simply committed to open access to markets. Closer to the mainland itself, the United States has variously treated Cuba as occupied territory, a place to subordinate without governing, and as an autonomous—but enemy—state.

These examples of overseas acquisitions and interventions leave out the most dramatic extensions of U.S. imperial power, namely those on the North American continent itself. The United States did not simply "expand" westward. It ruled for varying lengths of time territories and populations it did not immediately seek to integrate into a common national framework. It fought Mexico to determine whose imperium would incorporate what has now become the U.S. Southwest. It ruled Native American populations as what the Supreme Court in 1831 called "domestic dependent nations."[7] It acquired imperial domains by purchase, from Louisiana to Alaska, as well as by war. Acquisition of Hawaii was precipitated by nongovernmental mission and commercial activity.[8]

If the "American empire" turns out to be a question with a past, the current object of American attention—Iraq—has an imperial past as well. In some ways, a study of empires throughout history might well be entitled "Empire: From Iraq to Iraq," for among the earliest imperial formations were those that developed in ancient times along the Tigris and Euphrates rivers. Iraq, in short, has never been a pristine nation that is now experiencing intrusion on its sovereignty. The more recent past of the region included incorporation into the Ottoman Empire. In World War I, Ottoman forces in this space gave British invaders a fight they had not expected. The dismantling of the Ottoman Empire—along with that of the Habsburgs—only in some places gave rise to nation-states (with disastrous enough results in Central Europe), but the Middle East remained firmly within systems of imperial domination, and was given a tutelary, international imprimatur by the mandate system. Iraq became a British dependency. What followed was a typical empire story: a regional rebellion (tribal, it was called at the time, as such things sometimes are today) in Mesopotamia took place, and the British government was as usual trying to govern "on a shoestring."[9] But it had new technological means to do so: airpower. The repression of the Mesopotamian revolt was one of the earliest testing grounds for the use of bombing against an indigenous insurgency. It was cruelly effective—a few bombs could terrorize a village—and the rebellion was put down. But the episode revealed the limits of this configuration of new weaponry with the old imperial strategy of concentrating force, terrorizing a population into submission, and moving on. The ability of the British government to conduct routine administration was minimal; dropping bombs from the air reflected just how unsystematic empire was on the ground.[10] Soon, British strategy moved to finding a suitable client-ruler to take on the complex tasks of administering a heterogeneous population that Britain had ruled without considering it to be British: they found one among the Hashemites, whose Iraqi connections were tenuous, but could at least be passed off as from the region.

What is most important about this empire story is who remembers it and who ignores it. As Rashid Khalidi has pointed out, memories of empire are acute in the Middle East. People have witnessed many attempts by Europeans to pacify, civilize, and liberate them, and—as in Iraq—the assertions are hard to separate from the violence that was experienced with great immediacy.[11] Juan Cole's chapter in this volume describes three such episodes, the last of which is the present one. The absence of the Ottoman and British experiences from discussion of the American invasion of Iraq reveals the dangers of not using past experience of actual, historical invasion, occupation, and imperial rule in order to delineate, at the least, possible scenarios and contingencies. The past has indeed repeated itself, from "tribal" rebellions to the terror of air attacks.

EMPIRES, NATIONS, AND NATION-STATES

Such stories should be part of contemporary discussions of epochal transformation, crises of the state, and prospects for cosmopolitanism global order. During the 1990s it became commonplace to assert the end of the "post-Westphalian era" or the arrival of a "postnational constellation." The historical referents for this were illusory, however. After all, the Treaty of Westphalia signed at the end of the Thirty Years' War in 1648 did not usher in thirty years of peace and harmony, or even order, any more than the Wilsonian idea of self-determination gave the nation-state a secure place in Central Europe, let alone in European colonies.

Sovereignty has been a relative concept for a long time. Protectorates, such as Morocco and Tunisia until the mid-1950s, had their own nationality and their own "rulers" under imperial overrule; Egypt was at times under Ottoman rule, at times under British, and at times an independent state that did not, truly, rule itself. Iraq was a mandate until 1932, but hardly autonomous afterward. Client states and proxy wars characterized the cold-war era. All this implies that any search for precedents for understanding policy today should take into account what the precedents actually are, not fall into an artificial dichotomy of pure sovereignty and pure domination. The precedents, at the same time, existed in context, and just as struggles in the 1950s over the status of a protectorate like Morocco took place in relation to a field of anticolonial mobilizations, the loss of legitimacy of both these forms of domination reshaped options for the future, as did the reconfiguration of international politics through different kinds of multilateral organizations and the formation of new forms of sovereignty-compromising institutions like the European Union. Our case studies here can hardly draw out the policy implications of different sovereignty regimes, but they can at least suggest the importance of posing such questions with precision and attention to context, rather than abstracting singular lessons from a decontextualized past.

Following the trajectories of a number of imperial histories—however small a portion of the spectrum we have touched upon in this volume—points to the difficulty of seeing history, whether since Westphalia, the French Revolution, or the North and South American revolutions, as a teleology of "from empire to nation." It makes more sense to say that the nation-state *project* became *available* and increasingly prominent in both domestic and "international" affairs at some point after the seventeenth and eighteenth centuries. Claims were made in the name of the nation—for political voice, for autonomy, for resources. Some elites sought to align territory, economy, government, and culture. The alignments were never perfect and to the extent achieved were the products of both material and symbolic violence as well as of new systems of communications and transport, access to common education, vernacular language literatures, and mass participation in public affairs. Not only did empire coexist with nation throughout this period, but the existence of an "order" based on the sovereignty of states—national and imperial—was a fiction that enabled the construction of certain alliances, practices, and organizations.[12] That it was not simply a description is signaled by the violence, war, and disorder that followed Westphalia.

Conflicts were shaped in more ways than by the opposition of nation-state and empire. British and French conceptions of political order were shaped imperially, not just nationally.[13] The revolutions of North and South America were contests *within* empire—about the rules of membership—before they were struggles against empire.[14] The Haitian revolution also began as an attempt to redefine the French empire, as white planters, mixed-race property owners, and eventually slaves fought over the question of whether the rights of man and of the citizen would apply to a national, European France, or to an imperial, diverse, transcontinental France. Both the French revolutionary government and the Haitian rebels were operating in the space of empire; and as the latter evoked revolutionary principles, the former geared its own strategies around the reconfiguration of the rules of incorporation and differentiation, promising emancipation and citizenship for a time to colonial slaves, a policy reversed under a different vision of empire instituted by Napoleon.[15] The Napoleonic episode in turn was not a simple extension of France into Europe, but a remaking of France in the context of empire—a complex combination of different alliances with regional aristocracies or regional opponents of local aristocracies, a system of administration based on different rules for different places, and on harnessing populations in new and old territories to a war machine based on conscription.

The Napoleonic Wars may have stimulated various nationalist projects in Europe. Napoleon was defeated not by nation-states, however, but by other empires, notably Russia and Britain, both of whom drew on supranational resources. Just how one is to balance the tendencies within European states to draw on national ideas and reinforce national institutions, and how much they remained supranational, differentiated polities can be fruitfully debated. But the supranational forces of the major powers, from colonies, dominions, and protectorates overseas and from alliances and dynastic affiliations within Europe, were still horrendously in play in 1914, and the Great War hardly resolved the relationship of national and supranational political systems. Even after World War II, France kept trying to redefine itself as something other than a European nation-state—as the French Union (1946), and then as the French Community (1958). And opposition to this variously projected entity was as much focused on making citizenship real within Greater France as on exiting from it.[16]

While one could argue that empires were cosmopolitan and therefore good and nation-states were exclusionary and therefore bad, or that empires institutionalized racism and nation-states institutionalized self-determination and citizen participation in a polity, such arguments would be an oversimplification of a much more complex reality. The objective of these papers, therefore, is to bring out different forms of political organization and political imagination, and to enlarge our perspective on the forms of rule and the forms of contestation of rule that existed within imperial formations.

One is struck, when reading the accounts of empires past collected here, by the sheer durability of empires as political formations, compared to the relatively short time span in which the nation-state was the modal form of politics. The world of individual, sovereign nation-states dates only to the 1960s; until then nation-states were one of several forms of polity. It is only in hindsight that the inevitability of the world of nominally self-determining nations appears as such. The world of empires, in contrast, goes back over two millennia. A series of empires dominated China for most of that time, up to 1911; the Ottoman Empire lasted from the fourteenth to the twentieth centuries, and the Russian nearly as long. The distinction of nation from empire is not merely a neutral description of contrasting institutional forms. It is an ideologically charged political contrast. And it is informed by different implicit and explicit empirical examples. Indeed, as Sheldon Pollock notes in this volume, empires exist in a community of interpretation. One of the most important lineages of such interpretation considers Egypt, Alexandrine Hellas, Rome and then its split of East and West. This yielded Byzantium, which in turn gave way to the Ottoman Empire, whose emergence also came out of a world of steppe empires—the different Mongol empires—which shaped as well the rise of Russia and whose offshoots imposed dynasties on China. The Ottoman Empire took up a Mediterranean space which had been pioneered by Rome, and it was also influenced by the Persian Empire (which itself had roots back to struggles with Greece even before Alexander) and operated in an Islamic milieu that grew out of the early caliphates. After its conquest of Mecca and Medina, it took up the mantle of the caliphate itself—a claim which carried much weight until the destruction of the Ottoman Empire after World War I, a loss which still carries symbolic weight among many Muslims today.

Mughal India also traced roots to the Mongols and to Persia but also understood itself in relation to imperial complexes and successions in western and southern Asia (as evoked by Sheldon Pollock in this volume). And if the Holy Roman Empire was less exemplary in the West than its eastern counterparts, it was still part of a series that was linked to Spanish, Austro-Hungarian, Portuguese, French, British, and Prussian empires. Napoleon could see himself as both a direct inheritor of Charlemagne and the creator of a latter-day Roman empire, and even Republican empires—in Britain as well as France—looked back to Rome as they developed visions of what amounted to good imperial rule.

China, as Bin Wong makes clear, was one of the world's largest and most centralized polities, but the success of its rulers in creating and re-creating a series of imperial regimes within a vast space owed much to their sense of the limits of how far they could go in relation to local social practices and local elites. China—in both national ideology and much of western scholarship—is sometimes portrayed as a unique sort of polity, steeped in a set of traditions far more homogeneous than those of most empires. But more recent scholarship—such as that of Mark Elliott and Peter Perdue[17]—has brought Chinese history into dialogue with other empire stories, stressing not only the way dynasties of foreign origin—the Yuan of the thirteenth and fourteenth centuries and the Qing of the seventeenth to the twentieth—adapted to forms of bureaucracy and imperial ideology of older Chinese empires, but the way in which these rulers maintained their distinctiveness as a means of fostering coherence and authority among themselves. China's relations with its periphery—including areas of conquest and tributary states—as well as to the shifting political and commercial patterns in the rest of East and Southeast Asia and the back-and-forth commerce along the Silk Road and across the Indian Ocean tie it into the dynamics of imperial formations in western Eurasia and Europe.

The work of Sanjay Subrahmanyam (this volume) and Christopher Bayly in turn suggests that Portuguese and British empires were shaped by their interactions with the polities around the Indian Ocean.[18] We start to get a picture of world political history that looks rather different from that coming from the North Atlantic perspective that has been so dominant among English-speaking historians. Empire history suggests not the evolution of bounded societies that can be compared, but the consolidation and dissolution of structures of power in relation to each other—a pattern still relevant today.

Our case studies thus not only multiply the examples and reveal the durability of the empire form of a polity, but provide a basis for thinking about interactions among different sorts of political entities. Nation-states are neither wholly distinct from empires nor supplant them completely. Political mobilization—from the top (imperial reformers in the nineteenth-century Ottoman Empire, as Keyder shows) or from the bottom (the Haitain revolutionaries)—showed that political imagination often took up the spatial configuration and ideological framework of imperial regimes and tried to turn them into something that was different but still imperial. At the very end of the French Empire, some African political leaders were still trying to turn the empire into a federal system, and when France itself took the initiative to devolve power to self-governing individual territories, Léopold Senghor lamented the loss of the federal option as the "balkanization" of Africa, an interempire analogy that used the consequences of the breakup of Ottoman and Austro-Hungarian empires to make a point of the dangers which he feared from making national territories the only unit of governance.[19]

Supranational politics is thus neither new nor part of a sequence of change from empire to nation to some kind of postnational global configuration. Activists across borders, to use the phrase of Margaret Keck and Kathryn Sikkink, are operating today in a specific political conjuncture—whether their focus is issues of poverty, gender discrimination, health, or war and peace—but they are also the inheritors of a wide range of movements that brought together people across lines of geography and cultural difference.[20] Nor does al-Qaeda represent a wholly new form of cross-border organization, for the extension of empires across land and sea was accompanied by the growth of networks of traders, proselytizers, pirates, and others, who sometimes interacted with state-centered imperial institutions, sometimes fought against them, and sometimes cut across them.[21]

At the same time, moving "beyond the nation-state"—in the present as in the past—does not mean moving into an era of easy cosmopolitan democracy or shared sense of the "global." Such thought, flourishing in the 1990s, overestimated the extent to which economic interaction was mirrored by effective capacities for "subaltern" forces to mobilize across national boundaries, and it overestimated the capacities for effective action available to most individuals outside a fairly narrow cosmopolitan elite.[22] It almost certainly underestimated the extent to which states still mattered. It also underestimated the extent to which a decline in state capacities in some places would be an invitation to powerful states elsewhere to attempt to remake the world in their own interests, as well as the vulnerability of the United Nations to clashes among states, some projecting imperial might and others protecting more specifically national interests and projects.

But abjuring an easy cosmopolitanism or facile arguments for the submergence of states beneath a vaguely specified globality[23] should not derail more complex considerations of cosmopolitan ideologies and political connections. Pollock finds ancient precedents by contrasting different patterns of cultural imposition, tolerance, and mixing in earlier empires. The chapters of Snyder and Kelly most explicitly—and the others implicitly—urge us to think not just in terms of a dichotomy between sovereign and equivalent nation-states on the one hand and forms of dominance (empire, imperialism, hegemony) on the other, but to look at forms of institutionalized cooperation and transnational networks.

CONTEMPORARY IMPLICATIONS

The authors of our chapters are skeptical toward assertions that the situation we face today is wholly new and unprecedented, but they do not hold that it is the same old story repeated again. The implication is instead that in assessing the present conjuncture one needs to be precise about what is new and old, what is ephemeral and durable. Our most cherished images of ourselves—as with the nation-state—may well be a blip on a longer historical horizon.

What empires have been able to do, and the distinctive ways in which imperial projects go wrong, are important questions that take us from historical examples into contemporary debates. In addition to scholars of empire, we therefore included in this project a number of noted international relations specialists to help us think through the relationship between older imperial systems of rule and other forms of global power. Their work encourages us to ask whether the post–World War II dismantling of the European colonial system in Africa and South Asia and the corresponding rise of nationalism in those parts of the world, for example, fundamentally change the manner in which western powers behave toward less powerful countries in the global South. Has the Bretton Woods system of international financial institutions dominated by the World Bank and the International Monetary Fund so altered economic and political relations between rich and poor countries that it no longer makes sense to speak of an "empire" in which one powerful country—the United States—can act unilaterally with respect to another? Or, alternatively, is the post–World War II system of multilateral western "hegemony" giving way to a unipolar world that forces us back to the old concepts of empire or else a different formulation of extreme asymmetry in power relations?

Current global projections of U.S. power certainly unsettle both the relative autonomy of other states and the functioning of structures of multilateral relations. But this doesn't automatically make it political empire. In the first place, the United States seems clearly engaged in promoting a version of economic "globalization" that still relies on states. Globalization is ideologically presented as a sort of inexorable natural development, but of course it is in fact made possible by specific institutional structures that give it specific shape and consequences—including dramatic inequality. And as the United States seeks to put "suitable" new structures in place, it creates a situation—notably in Iraq—that unwittingly resembles in some ways the late "decolonization" or "developmental" phase of the great European empires, as Frederick Cooper discusses in his contribution to this volume. When France and Great Britain—after years of refusing to spend domestic resources on colonial development—finally got serious about such a task in the 1940s and 1950s, they quickly found that the costs of such an effort were more than domestic voters would tolerate. In the current moment, the political necessity of an exit is ahead of the strategy to get to one.

The economic dimensions of the current global situation cannot be overestimated. Yet to say that an empire, a unipolar power, or a global hegemon serves the interests of capital may reveal less than at first appears. Jomo K. S. and George Steinmetz both argue for conceptions of political economy that recognize new tendencies without positing a polarity between contempory "globalization" and past "imperialism." Capital has long had an ambiguous relationship to empire: needing state protection across distance at crucial moments, unwilling to pay the costs of maintaining imperial structures in others. It may be the case that political systems in our era have to serve the interests of capital to survive and meet other goals—without that requirement itself determining the choice of political systems. It would be more helpful, as Steinmetz suggests in this volume, to ask whether changes in the global capitalist structure (such as the accumulation regime he discusses) affect the timing of changes and forms of articulation among states, corporations, international bodies, and other actors.

Empires are located and spatially organized. They were not tight containers of economic processes, even if old trading companies tried to keep out "interlopers" and overseas empires at times deployed mercantilist strategies of favoring trade within the imperial unit. In some circumstances, their rulers sought to demarcate territory, but in others, as Stoler points out, the ambiguity of people's relationship to territory was crucial to strategies of control over earth-spanning structures. Some empires had clear and singular centers (Rome), and some did not (the Mongols). Some organized clear-cut boundaries, some not. Some were spatially contiguous, some not. But, as John Kelly stresses, the objects of rule include not only territories and trade but populations, and the process of rule has often produced complications and conflicts and run up against limits that have affected the possibilities of organizing production and exchange.

In the present conjuncture, it is arguable that what are often called the imperial projects of the United States are less efforts to extend political rule internationally than efforts to "manage" global affairs. The United States shows little inclination to make enduring commitments to Afghanistan or Iraq. Rather, each intervention seems to reflect a managerial orientation toward threats and emergencies. In such an analysis, the primary focus in each case is containment of potential damage to U.S. interests. But each intervention also pursues a longer-term agenda of restructuring local and regional relations in a way that will allow for the trade relations in which the United States is hegemonic but do not require enduring U.S. rule. They may serve the interests of capital at the same time. But it is worth noting that this managerial orientation towards international affairs is not at all unique to the U.S. government. It is shared with many other states and indeed with much of the global NGO community (including parts actively hostile to the Bush administration and American power). Humanitarian interventions may be much more attractive than preemptive wars, but they share this managerial orientation.[24]

Craig Murphy points to the contradictory tendencies within recent American policy—toward using power unilaterally and toward pushing a global order, with its attendant regulatory system, which allows capital to circulate freely and with the protections and legal guarantees it needs. Caglar Keyder fears that a new legal order—not just unilateral, coercive interventions—could suppress the specificity of local ways of regulating social life, just as Ottoman constitutionalism in the late nineteenth century undermined the legal pluralism of the earlier empire in regard to the different collectivities it embraced. Yet just as in the Ottoman Empire of the late nineteenth century, empirewide projects of reform were mediated through the relationships of Istanbul with provincial elites, the relationship of place, power, and market in today's world is complex and contested.[25] Iraq and Afghanistan are two places where coercive intervention reveals the limits of economic regulatory regimes and global capital flows. Much of Africa is a no-go area for capital, except in predatory and limited forms; the investor in Russia is well advised to have good relations with local mafias; and in China the state is a highly visible economic actor.

Once again, the lessons of studying past empires reinforce a cautious attitude toward claims made about the present. Coercive intervention can be a sign that economic and political systems are less systematic than we think. Empire builders are not the only actors involved. Not just resistance to conquest or nationalist mobilization, but quiet efforts to find alternatives to colonial institutions, to forge alternative commercial linkages, and to turn missionary teachings and ideologies of civilization and modernity into claims upon resources have repeatedly frustrated empire builders. Emperors do not necessarily get their way. Nor do presidents or CEOs.

Perhaps the most constructive aspect of the revival of empire talk in the last few years has been to force attention onto the issue of how one conceptualizes different modes of exercising power across space. But the lesson of such an examination may well be that what we need to do is not so much to extract parallels and explore analogies with past empires as to think more clearly about power *after* empire, when for the first time in world history this form is excluded from the realistic policy options. We have for some decades lived an illusion—the normalcy of nation-states, each of which is encased in its sovereignty in relation to other states equivalently constituted, like billiard balls bouncing off each other. This model has been projected backward—to Westphalia, to the French Revolution, to the Creole revolutions of the turn of the nineteenth century—but the nation-state form has actually been generalized for only a brief period of history, when the African and Asian empires fell apart in the 1960s—with hangovers extending to the 1970s in Portuguese Africa and in different ways to the Soviet Union, Eastern Europe, and South Africa in the 1990s. The empire form has not only been around for a long time, but it proved adaptable to the development of capitalism and communism as well, to changing technologies of warfare and new concepts of authority, as well as to reconfigurations of the relationship of land and sea, of contiguous territory and long-distance communications.

But if examining different empires might suggest more differences than parallels with current politics, the exercise opens up a variety of useful perspectives on the diversity of political forms, on the extent of connections across borders, on the complexity of on-the-ground interactions, even in the face of inequalities of power. At the heart of historical empires was not just occupation of territory but the incorporation of people—not as equivalents of others but nonetheless as members of a polity in which the exit option was sharply curtailed. Focusing on this essential dimension of historical empires underscores what is no longer in the political repertoire. It is far from clear that either sentimental evocation of a British empire or fearful evocations of the arrogance of the conqueror tells us much about the constraints or possibilities that a superpower faces today. Understanding what is out of the realm of imagination should help us focus on the spectrum of possibilities that actually exist, from unilaterialist to multilateralist interventions, from forms of shared sovereignty—as the European Union has become and the African Union might one day be—to international agreements set out in certain areas. If the essays in this book help to make clear what, historically, empires have and have not been, perhaps this will call attention to thinking with more precision about what options exist today and what do not.

At the same time, thinking about historic empires tells us something about power at its most extreme, something that may bear consideration in relation to claims being made about the potentials for good and evil in contemporary international politics. Most of the chapters in this collection have drawn attention to the limits of the most powerful empires, and indeed they have suggested—in regard to the long-lasting dynasties of China or the self-consciously modernizing empires of France or Britain, or the multinational Ottoman and Russian polities—that awareness of limits was one of the bases of imperial survival. The empire form itself entails limits by virtue of the distance and the diversity it embraces: the durability of empires has to a very large extent reposed on the ability to manage intermediaries, keeping agents traveling along circuits of empire and co-opting incorporated elites into at least a measure of self-interested affiliation. Empires have failed when other empires or other forms of long-distance connection eroded an imperial center's role in directing circuits of people, goods, and capital, not just when more localized— "national," "indigenous"—forms of affinity gave rise to solidaristic movements. Historical research has been particularly revealing on this point: empires have been made and unmade on the ground, in the formation and deformation of networks, in the alignment of previous trading routes and circuits of intellectuals.

The American occupation of Iraq is hardly the first occasion when conquest was the easiest part of the occupation of territory. Understanding the experience of empires from Babylonia to British East Africa might have suggested the importance of understanding how crucial the on-the-ground encounters are in shaping the possibilities of imperial control. The resurgence of guerilla activity after an apparent military victory, the complexity of cleavages within Iraqi society, the difficulty of an occupying army in securing plausible and cooperative elite cooperation, and even the grudging accommodation of much of Iraqi society are familiar subjects to students of empire. So too is the process of creeping colonization: the way in which limited objectives of conquerors have brought them into deeper involvement with the details of running a society: from administering justice among different members of the conquered society to building and maintaining a physical and social infrastructure. Once occupation—even without intention of long-term incorporation—is hitched to projects of societal reform, the possibility of creeping colonization opens wider, and the maintenance of empire on the cheap becomes more difficult to maintain. Numerous powers have tried to make empires into spaces of submission—laboratories for social experiments, sites where people could be made to work in ways that would be indefensible "at home," putty to be molded into something called "modernity" or "democracy." But empire space has not proven to be so tractable, and empires which did not appreciate the limits within which their projects could be developed suffered both challenges within colonial space and political movements that crossed divides between continents.

Lastly, thinking about empires helps us to analyze in subtle ways the long-term importance of cosmopolitanism and multiculturalism—two words used more often than they are examined. Empires were both coercive and heterogeneous. Day by day, politics was about managing, reconfiguring, and at times opposing this forced mixture. The ending of empires, as Rogers Brubaker aptly put it in regard to Eastern Europe, entailed the unmixing of people—a process at least as violent as their mixing had been.[26] If empires fostered myths of civilizational hierarchy, unmixing fosters myths of authenticity. In some former colonies, ideas of authenticity and indigeneity have served as rationales for local authoritarianism, while in some former metropoles the political energy once devoted to keeping conquered people inside the empire now goes to keeping their descendants out of the nation-state.

The value of thinking about the history of empires is not to re-create them, to treat them as models, or to use them as epithets. It is to recognize that the lessons of empire are plural and complex and that examining the specificity of contexts and the importance of trajectories helps us to appreciate the importance of thinking clearly about what is and what is not possible in the present conjuncture and about the importance of anticipating the consequences of whatever actions we take.

PART I

LESSONS OF EMPIRE

1. THE NEW IMPERIALISTS

MATTHEW CONNELLY

Scholars of empire have to ask themselves why, after several decades of research and teaching, almost all of it critical of imperialism and its legacies, we seem not to have had the slightest impact. For the first time in a century, proposals for a self-professed American empire are receiving serious and respectful attention. And rather than vigorously opposing such a project, academics are either wrong-footed or tongue-tied. Having habitually called U.S. foreign policy imperialist as a way to impugn its legitimacy, commentators on the left hardly know how to respond to this new atavism. As for full-time historians of empire, while contemptuous of the new imperialists' shoddy scholarship and intellectual dishonesty, they have hesitated to join a debate over the lessons of history for fear that it will merely provide a more usable past for a new generation of imperialists.

What is at stake in all the talk of empire is not whether America will acknowledge imperial ambitions and set about permanently occupying foreign lands. Bush has already disavowed the very idea and proclaimed that America works in the service of freedom. New imperialists like Niall Ferguson and Max Boot play the useful, if unacknowledged, role of providing a foil against which an administration that recognizes no limits to its actions abroad can appear moderate by comparison. If their opponents insist on crashing through a door now held wide open, they risk finding themselves in a sterile and self-contained debate about whether empires can ever be good. To the extent that anyone listens, it will only distract attention from the real business at hand.

Regardless of how it is justified or achieved, imperialism is the pursuit of unaccountable power. That is why it is corrupting and must be opposed. Historians can contribute by showing how, contrary to the new imperialists' portrayals, such power has often worked without the burden of territorial administration, through more informal means and on the cheap. And they can remind us how empires are often in denial. The British "Commonwealth," the French "Union" and "Community," and many more besides, claimed that they were different from all the rest—above all because they were the only ones that ever advanced universal values and unselfishly served humanity. The question is whether Americans will now fall prey to such delusions, and the answer may turn on what they understand of history—not merely the record of Britain, but of the many other imperial adventures, including their own.

This essay seeks to explain why imperialism has become fashionable by focusing on some of its most prominent proponents—including avowed imperialists such as Ferguson and Boot, as well as those like Antonio Negri and Michael Hardt who use imperial metaphors to describe the promise of a new transnational system. There is a long and honorable tradition of scholars drawing inspiration from the exercise of American power to offer new interpretations of imperialism. But the aforementioned authors are making a political rather than an intellectual intervention, and this analysis will therefore examine how it works politically. It will agree with other contributors that a new American empire in the classic mold is implausible, though pernicious misreadings of history can do tremendous damage before that particular lesson is relearned. For several decades powerful states have increasingly preferred to work in concert with international and nongovernmental organizations to create untrammeled power in particular domains, whether failed states or policy areas like population control. The vogue for empire may distract us from that more fundamental trend, and this essay will conclude by suggesting how we can—and must—come to grips with it.

I

How is it that empire was transformed from a term of abuse into an inspiration for reimagining America's world role? Most explanations begin by recounting America's recent martial exploits, the extent of its overseas base system, and its dominance of the seas, air, and cyberspace. Experts are quoted showing appropriate shock and awe. But the Pentagon's supremacy over all prospective competitors was no less apparent after the first Gulf War a decade ago, when the United States deployed even more aircraft carriers, air wings, and armored and infantry divisions. And at that time there were many more countries eager to collaborate, fewer declared adversaries, and barely an inkling of America's vulnerability to asymmetrical strategies.

If the first Gulf War did not inaugurate a new age of empire, it did reveal the public's appetite for the display of American military power. In the intervening years, an enormous market developed for television programs showcasing U.S. tactics and technology. Every new war now unleashes a ratings blitz to surpass the Olympics, with embedded reporters conducting onfield interviews and retired generals offering color commentary. For many, clutching their remote controls late into the night, meditating on U.S. preeminence is a guilty pleasure. Hearing America compared to Rome and imperial Britain—only bigger, and better!—adds gravitas, in the same way sports fans like to make comparisons to the greatest of years gone by. It is as if ESPN and the Discovery and History Channels could all be experienced at the same time.

Yet for some, raising the possibility that American power has become imperial is heard as a summons to a higher calling. For those eager to serve, good fun becomes high seriousness, as the fate of nations hangs in the balance. Even opponents, such as a shadowy new organization called the Committee for the Republic, seem eager to do battle. "The American Revolution was a nationalist revolt against the British Empire," its draft manifesto proclaims. "Our country was born as a defiant rejection of the legitimacy of imperialism."[1] Postcolonial theorists in academia have long imagined themselves to be engaged in a lonely, heroic resistance to empire and its legacies. But it is curious how many reach for imperial adjectives to add sex appeal to otherwise abstruse ruminations on race, class, and gender, such as *Imperial Leather* and *Knowledge and the Fantasy of Empire.* Certain of these works, such as Malek Alloula's *The Colonial Harem,* border on the pornographic in their determination to shock and titillate.[2]

Empire, in other words, has always had its pleasures, with the capacity both to amuse and instruct. All of the new imperialists understand that, and they cultivate and cater to the "pleasurable sentiment of Power," as it was once described to Britons applying to join the Raj. Boot's history of America's "imperial wars" promises "fascinating stories—tales of blunders and bravery, low cunning and high strategy, nobility and savagery—involving forgotten heroes of American history," such as "Fighting Fred" Funston and Smedley Butler. He invites a new generation of Americans to imagine themselves dressed in jodhpurs and pith helmets. Ferguson's account of the British Empire—to which he deems America the only apparent heir, however unworthy—was actually written to accompany a television series, with the wide margins and full-color illustrations of a coffee-table book. He too serves up the savagery and swoons over the more picturesque aspects of empire. "It would take a very hard-hearted anti-imperialist not to be moved by the sight of the changing of the guard at what is now the President's Palace," he declares on seeing the New Delhi designed by Edwin Lutyens, "as the great towers and domes glow in the hazy rays of dawn."[3]

Antonio Negri and Michael Hardt would appear to be just such hard-hearted anti-imperialists, purveying 413 pages of platitudes and pronunciamentos. Thus, we are assured that "the U.S. Constitution has remained more or less unchanged (except for a few extremely important amendments)," and that "the processes of ontological constitution unfold through the collective movements of cooperation, across the new fabrics woven by the production of subjectivity." Reviewers have held up such passages for ridicule. But one suspects this only bolsters the pride of those who read them as a rite of passage, strive to free the inner logic tortured and imprisoned therein, and thus share the authors' "irrepressible lightness and joy of being communist." Hardt and Negri intended their work as a manifesto for what they call, unhelpfully, "the multitude," who are meant to realize the liberating potential created by the decline of state sovereignty. But they, no less than Boot and Ferguson, believe that there is a new empire that already encompasses the globe, policed by American power, and that this development is both positive and inevitable.[4]

If there is a reason, and not merely an excuse, to consider the United States as an imperial power, it is because it requires that we ponder the world and our place in it, and begin to think more analytically, comparatively, and historically. First, thinking about empire is a way to think about power: what it is, how it works, and what it can and cannot do. This is not usually how Americans think about foreign policy, when they think of it at all. From Wilson to Roosevelt to Reagan to Bush, presidents have had to make extravagant promises of a New—and better—World Order to mobilize latent American power to meet threats abroad. After the Gulf War, this cultivated innocence was replaced not just by disappointment but a profound indifference. Network coverage of world news fell to less than a third of its cold-war peak and nearly vanished from most newspapers.[5] With intelligence budgets contracting, the CIA closed stations across Africa. As many as half of congressmen were said to lack a valid passport. During the 1996 Clinton-Dole presidential debate, the moderator almost had to beg the audience to ask even a single question about foreign policy. But national security seemed free and easy. It was health care that was expensive and uncertain.

September 11th brought palpable proof that power in itself does not guarantee security and can actually provoke new threats. Not since the Vietnam War has there been such a broad constituency for an activist and muscular foreign policy. Indeed, it is not just terrorism, but Americans' new consciousness of their collective power and their failure to prepare for the day when they would really have to use it that is feeding a pervasive insecurity. It can be measured by the number of flags waving from porches and pinned to lapels. Confronted with the possibility of empire, Americans now have to think harder about what those flags stand for.

And if it is indeed the case that there is no "peer competitor"—according to the Pentagon's lexicon—with which to compare American power, then we have no place to turn but history. History provides answers not just to such questions as "who's bigger," but to the more important question of how other great powers have sought to reorder the world, and with what results. Moreover, history reveals how Americans themselves have long grappled with the temptations of empire. History will not, alas, tell us what we should do now. It does not have all the answers, but it can at least prompt better questions.

II

Ironically, much of what we know about the history of empires was shaped by the example of American power. The authors of nearly every one of the more important theories of imperialism still in use today had the United States very much in mind when they were trying to explain Europe's long reign over the rest of the world. At their zenith, the European empires controlled almost half of the population and land mass of the globe. Yet for Ronald Robinson and John Gallagher, writing in the 1950s, when much of the world's map was still colored red as Her Majesty's Treasury bled white, imperial power could not be measured by its footprint. They were more impressed by the way nineteenth-century Britons exported capital and opened overseas markets without having to rule over new territories and subject populations. (Until the scramble for Africa, India was a mistake not to be repeated). This "imperialism of free trade" only required cooperative local rulers and the occasional display of firepower before the recalcitrant. Britain's global network of naval bases and entrepôts was but a volcanic archipelago compared to the massive "informal empire" seething beneath the surface. Formal rule was imposed only when imperial rivals intruded and local crises erupted.[6]

When Robinson and Gallagher were writing during the early cold war, Britain was America's most important overseas base, its unsinkable aircraft carrier. Labour and Tory leaders alike depended on U.S. protection and economic support if they were to retain what remained of their empire. Like African "subimperialists" of a century before, the bargain required that they provide access to markets and local stability. Reading Robinson and Gallagher's classic description of "the spirit of Victorian expansion," one cannot help but think of their American contemporaries—the Marshall Plan administrators, the Rotarians, the multinational executives—equally inspired by a moral duty both to do good and do well.[7]

In the 1960s a darker vision began to haunt the "world systems" theorists. They argued that Europeans started to expand outward half a millennium ago to hold the rest of the world in thrall. According to this view, a small core of industrializing nations enriched itself with raw materials at the expense of the periphery, permanently retarding its development. Authors like André Gunder Frank were first inspired by the contemporary example of Latin America, where the United States had assumed a neocolonial role in maintaining client regimes. For Frank, underdevelopment was not a condition, but a process.[8]

In the 1970s Edward Said was more interested in how imperialism colonized minds, dividing the world into discrete categories of civilized and savages, West and East, "us" and "them." For Said, orientalism was not just a field of scholarship that had grown up around a nineteenth-century fascination with the exotic "other," it was a whole way of ordering the world to keep Europeans on top. It continued into the present in the way the American media and pseudoexperts represented Arabs and Muslims, who were rarely given the chance to represent themselves.[9]

Finally, fifteen years ago Paul Kennedy discerned a pattern in "the rise and fall of the great powers." From the Habsburgs to cold-war America, each one began with a vibrant economy and sound finances. But in each case the steady accrual of new overseas commitments required ever larger military establishments, draining resources from more productive sectors of the economy and risking eventual bankruptcy. Writing at a time of unprecedented peacetime budget and trade deficits, Kennedy suggested the United States might one day meet the same fate and succumb to "imperial overstretch."[10]

All of these authors agreed that imperial power did not necessarily entail formal rule over people and territory. Indeed, territory and the responsibilities that came with it could be a positive liability. They taught us that imperialism is above all a set of relationships that depends on varying degrees of coercion or consent. Since they were all influenced by the example of American power, it is not surprising that they defined empires in a way that could encompass the United States (even if they did not always make the comparison explicit).[11]

The new imperialists, by contrast, are all emphatic about America's imperial identity. Indeed, they see this development as inevitable and inescapable. "America's destiny is to police the world," Boot proclaims. To Ferguson, given its manifest power, the United States is an empire in denial. Hardt and Negri emphasize more diffuse and unconventional forms of power, as we shall see. But they concede that the locus of military and financial might is at least partially centered in the United States, which plays the role of "peace police" in a new kind of transnational Empire, with a capital *E*.[12]

In one of the rare moments when they touch on the material basis for this new Empire, Hardt and Negri aver that "Imperial control operates through three global and absolute means: the bomb, money, and ether."[13] Readers will search in vain for a coherent account of nuclear doctrine, monetary regulation, or cultural production. But this same triptych can represent the different approaches of these new imperialists—their limitations as well as their complementarity. Reading the work of Boot and Ferguson provides both a reminder and a preview of how imperial power justifies and expresses itself, whether through bombs or money. And with Hardt and Negri we have a perfect example of how intellectuals become complicit by electing to withdraw to an ethereal plain of pure theory.

III

It is sometimes said that history is a great grab bag, out of which one can pull all kinds of curious objects and claim they prove things not just about the past, but the present and future too. Still, what Max Boot finds in American history, and the significance he assigns to it, is amazing. His purpose is to provide an upbeat account of

America's "imperial wars"—its innumerable punitive raids, fitful occupations, and occasional counterinsurgency campaigns. They allow him to make a number of points that have great political significance: the United States has a long tradition of launching wars without declaring war, without a vital interest, without popular support, without an exit strategy.[14] This argument poses a major problem for those who would oppose America's recent wars as an historical aberration. From this point of view, for instance, Robert Kennedy's successful argument during the Cuban missile crisis that an American president could not perpetrate another Pearl Harbor appears as nothing but salutary nonsense.

Still, finding instances in which America launched undeclared, unprovoked, unpopular, and open-ended wars does not, in itself, recommend the practice as a policy. Boot is therefore at pains to argue that all of these conflicts were "small wars," meaning that their cost could be managed. They were not necessarily small in their duration, violence, and devastation, but rather as measured from a strictly American perspective: by the extent of its mobilization and the expenditure of its blood and treasure. Thus, even the seven-year campaign to subdue the Philippines—in which marines were ordered to "kill and burn," target all those over the age of ten, and create a "howling wilderness"—seems small to Boot. In effect, some 200,000 civilians are interred in an unmarked grave, while we are asked to admire "a monument to the U.S. armed forces' ability to fight and win a major counterinsurgency campaign."[15]

The question of whether Filipinos had a right to self-determination or even self-defense hardly figures, since they are only bit players in this American "triumph." For Boot it is sufficient to note that U.S. occupation was more enlightened than that of some other imperial powers. More generally, he readily concedes that many of these "small wars" were launched with scant provocation and achieved little. But "whatever the specific causes of each war," he insists "we should not lose sight of a larger truth. Economists call it a yield curve: When cost is low, demand is high." Boot does not say whether this holds true of famine and pestilence as well. The main point is that, in the post–cold war world, "the price of exercising power appears low once again." Indeed, he breathlessly announces that "America's strategic situation today presents more opportunities than ever before for such entanglements."[16]

Still, why does he look on these entanglements as opportunities? Why does he assume that exercising power is a good in itself? Why does he presume that war will always be in demand if the cost is made to seem low? Quite simply, Boot wants us to think that war can be not only cheap and easy, but can also make us feel good. Of U.S. nineteenth-century expeditions, he asks: "What did they achieve? Sometimes a trade treaty; at other times, simply the satisfaction of having instilled fear of the Stars and Stripes." Even if punitive raids had no deterrent effect, they did "satisfy the human impulse to see wrongdoers punished"—such as those unfortunate miscreants unwilling to fire a twenty-one-gun salute to the flag. He allows that there will be setbacks, just as the British sometimes suffered defeats in expanding their empire. But he notes that this only "made them hunger for vengeance," and urges Americans to "adopt a similarly bloody-minded attitude." Boot, in other words, is a warmonger, and he knows that what he is selling appeals to base human instincts.[17]

A century ago, when Americans were first confronted with the question of whether to concede independence to the Philippines, there was also a great debate about the idea of empire. It was then that Kipling composed "The White Man's Burden," hoping to encourage Americans to undertake these "savage wars of peace," which now provides Boot with his title and his inspiration. Back then, opponents asserted that there was no precedent and no possible justification for the United States to subjugate other nations that only wanted their independence. But Theodore Roosevelt, along with his friend and ally, Senator Henry Cabot Lodge, pointed out that Americans had reached the Pacific only because they had waged unceasing struggle against all of the people who stood in their way. "We have a record of conquest, colonization and expansion unequalled by any people in the Nineteenth Century," Lodge exulted.[18] The atrocities in the Philippines soured Americans on this argument, and even Roosevelt worried about the brutalizing effect they had had on American officers. Now, in the figure of Max Boot, it has reemerged once again.

IV

Niall Ferguson also quotes Kipling in urging Americans to take lessons from the history of the British Empire. But whereas for Boot the question of what can be gained from imperial wars, other than instilling fear, seems incidental, Ferguson asks at the very outset "whether the Empire was a good or bad thing." In January 2003 he delivered a lecture at the University of London to fellow academics to explain that he could not provide a fully satisfying answer to this question before a television audience, or even in a book made for television. It required rigorous demonstration in charts, graphs, and tables of data. And it was best to focus on British India, where more than two-thirds of the empire's population lived, and where its reputation must therefore stand or fall.[19]

It would appear to be a tough case, since in India most of the empire's subjects actually died early deaths. Ferguson writes that under British rule life expectancy increased by 11 years, leaving for a footnote the fact that the increase was from 21 to 32, and that it took 130 years.[20] In fact, even in 1921, life expectancy in India was not more than 20 years. The census that year indicated the extraordinary mortality rate of 49.8 per thousand, meaning that every two years the population of India was literally decimated. The only measurable improvement came in the last three decades of the Raj, after responsibility for public health and sanitation had been turned over to local Indian governments. Even so, malaria continued to carry off a million or more every year, malnutrition remained general, and tuberculosis may have actually increased. As late as 1935 there were no qualified health officers in three-quarters of the municipalities of India.[21]

Without entering into such details, Ferguson acknowledged before his fellow academics that an average life expectancy of 20 years for most of the empire's subjects represented a grave injustice. But he insisted that was only part of the story, and not the most important part. The justification for British rule could be found in measures of investment, improvement of infrastructure, and agricultural production. He proceeded to argue that, by all these measures, Britain made extraordinary efforts to develop the Indian economy and integrate it in international trade networks. Britain brought globalization to India, in other words, and while globalization has winners and losers, in the long run we are all better off.

Unfortunately, no one lives to see the long run, as Keynes once quipped, especially not India's British subjects. In fact, there was a direct causal relationship between the impressive levels of external trade and investment in India and the appalling condition of its inhabitants. Infrastructure and irrigation projects created the very conditions that caused early death. First, the national web was structured to feed external trade, such that shipping rates were much lower for goods bound for ports than for those going to destinations within India. When monsoons failed to arrive, those areas best served by rails and roads were actually worse off, since grain reserves were more easily transported out of them and on to the highest bidders, from Liverpool to Singapore.[22]

Many infrastructure projects were undertaken as relief works in times of famine, which Ferguson holds up as evidence of good intentions, contrary to Mike Davis's indictment of these *Late Victorian Holocausts*. But as Davis and others have pointed out, they were often set up at such distances from famine-struck districts that many of the starving died struggling to reach the sites. Once there, men, women, and children were made to dig ditches and build roads for rations inferior to those given inmates at Buchenwald. Ferguson writes that "it is fashionable to allege that the British authorities did nothing to relieve the drought-induced famines of the period," which suggests that he is ready to dismiss this work without actually understanding it.[23]

In fact, these relief projects propagated disease. British engineers often designed roads without locating water supplies for the crowds of people who would use them, so cholera traveled with them. And new roads and rails along with irrigation schemes disrupted normal drainage routes, creating bogs and swamps—ideal breeding grounds for malaria. Even when, in 1897, Dr. Ronald Ross proved that mosquitos transmitted malaria, and hence that proper drainage would save lives, sanitation officers were pressured to downplay or dismiss these findings lest they interfere with the enormous profits to be made from irrigated agriculture. As Sheldon Watts points out, India was the most irrigated imperial possession in the world.[24]

When all else fails, Ferguson likes to spin what-if scenarios that are supposed to redeem British rule, asking us to consider whether, bereft of empire, they could have held out against Japan and Nazi Germany, or whether India would have been better off under the French. Professional historians do not take this kind of speculation seriously, since it requires entirely recasting world history with imponderable ramifications. As the writers of *Saturday Night Live* once asked, with no better answer, what if Spartacus had had a Piper Cub, could he have defeated the Roman legions? What we do know, and what is more to the point, is that even when the rulers of British India understood that their profits derived from the early deaths of their subjects, they still wanted their profits. London rejected the notion "that England ought to pay tribute to India for having conquered her," as Salisbury put it.[25] Instead, in good years as well as bad India transferred several millions of pounds of taxes to provide British investors with a guaranteed rate of return. British investment in its empire was hardly an alibi for the appalling condition of most of its inhabitants. In fact, it would be more accurate to say that it provided both the weapon and the motive in the early deaths of countless millions of unfortunates under British rule.

V

"The conquest of the earth, which mostly means the taking it away from those who have a different complexion or slightly flatter noses than ourselves, is not a pretty thing when you look into it too much," as Joseph Conrad famously observed.[26] It is worth looking into public health, in particular, because arguing that "empire is good for you," or at least better than the alternatives, is one of the favored tactics of the new imperialists. For instance, in advocating American empire the *Atlantic* correspondent Robert Kaplan cites the decline in infant mortality in Chile, which purportedly proves that the United States was right to back the overthrow of Salvador Allende.[27] One of the most compelling arguments for invading Iraq was that it would end a public health disaster that had claimed hundreds of thousands of lives, and the restoration of proper sanitation and health care is now a crucial test for the legitimacy of its occupation. Even "bloody-minded" Max Boot has suggested that public health improvements justified U.S. occupations of Cuba, Haiti, and the Philippines.

Of course, empire not only offers the promise of control over life and death, but also over *where* people are permitted to live. Bill Clinton justified intervening in Haiti as the only way to avoid a mass exodus, a concern that George W. Bush obviously shares. More generally, if less dramatically, a desire to deflect migratory movements has helped to motivate U.S. attempts to extend a free-trade zone to all the Americas, as well as the European Union's economic accords with African states. In this way, freeing the movement of capital and trade has been pursued as a means to control the movement of human beings.

Early in their study of *Empire,* Hardt and Negri offer a useful insight from Foucault, observing that world politics is increasingly a matter of biopolitics, "in which what is directly at stake in power is the production and reproduction of life itself." Like Ferguson, they see empire as a product of globalization, and for both it represents not only the increasingly fluid movement of capital, goods, and ideas, but people too. Since power and wealth can be accrued and deployed without controlling territory, political struggles focus on control over populations—control over life and death and movement as well as over what people want from life. But for Hardt and Negri biopower also promises liberation, because ultimately people cannot be controlled, even in the most literal sense. "A specter haunts the world," they declare, "and it is the specter of migration. All the powers of the old world are allied in a merciless operation against it, but the movement is irresistible. . . . A new nomad horde, a new race of barbarians, will arise to invade or evacuate Empire."[28]

Note the uncertainty, "invade or evacuate." They are not sure which. This is just one of many ambiguities in a book that revels in them. In other cases readers must infer what, specifically, Hardt and Negri have in mind when they describe the emergence of the new world that has displaced once-sovereign nation-states. "Throughout the years of the cold war," they write, "there was both a multiplication of international organisms capable of producing right and a reduction of the resistances to their functioning."[29] True enough, for some decades now students of world politics have tracked the proliferation of international organizations, professional associations, and activist groups that strive to make states conform to international norms. These include standards of financial accountability, fiscal stability, public health, safe working conditions, environmental conservation, and many, many more.[30] Yet all of these groups together do not, by themselves, have the wherewithal to uphold democracy and human rights or prevent genocide and wars of aggression. It was the United States that assumed the "role of guaranteeing and adding juridical efficacy," according to Hardt and Negri. "That is perhaps one of the central characteristics of Empire," they write, "that is, it resides in a world context that continually calls it into existence. The United States is the peace police." Note here again how, while pointing in opposite directions, the arguments of Hardt and Negri parallel those of Boot and Ferguson: America did not carve out a preponderant and privileged role; it was created by the "world context."[31]

Presumably, it is for this reason that they insist that their empire is not actually American and the United States is not its center. Indeed, it has no center. Real power is vested in markets for capital as well as cultural production and other kinds of immaterial labor, all of which transcend international borders. And if the greatest state merely serves this emergent system, then individual workers are entirely at its mercy. "[E]xploitation tends no longer to have a specific place," they write, ". . . we are immersed in a system of power so deep and complex that we can no longer determine specific difference or measure [sic]. We suffer exploitation, alienation, and command as enemies, but we do not know where to locate the production of repression. And yet we still resist and struggle." How do Hardt and Negri "resist and struggle"? By cheering on everything that appears to disrupt or subvert the orderly operation of political and economic power, from Tiananmen Square to anti-WTO protests to body piercing to Islamism. What do they offer as a program? Just three things: freedom to migrate, a guaranteed social wage, and something they call "free access to and control over knowledge, information, communication, and affects." They admit their proposals are still "rather abstract. What specific and concrete practices will animate this political project?" they ask. "We cannot say at this point."[32]

This may be because they have not, once, analyzed or even described the "specific and concrete practices" that animate their empire. Indeed, it not only has no center, it has no history: "Empire exhausts historical time," they claim; it "suspends history, and summons the past and future within its own ethical order."[33] We have heard this before: power is everywhere, and nowhere in particular. But this is no longer just a scholarly conundrum. It has become a dangerous illusion. On the one hand, it mystifies political and economic power, suggesting that it can arise and persist in some immaterial realm without the "specific and concrete practices" Hardt and Negri either cannot or will not describe. On the other hand, it makes imperialism nothing more than an "ethical order," a system of ideas that can be defeated by other ideas, by different ethics, by body piercing.

Hardt and Negri finally give away the game when they write that "all the elements of corruption and exploitation are imposed on us by the linguistic and communicative regimes of production: destroying them in words," they insist, "is as urgent as doing so in deeds."[34] Really now, are *all* the elements of exploitation imposed by linguistic and communicative regimes? Is there really any particular urgency in new rhetorical exercises that show no greater commitment to locating the production of repression or proposing concrete practices to resist it? Is it not rather more urgent, at this point, that we at least try to understand how words become deeds, that is, how particular individuals and institutions make decisions that mean life or death for millions of people?

VI

A specific research project can illustrate how this problem might be approached—in this case, through a history of "population control." The international campaign to control population growth was one of the most dramatic and unabashed assertions of biopower ever witnessed. It was also perhaps the single most ambitious project ever undertaken by "international organisms capable of producing right," especially the U.N. Development Program, the World Health Organization, the World Bank, leading universities, and one of the world's largest NGOs, the International Planned Parenthood Federation. It received hundreds of millions of dollars from the Ford and Rockefeller Foundations and multinational pharmaceutical corporations, but billions more ultimately came from the U.S. government. By working with and through these institutions and what would now be called public-private partnerships, policymakers sought to avoid criticism at home while assuaging political sensitivities abroad. By 1980 millions of family-planning workers and volunteers were encouraging and sometimes coercing most of the world's population to limit their fertility.[35]

This was an effort not only to make Hardt and Negri's "multitude" less multitudinous, but also to limit its movement. It was motivated in part by concerns about mass migration and included campaigns to discourage people from moving to cities. It also involved more subtle and profound forms of biopower, in which people were taught to control their own sexuality at the same time they were told that it was a concern for the nation, and even the world. The U.N.'s World Fertility Survey, for instance, had fieldworkers asking people in more than sixty countries how often they had sex and whether they had really wanted their youngest children—children who were often sitting beside them at the time. Drawing on the results, a worldwide "information, education, and communication" campaign was mounted to convince people to plan for smaller families. Every form of mass communication as well as "folk media" conveyed the message that they would be more beautiful, more healthy, and, not least, could afford to buy more things.

Such a quick sketch cannot reveal all of the complexities and paradoxes in the international campaign to control population growth. It was sometimes coercive, including cash payments for sterilization and outright compulsion. But separating sexuality from reproduction could be liberating too. It was designed and often implemented by international and nongovernmental organizations in the name of reproductive rights and health as well as environmental conservation. But it also empowered states with unprecedented forms of surveillance and the possibility of controlling the biological reproduction of the nation. It was driven and largely funded by the United States, but it was led by NGOs and U.N. agencies and survived later attacks by Republican administrations. Not for the first or last time, the United States fostered new norms and institutions that eventually escaped its control.

While this is only one example, it shows why it would be a mistake to underrate international and nongovernmental organizations as merely providing artificial flavorings and colorings in what Michael Ignatieff calls "Empire Lite." According to this view, imperialism is essentially the exercise of military might to protect the interests of great powers. In Bosnia, Kosovo, and Afghanistan, Ignatieff's three case studies, the U.N. and NGOs are allowed to help, and cannot help becoming complicit.[36] But the kind of international trusteeship that surfaces periodically in such places only represents the tip of the iceberg—to use Robinson and Gallagher's metaphor—and would never have emerged without a whole system of norms and institutions to support them. One might even call it an informal empire, though it is even more diffuse than its precursors. On the other hand, it includes terribly formal declarations, mandates, mission statements and—very rarely—rules of engagement.

In most cases, feeding refugees, training police, and supervising elections does not require shunting aside governments and taking their place—any more than Britain had to establish formal rule to create the conditions for profitable trade. And even when it does it is not inherently imperialist, pace Ignatieff, provided that it is accountable to the people most directly concerned. Again, the essence of empire is not military force, but the exercise of untrammeled power. And imperialists have long understood that an entrance exam or a vaccination program are less costly and more compelling instruments of influence, especially when infused with an appealing idea—like *mission civilisatrice* or *médecins sans frontières*.

The potential power of international and nongovernmental organizations is most obvious when it takes the place of "failed states." But when they work in concert with local governments in discrete domains it may be even greater—as great as any empire. Thus, British and French authorities almost never risked promoting birth control for fear of a backlash, even in colonies where population growth seemed out of control. Their malaria eradication campaigns often seemed pathetic compared to those of the Rockefeller Foundation and the World Health Organization, in part because they could not command the same degree of cooperation. Similarly, the World Bank has collaborated with governments in gargantuan hydroelectric projects that have uprooted the populations of whole regions, and the IMF has pressed austerity programs that few colonial regimes could have safely inflicted on subject populations.

Nevertheless, international and nongovernmental organizations are not yet integrated in the kind of all-encompassing, transnational empire imagined by Hardt and Negri. They probably cannot be, even leaving aside the other actors in world politics—multinationals, the media, diasporas, etc. The reason is that even seemingly universal ideals, such as maternal and child health, gender equality, national self-determination, or environmental conservation, invariably come into conflict when applied in particular cases. Thus, in the case of population control, these goals mobilized different constituencies that were continually and bitterly fighting over strategy and tactics until the very idea of trying to control other people's fertility—even to save the earth—was utterly discredited. Similarly, the apparently noncontroversial idea of preventing genocide has not created an agenda for concerted action, but an arena for acrimonious debate.

The problem of conflicting and sometimes incommensurable values makes it all the more important that any outside intervention, however well meaning, ultimately answers to its presumed beneficiaries. It also shows why imperialism must be studied not in the abstract, but where it lives and breeds—not merely international trusteeships in "failed states," but also discrete domains like population control. Examining such cases suggests that, far from being exhausted, history might actually have far more to tell us about the world we live in today than the kind of scholasticism exemplified by Hardt and Negri. Yet, unlike Boot and Ferguson, it requires that we treat the study of empire not as a source of cheap thrills, or easy alibis, but as a way to grapple with the changing nature of international politics. And rather than striving to glean meaning from continental philosophy, we might instead examine the actual archives of the World Bank, U.N. agencies, leading foundations, and the largest NGOs. They are not only more relevant, but also more accessible, with staff ready and eager to help researchers who are serious about exploring their inner workings and their interaction with the most powerful states and multinational corporations.

We will never realize the contemporary potential for empire or the possibilities for fighting it if we assume it will be anything as simple as a Manichean struggle between the United States and the United Nations, multinational corporations and transnational NGOs, avowed imperialists like Boot and Ferguson and those, like Hardt and Negri, who claim to speak for some imagined "multitude." As scholars, we must work harder to illuminate the complex interconnections and complicities between them, and bring those findings to the broadest possible public. And it is that very complexity that commands us to speak and write clearly and with all the specificity and evidence we can muster. If we do not, then the American academy, that most sovereign of institutions, will have to admit that it has become nothing more and nothing less than a finishing school for new imperialists.

2: THE HISTORY OF LESSONS: LAW AND POWER IN MODERN EMPIRES

EMMANUELLE SAADA

On August 27, 2003, the Pentagon's special-operations chiefs organized a screening of *The Battle of Algiers* in the army auditorium. The 1965 Italian movie by Gillo Pontecorvo is a powerful account of the tactical complexities of the war in the Casbah in 1957, documenting both the escalation of violence by the Front de Libération Nationale (FLN) and the French army, and the difficult decisions that members of both groups faced as the situation grew more polarized.

Sensitive to the worsening violence in Iraq, Pentagon officials thought they could draw "lessons" from the French failure in Algeria. The flyer announcing the screening offered a pedagogical perspective: "How to win a battle against terrorism and lose the war of ideas. . . . Children shoot soldiers at point blank range. Women plant bombs in cafés. Soon the entire Arab population builds to a mad fervor. Sound familiar? The French have a plan. It succeeds tactically, but fails strategically. To understand why, come to a rare showing of this film."[1]

The thinness of the analogy offers some easy targets, from the naive "orientalism" that binds Algerians and Iraqis into uniform "Arabs," to the naturalization of the "imperialist's" position that allows U.S. officers to see themselves in the shoes of the French, to the erasure of the crucial historical background to the battle of Algiers— colonial urban development and segregation, the demographic explosion (caused in no small part by colonial health and social policies), the transformation of gender relations introduced by colonial domination, the deep-seated and widely shared Algerian agenda for national independence, the complex coalitions among factions that led to the FLN victory, and the international context of anticolonial movements. A military historian, finally, might emphasize the specificity of the tactical and strategic moves that shaped the battle of Algiers and made it a watershed moment in the Algerian war.

Yet the comparative impulse at work here is powerful and, in this case, points to an emerging bundle of assumptions about both empire and historical analysis among an extended network of issue entrepreneurs and audiences—in the Pentagon and elsewhere. We could ask both narrow and more general questions about the groups that compose this network—beginning, perhaps with questions about the culture of the Pentagon and about what informs the historical worldviews of its officers. A serious ethnography of the American military elite and an understanding of its historical perspective would be valuable in understanding what kinds of lessons are likely to be drawn.

As a more general framework, the recent surge in "empire talk" in the American popular media (displacing earlier "globalization talk") is evidence that officers are not alone in believing that there are "lessons of empire"—both military and geopolitical. Professional historians and social scientists play a leading role in shaping this debate. Sometimes they make use of the notion of "empire" as a metaphor, sometimes as an analytical device, and somewhat less often as a reservoir of "lessons." Their thinking on this matter is prevalent in that part of the media and intellectual field closest to the field of power: in reviews like the *National Interest,* in think tanks like the American Enterprise Institute or the Project for the New American Century, and maybe at the Pentagon itself. They have also found outlets in the mainstream media, which has developed an interest in the historian qua expert comparable to that shown economists and specialists of international relations.

Although we need not let the terms of this debate frame our own thinking about empire, it is difficult to ignore them and their potential effects on the "imperial" formations themselves. Since participants in the debate have recourse to historical data as a means to legitimate a political stance, it seems important not only to understand their use of the history of empires but also to question the historiography it entails. Drawing from the example of modern French colonialism, I would suggest that the imperial histories from which lessons are currently drawn miss a crucial aspect of the modern colonial experience: *the reorganization of the modes of exercising power it entailed on both the domestic and international fronts.* Our understanding of both imperial formations and the United States' current projection of power is impoverished as a result.

THE TERMS OF A DEBATE

One could make a good case that this turn toward historical comparison is itself a characteristic feature of imperial projects: empires—at least European empires—frequently represented themselves as inspired by the "lessons of (former) empires": the ancient Roman Empire was a central referent for the Holy Roman Empire and the Carolingian Empire, and, through them, for the Napoleonic Empire.[2] The French case was somewhat more complicated. In the late nineteenth century, French politicians avoided the term *empire* due to its association with the Napoleonic regimes that twice ended republican governments. But Rome remained a ubiquitous referent for their colonial doctrine. It was used in the ideological construction of a sharp contrast between French and British modes of colonial domination, especially the distinction between *assimilationist* and *differentialist* attitudes toward the *indigènes*. The French colonial style was depicted as a direct continuation of Roman practices of assimilation. Colonial legal theorists, in particular, were fascinated by the extension of Roman law and its long-term influence on European legal systems.

The current public debate on imperial comparison is similarly complex and needs closer examination: it bears less on the actual "tactical and strategic" lessons that can be drawn from imperial experiences than on the characterization of the United States as an empire. One could reasonably ask why this terminological debate has attracted so much attention, when the fact of U.S. supremacy is not questioned. What difference does it make to speak of the United States as an empire or (only as) a *hegemon*?[3] Though the authors are not always eager to acknowledge it, the debate over the characterization has much more to do with political agendas than with a desire for analytical accuracy. At the top of the list is the desire to salvage the notion of empire from the bad press it received from "a generation of 'postcolonial' historians anachronistically affronted by its racism" and more broadly to rehabilitate it from the various anti-imperialistic critiques of the 1960s and 1970s.[4] Those who reject the characterization of the United States as an empire—and who prefer, like Robert Kagan, to speak of a "global *hegemon*"—do so in part to "eschew the labels of Marxism and Leninism" on the way toward affirming that the "expansion of the free market is not, in fact, imperialism."[5] This leads Kagan to assert that the "essence of American policy" is "not imperialist" because it is based on the belief that the "expansion of American power is a good thing for America and for the world." This argument is challenged by those who, like Niall Ferguson, insist on the imperial dimension of current American power, noting especially the continuity of the rhetoric of the "mission civilisatrice et libératrice" from European imperialism of the nineteenth century.

Beyond this "definitional matter," Ferguson and Kagan agree that "the United States has a critical role in maintaining world order." Kagan's objective is to "constantly argue the case for why the United States must remain engaged in the world, why it must have more constancy."[6] Ferguson's position is only marginally different, advocating a more direct and long-term engagement in some of the troubled parts of the world. Interestingly, here the "objective lessons" of history become "political lessons." In his book on *Empire,* Ferguson noted that history teaches us that U.S. policy *will* shift from indirect to direct rule.[7] In his many interventions in the public debate, he has repeatedly argued that it *should* do so: "Americans need to go there. If the best and brightest insist on staying home, today's unspoken imperial project may end—unspeakably—tomorrow."[8]

This is not the place to take issue with the political agenda articulated in this debate, but rather to observe that it rests on a deeply problematic colonial historiography. The basic categories that Kagan and Ferguson deploy (*direct* vs. *indirect rule*; *formal* vs. *informal empire*) are the product of nineteenth century "colonial (administrative and legal) science" and were appropriated by the colonial actors themselves reflecting upon their own practices. Those categories had more to do with ideological constructions and the "politics of comparison" than with an accurate description of actual practices of rule: the opposition between *direct* and *indirect rule* was to a large extent the construction of metropolitan intellectuals and politicians in both France and Great Britain.[9] As historians, we cannot appropriate those categories uncritically, leaving out a genealogical analysis of their production and usages.

There are other troubling aspects of this demonstration. Ferguson, like others, advocates greater U.S. financial involvement in direct "institution building" (in Iraq and Afghanistan). He underscores that empires were not "built on the cheap."[10] This does not take into consideration the complex reality of colonial investments, which were frequently conceived, and ultimately implemented, on the cheap. In 1900, for example, a French law required that the colonies be self-financing. For the most part, the metropolitan political class believed that the empire would not be acceptable to the public if it had any substantial cost. Governors had to levy enough taxes to balance their local budgets and to intervene directly in infrastructure building and the establishment of a working class. This had enormous consequences for patterns of colonial rule and for French metropolitan economic history.[11]

Among the other debatable "lessons": Ferguson laments that the youth of the American elite shuns direct involvement in the civil administration of territories currently occupied by the United States. The French elite had the same reluctance. The French colonial administration was populated overwhelmingly by men who came from peripheral regions (Corsica) or from other colonies (mostly the Caribbean "old colonies").[12]

One could continue in this vein. The important point is that all of these claims rely on assumptions about the integrity and coherence of imperial projects, setting up a comparison between a self-confident (British) imperialism and the "organized hypocrisy" of American "Empire in denial." Ferguson strongly advocates that the United States should "go there" and "stay there for a while." When he compares the forty years of British involvement in Iraq with the few months of (originally) planned U.S. presence, he neglects the contingencies that shaped both the conquests and the decisions to stay. He forgets that the time frame of the colonial presence was *always* in question, from conquest to decolonization. In the French case, in the writing of administrators and other members of the colonial elite, the anticipated end of the colonial presence *always* colored perceptions of the situation.

Older historiography often elides this dimension, placing actions within a narrative of empire that was not always perceived or believed at the time. The traditional periodization of French colonial rule is an example of this tendency. Colonial historians of France often identify a period of "stabilization" of the colonial societies after World War I and the end of the most obvious military aspects of conquest.[13] By this time, the economic infrastructure and the main colonial administrative and educational institutions were in place, and burgeoning colonial cities had begun to attract women and provide services for children. But by the 1920s, modern movements of colonial contestation had also emerged across the empire, from Indochina to North Africa to the metropole itself. These were perceived as major threats by colonial administrators. As the most insightful historical scholarship has shown, "Tensions of Empire" always ran deep.[14] The "imperial project" was always evolving, always precarious, and marked by an uncertain time frame.

The very notion of "Empire in denial" or "hypocrisy" misses something important about the complexity of these imperial arrangements. In France, the "Empire" was never officially recognized as such, and never formally organized into a clear system of administration. The relationship between the metropole and the colonies was specified only once, during the Second Empire, in the *Senatus-consulte* of 1854, and then only in the loosest legal terms. Subsequent republican governments never replaced this framing document, even though its constitutionality was often called into question. This persistent reluctance to formalize empire meant that the administrative organization of the colonies was never really "imperial": among the territories under French rule, there were colonies (overseen by a Ministère des Colonies after 1894), protectorates and mandates (under the Ministère des Affaires Etrangères), and three fully French *départements* in Algeria. The word *empire* itself was used only rarely before the interwar period. For the republicans, it smacked too much of the Napoleonic empires. For a long time, it also connoted a mode of domination through conquest at odds with the "spiritual" universalism of the "Great Nation." According to Michelet's "Picture of France," which opens his monumental *History of France,* "Great Britain is an empire; Germany is a country—a race; France is a person."[15] *L'Empire, c'est l'autre.*

The "lessons of Empire" raise a further historiographic problem. The continuity posed between the "British World Order" and "U.S. global power" is built on a history of the British Empire centered on its role as the worldwide propagator of liberal capitalism. Ferguson's main historical point is that the nineteenth-century empire "pioneered free trade, free capital movements and, with the abolition of slavery, free labour." It developed a "global network of modern communications. It spread and reinforced the rule of law over vast areas."[16] In a word, it is the first moment of a linear and irresistible history of "globalization."

It is easy to point out the semantic similarities between this historical representation of Britain and the discourse of American leaders of the 1990s and 2000s. They appear in the *National Security Strategy* document of September 20th, 2002, submitted by the Bush administration to Congress as the annual report on the nation's strategic security objectives. Echoing British imperial lingo, this document lists the objective to promote "free trade that provides new avenues for growth and fosters the diffusion of technologies and ideas that increase productivity and opportunity."[17] But beyond rhetorical similarities, the hypothesis of a continuity of "imperial globalization" ignores the vast amount of historical scholarship that demonstrates that liberal capitalism was never a ready-made product to be exported, but rather something shaped by colonial and imperial histories. It also completely neglects the granularity of colonial rule over different territories and the very diverse modes of economic engagement that accompanied that rule. In the French case, there never was free trade but rather a system of heavy taxation that strongly favored the metropole; the mobility of capital was extremely limited and colonial banks were under the direct control of the state; "forced labor" was prevalent throughout the empire; the movement of populations was tightly restricted and controlled.

POWER

Arguably the most striking limitation of the current debate over "lessons of Empire" is the lack of interest in the close analysis of both the "colonial order" and "global power"—of their modes of exercise, their concrete effects, and the kinds of resistance they produce. The public face of this debate offers many breathless accounts of the current extent of U.S. "power." Often, its hegemonic position is compared favorably with that of Rome and the British Empire. In "The Greatest Superpower Ever," Paul Kennedy, who not so long ago worried about "imperial overstretch," observes: "Nothing has ever existed like this disparity of power; nothing." Lists of the various "indicators" of U.S. power are a favorite form of supporting evidence for this discourse.[18]

Most of the time, the indicators used to quantify U.S. "world power" are borrowed from the military, economic, and cultural fields. Ferguson refers to these traditional categories as the "three pillars of power" and bases his characterization of the United States as an empire on the existence of "750 military bases in 130 countries," a "contribution to global economic output of 31 percent," and indications of American dominance in world cinema and television.[19] Here and in other contributions to the debate, the "qualitative" dimension of power is left aside except for occasional loose invocations of "soft" and "hard" power.[20]

Power, always invoked as the fundamental explanatory variable, is never explained except through recourse to rough psychologizing. This is above all the case in Robert Kagan's characterization of the United States as a "non-imperialist *hegemon*." In circular fashion, the gap between a "Kantian," "post-modern" Europe, which has shed "power politics" in favor of collective obedience to international rules and a "Hobbesian" United States, which still believes that "power is the ultimate determinant of national security and success," is explained by . . . the "power gap."[21] The psychology of power offered here is simple enough: those who have power tend to believe in its effectiveness and have recourse to it more readily than those who do not have it and must make do without it.[22] European countries used to "believe in power" and act according to the principles of "*Machtpolitics.*" But the successive tragedies of the European twentieth century made them forgo it. After the demise of the Communist bloc, this left the United States as the only actor able and willing to fight in the new "jungle."[23] Imperialism plays a prominent role in this historical demonstration, since decolonization is regarded as a fundamental step in the European rejection of power.[24] It also figures centrally in Kagan's psychology of power, made up of "urges" and "atavism" and a nostalgia for Europe's role in shouldering the "white man's burden": "Maybe concern about America's overweening power really will create some energy in Europe. Perhaps the atavistic impulses that still swirl in the hearts of Germans, Britons, and Frenchmen—the memory of power, international influence, and national ambition—can still be played upon. Some Britons still remember empire; some Frenchmen still yearn for *la gloire*; some Germans still want their place in the sun. These urges are now mostly channeled into the Grand European Project, but they could find more traditional expression."[25] The Kiplingesque references—veiled here but explicit in the conclusion of Ferguson's book—suggests that beyond the terminological debate lies the conviction that white men have a continuing mission to shape world history.[26]

Like the other participants in the debate about American "empire," Kagan never specifies what he means by "power."[27] In his text, power has a polymorphic, almost metaphysical dimension, which makes it useful for bridging different arguments and more generally covering loose argumentation. As Max Weber argued with respect to the analogous German term *Macht,* such uses of "power" are in need of qualification. Most importantly, Kagan's use of the term supports the "double standard" that is central to his vision of U.S. dominance. Power has to prevail in the "jungle," while norms apply—potentially—to the actors in the "civilized world": "The problem is that the United States must sometimes play by the rules of a Hobbesian world, even though in doing so it violates Europe's post-modern norms. It must refuse to abide by certain international conventions that may constrain its ability to fight effectively in Robert Cooper's jungle. It must support arms controls, but not always for itself. It must live by a *double standard.*"[28] Kagan's notion of a "double standard" takes us much closer to the historical complexities of imperial rule than Ferguson's account of the empire qua globalization. The tensions of this double standard—the dialectic of "power" and "norms"—have deeply informed the historical dynamics of modern imperialism.

Kagan's distinction between "Hobbesian rules" and "Kantian norms" reactivates the classical opposition between the "realism" of "power politics" and the "idealism" associated with the "international rule of law." It sees international relations as the primary stage for this conflict of values. But as the French imperial experience abundantly illustrates, the "double standard" was never limited to dealings between sovereign nations: it becomes a characteristic mode of governance *within* empires. It comes to describe, in particular, a range of internal distinctions between people ruled by "law" (Kantian norms) and those governed by less formalized "rules," such as customs or forms of state violence. These distinctions form one part of the broader "tensions of empire," with their dialectics of persuasion and coercion, inclusion and exclusion.[29] And yet at no point are we dealing with an absence of law. The double standard can not be reduced to the classical opposition between a Hobbesian "rule of men" and the "rule of law"—between an anarchic time and the emergence of law-bound society. In both the French colonial empire and the current U.S. actions, legal regimes encompassed both "norms" and "rules." They were the lens through which power was understood, exercised, and legitimated. They formalized the logic that justified indefinite rule over foreign territories, that extended human and political rights to some, and that permitted others to be excluded, detained, tortured, or killed.

THE RULE OF LAW

French colonizers legitimated their enterprise by affirming that they would bring the "rule of law" to populations that were still slaves to (barbaric) customs. They did so arguing that colonization would bring an end to "despotism," propagate the values of the "Great Nation," and get rid of "barbaric customs" such as human sacrifices and slavery, which ran counter to "respect for human personality and dignity."[30] We hear almost identical language in U.S. pronouncements such as the September 2002 *National Security Strategy* document, which argues that "America must stand firmly for the nonnegotiable demands of human dignity: the rule of law; limits on the absolute power of the state; free speech; freedom of worship; equal justice; respect for women; religious and ethnic tolerance; and respect for private property."[31] Similarly, the list of accomplishments in Afghanistan and Iraq cited by President Bush in his third State of the Union address dealt almost exclusively with the establishment of law and steps toward the (eventual) restoration of Iraqi sovereignty.[32]

Then, as now, *sovereignty* was a central concern. For the French, the consolidation of the Empire and the emergence of the Third Republic in the last decades of the nineteenth century were accompanied by intense political and theoretical debates about the nature of the state and its modes of domination. These questions were perceived as closely linked.

At the center of these debates was the distinction between territorial and national sovereignty. For the legal theorists of the late nineteenth century, the sovereignty of the *ancien régime* was exclusively territorial in that it "derived from the King's right on the territory." National sovereignty, in contrast, was the major invention of the French Revolution, and was by definition impersonal and detached from this material (territorial) connection. The colonial exclusion of indigenous populations from citizenship challenged this distinction: it reactivated territorial sovereignty for the subjects of empire while barring them from participating in national sovereignty.[33]

International law, at the time, did not so much counterbalance this development as ratify it. International law developed quickly in the late nineteenth century in response to the need for restraints on the European competition for colonial empires. But the legal norms developed in this context applied more to relationships between Western European states than to their handling of conquered peoples, who were denied any form of sovereignty over the territory they inhabited. Non-European nations and peoples were not considered equal players in the field of international law, and the conquering nations were free to define the terms of their domination. A double standard very similar to that articulated by Kagan prevailed: norms of good colonial behavior were spelled out in the legal documents drafted at the Berlin conference in 1884–85 and the Brussels conference of 1890. On the ground, coercive and often violent regimes of colonial rule were put in place.

However we interpret American concern for Iraqi sovereignty and rule of law, it would be a mistake to understand such promises solely in terms of the degree of their implementation, or to judge their authors solely on their good or bad faith. Legality plays a deeper role in these contexts. With John Comaroff, one could argue that, fundamentally, "cultures of legality were constitutive of colonialism, *tout court*."[34] French colonial actors thought about their projects and practices through the prism of legal categories. This was true even at the most basic level of the acquisition of territories: French property law, for instance, provided the conceptual basis for distinguishing between the discovery, occupation, conquest, and cession of territory.[35] These were not merely ex post facto technicalities: they had much to do with how land was partitioned and controlled, with significant consequences for the local populations. In New Caledonia and Algeria—the two territories most subjected to French agricultural development—land outcomes were very different. The ostensible "occupation" of the former was the basis for a radical denial of indigenous property and the building of reservations for the local population. In contrast, Algeria had been "conquered"—a notion that implied some degree of recognition of indigenous rights to property and a distinction between "French" and "Muslim" land.[36]

Legal categories are also central to the U.S. administration's conception of power, as the transfer of Iraqi sovereignty suggests. For American administrators, whose political culture hinges on a modern notion of legitimacy, sovereignty is the primary way of thinking about political stability. The pervasiveness of the culture of legality is also visible in the mobilization of legal experts by the administration to justify unusual forms of interrogation since September 2001, both in the United States and abroad: the dialectics of "power" and "norms" have never been more intense.

CUSTOMS AND LAWS

It did not take long for colonial administrations in all parts of the French Empire to realize that forcing French "rule of law" on the indigenous populations was practically impossible. In addition, it went against the pledges made by the French state in all cession treaties to "respect the religion" of the indigenous peoples.[37] The "double standard" of law and rules finally prevailed. While French law applied to French *citizens* in the territories, indigenous *subjects* remained subjected to their "customary" rules—liberally interpreted, codified, and transformed by colonial administrators.

This dualism rested on two assumptions: the first was an organic conception of law, understood as strongly linked to other social institutions and, in the last instance, to the authoring race itself. As such, law could not be easily reformed or exported. The second idea was the strong connection between private and public law—between norms of civility and political participation. For the French, it was *because* the *indigènes* followed their own customs in their private dealings that they were refused civic rights. In effect, and despite the official claims of French republicanism, citizenship in the empire was never abstract or universal: it was predicated on norms of private behavior, from which legal status and associated political rights were derived.[38]

The "double standard" entailed obvious contradictions which *indigènes* were quick to point out and use strategically. The unstable conjunction of the rhetoric of the "rule of law" and the government of *indigènes* through customs appeared most clearly in regard to the question of secularization in Algeria (perhaps the most difficult issue that contemporary France inherited from its colonial projects). The 1905 law of separation of church and state was proclaimed valid in principle in Algeria, but governors regularly postponed its application. Local administrators, not imperial policymakers, preserved French control of Islam in Algeria, maintained through the hiring of imams and the subsidization of mosques. The religious sphere was seen as a site of potential contestation of French authority, and therefore remained part of French strategies of governance. From the 1920s onward, religious and secular political movements (including the Communists) joined forces to call for a true separation of church and state—for the application of "Republican law" to Algeria. In 1946, they appealed directly to French public opinion and to the highest level of the metropolitan state for the enforcement of republican principles. Denouncing the double standard thus became a powerful political tool for contesting the colonial order.[39] The threat was radical because the double standard ran through so many aspects of colonial rule. In the end, it proved enormously difficult to sustain over time. We should be very mindful of similar dynamics at work in Iraq, as Shiite leaders move ahead of their American "liberators" in making democratic demands.

The distinctions entailed by the double standard were endlessly negotiated, circumvented, and re-inscribed. The civil code and customary law overlapped in many ways: in appellate courts in most territories, French judges applied customary law and, in the process, deeply transformed it by basing decisions on their own legal categories and senses of justice. In Algeria, this opened the space for otherwise silenced populations, notably women, to make claims.[40] In several instances, *indigènes* were offered the possibility to "opt for French law" on an ad hoc basis in their private dealings.

A more or less continuous process of ad hoc adjustments greased the wheels of empire, but also undermined colonial legal pluralism—the practice of maintaining coexisting but separate legal systems.[41] As in the more blatant contradictions of the double standard, individuals and groups found strategic uses for these gaps and overlapping jurisdictions. It should come as no surprise that the United States has reproduced this dilemma in its own projects of legal reform. Tensions were visible in the handling of the new Iraqi constitution, especially regarding the challenge of reconciling normative systems modeled after American notions of "rule of law" with those left in place in order to respect religious (and other) traditions. In a gesture probably intended to ensure that legal reform did not put itself at odds with core values of Iraqi society, the position of senior constitutional adviser to the Coalition Provisional Authority was given to Noah Feldman, a law professor trained in classic Islamic thought. Feldman's main academic contribution to date, *After Jihad: America and the Struggle for Islamic Democracy,* is strongly reminiscent of the kind of conceptual and practical synthesis between "customs" and "law" that pervaded the French Empire. This continuity is perhaps most striking in its effort to reconcile the Koran with modern democracy. Examining traditional religious law, Feldman concludes that the "rule of God" does not preclude the "rule of the people" and that Islamic democracy might require a more flexible notion of equality that accommodates some degree of discrimination against non-Muslims and women.[42]

Here we have not a solution to the double standard, but the recycled terms on which it is likely to be rebuilt.

COLONIAL PUBLIC ORDER

Legal pluralism also had a more coercive side dedicated to maintaining public order. The key legal instrument for this purpose was the *Code de l'indigénat,* the special criminal law applicable to indigenous peoples. Contrary to all republican legal principles, the *Code* defined crimes specific to the *indigènes* and gave the colonial executive branch entire discretion over judgments and punishment. It provided thin legal cover to an array of violent and repressive acts by the colonial state. The first *Code de l'indigénat* was approved by Parliament in 1881 for application in Algeria. Criticized by some as a "legal monster," the *Code* was provided only a limited term of seven years. The assumption was that once "colonial violence" had cleared the Algerian "jungle," the rule of law would finally prevail. (One finds strong echoes of this line of reasoning in Kagan's claims). This temporary solution to the tension inherent to the "double standard" was reenacted every seven years until 1944 in Algeria, 1946 in other colonies. At each new parliamentary vote on the question, there was a pledge that it was only a provisional measure.[43]

The colonial situation, like the current "war on terrorism," was characterized by constant crisis and the continual reaffirmation of a transitory "state of exception" necessary before the rule of law can finally prevail. Regimes of rights specific to *indigènes* were supposed to be replaced by the civil code once cultural assimilation was achieved. Needless to say, this temporary horizon constantly receded. It took World War II to finally abolish the *Code de l'indigénat.* Meanwhile, it became the most infamous symbol of colonial domination for the Algerians and all other French colonial subjects.

Regulations such as the Patriot Act (2001) and the Military Order of November 11, 2001, on the "detention, treatment and trial of certain non-citizens in the war against terror" raise analogous questions of the relationship between "power" and "violence." They also entail a distinction between those who are entitled to the *rule of law* and those who are submitted to less formal and often more violent state sanction—i.e., those to whom the Fifth and Sixth Amendments do not apply. Although the Supreme Court has historically held that those amendments applied to noncitizens—such as permanent alien residents "physically present" in the United States—citizenship and place of legal residence have recently become increasingly determining factors as diverse populations are swept into the war on terror.[44]

In the last months of 2003, the American legal system registered a number of successful challenges to these encroachments on established rights—notably the concept of due process. These challenges led to groundbreaking decisions by the Supreme Court at the end of June 2004: in the *Hamdi v. Rumsfeld* and *Rasul v. Bush* cases, the Court decided that citizens and noncitizens alike seized during military operations could not be held without access to American courts. In affirming the rights of those deemed "enemy combatants," the Court rejected the administration's legal argument that by virtue of separation of powers, the executive branch could impose open-ended detentions. On the contrary, the Court declared that "state of war is not a blank check for the president when it comes to the rights of the nation's citizens."[45]

The confrontation between the executive and the judiciary is a recurrent pattern in moments of crisis of the colonial order: during the Algerian War, the manipulation of criminal justice by the French military took a very similar path toward summary forms of justice and ultimately torture.[46] The revelations of acts of torture and humiliations at the Abu Ghraib prison and the indications of a widespread and organized system of torture and abuse are reminiscent of the French debates raised by the torture of "terrorists" following the battle of Algiers. These debates generated public questioning about national identity and character in terms similar to those seen in the American press in May 2004—questions of national dignity and honor were paramount—and hastened the end of the Algerian War.

TECHNOLOGIES OF POWER

Before concluding, it is worth noting that this relationship between national and imperial organization of power is not limited to the legal sphere and to regimes of rights. It also informs changes in the technologies of power. Here again, the comparison between the current situation and the colonial state is striking. In both cases, improved control of the movement of populations is a primary goal. In many ways, empires have always been characterized by the porosity of their outer frontiers, combined with acute attention to the control of movements from the periphery to the center.[47] Such control is now the main preoccupation of U.S. immigration policy, shaped by a terrorism-induced desire to "exclude the Barbarians."[48] This effort involves the implementation of improved identification systems—among them, the improved Integrated Automated Fingerprint Identification System (IAFIS)—to better identify aliens wanted in connection with criminal investigations in the United States or abroad. But this identification apparatus also potentially applies to American citizens: in the wake of the Patriot Act, general biometric databases are receiving new attention and the discredited project of a national identification system has reemerged. This trajectory is reminiscent of the French construction of a state apparatus for the identification of citizens and subjects. The colonial setting was the laboratory for the "identifying state," initially with identity papers in Algeria in 1882. Only later was it applied to immigrants in France (1917) and ultimately to the entire French population in the early 1950s. Modern screening techniques were also tested first on colonial immigrants to France before becoming standard border-control practice.

As I have stressed through the example of the French Empire, one of the most striking lessons of empire is that the "European experience of state formation was predicated on its colonial experience."[49] Although I have suggested reasons for skepticism about the grander geopolitical lessons sought by Ferguson, Kagan, and others, I would argue that we can be fairly certain about the applicability of this one, and rightly concerned about its implications for the current situation. Because of its new modes of projection of power, the American state is undergoing a reorganization in the dialectic of law and power, at home and abroad. In France, this process was slow and incremental, following a logic that was not articulated at the outset. Although it is too early to judge, the war on terror seems both clearer and faster in its unfolding. This is a challenge for historians but perhaps also a more powerful occasion for critique.

3. IMPERIAL FORMATIONS AND THE OPACITIES OF RULE

ANN LAURA STOLER[1]

For colonial studies—a field devoted to the nature of European empires, their rationales and representations of rule—thinking critically about empire invites pointed questions: how might its conventions hinder or help an assessment of what constitute imperial conditions and imperial effects? Do its analytic frames allow or dissuade speaking to contemporary debates? And not least, what does and should *effective*, rather than applied, knowledge about empire look like now?

Empire, imperium, imperialism, and colonialism are now—and have long been—terms with multiple referents and conflated meanings. Nor are academics surprised (as we might have been, just two years ago) by the staggering appearance (and disappearance) of these terms in public fora as sources of metaphoric might, evocative analogy, and instructive comparison. *Foreign Policy,* the *New York Times, Pacific News Service, Le Monde Diplomatique, Rhodesian.Net* and *Workers Online* are all tracking the movements of "imperial America" and the "consequences of empire," with comparisons and conclusions as varied as the political positions they express.

Viewed from left, right, center, academic corridors, or the mainstream press, it is striking how sure some commentators seem about what empires are and were, and how they work "then" and now. Michael Ignatieff writes in the *New York Times,* it's empire and we better get used to it.[2] Immanuel Wallerstein contends that the wool has been pulled over our collective eyes, and that the United States is an empire if not in free-fall, then in serious demise.[3] Political theorists Michael Hardt and Antonio Negri identify a radical shift from imperialism as we/they knew it—one of "fixed entities"— to Empire with a capital *E,* one "deterritorialized," hybrid, global, inhabited by multitudes, unbounded, and limitless.[4] Dinesh D'Souza's "two cheers for colonialism" and Niall Ferguson's best-selling *Empire* hint at a new stance among those who no longer feel compelled to secret their affection for the British Raj or disdain for a postcolonial scholarship that condemns the nostalgias these once quiescent devotees of empire have long harbored.[5]

Empire is more than a current watchword: according to the conservative *Washington Times,* it has "suddenly" become "hot intellectual property within Washington's beltway."[6] The assertion of temporal immediacy and of real-world value prompts questions about what new political interests make empire "hot" today, what forms of knowledge are staked out as credible, what accrues to those with proprietary claims on how empires once operated, and how does a subject of historical study once deemed too remote for political pragmatists "suddenly" become repositioned at center stage?

Certainly empire is not "hot" because it is new or because the United States just acquired one. Scholars, politicians, and public intellectuals have vehemently disagreed about imperial practice and abuse, about imperial stretch or "overstretch" of the U.S. polity since the mid-nineteenth century. Favored examples might include Mark Twain's anti-imperialist satire in 1867 on the U.S. government's plan to buy the island of St. Thomas, his outrage at the U.S. initiative to recognize the Congo Free State in 1884 in the wake of King Leopold's campaign of carnage in the name of progress, or his incessant condemnations at the turn of the century of the U.S. Philippine war.[7] Some point to W.E.B. Du Bois's 1915 appraisal that World War I was not a battle in Europe but one over black bodies and imperial contests over Africa.[8] William Appelman Williams's insistent arguments in the 1950s against American exceptionalism and his tracing of U.S. imperial interventions back to the 1780s is quoted by any serious student of U.S. expansion.[9] And students of U.S. interventions in Latin America, the Middle East, and Southeast Asia have never hesitated to call the structured violence of occupation, annexation, scramble for access to ports and raw materials, capital expansion, and the dislocations that followed—despite the United States' lack of "colonies proper"—by their imperial name.

What has changed then is not the declaration of empire, but the force field in which it operates, the breadth of its metaphoric extensions, and the scope of the public for whom it has been readied for consumption. What has changed dramatically is not only the currency of empire as an evocation of the moment but the alternate density and absence of historical referents called upon; the cross section of, and *crossover* between, scholars and national policy advisors who (many for the first time) find themselves sharing a common language and not always, as we might expect, with wildly different understandings of how it should be used.

Political pundits and scholars of the long nineteenth century "age of empire" are contesting whether British imperial strategies in Asia and Africa have lessons to teach us and whether these are useful ones or not. Washington's political advisors have never been short on historical sound bites, but those circulating are about peoples that have been off their radar, in places rarely acknowledged as relevant. Now the exercise of French colonialism in Algeria in the 1950s is deemed openly pertinent to the tactics of torture and moral ethics of intervention. What Social Science Research Council President Craig Calhoun—in a call for papers on "lessons of empire" in fall 2003—rightly identified as a "disconnect" between what academics do and what discourse pervades the public domain may not be in the terms used but in the quixotic oscillation between shared and contested meanings assigned to them. I pose two related questions: (1) why have students of colonial studies been so absent from these debates, and (2) how might we/they reframe and thereby relocate the grounds of these charged conversations?

If colonial studies once worried that it had positioned itself too comfortably "safe for scholarship," it is (and should be) not so now.[10] Conservative journals like the *National Interest* share with students of imperial history a focused interest in the perils and promises of empire past and present, as political elites and their advisors ponder what a measured imperial vision might destroy or ably serve in Afghanistan or Iraq. Eric Hobsbawm writes forcefully in *Le Monde Diplomatique* that today's American empire "has little in common" with the nineteenth-century British Empire and proceeds point by point to dismiss any productive comparison.[11] Alternately, British imperial historian A.G. Hopkins's feature essay in the *New York Times* declares that the lessons of the "civilizing mission" (defined as "underestimated" difficulties, unrealistic plans, wrongheaded premises) were unlearned at the time, and should be better learned today.[12]

Few have missed the fact that the dominant rhetoric of an American imperium celebrates that which was once denied, if not condemned. Long having claimed that the United States is an empire in denial, critics and advocates of empire now find it in openly cautious—to expectant—celebration. On both sides are a new set of descriptive referents. Thus a former member of Reagan's Department of State, Robert Kagan's "benevolent empire" ("a better international arrangement than all realistic alternatives") or advisor to Tony Blair, Robert Cooper's "cooperative, new liberal empire," or the equally applauded "voluntary empire," "humanitarian imperialism," or "empire by invitation"—all such formulations celebrate the advent of a beneficent macropolity endowed with consensual rather than coercive qualities.[13]

Empire's critics also have a new coinage for an empire that until recently refused to call itself by that name. Michael Mann's "incoherent empire" cannot, he writes, "control occupied territories like the Europeans used to" with practices in Afghanistan and Iraq "too rudimentary to be considered imperial."[14] Others insist on the "invisible" qualities of U.S. empire and a more secret one in its new manifestation, but here again the question is obvious: less visible than what and invisible to whom? "Humanitarian imperialism," "the arrogant empire," "the conceited empire," "the quasi-empire," "the invisible empire," or alternately, the "global" one, implicitly and explicitly call upon comparison with received accounts and tacit features of what European empires were known to be: coherent, full-blown, visible, blatantly coercive, overtly exploitative, territorially distinct, and not humanitarian. But were they?

These amplified assertions of empire as an appropriate scale of analysis, as a model of practice, and as invitation to think with about contemporary global politics on the cusp of the twenty-first century challenge academic know-how and expertise. But they have also caught some students of colonial and postcolonial studies analytically off guard. It is no accident that recent debates on the new imperialism and the rise and demise of American empire are not drawing in—and on— the allegedly expert witnesses to imperial history that students of colonialisms claim to be.

Disputing whether politicians and the press are using the vocabulary of empire "correctly" may be an instinctive scholarly move, but it is not clear that such correctives matter to the current debates. If not directed at the terms used, should it be at the misrecognitions and assumptions that favor ambiguous analogies to be drawn? *How* does it matter, that in the public domain, imperial metaphors are conflated with contextualized comparison? The task may be to provide alternative histories and genealogies of the present, or studied appraisals of how caricatures of what empires are supposed to have once condoned or condemned are now rendered salient, self-evident, politically efficacious and "true." One path leads to a reassessment of claims about empires past; the other places emphasis less on the past than on what constitutes the current habitus of belief, on the sedimented histories through which these notions of empire circulate, on the weight and currency that nourish them now.

WHAT HISTORY LESSONS?

In September 2003 the *New York Times* reported on the Pentagon's screening of *The Battle of Algiers*—a film documenting the brutal interrogations of Arab suspects in the war against France, snidely noting that the film was once de rigueur viewing as a "teaching tool for radicalized Americans and revolutionary wannabes opposing the Vietnam War."[15] At the Pentagon the viewing had another goal. The forty officers and civilian experts attending were "urged to consider and discuss the implicit issues at the core of the film," "the advantages and costs of resorting to torture and intimidation in seeking vital human intelligence about enemy plans."

The Battle of Algiers, once banned in France for exposing what French nationalists and most French nationals preferred to deny, now relocates itself as a "preserved possibility," a colonial lesson that in some tempered or heightened form might serve the Defense Department well. One response might be to endorse that viewing but suggest that someone who lived that struggle be there to contextualize the history of that violence and the message of the film. Or should one campaign for its showing across the country in blockbuster theaters with the billing "what the Pentagon considers relevant and you should too"? (Film festivals across the country did just that and featured it for months following the Pentagon screening, advertising its "astonishing immediacy"—a "suspenseful thriller, " "as relevant today as it was in 1965.")[16]

Or should academics do what they are paid to do: make our undergraduates watch the movie and study what produced the conditions for French license to torture and the tactical violence of the Algerian response, and compare both to the School of the Americas' torture manuals that have trained its graduates since 1946?[17] Or is all that unnecessary? After all, the Pentagon did follow the recommendation of its "Special Operations/Low-Intensity Conflict," "civilian based" organization and asked whether winning a battle through torture was not a way to win a war.[18]

However viewed, there is little doubt that two years ago few students of colonialisms would have predicted a showing of *The Battle of Algiers* in 2003 to political strategists in Washington—especially when the French public still largely rejects that French systems of colonial rule in North Africa are not just unseemly reminders of an ugly past but basic to the tensions and making of modern France.[19] The lessons to learn and teach could be geared in any number of directions. An exercise in "lessons of empire" might answer back that *categories imposed by imperial rule do matter but precise definitions of empire do not;* or that imperial states and their administrative apparatus never achieved command over the shifting terrain of categories they helped to create or over quixotic shifts in who "belonged." When political science professor James Kurth writes in the *National Interest* that American empire is based on "ideas more than empires of the past," it is hard to summon his historical referents.[20] Colonial empires were always dependent on social imaginaries, blueprints unrealized, borders never drawn, administrative categories of people and territories to which no one was sure who or what should belong.[21]

EMPIRE VS. HUMANITARIAN REPUBLIC?

The current framings are familiar—and not. Republican liberty vs. imperial reach and responsibility, violent intervention in the name of humanitarian sympathies, the proper weighting of consent vs. coercion, the "soft" vs. "hard" tactics of empire are contrasts and connections that students of colonialisms have schooled themselves to treat not as contradictions of empires but as part of their standard architecture. Still how these terms appear now seem at once resonant and oddly askew in their usage and form.

Michael Ignatieff's *New York Times* feature article, "American Empire: The Burden," is a good example. In January 2003, the essay seemed at once brazen and historically naive. It acknowledged the previously unacknowledged—both that the deep denial of empire *is* a major part of early-twentieth-century American history and that United States foreign policy was and remains about "enforcing [a global] order."[22] On the other hand, it caricatured what empire once was and what "empire lite" looks like today, one whose "grace notes" are "free markets, human rights and democracy" as if these liberal impulses were new imperial inventions.[23] If "empire lite," is, as he contends, "no longer in the era of the United Fruit Company," participants in a strike of United Fruit workers protesting the continued use of insecticides banned in the United States (reported in the *Times* of the same week) might not agree.

Ignatieff's story hinges on what he identifies as "the real dilemma": "whether in becoming an empire the U.S. risks losing its soul as a republic," as if these were ever mutually exclusive categories. Students of empire could easily argue otherwise: that colonial empires have not only long coexisted with metropolitan republics but in dynamic synergy with them. The "grace notes" of "human rights" are not embellishments at all. To posit that the impulses that guide this form of imperial rule in a postimperial age are confusing because they are "contradictory" rehearses both a fictive model of colonialisms and a misconceived one. Civic liberties and entitlements like those lauded in the making of republican France were forged through the extension of empire. Racism was written into the very definition of republican liberties in the United States as well as France: the "color of liberty" was decidedly white, not North African, not Vietnamese and, in Haiti, Creole but not black.[24] That "America's empire is not like those of times past, built on conquest and the white man's burden" is both true and false.[25] Appeals to moral uplift, appreciation of cultural diversity, and protection of "brown women and children" against "brown men" were based on imperial systems of knowledge production enabled by, and enabling, coercive practices. These were woven into the very weft of empire—how control over and seizure of markets, land, and labor were justified, worked through and worked out.

Treating humanitarianism as the ruse, the mask or "the packaging" of empire misses a fundamental point.[26] In Norman Mailer's quest for the "logic of the present venture," military intervention in Iraq, he takes Bush's underlying dream to be a striving for "World Empire"—a commitment to empire as the subtext of flag conservatives. Then doubting whether he has it "right," he wonders if "perhaps they are not interested in empire so much as in trying in *true good faith* to save the world"— as if "good faith" was ever incompatible with imperial projects.[27] Compassionate imperialism was not the false advertising of imperial projects. Social hierarchies were bolstered by sympathy for empire's downtrodden subjects.[28] Sympathy conferred distance, required inequalities of position and possibility, and was basic to the founding and funding of imperial enterprises—these were core features of empire that the elaboration of such sentiments helped to create.

One could argue that the current debates about what constitutes empire—who has one and who does not—feeds a historically ill-formed public discourse and that a measured response would be to fight ignorance, to insist the Americans recognize their history. Just before his death, Edward Said criticized a North American public, schooled to be passionate about the history of the American revolution, quilt making, and small-town heroes, but not about the "sacroscant altruism" of U.S. innocents abroad and their well-meaning "do-good" state.

Students of colonial empires could easily document that claims to universalism are founding principles of imperial inequalities, in the past as in the present. Histories of empire resonate with contemporary racial formations in the world and set the conditions of possibility for the uneven entitlements they foster. We might step back and ask not only what is new (as many have), but why "newness" is always a part of imperial narratives. The U.S. empire was considered "new" at the turn of the twentieth century, "new" by Du Bois in 1920, and again in 1948 an "entirely new concept in the long history of political thought and action."[29]

IMPERIAL FORMATIONS AS STATES OF EXCEPTION

One would imagine that colonial studies could offer useful tools of analysis, and on some counts it does. But some cherished concerns get in the way. One has been a fixation on empires as *clearly bounded geopolities:* the notion that the color-coded maps empire's geographers designed and traced with linear precision were indeed fixed realities. Why this focus, when so much of the historical evidence points in another direction—not at fixed boundaries, but at fluid, ill-defined ones; not at empires as steady states but as states of becoming, of contested and changing relations? As historian Thongchai Winichakul has argued, imperial maps were a "model for, rather than a model of, what [they] purported to represent."[30] Imperial ventures are and always have been both "deterritorialized" and re-territorialized, both more and less marked, opaque and visible in ways we did not foresee. Second, colonial studies has predominantly focused on *European* empires, with France, Britain, Belgium, and the Netherlands establishing the ur-cases for what constitute the foundational strategies of rule. What Hannah Arendt called "continental imperialisms" or contiguous empires, such as the Habsburg or Ottoman empires, have been treated as incommensurate kinds.[31]

Third, European empires have not only been equated with their colonial variants, but more significantly, reduced to only certain features of them, such that outright conquest, European settlement, and legalized property confiscation are taken as defining attributes. Deviations from that norm become just that: aberrant, quasi-empires, exceptional cases, peripheral forms. Not least, our vocabularies have long been misleading and inadequate. "Internal colonialism" already presupposes a form apart from the real and dominant version. Elsewhere scholarly vocabulary defers to the terms of empires themselves—"indirect rule" and "informal empire" are unhelpful euphemisms, not working concepts.

Some have argued that the "stable canon" of colonial and postcolonial studies both has been skewed toward a focus on Europe and its former colonies and has been "overly committed to literary and historical perspectives." But I would argue that it has not been historical enough—that it has flattened out the relevant range of blurred genres of rule on which modern empires have flourished. Distinctly marked boundaries, transparent transfers of property, and even clear distinctions between colonizer and colonized represent a specific range of imperial forms and a narrow range of their orientations.

Students of the colonial embrace the notion that racial categories were murky and porous, but not that imperial jurisdiction was as well. The legal and political fuzziness of "dependencies," "trusteeships," "protectorates," and "unincorporated territories" were all part of the deep grammar of partially restricted rights in the nineteenth- and twentieth-century imperial world. Most importantly, those who inhabited those indeterminate spaces and ambiguous places were rarely beyond the reach of imperial will and force. They were not out of imperial bounds.[32]

Colonial studies has produced a representational archive of empire that almost seems to mimic that of well-bounded nation-states. Boundaries matter to nation-states in ways that for vast imperial states in expansion they cannot. So what if one starts from another premise, that this model of empire represents a tunnel vision, one scripted, limited, and endorsed by imperial states themselves? What if the notion of empire as a steady state (that may "rise or fall") is replaced with a notion of imperial formations as supremely mobile polities of dislocation, dependent not on stable populations so much as highly movable ones, on systemic recruitments and "transfers" of colonial agents and native military, and on a redistribution of peoples and resources, relocation and dispersions, contiguous and overseas? What if we begin not with a model of empire based on fixed, imperial cartographies but one dependent on moving categories and moving parts whose designated borders at any one time were not necessarily the force fields in which they operated or the limits of them? Hardt and Negeri define the new empire as one marked by "circuits of movement and mixture" but there were no colonial empires that were not.

Blurred genres are not empires in distress but imperial polities in active realignment and reformation. "Semblances of sovereignty" and contestation and congressional debate over the application of U.S. law beyond the territory of the United States, as Alexander Aleinikoff has so powerfully argued, have been an enduring feature of United States history. As he has put it, "Sovereignty meant more than control of borders. It also implied power to construct an 'American people' through the adoption of membership rules"—and strategic exclusions from them. The very concept of the British Empire should be traced through a genealogy that passes through Wales, Scotland, Protestant Ireland, the Caribbean and North America. The French Empire too was a single "France," but a differentiated one, in which Napoleon's continental expansion was part of an older and more recent pattern of expansion overseas. What is striking is not the absence of these liminal and disparate zones (and debates about them) in the histories of imperial formations, but the scant treatment of them. Ambiguous zones, partial sovereignty, temporary suspensions of what Hannah Arendt called "the right to have rights," provisional impositions of states of emergency, promissory notes for elections, deferred or contingent independence, and "temporary" occupations: these are conditions at the heart of imperial projects and present in nearly all of them. We need only look to the history of the British mandate in the early-twentieth-century Middle East, to contests over the Falkland Islands, to the terms of the Moroccan French protectorate, to the "unincorporated territory of Cuba," to the "temporary acquisition" of Guantanamo Bay at the turn of the century (or to the "rights-free zone" of Guantanamo today), or to American Samoa, whose inhabitants are considered U.S. nationals but not U.S. citizens. What do they have in common?

All are founded on *gradated variations and degrees of sovereignty and disenfranchisement*—on multiplex criteria for inclusions and sliding scales of basic rights. Each generated imperial conditions that required constant judicial and political reassessments of who was outside and who within. Each required frequent redrawing of the categories of subject and citizen, fostering elaborate nomenclatures that distinguished among "resident alien," "naturalized citizen," "national" "immigrant," or "U.S. citizen" without voting rights—as in the case of Guam.[33] All produced scales of differentiation and affiliation that exceeded the clear division between ruler and ruled. These are enduring forms of empire, force fields of attraction and aversion, spaces of arrest and suspended time. In imperial discourse, they are framed as unique cases—but they are not exceptions to imperial formations.

It is often assumed that guardians of empire were intent to clarify borders, establish "order," and reduce these zones of ambiguity. I would argue the opposite: that architects of imperial rule have invested in, exploited, and demonstrated strong stakes in their proliferation.

The observation invites a re-viewing of claims to U.S. exceptionalism: the notion that the U.S. is not really an empire because it has been "uninterested" in having colonies; that colonial America ended with the American revolution; or that reference to "the colonial" or "empire" reduces to a scholarly affectation. Viewed through a broader range of imperial forms, those terms signaling the ambiguous sovereignties of U.S. imperial breadth—unincorporated territories, trusteeships, protectorates, and "possessions" are not the blurred edges of what more "authentic," nonvirtual, visible empires look like, but variations on them. Puerto Rico, "inside and outside the constitution,"and Guantanamo, "both belonging to but not part of the United States," are both characteristic of what defines American empire itself.[34]

The United States *has* mastered this art of governance, but again, ambiguous domains of jurisdiction and ad hoc exemptions from the law on the basis of race and cultural difference are guiding and defining principles of imperial formations.

Students of colonial history should know it well. Edward Said insisted that the discursive and material configuration of power that defines orientalism describes not only a cultural enterprise in France and England but a political enterprise in the United States. In his preface to the twenty-fifth anniversary of the book's publication, he put it simply:

> Every single empire in its official discourse has said that it is not like all the others, that its circumstances are special, that it has a mission to enlighten, civilize, bring order and democracy, and that it uses force only as a last resort.[35]

These are consequential claims: one dismisses U.S. exceptionalism, the second more importantly holds that *discourses of exceptionalism are part of the discursive apparatus of empires themselves.* I would extend Said's insight: imperial states by definition operate as states *of* exception that vigilantly produce exceptions to their principles and exceptions to their laws.[36] From this vantage point, the United States is not an aberrant empire but a quintessential one, a consummate producer of excepted populations, excepted spaces, and its own exception from international and domestic law.

Whether we look to the Netherlands Indies, French Indochina, French Algeria, or British Malaya, each of their legal histories track prolonged exercises in forms of incorporation and differentiation that reshuffled and attenuated which populations and which social kinds (and in what distribution of spaces) had, at any specific moment, a "right to have rights" to education, labor protection, health care, or housing. Protracted debates—over who were to be classified as "white," "European," "mixed-blood," or "native Christian," who was subject to land tax and who not, who could hold property—were protracted exercises in developing regulations for selective populations and in setting out special conditions for suspension and reinvention of the laws applied to them.

Agamben's definition of a state of exception as a "threshold" between inside and out has more resonance still. Imperial formations and the varied degrees of sovereignty they afford could be understood as extended and extensive examples of macropolities whose thick or thin thresholds of ambiguous political status and territorial autonomy are fundamental to their technologies of rule. Imperial architectures are not wholly visible or wholly opaque. *Oscillation* between the visible, secreted, and opaque structures of sovereignty are features of them.[37] The creative lexicon of U.S. interventions then suggests not a marginal imperial form, but a more comprehensive picture of the varied and changing criteria by which empires sanction appropriations, occupations, and dispossessions.

What distinguishes this moment instead may be the accentuated *amorphous form* of power that the United States has assumed—and the justifications for a just war based on it. But how new was this? One could argue that the invisible boundaries outlining "the western hemisphere," drawn by the Monroe Doctrine in 1823, set the conditions of possibility for a geopolitical zone not to be subject to European empire but to a still emergent North American one.[38]

Students of imperial history count on a solid archival trail to track, on elaborated cultures of documentation for which agents of empire were rewarded and invested their careers. We are less versed at identifying the scope of empire when the contracts are not in written form, when policies are not labeled as confidential and designated as state secrets. Yet being an effective empire has long been contingent on partial visibility—sustaining the ability to remain an unaccountable one.

THE ENEMY WITHOUT AND WITHIN

Some issues have been largely absent from the current debate. At least one would entail knowing more about both what kinds of new agents of empire are in formation and what kinds of new subjects this empire is producing. Both are questions deeply tied, as postcolonial scholars have long insisted, to earlier imperial movements of labor, bureaucracies, and technological expertise across the globe. But they are also intimately linked to deep genealogies of trade, religious, and family networks that have moved obliquely to imperial routes and often in contradistinction to them.[39] The question demands a sense of what an ethnography of empire should look like: what new social distinctions are fortified, what movements of people it compels, what countermovements it provokes, what gender politics it gives rise to, what kinds of histories it arrests, reanimates, or seeks to trace.

Hannah Arendt argued that what distinguished totalitarian from imperial expansion was that the former recognized no difference between a home and foreign country while the latter depended on it.[40] But Arendt did not anticipate how much decolonization and the changing face of capital investment would not only bring the empire back home but collapse some of that difference. One profound imperial effect is a reconfigured space of the homeland, its defense, and who has what rights in it.

The language is familiar: the potential of an "enemy in disguise," an enemy who has surreptitiously entered the nation's ranks, perhaps even one linguistically indistinguishable who might not miss a cultural cue. It is not Bush alone who imagines a hidden enemy and interior frontiers that have to be safeguarded with artillery, computer surveillance, and duct tape. James Kurth envisions the advent of "two nations" (a term Andrew Hacker used to characterize what it means to be black in white America: namely, separate, hostile, and unequal).[41] For Kurth, it is Europe that will be internally divided as if "two nations"—one white, "secular, rich, old and feeble," the other an "anti-European nation" of colonial peoples, "Islamic, poor, young and virile." In his version, the "foreign colonizing nation will be the *umma* of Islam, and the colonized entity will be Europe" itself.

In Kurth's social imaginary, the enemy is not only to the south and east, but increasingly internal and domestically located, displacing whites in the north and west. In his "melancholy tale of empire and immigration" is a sober "warning" and "prophesy" for America, one that leads him to transpose terror into an explicitly racialized formulation. And so he asks whether "imperial immigration" may cause the United States also to become two nations, with "the coming of a Latino nation that would be poor, young and robust," accompanied by a "widespread fear of Latino terrorism." Samuel Huntington, in his series of articles on the "Hispanic Challenge" and in his new book, *Who We Are: The Challenges to America's National Identity,*[42] rehearses a similar argument, with unabashed reference to fears of a dark demographic tidal swell: "the most immediate and most serious challenge to American's traditional identity comes from the immense and continuing immigration from Latin America, especially from Mexico, and the fertility rates of these immigrants."[43] Race war/religious war/civilizational battle lines thread through these imaginaries, pulling up deep histories on which colonial empires were built. One could argue that the Euro-American public is susceptible to such visions because they are embedded in notions of racialized distinctions and profilings that recuperate and replay the historical anxieties of who is really "us," who gets to be called "white," and who is just "passing."

Foucault's notion that modern states take as their project that "society must be defended" against its enemies without and *within* confronts the deep logic of such arguments, making sense of how macropolities enlist their own citizens to police themselves, murder others, and accept the deaths of their soldier-children in the name of the greater good.[44] This notion that "society must be defended" condones the moral right to murder those "outside," as it produces not only state-sanctioned disenfranchisements, persecutions, and internments, but a dangerous overproduction of popular seat-of-the-pants profiling by "good citizens."

On the contemporary landscape, this has manifested in concrete ways. In the name of "national security" and the "fight against terrorism," the government targets "nonimmigrant aliens" and "enemy aliens" from over twenty-two countries, launching what the ACLU calls "one of the most serious civil liberties crises our nation has ever seen."[45] All true Americans must take part in this "defense." Being "on the alert" in the United States has become the job of park rangers, subway riders, and everyone who enters a public space. Vigilance and suspicion join with tolerance and compassion as sources of national pride and patriotic duty. In Dearborn, Michigan, those of the Arab and Muslim population must prove their loyalties and protect their property, not only with U.S. flags flown on their lawns and storefronts as after 9/11, but by accepting to help "sensitize" the FBI.[46]

Fear of an omnipresent, invisible "hidden force" and a secret intelligence apparatus to combat it are standard features of imperial administrations. A fear of pan-Islamism among Dutch colonials on the cusp of the twentieth century produced fingerprinting, kilometers of crime profiles, and secret-operations offices of "defense" and preemptive imprisonment. Updated and digitized, these are not unlike Department of Homeland Security practices. An Internet alert (quickly identified as a "false alarm") warning people not to open UPS packages or allow possible "terrorists disguised as UPS drivers" to enter one's home was not unrelated to that narrative. That colonial states policed and protected the privileges bestowed on some by making them police the moral values, familial forms, and political affiliations of those within their communities and of those suspected of really being "others" again is not unlike the social vigilantism today. What different polities have been willing to call themselves—what Arendt called "the wild confusion of historical terminology"—and how they have sought to compare themselves to, and label others, are part of the affective space of empires themselves.[47] There is no "pinning them down"—these are strategically malleable *active ingredients,* not dead metaphors in the making of consensus, in the building of popular support, in the making of what counts as benevolence, and what passes—when and for whom—as legitimate rule.

One sobering lesson we have learned about key symbols and powerful discourses in and out of colonial contexts: they are resilient in the face of contrary evidence. Like racisms they thrive smugly unchallenged by empirical claims. If the regimes of truth that underwrite contemporary understandings of empire are out of sync with what have been taken to be fundamentals of imperial rule, we need to identify what is singular about the contemporary situation and reassess the limits of what was assumed the case for our prototypic examples.

The question may not be whether current representations of an omnipotent or defunct American empire help or hinder understanding the contemporary situation, but rather why these representations surface in the form they do, what resonance they have—whether accurate or not. Reassessing what we think we know about empire (its historical specificities, its aftereffects, its durabilities) entails reassessing what counts as evidence and what does not. Some of the "lessons" may stretch us to find new ways to demonstrate that the "results" of empire are intimately bound to who, where, and what we are asking. To enter the debate may be to relocate what counts as knowledge and the force field of it.

PART II

EMPIRES AS AGENTS OF CHANGE

4. MODERNIZING COLONIALISM AND THE LIMITS OF EMPIRE

FREDERICK COOPER

A few years ago, with-it scholars were claiming that the nation-state was dying and that new forms of global connections would shape the world order. Now the state is back, and in one instance in a form so powerful that public intellectuals call it an empire. Earnest liberals lamented the imperial arrogance of the United States government, but then some feisty conservatives seized the terrain and asserted that indeed the United States was an empire and that its unembarrassed exercise of state power would be good for the world as a whole.[1]

The argument that the nation-state is withering away was just as wrong on September 10, 2001, as it is today, and what is particularly striking—and in some ways ominous—about the way the United States projects its power is that it is not like an empire. The relationship between territorially bounded institutions and transterritorial linkages has long been a shifting one, and the current phase of history is no exception to this pattern. But the examination of how it is shifting in this conjuncture is not promoted by arguments that dissolve the problem, either by proclaiming the death of the state or dominance of one state.

Empire is being used more as a metaphor than as a category that designates a particular form of polity. But some of the most crucial questions we face are about the structures through which power is exercised in an asymmetrical world order, about the institutions that can conjugate territorial and deterritorialized processes, about the forms of shared sovereignty that the European Union and other units of international cooperation entail, and about the governance of multicultural polities. The virtue of thinking about empire historically is that it cuts the nation-state down to size. We need not see history as a succession of coherent epochs: from empire to nation to postnational globality. Recognizing the continuing importance of empires well into the twentieth century and the importance of political movements that sought to change as well as replace empires points to a more general issue of continued relevance: the range of possibilities for exercising power. In past as in future, communities may be imagined, but not all imaginings are national ones.[2]

A useful beginning in examining the specificities of intrusive, sovereignty-compromising, transformative political forms is to distinguish among the imperial, the hegemonic, and the colonial.[3] Yet those distinctions say both too much and too little: not enough to distinguish the vast differences in process and effect within each, too much to understand the ambiguity and the interplay among them. If one grants that the U.S. position on Iraq is not about empire in the formal sense— asserting long-term sovereignty over Iraq—and therefore is either hegemonic or imperial but not colonial, one quickly arrives at a problem that is indeed quite colonial. Take the following catalog from a recent op-ed piece in the *New York Times:* in Iraq, the United States faces

> at least a decade's worth of reconstruction and improvements. This will include rebuilding ports, farms, roads, telecommunications systems, power plants, hospitals and water systems, as well as introducing a medical benefit plan, a national pension scheme, and new laws for foreign investment and intellectual property rights. The country needs a revised criminal code and judiciary system, a new tax code and collection system, and an electoral voting system with appropriate technology. . . . The total bill is likely to be at least $200 billion over a decade.[4]

This definition of the task rings a bell for an historian of the British and French Empires in Africa. It does not sound like colonialism in general, but very much like the colonialism of the post–World War II era, when the leading colonial powers, trying to reestablish their legitimacy and make their empires more orderly and productive, acknowledged the mediocrity of their past economic and social contributions to the colonies and proclaimed a new policy of "development." The goals of the British Colonial Development and Welfare Act (passed in 1940 and put into operation in 1945) and the French Investment Fund for Economic and Social Development of 1946 sound remarkably like those mentioned above. And the effort lasted about one decade, when British and French governments, frustrated by the difficulties of such a transformative project, realized that their taxpayers would not be willing to pay the bill to carry them through, that the interventions would produce more conflict than they would appease, and that giving up empire—once the goals were set so high—was more prudent than trying to make it work.

Looking further back, the now quite large history of empires goes against much of the polemical usage of the concept of empire, stressing that empire is a form of limited rule, limited both in relation to the exercise of totalizing power and to the will and ability to transform societies. When Britain and France rather belatedly got serious about using colonization as a tool of social transformation, they very quickly backed off.[5] So let me examine in more detail the notion of limits of empire—even in cases of extreme power asymmetry—and the contradictions of modernizing colonialism.

CIVILIZING MISSIONS, DEVELOPMENT
PROJECTS, AND THEIR LIMITS

In proclaiming a "civilizing mission," certain leaders in the French Third Republic in the 1870s were trying to convince colleagues and voters that colonial conquest was not necessarily too adventurous for a bourgeois society or too militaristic for a republic. The new subjects would neither be fully incorporated nor held in a state of permanent otherness. That was congruent with older notions of the French Empire as an inclusive but differentiated polity: it had a core in European France; "old colonies," notably in the Caribbean, where since 1848 all inhabitants were citizens; outposts in South Asia and Senegal where inhabitants had some of the rights of citizens; and Algeria, which was an integral part of the metropole, but which excluded the majority of the population from citizenship. In the late nineteenth century, France was acquiring "new colonies," whose people would be subjects but not citizens, and protectorates, which were states that had voluntarily ceded part of their sovereignty to France while retaining their own "nationalities." The republican colonizers claimed that France could take on new subjects as long as it committed itself to "civilizing" them and giving them citizenship as they proved their worth. This processual vision of colonization presumed that the empire was a unit of political and moral significance. The Saint Domingue (Haitian) Revolution of 1791–1804 had much earlier put on the table the question of whether the Declaration of the Rights of Man and of the Citizen applied to the colonies, barely after it had been issued in Paris.[6]

The British had no analogous citizenship construct—all were subjects of the queen—but the antislavery movement had an even greater impact in insisting that how people in the empire were treated, whatever their color or culture, could be a stain on the British flag. Conquest in the late nineteenth century was in large part made meaningful to the British public, or that part of it which cared, because the influential missionary lobby had since the 1860s put forth a picture of Africa as a benighted continent, still distorted by an internal slave trade, ruled by tyrants and in need of redemption. The experience of the empire, however, was already ambiguous: hopes of redeeming the already British slaves of the West Indies had been dashed by the unwillingness of many of those ex-slaves to play the role of dutiful free laborer assigned to them, and they had been increasingly portrayed as racial exceptions to the rule of optimizing behavior under free markets and just government. The notions of redemption and unredeemable inferiority coexisted uneasily in imperial discourse at the end of the nineteenth century.[7] And alongside this ambivalence, officials read the risks of pushing too hard in different ways: the Indian Mutiny of 1857 led the government to insist that India be governed firmly but carefully.

Empires were both incorporative and differentiated polities. Too sharp differentiation and the intermediate authorities on whom the center depended would have no stake in cooperation; too much incorporation and demands for political voice or autonomy would be enabled. That certain issue networks in France and Britain saw the space of empire in moral terms and argued that enslavement or abuse of subject populations violated imperial integrity did not prevent imperial governments and settlers from being brutal or exploitative, but it did insure that scandals would be a periodic feature of imperial governance in democratic states: over slavery, massacres, colonial wars, forced labor, and poverty.

The politics of imperial reformers interacted uneasily with political movements among colonized populations themselves, but such movements did not limit themselves to a dichotomous choice between demanding full participation in an imperial polity on that polity's own terms or the transformation of difference into national autonomy. Different forms of cultural assertion and different claims to political voice and representation—from turning colonies into departments of France, to turning empire into a federation of distinct nationalities, to other forms of transnational connection (pan-Islamism, pan-Africanism)—were parts of political mobilization within and against empires. Until the very end of colonial rule, the overlap of these different sorts of movements underscored the importance of empire as a unit in which political morality, rights, and well-being were debated and marked the instability of the balance of inclusion and differentiation. That empire, over the last two hundred years, has provoked debate within imperial metropoles, organizing by international networks, and opposition and mobilization within colonies—using and challenging the ideologies of imperial powers themselves—lies behind concerns voiced today over the political consequences of how the United States or another power acts when it intervenes forcefully outside its borders.[8]

Actually ruling an empire was more complicated than civilizers, reformers, and redeemers admitted. The great advantage of a conquering power in the age of the telegraph and Maxim gun was the ability to concentrate forces and then move onward. Colonization meant raiding a village, visibly terrorizing its population, seizing the cattle, burning the huts, and going elsewhere. Routinizing control was another story, and it meant going against the logic of any civilizing mission or project of building a new political order. The only way to administer the large spaces and dispersed populations of Africa was to co-opt local elites into doing the dirty work. "Indirect rule" was a fact in Africa—as it had been in many other empires—long before it was a doctrine. Moreover, both France and Britain treated as sacrosanct an old imperial doctrine: colonies should pay for themselves. Even the famous imperial advocate Sir John Seeley said in regard to India in the 1880s, "It is a condition of our Indian Empire that it should be held without any great effort." British and French colonialism, at least up to World War II, was colonialism on the cheap: the colonies were supposed to pay the costs of their own repression.[9]

Niall Ferguson, in the body of his book *Empire,* makes clear that British rule was constrained by its cheapness and reliance on intermediate authorities, then contradicts himself at the end by insisting that British rule meant rule of law, fair and honest government, the maintenance of peace, and free-market policies. It neither had the will nor the capacity to play such a role, certainly not in Africa, where its rule in much of the continent depended on rigidifying the power of local authorities; on using a "customary" law that was reified as it was codified; in settler colonies, on arbitrary seizure of land from Africans and the prevention of African ownership of land elsewhere; and on the segregation of public facilities. Economic policy favored British import-export firms over indigenous commercial networks, and as Ferguson admits, invoked "imperial preference" to restrict trade beyond the sterling block when it suited British needs. If the British Empire disseminated lessons in law and free markets to the "white" colonies, Africans were taught something else.[10]

At times, officials in the early years of African colonization sought to turn African cultivators or African slaves into wage workers or productive farmers. The zeal behind such efforts quickly burned out, partly because the very authorities on whom rulers depended were likely to have an interest in maintaining people in a dependent status (even if slavery was formally ended), partly because the need for export crops was too acute for authorities to ask too many questions about how they were produced, and partly because new actors, notably white settlers, pushed for short cuts around "free" labor principles. By winks and nods, officials—sometimes over the protests of missionaries—accommodated themselves to a variety of forms of labor organization in African territories. By World War I, officials were congratulating themselves on having the wisdom not to change African society too much.

In the early 1920s, French and British governments rejected "development" programs that would have used metropolitan funds to foster a more systematic usage of African resources, both in the name of the old doctrine of each colony paying its way and because key figures did not want to upset tacit arrangements with African local authorities.[11] Private capital investment was little more aggressive, as British capital exports went to old colonies and dominions, Europe, and the United States, and what little went to Africa went overwhelmingly to mines.[12] Throughout this time, islands of export productivity were carved out: mining zones surrounded by vast impoverished areas from which back-and-forth migrant laborers could be recruited; areas of white settlement where farmers received considerable help from the state in recruiting and disciplining labor; and areas of cultivation by African farmers, small or medium scale, who used family labor, tenants and clients, and sometimes wage labor. Attempts to build either an indigenous or a settler capitalism ran up against the situation that most Africans had some land resources, even if these were squeezed by alienation, that colonial economies opened up new niches which were alternatives to subservience to an employer, and that employers themselves did not necessarily want to play by the rules of a wage-labor economy.[13] Infrastructure focused on the narrow pathways of an import-export economy. Urban centers provided little infrastructure for long-term workers and families. Such an economic structure permitted some firms to make large profits, but gave every incentive to Africans to find alternatives to full involvement in a wage-labor or cash-crop sector.

TOWARD DEVELOPMENTAL COLONIALISM— AND THE END OF EMPIRE

The mediocrity of colonial economic performance made it easier for colonial powers to slough off the dislocations of the 1929 Depression into a countryside that they did not have to examine. By the end of the decade, however, British officials began to recognize that even weak economies in Africa and the West Indies produced social dislocation, particularly in the narrow channels of communication and islands of wage-labor production. When production haltingly increased (and with it inflation), a wave of strikes began, from Barbados to Mombasa. The Colonial Office, through a series of commissions and internal arguments, finally came to recognize the woefully inadequate infrastructure and the poverty in both its old, West Indian, and new, African, colonies. With the passage of the Colonial Development and Welfare Act of 1940, it finally committed metropolitan funds, with the specific intention of strengthening colonial economies for long-run development and improving the welfare of at least those colonial subjects in the "modern" sector. It was only then that the piecemeal and underfunded initiatives of colonial governments in the realm of health, agricultural technology, and urbanism were aggregated under the rubric of "development."

During the brief Popular Front rule in 1936–38, the French government also undertook an autocritique of its initiatives in Africa, and found them wanting: too much coercion, not enough incentive for Africans to participate voluntarily in export production, feeble infrastructure. But once again the legislature refused to spend money on development programs. The right-wing government of Vichy in the early 1940s came up with a plan for the unblinking and systematic exploitation of Africa, but not with the money to implement it. The war, the strike wave—which hit French Africa right after the war—and other conflicts within African colonies, the turmoil in other colonies, notably Vietnam and North Africa, and the changed international environment put pressure on the French government, like the British, to articulate and implement an effort to make colonialism progressive, hence the postwar development drive and various efforts at political reform. Unlike the older category of "civilization," development focused on concrete changes and potentially measurable progress. While the category marked a hierarchy between those who had achieved development and those who had not, it also constituted a language in which claims could be posed for the resources to advance along the path.

But the development framework did not bring social questions under control. Labor was a restive force, which British and French officials tried to domesticate by importing to Africa the techniques of industrial relations. Given the vast and still untransformed African countryside, trying to define, train, and acculturate an African workforce in the key sites of production and commerce in mines and cities and along railroads meant separating it from its rural origins, a policy known as "stabilization." This meant paying wages adequate to support a family and bringing the next generation of workers up under the surveillance of experts in nutrition, education, and labor relations. Labor unions realized the vulnerability of colonial regimes to collective action in the narrow channels of a colonial economy, as well as the vulnerability of the ideological efforts to demonstrations of discontent. Once the colonial regimes were no longer able to defend a racially defined boundary, the claims to "equal pay for equal work"—posed in the very language of developmental colonialism—were hard to shunt aside.

The French case is an especially vivid demonstration of the volatility of a supranational polity, in which the effort of the metropole to define itself as the model and reference point for progress leads, unintentionally, to an escalation of claims placed in the language of imperial ideology. In 1946, the French legislature, which then contained a small minority of colonial representatives, passed a law that abolished the distinction between subject and citizen. The citizenship law may have been intended to give Africans a minority voice in French institutions while denying them control over their own destiny—meanwhile inscribing Greater France as indissoluble and unitary. But the effect was more profound than that. Once the normality of racial distinction was stripped from imperial ideology, the notion of empire as a political and moral unit became an empowering one for social movements. Trade unions claimed equal pay for equal work; veterans claimed full benefits; students rejected inferior schooling; political parties demanded more spending on health care and urban amenities—all within a rhetoric of French citizenship.[14]

Such arguments were underscored by various forms of collective action, but they also appealed to officials whose own hopes for remaking empire depended on Africans taking seriously the premises of modernizing imperialism. While African political movements did increasingly claim more autonomy, they also made full use of imperial institutions and the rhetoric of citizenship to make claims. A French minister in 1956 summed up the turn that late imperial politics had taken: citizenship had come to mean "equality in wages, equality in labor legislation, in social security benefits, equality in family allowances, in brief, equality in standard of living."[15]

It is thus only in the last phase of colonial rule that something like the project of a reformist imperialism was implemented with any degree of seriousness. And this effort was short-lived. The basic problem with developmental colonialism was twofold, and both are quite relevant to considerations about the present. One problem was domestic: the empires of France and Britain had been empires-on-the-cheap. Postwar colonialism promised to be expensive.[16] And this promise was soon fulfilled. The development effort clogged on the retrograde infrastructure of African colonies, while African workers were in a good position to claim higher wages and benefits and this drove up the costs. The colonial archives betray the frustration of officials in the early 1950s at the slowness of results on the development front. Domestically, empire was becoming a hard sell, and by the mid-1950s, the cost was being questioned in the press and legislature in France and Britain.[17]

The second problem was in Africa itself. The reformist effort produced more conflict than it alleviated. Trade unions became confident and escalated their demands. The most successful farmers complained of discrimination in produce markets, while the least successful complained—and sometimes revolted—because of the loss of security in a more competitive environment.[18] All this followed when the logic of empire met the logic of the welfare state, with the logic of immutable racial distinction no longer available. The responsibility of the state became the empire as a whole, and social and political organizations throughout the empire were prepared to raise issues of equivalence and equality in imperial space.

In the end, it was the French and British governments that blinked: they could not accept the costs of modernizing colonialism, when the political and economic benefits were so uncertain. In French Africa, Africans were still debating whether to push for more autonomy or a fuller French citizenship when the French government decided to devolve most power, including that over the budget, to the individual colonial territories. The unit in which citizens would seek equality—and the resources to pay for it—would become the territory, not the empire. For France, as for Britain, this meant effectively renouncing the power of imperial control, but for Africans who took the bargain it meant renouncing claims on those resources in favor of territorially bounded power.

The colonialism that collapsed first in Africa was colonialism at its most reformist. The oldest and least dynamic of the African colonizations, that of Portugal, would be the last to go. It is important to think beyond the common notion of an obdurate, unchanging colonial edifice falling before the assaults of heroic uprisings.

The uprisings in sub-Saharan Africa, notably in Madagascar, Kenya, and Cameroon, were put down successfully; so too, for that matter, was the military side of Algeria.[19] But the threat came from collective action within the colonial edifice too, from Africans who turned the modernization arguments of Britain and France into claims to resources and whose strikes, demonstrations, and other campaigns—in the shadow of Algeria, Suez, Vietnam, and other colonial crises—forced Britain and France into a cost-benefit calculation about colonies that they had not needed to make before.

IMPLICATIONS

What does this history signify for the present world conjuncture? It reveals alternative models for empire. The idea of empire as a transformative mechanism is indeed available, but one has to be careful about how one locates it. The precedents for it are not the "British Empire" or the French civilizing mission writ large. Rather, initiatives to systematically remake colonized societies appear as alternatives within colonial regimes, against other visions of colonization, from ruthless, dehumanizing extraction to the deliberate conservation of pacified indigenous communities, with a big dose of low-cost improvisation thrown in. The precedent regarding interventionist imperialism appears quite relevant to today's concerns, but not in the way advocates of the empire model would have it: it is a precedent for getting out when the costs get high.[20] If advocates of passing the imperial mantle from Britain to the United States worry whether Americans have the will to take on an imperial mission, the British experience should in fact reinforce their anxieties.

The other model of colonialism that seems quite relevant is what Ferguson—but not where he draws the lessons for today—calls "butcher and bolt": the tendency of colonizing regimes to pacify or punish, move on, and do a poor job of establishing routine administration. That may well be—indeed that is Ferguson's worry—what the Bush administration has in mind.[21] In Iraq, however, bolting is proving the more difficult task.

Still another model of supposedly benevolent colonization is more consistent with a conservative administration's view of the world: a more minimalist view of keeping a colonial peace under which divided, "primitive" people are kept off each other's throats and given the chance to develop more productive agriculture and commerce under some predictable, if not exactly fair, administrative and judicial control.[22] Familiarity with the past again should lead to skepticism about this future. The colonization of Africa extinguished certain forms of conflict—one need not invent a romantic image of pacific Africa to question the idea of a colonial peace. But the roots of present-day African conflicts lie significantly in the ethnicization that the colonial strategy of ruling through indigenous elites—frozen in place by the colonizing authority—fostered out of more shifting patterns of cultural difference and the efforts of rulers to recruit clients and followers. Rule of law was hardly a colonial accomplishment: such a notion was cut across by racial segregation in employment, residence, and public accommodations, and by the notion that Africans should be ruled by "custom" and that their land could only be "communal." When after World War II British and French governments at last tried to reduce, with the notable exceptions of colonies of white settlements, the racial exclusions that were part of daily life in the colonies, that was part of the ambitious modernization of imperialism, with all the costs and conflicts that this entailed. As an American administration not noted for its reformist social agenda seems to be discovering in Iraq, establishing rule of law, predictability in economic transactions, and intercommunal respect may well be among the most expensive, least certain, and long-term processes there are. Only the blindness of certain conservatives to the complexity of social life and their unawareness of the conflict-ridden histories of twentieth-century empires makes it possible for them to see colonial occupation as a precedent for establishing legality and transparency in administration.

Ferguson's argument for the passing of the imperial mantle from Great Britain to the United States is, in the end, not an argument about empire at all. The bulk of his book *Empire* is scrupulous enough to dissociate "empire" as a political form from rule of law, honesty, concern for others, and the generalization of the benefits of economic development. In the concluding pages, these virtues are linked not to the messy and often sordid story of empire, but to the image of a British man assuming the "White Man's Burden" and saving those people who cannot save themselves.[23]

But the brief episode of modernizing imperialism, British and French style, in the 1950s, still bears thinking about, not so much for what it was as for its unintended consequences: the escalation of claims phrased within the language of postwar imperialism. This story is a reminder that the terms of politics are not static and that policies which take a world power deeply into the affairs of another state will likely have repercussions far beyond their intended objective. We need to think precisely about the specificities of institutions and the possibilities of different languages by which political movements make claims and challenge established orders. We are not stuck with a choice between a politics of nation-states and citizenship and an amorphous globality or between inviolable sovereignties and unrestrained interventions. The sooner we start thinking with care and precision about the space in between the better.

5. LEARNING FROM EMPIRE: RUSSIA AND THE SOVIET UNION[1]

RONALD GRIGOR SUNY

The two states that ruled over the great Eurasian expanse from the Pacific to east-central Europe have both been characterized as empires. While tsarist Russia was in its own self-definition unquestionably an empire, the Soviet Union rejected such a characterization, which was usually applied to it only by its enemies. In this chapter I explore the nature of these two large contiguous states with reference to a set of concepts of empire and nation. The issue of whether the USSR should be considered an empire remains controversial. If it is imperial, in what sense? Is there something about the imperial nature of tsarism or the Soviet Union that contributed both to their success for however long they lasted and to their ultimate demise? My argument is that a "dialectic of empire" linked success to failure.

Empire, like nation-state, is best understood as a historically constructed state form that combines both objective and subjective elements. Rather than a straightforward definition based on objective characteristics, I propose thinking about empire, nation, and nation-state as forms of political practice and understanding.

Among the various kinds of political communities and units that have existed historically, empires have been among the most ubiquitous, in many ways the precursors of the modern bureaucratic state. Borrowing from the definitions of empire of John A. Armstrong and Michael W. Doyle, I consider *empire* to be a particular form of domination or control, between two units set apart in a hierarchical, inequitable relationship, more precisely a composite state in which a metropole dominates a periphery to the disadvantage of the periphery.[2] Imperialism, then, is the deliberate act or policy that furthers a state's extension or maintenance for the purpose of aggrandizement of that kind of direct or indirect political or economic control over any other inhabited territory which involves the inequitable treatment of those inhabitants in comparison with its own citizens or subjects. The key characteristic of empire is inequitable rule by one legally distinctive group over another; the "domain of empire is a people subject to unequal rule."[3] Inequitable treatment might involve forms of cultural or linguistic discrimination or disadvantageous redistributive practices from the periphery to the metropole (but not necessarily, as, for example, in the Soviet empire).

Inequality and subordination in empire involve defined markers of difference, e.g., ethnicity, geographic separation, or administrative distinction.[4] If peripheries are fully integrated into the metropole, as various appanage principalities were into Muscovy, and treated as well or badly as the metropolitan provinces, then the relationship is not imperial. Very importantly, the metropole need not be defined ethnically or geographically. It could be the ruling institution. In several empires, rather than a geographic or ethnic distinction from the periphery, the ruling institution had a status or class character, a specially endowed nobility or political class, like the Osmanli in the Ottoman Empire, or the imperial family and upper layers of the landed gentry and bureaucracy in the Russian Empire, or, analogously, the Communist *nomenklatura* in the Soviet Union. In my understanding, neither tsarist Russia nor the Soviet Union was an ethnically "Russian Empire" with the metropole completely identified with a ruling Russian nationality. Rather, the ruling institution—nobility in one case, the Communist Party elite in the other—was multinational, though primarily Russian, *and* ruled imperially over Russian and non-Russian subjects alike. In empire, unlike nations, the distance and difference of the rulers was part of the ideological justification for the superordination of the ruling institution. The right to rule in empire resides with the ruling institution, not in the consent of the governed.

All states have centers, capital cities, and central elites, which in some ways are superior to the other parts of the state, but in empires the metropole is uniquely sovereign, able to override routinely the desires and decisions of peripheral units.[5] The flow of goods, information, and power runs from periphery to metropole and back to periphery, but seldom from periphery to periphery. The degree of dependence of periphery on metropole is far greater and more encompassing than in other kinds of states. Roads and railroads run to the capital; elaborate architectural and monumental displays mark the imperial center off from other centers; and the central imperial elite distinguishes itself in a variety of ways from both peripheral elites, often their servants and agents, and the ruled population.[6] The metropole benefits from the periphery in an inequitable way; there is "exploitation," at least there is the perception of such exploitation. While subordination, inequitable treatment, and exploitation might be measured in a variety of ways, they are always inflected subjectively and normatively.[7] That, indeed, is the essence of what being colonized means.

To sum up, empire is a composite state structure in which the metropole is distinct in some way from the periphery and the relationship between the two is conceived or perceived by metropolitan or peripheral actors as one of justifiable or unjustifiable inequity, subordination, and/or exploitation. "Empire" is not merely a form of polity but also a value-laden appellation that as late as the nineteenth century (and even in some usages well into our own) was thought of as the sublime form of political existence (think of New York as the "empire state"), but which in the late twentieth century casts doubts about the legitimacy of a polity and even predicts its eventual, indeed inevitable, demise. Thus, the Soviet Union, which a quarter of a century ago would have been described by most social scientists as a state and only occasionally, and usually by quite conservative analysts, as an empire, is almost universally described after its demise as an empire, since it now appears to have been an illegitimate, composite polity unable to contain the rising nations within it.

This ideal type of empire, then, is fundamentally different from the ideal type of the *nation-state.* While empire is inequitable rule over something different, the practice of rule in a nation-state is, at least in theory if not always in practice, the same for all members of the nation. Citizens of the nation have a different relationship with their state than do the subjects of empire. A *nation,* the body of citizens that conveys legitimacy to the ruling elite of the nation-state, is defined as "a group of people who imagines itself to be a political community that is distinct from the rest of humankind, believes that it shares characteristics, perhaps origins, values, historical experiences, language, territory, or any of many other elements, and on the basis of their defined culture deserves self-determination, which usually entails control of its own territory (the "homeland") and a state of its own."[8] Neither natural nor primordial but the result of hard constitutive intellectual and political work of elites and masses, nations exist in particular understandings of history, stories in which the nation is seen as the subject moving continuously through time, coming to self-awareness over many centuries.[9]

From roughly the late eighteenth century to the present, the state, the territorially bounded authorities that increasingly held the monopoly of legitimate violence, merged with the "nation," and almost all modern states claimed to be nation-states, either in an ethnic or civic sense, with governments deriving power from and exercising it in the interest of the nation. Although the discourse of the nation began as an expression of state patriotism, through the nineteenth century it increasingly became ethnicized until in most cases the "national community" was understood to be a cultural community of shared language, religion, and/or other characteristics with a durable, antique past, shared kinship, common origins and narratives of progress through time. Modern states legitimized themselves in reference to the people constituting the nation, which in the decades after the French Revolution was increasingly seen as the source of sovereign power.[10] Against the claims of dynastic rulers and multinational empires, nationalists strove to take power in the name of the nation and to make the nation and the state congruent. As once viable imperial states became increasingly vulnerable to the appeals of nationalisms, that in turn gained strength from the new understanding that states ought to represent, if not coincide, with nations, the simultaneous rise of notions of democratic representation of sub-altern interests accentuated the fundamental tension between inequitable imperial relationships and horizontal conceptions of national citizenship. Though liberal states with representative institutions, styling themselves as democracies, could be (and were) effective imperial powers in the overseas empires of Great Britain, France, Belgium, and the Netherlands, the great contiguous empires resisted democratization that would have undermined the right to rule of the dominant imperial elite and the very hierarchical and inequitable relationship between metropole and periphery in the empire. While empires were among the most ubiquitous and long-lived polities in premodern history, they were progressively subverted in modern times by the powerful combination of nationalism and democracy.[11]

The nation-state was not, however, the inevitable future for nineteenth- and twentieth-century empires. Three outcomes became imaginable in the half century after World War I:

1. disintegration into a number of purported nation-states (which was the fate of the Austro-Hungarian Empire and the Ottoman Empire);
2. reconfiguration as a *multinational state* based on recognition of differentiation between the various populations but with no subordination or inequitable dominance but equality among all parts of the population to the degree possible, and the formation of a single political community that does not coincide in all ways with the various cultural communities; and
3. reconfiguration as a nonimperial, non-nation-state that conceived of itself as an alternative to the state form altogether (i.e., the Soviet Union). But the fate of this model was to fall between the state practices of nation making and imperial rule.

Empire and nation-state/multinational state stand at opposite ends of a spectrum of state practices and perceptions. In actually existing states the actions of ruling elites may shift from more inequitable and differentiating imperial practices to practices that promote horizontal equivalency among citizens; movement in the other direction also occurs. In other words, no state is safe from reversion to empire or movement toward homogenizing, nationalizing practices. The argument here is that states that act as empires may also engage in nation making (and vice versa), but that these two state practices are contradictory and difficult to reconcile, that one tends to subvert the other and lead to an erosion of the stability and legitimacy of the state. This argument is well borne out in the histories of tsarist Russia and the Soviet Union and tells us much about the present problems of state building and foreign policy of the current Russian Federation.

MODERNIZING EMPIRES

In the last two centuries state authorities in the great contiguous empires of Europe attempted to homogenize the differences within the state in order to achieve the kinds of efficiencies that accompanied the more homogeneous nation-states, but for a variety of reasons they ultimately failed. What was once possible in medieval and early modern times when quite heterogeneous populations assimilated into relatively homogeneous protonations, perhaps around common religious or dynastic loyalties, became in the "age of nationalism" far more difficult, for now the available discourse of the nation with all its attendant attractions of progress, representation, and statehood became available for anyone to claim. At the same time the appeals of popular sovereignty and democracy implied in the nation form challenged the inequity, hierarchy, and discrimination inherent in empire, undermining their very raison d'être.

Modern empires were caught between maintaining the privileges and distinctions that kept the traditional elites in power or considering reforms along liberal lines that would have undermined the old ruling classes. While the great "bourgeois" overseas empires of the nineteenth century were able to liberalize, even democratize in the metropoles, at the same time maintaining harsh repressive regimes in the colonies, it was far more difficult to pursue different policies in core and periphery in contiguous empires than in noncontiguous ones. A democratic metropole easily coexisted with colonized peripheries in overseas empires, as the examples of Britain, France, and Belgium show, but it was much more destabilizing to have constitutionalism or liberal democracy in only part of a contiguous empire. In Russia the privileges enjoyed by the Grand Duchy of Finland, or even the constitution granted to Bulgaria, an independent state outside the empire, were constant reminders to the tsar's educated subjects of his refusal to allow them similar institutions. This major tension of contiguous empires encouraged some kind of separation or apartheid to maintain a democratic and nondemocratic political order in a single state. But, as the governments of South Africa and Israel would discover in the twentieth century, this was a highly unstable compromise.

Responding to the challenges presented by the efficiencies of the new national states, imperial elites promoted a transition from "ancien régime" empires to "modern" empires, from a more polycentric and differentiated polity in which regions maintained quite different legal, economic, and even political structures, to a more centralized, bureaucratized state in which laws, economic practices, even customs and dialects, were homogenized by state elites. The more modern empires adopted a number of strategies to restabilize their rule. In Russia the monarchy became more "national" in its self-image and public representation, drawing it closer to the people it ruled. In Austro-Hungary the central state devolved power to several of the nonruling peoples, moving the empire toward becoming a more egalitarian multinational state.

In the Ottoman Empire modernizing bureaucrats abandoned certain traditional hierarchical practices that privileged Muslims over non-Muslims, and in the re-forming era known as *Tanzimat* they attempted to create a civic nation of all peoples of the empire, an Ottomanist idea of a new imperial community. In the last two decades of the nineteenth century the tsarist government attempted yet another strategy, a policy of administrative and cultural Russification that privileged a single nationality. The Young Turks after 1908 experimented with everything from an Ot-tomanist liberalism to pan-Islamic, pan-Turkic, and increasingly nationalist recon-figurations of their empire.[12] But modernizing imperialists were caught between these new projects of homogenization and rationalization, and policies and struc-tures that maintained distance and difference from their subjects as well as differen-tiations and disadvantages among the peoples of the empire. Modernizing empires searched for new legitimation formulas that softened rhetorics of conquest and di-vine sanction and emphasized the civilizing mission of the imperial metropole, its essential competence in a new project of development.

Given the unevenness of the economic transformations of the nineteenth and twentieth centuries, all within a highly competitive international environment, most states, even quite conservative imperial states like the Ottoman and Romanov em-pires, undertook state programs of economic and social "modernization." Needing to justify the rule of foreigners over peoples who were constituting themselves as na-tions, the idea of developing inferior or uncivilized peoples became a dominant source of imperial legitimation and continued well into the twentieth century.[13] Deeply embedded in both national and imperial state policies, however, is a partic-ularly subversive dialectic in imperial developmentalism. Its very successes create the conditions for imperial failure. If the developmentalist program succeeds among the colonized people, realizing material well-being and intellectual sophistication, ur-banism and industrialism, social mobility and knowledge of the world, the justifica-tion for foreign imperial rule over a "backward" people evaporates. Indeed, rather than suppressing nation making and nationalism, imperialism far more often pro-vides conditions and stimulation for the construction of new nations. Populations are ethnographically described, statistically enumerated, ascribed characteristics and functions, and reconceive themselves in ways that qualify them as "nations." Not acci-dentally the map of the world at the beginning of the twenty-first century is marked by dozens of states with boundaries drawn by imperialism. And if clearly defined and articulated nations do not exist within these states by the moment of independence, then state elites busily set about creating national political communities to fill out the fledgling state.

Developmentalism, of course, was not the project of "bourgeois" nation-states and empires alone, but of self-styled socialist ones as well. The problem grew when empires, which justified their rule as agents of modernity and modernization, as instruments of development and progress, achieved their stated task too well, supplied their subordinated populations with languages of aspiration and resistance (as Cooper and Packard put it, "What at one level appears like a discourse of control is at another a discourse of entitlement"[14]), and indeed created subjects that no longer required empire in the way the colonizers claimed. This dialectical reversal of the justification for empire, embedded in the theory and practice of modernization, was, in my view, also at the very core of the progressive decay of the Soviet empire. In a real sense the Communist Party effectively made itself irrelevant. Who needed a "vanguard" when you now had an urban, educated, mobile, self-motivated society? Who needed imperial control from Moscow when national elites and their constituents were able to articulate their own interests in terms sanctioned by Marxism-Leninism in the idea of national self-determination?

The end of empire, in this argument, is best understood as arising from two factors: the delegitimizing power of nationalism and democracy that severely undermines imperial justifications; and the subversive effect of other legitimizing formulas, like developmentalism, that produce precisely the conditions under which imperial hierarchies and discriminations are no longer required. In modern times the end of empire must be placed in the context of the institutional and discursive shifts that have taken place with the rise of the nation-state. Historically many of the most successful modern states began as empires, with dynastic cores extending outward by marriage or conquest to incorporate peripheries that over time were gradually assimilated into a single, relatively homogeneous polity. By the late nineteenth century empires were those polities that were either uninterested or had failed in the project of creating a nation-state. The fragility of twentieth-century empires was related to the particular development of the nation as the dominant source of political legitimation, its claims of popular sovereignty with its inherently democratic thrust, and its call for a cultural rootedness alien to the transnational cosmopolitanism of European dynasts and aristocrats.

RULING THE RUSSIAN EMPIRE

Despite the tendency of postrevolutionary historians to see it as a failure, the tsarist empire can easily be appreciated as one of the most successful empires in history. Over several centuries it maintained effective control over a vast continent peopled by over a hundred different ethnicities, which at one and the same time were living in different historical epochs. Nomads and illiterate hunters and gatherers were subjects of the same emperor as were the sophisticated Europeanized urban dwellers of Moscow and St. Petersburg. The legitimacy of the tsar's dominion was only infrequently questioned before the nineteenth century, and even up to the early twentieth century primarily by a small number of oppositional intellectuals. At first the ruling elite's distance from the population gave it the aura and mystery that justified its power. In his study of the rites, rituals, and myths generated by and about the Russian monarchy, Richard S. Wortman argues that the imagery of the monarchy from the fifteenth to the late nineteenth century was of foreignness, separation of the ruler and the elite from the common people.[15] The origin of the rulers was said to be foreign (the Varangians were from beyond the Baltic Sea), and they were likened to foreign rulers of the West. "In expressing the political and cultural preeminence of the ruler, foreign traits carried a positive valuation, native traits a neutral or negative one," writes Wortman.[16] Even the models of rulership were foreign—Byzantium and the Mongol khans—and foreignness conveyed superiority. Later, in the eighteenth and nineteenth centuries, the myth of the ruler as conqueror was used to express the monarchy's bringing to Russia the benefits of civilization and progress, and the ruler was portrayed as a selfless hero who saved Russia from despotism and ruin.

With the annexation of Ukraine (1654) and Vilnius (1656), the monarch was proclaimed "tsar of all Great, Little, and White Russia."[17] The state seal of Aleksei Mikhailovich, adopted in 1667, depicted an eagle with raised wings, topped with three crowns symbolizing Kazan, Astrakhan, and Siberia, and bordered by three sets of columns, representing Great, Little, and White Russia. The tsar, now also called *sviatoi* (holy), further distanced himself from his subjects "by appearing as the supreme worshipper of the realm, whose piety exceeded theirs."[18] Finally, toward the end of the century, Tsar Fedor referred to the "Great Russian Tsardom" (*Velikorossiiskoe tsarstvie*), "a term denoting an imperial, absolutist state, subordinating Russian as well as non-Russian territories."[19] In this late-seventeenth-century vision of empire Great Russia, the tsar and state were merged in a single conception of sovereignty and absolutism. State, empire, and autocratic tsar were combined in an elaborate system of reinforcing legitimations. In Russia, according to Wortman,

> The word *empire* carried several interrelated though distinct meanings. First, it meant imperial dominion or supreme power unencumbered by other authority. Second, it implied imperial expansion, extensive conquests, encompassing non-Russian lands. Third, it referred to the Christian Empire, the heritage of the Byzantine emperor as the defender of Orthodoxy. These meanings were conflated and served to reinforce one another.[20]

Not only was the tsar the holy ruler, a Christian monarch, the most pious head of the Church, but also a powerful secular ruler of a burgeoning bureaucratic state, a conqueror, and the commander of nobles and armies. With Peter the Great the Christian Emperor and Christian Empire gave way to a much more secular "Western myth of conquest and power."[21] "Peter's advents gave notice that the Russian tsar owed his power to his exploits on the battlefield, not to divinely ordained traditions of succession," according to Wortman, "The image of conqueror disposed of the old fictions of descent."[22] Peter carried the image of foreignness to new extremes, imposing on Russia his preference for beardlessness, foreign dress, Baroque architecture, Dutch, German, and English technology, and a new capital as a "window on the West." He created a polite society for Russia, bringing women out of seclusion into public life, culminating in the coronation of his second wife, the commoner Katerina, as empress of Russia. He took on the title *imperator* in 1721 and made Russia an *imperiia*. "Peter's ideology was very much of the age of rationalism," writes Wortman, "his contribution to the 'general welfare' of Russia legitimating his rule."[23] The emperor was "father of the fatherland" (*Otets otechestva*), and "now the relationship between sovereign and subjects was to be based not on hereditary right and personal obligation, but on the obligation to serve the state."[24]

By the eighteenth century Russia was an empire in the multiple senses of a great state whose ruler exercised full, absolute sovereign power over its diverse territory and subjects. Its theorists consciously identified this polity with the language and imagery of past empires. "Peter the Great bequeathed to his successors a daunting image of emperor as hero and god," benefactors who "subdued the forces working for personal interests against the welfare of all."[25] His successors, four of whom were women, were backed by guards regiments who decided struggles for the throne. "The guards' regiments and the court elite advanced the interests of the entire nobility in defending an alliance with the crown that lasted until the accession of Paul I in 1796."[26] "In this system, the term general welfare came to mean the advancement of noble interests."[27] The eighteenth-century monarchs combined aspects of the conqueror and renovator "while they maintained and reinforced the stability that would preserve the predominance of the serf-holding nobility. The conqueror was also the conserver, who helped defend and extend the elite's authority."[28]

As Europe went through the fallout from 1789, Russia represented the most imperial of nations, comprising more peoples than any other. In its own imagery Russia was the Roman Empire reborn. As the discourse of the nation took shape in and after the French Revolution and the Napoleonic wars, as concepts of "the people" and popular sovereignty spread through Europe, the traditional monarchical concepts of the foreign tsar held at bay any concession to the new national populism. Russian resistance to Napoleon, as well as the expansion of the empire into the Caucasus and Finland, only accentuated the imperial image of irresistible power, displayed physically on both battlefield and parade ground by the martinet tsars of the early nineteenth century.[29] Russian authorities resisted portraying the great victory as a popular triumph and instead projected it as a divinely ordained triumph of autocracy supported by a devoted people.

Russia emerged from the Napoleonic wars even more imperial than it had been in the eighteenth century. Now the possessor of the Grand Duchy of Finland, the emperor served there as a constitutional monarch and was to observe the public law of the Grand Duchy, and in the Kingdom of Poland (1815–1832), he served as *Tsar' Polskii*, the constitutional king of Poland. According to the Fundamental Laws codified in 1832, "the Emperor of Russia is an autocratic [*samoderzhavnyi*] and unlimited [*neogranichennyi*] monarch," but his realm was governed by laws, a *Rechtsstaat*, and was distinct from the despotisms of the East.[30] The tsar stood apart and above his people; his people remained diverse not only ethnically but in terms of the institutions through which they were ruled. Victorious Russia, the conservative bulwark against the principles of the French Revolution, was in many ways the antithesis of nationalism.

While expanding in territory and upholding the traditional principles of autocracy and orthodoxy, the Russian monarchy, at least up to the time of Nicholas I (1825–1855), imagined Russia as a modern Western state. But the "West" had changed since Peter's time. No longer embracing the ideal of absolutism, Europe increasingly embodied the principles of nationality and popular sovereignty, industrialism and free labor, constitutionalism and representative government. The task for the ideologists of empire in mid-century was to reconceive Russia as "modern" and rethink its relationship to its own imagined "West." The threat presented by innovative ideas to absolutism became palpable with the Decembrist rebellion of 1825, and state officials themselves attempted to construct their own Russian idea of nation, one that differed from the dominant discourse of the nation in the West.

Nicholas's ideological formulation, known as "Official Nationality," was summed up in the official slogan "Orthodoxy, Autocracy, Nationality [*narodnost'*]." Elaborated by the conservative minister of education, Sergei Uvarov, Official Nationality emphasized the close ties between the tsar and the people, a bond said to go back to Muscovy. Russians, it was claimed, had chosen their foreign rulers, the Varangians, and worshiped their successors. Russia was distinct in the love of the people for the Westernized autocracy and their devotion to the church. At the heart of Official Nationality lay the image of Russia as a single family in which the ruler is the father and the subjects the children. As an authentically Christian people, Russians were said to be marked by renunciation and sacrifice, calm and contemplation, a deep affection for their sovereign, and dedicated resistance to revolution. At his coronation, which was delayed because of the Decembrist mutiny of progressive nobles, Nicholas bowed three times to the people, inventing a new tradition that continued until the dynasty's fall. At the same time he nationalized the monarchy more intensively. At the ball that followed the coronation, nobles danced in national costumes surrounded by Muscovite decor. Russian was to be used at court; Russian language and history became required subjects at university; churches were built in a Russo-Byzantine style; a national anthem, "God Save the Tsar," was composed, under the emperor's supervision, as well as a national opera, *A Life for the Tsar*, by Mikhail Glinka, which incorporated folk music to tell the tale of a patriotic peasant, Ivan Susanin, who leads a band of Poles astray rather than reveal the hiding place of the future tsar.[31]

Official Nationality was an attempt to make an end run around the western discourse of the nation and to resuture nation to state, to the monarch and the state religion at the moment when in Western Europe the political community known as nation was becoming separable from the state, at least conceptually, and was fast gaining an independent potency as the source of legitimacy.[32] In contrast to the discourse of the nation, tsarist ideology resisted the challenge to the ancien régime sense of political community (and sovereignty) being identified with the ruler or contained within the state. Generalizing from the Russian case, Benedict Anderson sees "official nationalisms" as a category of nationalisms that appear after popular linguistic nationalisms, "*responses* by power-groups—primarily, but not exclusively, dynastic and aristocratic—threatened with exclusion from, or marginalization in, popular imagined communities." Official nationalism "concealed a discrepancy between nation and dynastic realm" and was connected to the efforts of aristocracies and monarchies to maintain their empires.[33]

The tsarist empire tried to extend official nationalism, first bureaucratic then cultural Russification, to suppress non-Russian nationalisms and separatisms, and to identify the dynasty and the monarchy with a Russian "nation." But all of these various and often contradictory attempts foundered before opposing tendencies, most significantly the powerful countervailing pull of supranational identifications of Russia with empire, Orthodoxy, and Slavdom. As an imperial polity, engaged in both discriminating as well as nationalizing policies in the nineteenth century, the Russian state maintained vital distinctions between Russians and non-Russians, in their differential treatment of various non-Russian and non-Orthodox peoples, as well as between social estates. The Great Reforms of the 1860s did not extend *zemstva* (local assemblies) to non-Russian areas. Whole peoples, designated *inorodtsy*, continued to be subject to special laws, among them Jews, peoples of the North Caucasus, Kalmyks, nomads, Samoeds and other peoples of Siberia. The Church's own educational reformer, N. I. Il'minskii, established a network of missionary schools in local languages so that "the heathen" could hear the Gospel in their own language.[34] Yet at the same time concerted efforts were made to Russify other parts of the population. The government considered all Slavs potential or actual Russians, and officials restricted Polish higher education and the use of Ukrainian.[35]

In its last years the tsarist upper classes and state authorities were divided between those who no longer were willing to tamper with the traditional institutions of autocracy and nobility and those who sought to reform the state to represent the unrepresented, reduce or eliminate social and ethnic discriminations, and move toward forming a nation.[36] But the resistance to social egalitarianism or ethnic neutrality overwhelmed nation-making processes. The famous attempt to establish elective *zemstva* in the western provinces precipitated a political crisis. If the usual principle of representation by estate were observed, local power would pass into the hands of Polish landlords, but when a system of representation by ethnic curiae was proposed, the law was defeated in the conservative upper house of the Duma because it compromised representation by estate. A law on municipal councils in Poland's cities collapsed before the resistance by anti-Semitic Poles, who feared Jewish domination of the municipal legislatures. Russian nationalists triumphed briefly in 1912 when the region of Kholm (Chelm), largely Ukrainian and Catholic in population, was removed from the historic Kingdom of Poland and made into a separate province.[37] In each of these three cases particularistic distinctions about nationality and class dominated the discussion and divided the participants. Universalist principles about allegiance to a common nation were largely absent.

Tsarism never created a nation within the whole empire or even a sense of nation among the core Russian population, even though what looked to others like imperialism was for the country's rulers "part of larger state-building and nation-building projects."[38] Tsarist Russia managed only too well in building a state and creating an empire; it failed, however, to construct a multiethnic "Russian nation" within that empire. The history of tsarism is of an empire that at times engaged in nation making, but nationalizing state practices were always in tension with the structures and discourses of empire. The imperial tended to thwart if not subvert the national, just as the national worked to erode the stability and legitimacy of the state. After relatively successfully conquering and assimilating the Orthodox Slavic population of central Russia (Vladimir, Novgorod, other appanage states), Muscovy set out to "recover" lands with non-Slavic, non-Orthodox populations, like Kazan. In some areas the tsarist regime managed to create loyal subjects through the transformation of cultural identities, but its policies were inconsistent and varied enormously. It neither created an effective civic national identity nor succeeded (or even tried very hard) forging an ethnic nation, even among Russians.

Russia was a composite state with unequal relations between a "Russian" metropole, which itself was a multiethnic though culturally Russified ruling elite, and non-Russian populations. For all the haphazard nationalizing efforts of the ruling institution, both the programs of discrimination and inequity between metropole and periphery and the resistant cultures and counterdiscourses of nationalism of non-Russians prevented the kind of homogenization and incorporation of the population into a single "imagined community" of a Russian nation. Though tsarist Russia's collapse did not occur because of nationalisms from the peripheries, but because of the progressive weakening and disunity of the center, much of the legitimacy of the imperial enterprise had withered away by 1917. As Russians suffered defeats and colossal losses in World War I, the fragile aura of legitimacy was stripped from the emperor and his wife, who were widely regarded as distant from, even foreign to, Russia. What the dynasty in the distant past had imagined was empowering, their difference from the people, now became a fatal liability. Elite patriotism, frustrated non-Russian nationalisms, and peasant weariness at intolerable sacrifices for a cause with which they did not identify combined lethally to undermine the monarchy. The principles of empire, of differentiation and hierarchy, were incompatible with modern ideas of democratic representation and egalitarian citizenship that gripped much of the intelligentsia and urban society. When the monarchy failed the test of war, its last sources of popular affection and legitimacy fell away.

EMPIRE AND NATIONS IN THE SOVIET UNION

Empire has become the preferred word to describe the Soviet Union now that it is gone. A highly normative term, it was most notably applied in the 1980s to "the evil empire" and only later, less pejoratively, as the "affirmative action empire" or the "empire of nations" in which "imperialism [w]as the highest stage of socialism."[39] Whereas it is doubtlessly true that the USSR was imperial in its relationships with Mongolia and the bordering states in east-central Europe, to consider the Soviet Union itself as a contiguous empire requires something more than just a typological distinction. What does "empire" tell us about how the USSR worked; why it succeeded for so long in maintaining relative ethnic peace within its borders; and what utility does empire give us in understanding the Soviet disintegration?

Like such contested words as *revolution* or *modern, empire* is essentially a comparative term. It gains in conviction insofar as it robustly links shared characteristics and dynamics of a set of polities and sharply distinguishes that set from other political structures. Much comes down to how one defines empire. Too broad and inclusive a definition—like that employed by Francine Hirsch ("a state characterized by having a great extent of territories and variety of peoples under one rule")—or avoiding a definition altogether leads to conceptual confusion.[40] Several historians and political scientists have raised objections to applying the term *empire* to the Soviet Union. Terry Martin points out that "the Soviet Union was a highly centralized, unitary state. Peripheral subjects (understood here as non-Russians) were not subjected to legal discrimination, nor indeed to different laws; they were not discriminated against economically due to their 'peripheral' status; they were ruled like 'core' subjects. They were indeed dominated, but so too were majority Russian regions."[41] Yuri Slezkine is willing to concede that the USSR may have been an empire according to some definitions but calls for more careful and critical evaluation of the notion that it was a colonial empire comparable to the British, French, or Dutch empires. His view of the relations of Russia to the rest of the Soviet Union differs markedly from Martin's, however: "[N]o matter how ill-defined the mother country and how peculiar its relations with the other administrative units, Russia was treated differently from them all, if sometimes by omission, and the Russians were seen as the imperial nation, if not always to their benefit. The USSR may differ from Western colonial empires on many important counts, but it seems eminently comparable to them."[42]

If we think of the practice of empire (imperialism) as differentiating and subordinating, while usurping the sovereignty of the subordinated, then the Soviet Union appears to fit the concept of empire quite well. But if we think of the practice of nation making as homogenizing, making equivalent and equal, while recognizing the populace as sovereign, then the Soviet Union appears to be engaged in nation making (both at the level of the various nationalities and in the creation of a "Soviet people"). In its first decades the Soviet Union increased power at the center, while the peripheries, both ethnonational and the people (*narod*) as a whole, lost the power to make the crucial decisions in their political life. At the same time the Soviet state engaged in practices that rationalized and standardized its relations with its subjects, mobilized them with a civilizing discourse about progress and modernity, while differentiating among its constituent peoples, ethnicizing dozens of cultures, and in a real sense creating nations within an "imperial" federation. At certain times, though at different levels (all-Union and specific nationalities), the imperial practices dominated, even overwhelmed the nationalizing tendencies (e.g., in the Stalin years). At other times, nation building at the sub–all-Union level dominated (e.g., in the 1920s, the heyday of the "affirmative action empire"); and at others, central power weakened and subordinate nationalized elites increased their autonomy (within strict limits) at the expense of the central authorities (a kind of indirect rule was established in some republics). In other words, the USSR looks a lot like other modernizing empires but disguised as an anti-imperialist multinational state.

The original Soviet state was ideologically conceived as temporary, provisional, transitory from the era of capitalism, nationalism, and imperialism to the moment of successful international socialist revolution. That "state," which in one sense was to be the negation of states as they had hitherto existed, was at the same time the carapace of the first socialist government, the vehicle for the Bolshevik party to carry out its program of disempowering the "bourgeoisie" and the old ruling classes, ending an imperialist war, and spreading the international civil war beyond the bounds of Russia. In the understanding of its paramount leaders, the Soviet Union was at one and the same time an anti-imperialist state, a federation of sovereign states, a voluntary union, a prefiguration of a future nonstate, dedicated (initially, at least in Lenin's view) to be an example of equitable, nonexploitative relations among nations, a model for further integration of the other countries and the fragments of the European empires. All of these claims were easily dismissed by its opponents as self-serving and disingenuous. Yet for the Bolshevik leaders anti-imperialism was both a model for the internal structure of the USSR and a posture to attract supporters from abroad. Like Woodrow Wilson, Lenin was a major contributor to the delegitimizing of imperialism and empires, and anti-imperialism remained until the end of the USSR a powerful trope in Soviet rhetoric.

The Soviet Union became an empire despite the ideology and intentions of its founders. But given the imperatives of a minority party holding power in conditions of civil war, foreign intervention, and state collapse, the forcible regathering of Russian lands carried out by the Communist Party and the Red Army created an inequitable relationship between center and periphery that was enforced by the greater physical power and the determined will to use violence of the Bolsheviks. Thus, almost from its inception the Soviet Union replicated imperialist relations. The power of the metropole, which should be defined as the ruling institution of the central party/state apparatus, as well as the demographic weight of Russia, was far greater than any opposing social institution or any of the other units of the new state or, indeed, of all of them combined. Concessions were made to the perceived power of nationalism, which was believed to be the product of and contingent on imperialist oppression. However appropriate nationalism might be for a certain stage of history, Lenin believed that it was soon to be superseded. Political and cultural rights for non-Russians and the systematic constraint of Russian nationalism, along with the development of a socialist economy, would be sufficient to solve the "national question." There would be nations without nationalism in the Soviet federation.

Relations between the Soviet metropole and its peripheries were different on the political, cultural, and economic levels. Politically, certainly most pronouncedly in the first decade of Soviet rule, power was somewhat diffused, with bargaining taking place between the center and the republics and autonomies. In the cultural sphere, the policy of *korenizatsiia* (indigenization) stressed promotion of the "native" culture and local elites. The new state attempted to incorporate elites that were not hostile to Soviet power and to allow the development of "nations" within the

Soviet federation, but the political order in which a single party monopolized all decision making everywhere constrained from the beginning and ultimately undermined local centers of power. As the regime became ever more centralized and bureaucratized in Moscow, the inequitable, imperial relations between center and peripheries became the norm until actual sovereignty existed only in the center.

In the economic sphere the emphasis was on efficiencies that very often disregarded ethnocultural factors. While creating national territorial units with broad cultural privileges, the new government's overwhelming concern was that the new multinational federal state be a single integrated economy. On this point there was to be no compromise. Economic policy was statewide, and each federal unit was bound to others and to the center by economic ties and dependencies. An intense debate raged in the Communist Party in the 1920s over the priority of economy over national culture, with the more-economically oriented, like Avel Enukidze, promoting administrative division of the country according to an economic rationale (*raionirovanie*), and officials in the People's Commissariat of Nationality Affairs (Narkomnats) and representatives of various non-Russian peoples favoring boundaries that corresponded to ethnicity.[43] While much attention was paid to regional and cultural particularities, at least in the 1920s, over time economic regionalization became an extraethnic practice, and party members were regularly encouraged, even in the 1920s, to consider specialization, education, and training over ethnic qualifications in cadre policy.[44]

The USSR, as Rogers Brubaker and others have pointed out, was one of the few states (present-day Ethiopia seems to be another) that allowed national formation not at the level of the state itself but at the level of the secondary units within the state, the union republics.[45] There was shockingly little effort to create a "Soviet nation." While everyone in the USSR carried a passport inscribed with a nationality, no one was permitted to declare him- or herself a Soviet by nationality. The Soviet idea of nationality was based on birth and heredity, the nationality of one's parents, but with its almost racial finality nationality was rooted in the substate units. The nations of the Soviet Union were based on what were conceived as preexisting ethnic, religious, or linguistic communities, and in some cases on earlier polities, but whatever the degree of national cohesion and consciousness in 1917 (generally fairly low), for both ideological and politically expedient reasons Soviet political leaders promoted national construction among the non-Russian peoples. The effect of this dualistic policy, which at one and the same time stressed a kind of ethnically blind modernization and yet encouraged ethnocultural particularism and local political power within bounds, was to create increasingly coherent, compact, and conscious national populations within the republics, while promising an eventually supraethnic future, full of material promise.

With the agenda ultimately set in Moscow, the relationship between center and republics was one of subordination of the non-Russian periphery to the "Russian" (more accurately, Soviet) metropole. In some periods local elites had considerable influence, but their effective participation in the political, economic, or cultural life of the country required a cultural competence in Russian and a loyalty to the entire Soviet project that superseded local identities and loyalties. Through generous rewards of power, prestige, and influence, along with severe punishments, the Soviet center attracted "the best and the brightest" among the national elites, many of which were created during Soviet times, to collaborate with the all-Soviet rulers. The costs of refusing to work in this way or of displaying "local nationalism" were extraordinarily severe. But the Soviet recruitment of native elites had different effects on different members of the non-Russian elites. Those who were particularly competent in Russian and Soviet cultural practices (and were from certain nationalities like the Baltic peoples, Ukrainians, and Armenians—and Jews in the early Soviet years) became part of a cosmopolitan Soviet elite, highly mobile, largely interchangeable, and dedicated to the larger Soviet (imperial and developmental) project. These men (and they were usually men) were the carriers of Soviet culture, enforcers of party policy, agents of the center in the peripheries. Leonid Brezhnev was such a figure. Born in Ukraine of Russian parents, he served in several republics, rising to be first secretary of Soviet Moldavia and later first secretary of Soviet Kazakhstan.

But in Moldavia, Kazakhstan, and other republics, there was a local native elite of people skilled in the language, culture, and native practices of the people of that republic. Among them were Armenian poets, Georgian musicians, Estonian politicians whose Estonian was far better than their Russian, and others whose skills and interests aided them in making national rather than all-union careers. In the early Soviet period these "national Communists" were frequently the targets of antinationalist campaigns, and a whole generation of such builders of the early Soviet republics was destroyed in the Stalinist purges. But later as the hold of the center loosened on the peripheries, as a policy of indirect rule replaced the hypercentralization of Stalinism, native cadres with local ties and constituencies were content to pay lip service to the ideology of Sovietism and to sponsor both local nationalisms and economic practices that basically ripped off the Soviet state. As the center itself abdicated much of its control over the country during the Gorbachev years, non-Russian (and it turned out, even Russian) Communists were torn between those who wanted to preserve the larger state (without its imperial aspects) and those ready to move off into a separate sovereignty.

With decisions on political and cultural issues taken primarily at the center, the fate of the Soviet nations was dictated by the imperatives of Soviet state building. In the 1920s particularistic ethnic cultures were encouraged to the detriment of Russian national culture. In the 1930s and 1940s Soviet patriotism as an elaborate Russian costume drama overwhelmed the simultaneous national imitations at the republic level. In the 1950s and 1960s the higher status of Russian culture and language led to spontaneous erosion of national affiliation in various republics, only to produce its own backlash of republic-based unofficial and semiofficial nationalisms.[46] But a state policy that both promoted cultural differentiation and assimilation into a higher Russo-Soviet culture was creating a polity that was inherently unstable. By the 1970s and 1980s consolidated and conscious nations in the Caucasus, the Baltic republics, and elsewhere faced an aging central authority that gradually lost its will and commitment to the socialist project. For many national intellectuals and local politicians dedication to the nation offered an intellectual and emotional charge that the revolution and Marxism-Leninism had long since lost.

Among the many ironies to Soviet history, certainly a principal one must be that a radical socialist elite that proclaimed an internationalist agenda that was to transcend the bourgeois nationalist stage of history in fact ended up by making nations within its own political body. Another irony is that the very successes of the Soviet system—not least this making of nations, but also the industrialization, urbanization, and mass education of the country—made the political system that had revolutionized society largely irrelevant. Instead of legitimizing the system, as it had done earlier, modernization undermined it at the end by creating the conditions and the actors that were able to act without the direction of the Communist Party. This dialectic of empire took on a revolutionary coloration in the Soviet case. Whatever the intentions of the Bolsheviks, they succeeded only too well in creating the conditions for their ultimate demise.

Like other great empires in the modern world, the Soviet Union was a modernizing state. It was not interested in preserving but transforming social and cultural relations. But at the same time it built and then petrified a hierarchical, inequitable, nondemocratic political structure that progressively became an obstacle to further political—and to a large extent, social, economic, and cultural—development. Increasingly irrelevant and burdensome to the population, the arteries of the state structure hardened along with those of the Politburo members, setting the stage for political decay, economic corruption and decline, social alienation, and ultimately a crisis of legitimacy. The time arrived when younger leaders understood that the political structure had to change or society and the economy would simply continue to stagnate.

Reform ultimately led to revolution; renewal and restructuring to collapse and disintegration. When the center weakened, many of the non-Russian elites (and in some cases the people as well) acted to free themselves of the metropole's grip. As in the fall of tsarism, so in the Soviet demise, nationalism was not the primary cause of the collapse of the Soviet system. The erosion of central power, dependent as it was on elite cohesion and belief in its right to use its power to maintain order (the evaporation of political will and confidence), precipitated the centrifugal forces that tore the USSR into new states. Until the August 1991 coup, centripetal forces remained quite strong. But in its aftermath there was a scramble to abandon the sinking ship that seemed unable to steer a new course away from imperial practices. The Soviet empire collapsed in the context of (and because of) a failed attempt by top Soviet leaders to transform the USSR into a more "modern," "Western-style," "civilized" multinational state and system. This involved economic reform, eventually marketization; political reform leading eventually to democratization; and once embarked on democratization, the end of empire and the creation of a new form of multinational state. The problems were formidable, perhaps insurmountable, yet the centripetal pull of the center remained competitive until the August 1991 coup. Gorbachev and his closest comrades by the late 1980s were convinced that the empire, which they believed had many of the cohesive characteristics of a nation, had to be transformed, but his sincere hope that the end of empire did not also mean the end of the Soviet state was shared by few of those about to make history.

THINKING ABOUT THE PRESENT

In his speech on September 7, 2003, President George W. Bush presented the war and occupation in Iraq as the "frontline of freedom" in the ongoing global war on terrorism. The invasions of Afghanistan and Iraq were not imperialist adventures, in the administration's view, but defenses of civilization against barbarism, the necessary, unavoidable means to bring the advances of democracy, the free market, law and order to the Islamic world. To students of empire the rhetoric and actions of the Busheviki conjure up familiar images of other imperialisms. Yet, the current American global effort falls short of qualifying as empire by most definitions of empire. According to their stated goals American actions are not directed at appropriating the full sovereignty of another people. As policies based on a fantasy vision of the Middle East and Central Asia grind to a halt and America's leaders scramble for exit, their promise is expressed ever more loudly that sovereignty will be restored to the indigenous peoples of Afghanistan and Iraq. A "logic of sovereignty," in the words of the French, will replace the "logic of occupation."

Certainly the United States has had episodes of imperialism, most notably at the end of the nineteenth century. Yet in the first years of the twenty-first century the United States is engaged in consolidating its economic and political *hegemony* over much of the globe, rather than establishing an empire in the conventional sense. Since World War II, American dominance has replaced the Japanese in Asia and the

Pacific, the British in the Mediterranean and Middle East, and now the Soviets in Central Asia and the Caucasus. While diplomacy, persuasion, and economic clout are the preferred means of expansion and stabilization, at times this activist policy has required short-term military interventions, usually followed by rationalized retreat. The United States, then, does not fit the definitions of empire presented in this chapter (which others would call colonialism or formal empire). It does not aim at permanently appropriating the sovereignty of another country, for it much more effectively dominates through its military presence around the globe, its economic power, and its cultural appeal. Rather than imperialism in the sense used in this account, the United States engages in global hegemony.

Just as the Russian Empire was both empowered and constrained by its ideological justifications for empire, just as the Soviet empire was motivated and ultimately thwarted by its "socialist" developmentalist discourses, so the American establishment is both driven and restrained by the ideas and identities to which Americans subscribe as well as the political structures in which they become manifest. In its own self-construction, repeated and reinforced by politicians, government spokesmen, and the media, the United States is a unique country, exemplary in its freedoms, its democratic constitution and values, and its altruistic approach to the rest of the world. It wishes nothing for itself, except to extend the blessings that it enjoys to the rest of the world, blessings summed up by President Bush as "decency, freedom, and progress." Such language is certainly self-serving, but in the structures and practices of democracy it takes on a power of its own. Whether those who express them sincerely believe these phrases or not, such discursive constructions define the range of the possible. Discourses can cut in many ways at once and quickly escape the hold of those who express them. Expressed American values would seem to preclude extended usurpation of the sovereignty of another people, colonialism, or even overt exploitation of the resources of another country. This is not to say that horrors associated with war, profit, racial and religious discrimination, and the self-interest of the dominant do not and will not occur, but they must be disguised, interpreted, and are always subject to challenge from others who will appeal to what they consider the proclaimed core values of American society. The same language of freedom, progress, and democracy easily turns, as the Busheviki have demonstrated, into justifications for the overthrow of tyrants, massive buildups of armed forces abroad, and the repeated violation of other nations' sovereignty.

A far more significant restraint on American empire is the reluctance of many Americans (and limited capacity of the country) to spend resources and manpower outside the boundaries of the United States. From its founding the country has been wary of foreign entanglements, at least outside its own hemisphere, and the tradition first stated in Washington's farewell address has remained part of the rhetorical arsenal, earlier of conservatives and isolationists, today of liberal anti-interventionists and pacifists. American aversion to taxation, combined with a lack of interest in and knowledge of the outside world, has hardly been tempered by the sense of threat after September 11th. The costs of empire have already been enormous, are likely to grow, and will set the most powerful limits on American expansion.

This leads us, finally, to consider the ways in which the international context contributes to the stability and fragility of empires, not only in the sense that a highly competitive international environment presents empires with difficult challenges economically and militarily but also at the level of dominant understandings of what constitutes legitimacy for states. Through the twentieth century international law and international organizations, such as the League of Nations and the United Nations, established new norms that sanctioned national self-determination, nonintervention into the affairs of other states, and the sovereign equality of states. Despite the unilateralism of the Bush administration, the international community has demonstrated the increasing importance of international institutions, like the United Nations, the need for cooperation and collaboration among the most powerful states, and the costs of trying to go it alone. After both world wars new states and former colonies were quickly accepted as fully independent actors in the international arena. This acceptance set the stage for 1991, when the former Soviet republics—but no political units below them—were quickly recognized as independent states with all the rights and privileges appertaining.

In the post-1945 period particularly, the wave of decolonizations constructed empires as antiquated forms of government, justifiable only as transitory arrangements that might aid in the development of full nation-states. This justification of empires was read back into the retrospective histories of empires. As Miles Kahler puts it, "The empire-dominated system of the early twentieth century swiftly tipped toward a nation-state dominated system after World War II; in dramatic contrast to the 1920s and 1930s empires were quickly defined as beleaguered and outdated institutional forms."[47] Kahler notes that the two dominant powers of the post–World War II period, the USA and USSR, were both "rhetorically anti-colonial, despite their own imperial legacies," and American economic dominance, with its liberal, free-trade approach, "reduced the advantages of empires as large-scale economic units."[48] Thus, both on the level of discourse and on the level of international politics and economics, the early twenty-first century appears to be a most inhospitable time both for formal external empires and contiguous empire-states. The limits of global hegemony, however, have yet to be determined.

6. EMPIRES OF LIBERTY? DEMOCRACY AND CONQUEST IN FRENCH EGYPT, BRITISH EGYPT, AND AMERICAN IRAQ

JUAN COLE

Below, I consider the rhetoric of empire in three major episodes during the past two centuries, with reference to the Middle East. Not all of these wars can be considered "imperialist" in precisely the same way, nor are the legal bases for the wars the same in all cases. They do, however, share certain key attributes. The proponents of war in the case of the French invasion of Egypt in 1798, the British invasion of Egypt in 1882, and the American invasion of Iraq in 2003, all represented themselves as saviors and liberators of the peoples of the country invaded. This rationale for war probably first emerged with Napoleon and the expedition against Egypt, since a French Republic dedicated to the Rights of Man could hardly wage war employing the old, cynical language of mere power and subjection of the enemy. In each case the ruling cliques of the countries invaded were decried as despots who oppressed the local population and menaced the interests of the West.

In each case, the country invaded possessed economic or strategic assets of great importance to the invader, though these were played down in the speeches politicians and military men gave about the war. France needed Egyptian wheat and saw holding Egypt as a way to challenge British domination of the Mediterranean and of India. The British in 1882 desperately needed to protect their control of the Suez Canal, which had become essential to their imperial interests in Africa and Asia. The Bush administration in 2003 sought an oil ally that could substitute for what they saw as an increasingly unreliable Saudi Arabia. In each case, the invaders attempted to locate local collaborating elites who might help establish a sister regime to that of the western invader. The French sought a French Directory similar to, but subordinate to, their own. The British in Egypt restored a viceroy to his throne and ultimately authorized a toothless Chamber of Deputies, ultimately leaving Egypt a constitutional monarchy in the grip of big landlords. The Americans appointed a supposedly representative Interim Governing Council, the explicit task of which was said to be preparation for democratic elections and the dissolution of a socialist economy in favor of laissez-faire. (Some Bush administration figures, such as

Dick Cheney and Donald Rumsfeld, seemed prepared to accept rather less than democracy, just as Lord Cromer [1841–1917], who served as the first British viceroy of Egypt from 1882–1907, had done in the "veiled Protectorate" on the Nile.)

France under the Directory, Gladstone's Great Britain, and the contemporary United States represent very different political systems. All three had, however, regular elections, a regime of citizen rights, and a relatively unregulated economy. To any extent that they exhibited classical features of what political philosophers tend to call liberalism, their military activity poses a puzzle. That is, it has been widely held that liberal regimes are peaceable by nature. As to liberalism, Michael Doyle notes that

> There is no canonical description of liberalism. What we tend to call *liberal* resembles a family portrait of principles and institutions, recognizable by certain characteristics—for example, individual freedom, political participation, private property, and equality of opportunity, that most liberal states share, although none has perfected them all.[1]

This definition of *liberal,* of course, is a technical one and has nothing to do with its popular use in contemporary American society as an antonym to *conservative.* Historians would consider both U.S. conservatives and liberals to be general heirs to the liberal political philosophy. It is in any case more useful to talk about liberal elements in ruling regimes than about the phenomenon as a Platonic ideal that is universally applicable. "Liberal" motifs tended to be thrown up by three great modern revolutions: the 1688–89 Glorious Revolution in Great Britain, the American Revolution that began in 1775, and the French Revolution of 1789. All three events constituted structural turning points that appealed at least in part to the principle of popular sovereignty and implied the legal equality of citizens, as opposed to the hierarchy of rights and duties of subjects in absolute monarchies. These turning points established discourses of the rule of law rooted in representative institutions.[2]

I argue here that the rhetorical premises of liberalism, once accepted, make it difficult for leaders and politicians to glory publicly in the subjection of other peoples, since to subject them robs them of popular sovereignty, the constitutive characteristic of the human being in liberalism. Rhetorical strategies thus have to be developed that justify empire without appearing to attack the principle of popular sovereignty. The question is not behavior, since states with a liberal system in the metropole have clearly maintained empires abroad. The question I am raising is one of political language. The early modern language of empire, or the justifications for war used by twentieth-century fascist states, assumed that human beings were unequal and best organized into social hierarchies, with the stronger "people" (or later "race") on top. The stronger had a right, perhaps an obligation, to conquer the inferior and the weak. We are told of Mussolini that "the later Duce's underlying assumption . . . was that life was struggle. History was an endless succession of conflicts between elites, states, and tribes. In each epoch a particular elite or state set the tone. By definition, dominant elites or states were fittest."[3] Hierarchy and dominance are keywords for illiberal political philosophies.

Because more democratic systems accept the legal equality of all citizens, their leaders cannot so easily make explicitly hierarchical claims to power and rule. No essential basis for inequality can be admitted. Elites in parliamentary regimes have therefore developed rhetorical strategies to justify such hierarchies and inequalities. One such strategy is juvenilization. The excluded populations are coded as childlike and unready for political participation as autonomous citizens. This approach has the advantage of implying that the inequality is temporary, since over time children do grow up. Thus, women, unpropertied workers, and racial minorities have all at one time or another been juvenilized and deprived of political standing within liberal societies. This strategy, however, is unstable and susceptible of being blunted and defeated over time, when the excluded populations can mobilize enough resources and make sufficiently powerful appeals to the ideals of political equality. Notoriously, the juvenilization of foreign conquered subjects was a leading strategy for proponents of imperialism. Colonial subjects were defined as not truly adults, as needing a long apprenticeship for a very distant self-rule.

Sociologist Joseph Schumpeter defined imperialism as "an objectless disposition on the part of a state to unlimited forcible expansion."[4] By "objectless" he meant that the war had no legitimate goal of fending off imminent attack, for instance. His definition implies that the imperial state aggressively takes, holds, and administers territory beyond its borders directly. Schumpeter believed that such a disposition was incompatible with liberal, democratic, capitalist regimes. He dismissed the colonial wars of conquest of the nineteenth century as products of leftover mercantilism, which he thought was being jettisoned in the early twentieth century, leading to peace. (Mercantilism, or state-promoted monopoly capitalism, was an early modern economic doctrine.) Schumpeter clearly was mistaken.

I argue here that the imperial temptation persists whether regimes favor mercantilism, laissez-faire, or the socialism of managed capitalism. Foreign conquest always at least seems to offer economic benefits to the metropole, regardless of its economic system. Material reward is only one of a number of motivations that impel politicians otherwise influenced by democratic ideals to seek empire, which include strategic competition with imperial rivals, resentment of mistreatment by weaker states, and fear that weaker states might nevertheless prove able to inflict damage on the interests of the liberal state. Imperialism as a ruling strategy has the disadvantage of imposing costs on the metropole, insofar as it requires the direct administration or at least close dominance of the conquered society. There are material costs. India often cost Britain more to run than it received in tax revenues, even if British private business benefited from a captive market. There are political costs. The public in the metropole sometimes objects to the military sacrifices made by its children serving abroad, or feels guilty about the massacres and repression necessary to keep the colonial subjects down. Soft imperialism, or neoimperialism, whereby stronger states dominate by more subtle mechanisms (offer or denial of loans, behind-the-scenes military threats, and covert operations), is generally less costly and has been increasingly favored since the end of World War II. Here, I interrogate the main rhetorical justifications for three cases of imperial conquest, and the discontents that developed with these rationales.

THE FRENCH REPUBLIC OF EGYPT

The French Directory of 1795–1799 represented a brief period of parliamentary liberalism sandwiched between the Terror and the Triumvirate. Napoleon Bonaparte played a crucial role in ushering it in, through his intervention against royalists in 1795. But he also ended it, with his coup of November 9, 1799. During the intervening years, the French legislature consisted of a bicameral, elected parliament, with a Senate and a lower house or "Council of 500." The legislature in turn appointed a collective five-man executive, the Directory. The Directory-era politicians attempted to steer a course between the excesses of Robespierre and the threat of resurgent royalism. Their class base was the bourgeoisie, and they came to be viewed as corrupt champions of the interests of the nonaristocratic wealthy. Although it engaged in parliamentary elections and politics, the new elite was distinctly nervous about the growth of popular political parties.[5] The government fought a number of wars, notably in Italy and Egypt, in part to distract the public from domestic economic woes and in part in search of loot or strategic advantage. The Directory is the only period of republican French liberalism before the advent of the Third Republic in 1870.

As he prepared his troops for their attack on Egypt on May 9, 1798, Gen. Bonaparte gave a stirring speech in which he compared the French army assembled in Toulon to the Roman troops who had fought at Carthage. The rhetoric of imperialism typically attempts to rehabilitate earlier imperial ventures, and to make them justificatory reference points for present ones. But politicians at all influenced by liberal ideals must downplay elements of empire about which previous Caesars and sultans were often quite open, which is the attractions of plunder, tribute, and power. Bonaparte told his troops, "The genius of liberty, which has since its birth rendered the Republic the arbiter of Europe, is now headed toward the most distant lands."[6] The French are thus both to be like the Romans at Carthage and unlike them. They represented the triumph of European civilization in recalcitrant Africa, but their raison d'être was not vengeance or simple conquest, it was the implantation of liberty abroad. It may well be that Bonaparte here gave the first liberal imperialist speech.

Tellingly, Bonaparte exceeded his authority and promised his men plots of land on their return, which the Directory had not authorized him to do. The pledge had to be excised from printed versions of the speech, but its oral rendition no doubt raised unrealistic hopes among many of the troops. Imperialists in more democratic societies cannot merely depend on paid mercenaries, but must promise citizen-soldier conscripts that their efforts will bring them security and a better life on their return. Heartened by this mendacious promise, the soldiers cried out, "The Immortal Republic forever!" The troops engaged in a Republican ritual that evening in which they planted a tree of liberty with the inscription, "It grows each day."[7] The military employed this tree-planting ceremony to reinforce French solidarity, and, as Lynn Hunt has argued, to replace the old charisma of monarchy with a new symbolic universe centered on the body of the republic.[8] A young officer at Toulon, Michel de Niello Sargy, later wrote, "I was far from having any idea of the nature of the armament that was prepared, and even less of its destination, when I threw myself—like so many other young persons—into that audacious expedition. I was seduced by the renown of the general in chief and by the glory of our arms. It was a delirium, a nearly universal compulsion."[9]

Some in the invasion force, however, could see through the rhetoric of egalitarianism and came to despise Bonaparte's increasingly imperial airs. The uniform designer Bernoyer visited Bonaparte's flagship, the *Orient,* while en route to Alexandria and saw the general's quarters. He said the receiving room "was more made to accommodate a sovereign, born in flabbiness and ignorance, than a republican general, born for the glory of his country." The officers gambled on a gold table, "as though we were setting out to conquer Peru." He added that there "reigns here a most severe discipline among the troops, and with the general they observe the strictest etiquette. They seek to copy the former usages of the court, which usages seem just as ridiculous to us as those of a great feudal lord would be in the middle of a camp of Spartans."[10] The realities of hierarchy and opulence at the top starkly contrasted for Bernoyer with the Republican sentiments of the official speeches.

After taking Malta, Bonaparte sent out from his flagship a proclamation dated 12 June. He wrote, "Soldiers, you are about to undertake a conquest of incalculable import for the civilization and commerce of the world. You shall inflict on England the surest and most palpable blow, while awaiting the opportunity to administer the coup de grace."[11] He bitterly criticizes the slave-soldier elite or Mamluks, who ruled Egypt as Ottoman vassals, on two grounds. First, they had been favoring British commerce and humiliating French merchants. Second, they had oppressed the hapless Egyptians with their tyranny and expropriations. He thus combined national economic grievance with a universalistic appeal to liberating the foreign victims of despotism. The intervention is necessary because a despot is harming both the imperial power and his own people. By helping the downtrodden abroad, the empire is helping itself simultaneously. This dual goal of any intervention helped justify it to the weary public in the metropole, and aimed at reducing xenophobia in the conquered state.

Bernoyer initially shared the optimism of liberal rhetoric. He wrote home that in Egypt tyranny still exercised absolute power, starving its subjects in the midst of abundance. "Bonaparte," he wrote confidently back to his wife in summer of 1798, "will without doubt end this state of affairs."[12] He observes of Egyptian homes, "Their dwellings, which prosperity, the daughter of liberty, will now enable them to abandon, are adobe huts." Note his confidence that parliamentary elections and a rule of law always equate to economic betterment, whereas political oppression runs the country into the ground. Here, the "liberal" term of the phrase refers both to elections and to capitalism. Commerce, its theorists insisted, was hamstrung by despotism but unleashed by liberal institutions. He saw poverty at home as the fault of the indolent poor, but saw poverty abroad as an indictment of the foreign despot. A scientist, or "savant," who accompanied the expedition and wrote an anonymous memoir, chimed in: "The people of Egypt were most wretched. How will they not cherish the liberty that we are bringing them?"[13] He accuses the Ottoman-Egyptian elite of usurping most of the country's land, while imposing on the rest of the population a cloud of taxes and imposts, barely leaving the peasantry with enough to keep body and soul together. Like Bernoyer, the savant sees the rags in which many poor Egyptians attempt to cover themselves as an indictment of the slave-soldier Beys: "Everything one sees announces a country of slavery and tyranny." He complains of lack of justice and summary executions and mulcting.

Of a September festival held by the French in Egypt, the anonymous savant writes: "It was a truly interesting spectacle for the French to see the tricolor pavilion, emblem of their liberty and of their power, floating above that antique land, from which the greater part of the nations derived their knowledge and their laws; to see that from Alexandria to Thebes and then from Thebes to the Red Sea, all recognized the domination of their fatherland."[14] These French thinkers of the Directory era seemed unable or unwilling to recognize any contradiction between such a discourse of subjection and the ideal of liberation to which they simultaneously appealed. Here the "liberty" invoked is the liberty of the French, which is symbolized by the tricolor. Yet the tricolor's presence everywhere in Egypt is at the same time a symbol of the "domination" by the *patrie,* by the fatherland, of this second land.

At times, the discourse of liberty was discarded altogether, in favor of frank acknowledgment of the realities of power. The "domination of the fatherland" was clearly more important than the exportation of liberty. Bonaparte wrote to General Menou about organizing the port city of Rosetta, "The Turks can only be led by the greatest severity. Every day I cut off five or six heads in the streets of Cairo. We had to manage them up to the present in such a way as to erase that reputation for terror that preceded us. Today, on the contrary, it is necessary to take a tone that will cause them to obey, and to obey, for them, is to fear."[15] (This harsh treatment of local Muslims contrasted with the way in which Bonaparte insisted that Coptic Christian tax collectors be virtually coddled.) The French of this generation had extensive experience with terror and its coercive properties. Although many of the officers and savants despised Robespierre and the sans-culottes, at whose hands some of them suffered, they had not entirely abandoned his dictum that terror is merely an aspect of justice.[16] In the fall of 1798, fifteen Frenchmen plying the Nile were set upon and killed by the villagers of Alkam. Among the dead was Julien, an aide-de-camp of Bonaparte. "The General, severe as he was just, ordained that this village be burned. This order was executed with all possible rigor. It was necessary to prevent such crimes by the bridle of terror."[17]

The "crimes" grew in enormity over time, including the popular uprising against the French in Cairo, launched in October of 1798. Afterwards, the savant acknowledged the necessity of getting "these fanatical inhabitants" used to the "domination" of "those whom they call infidels." He adds, "We must believe that a Government that guarantees to each liberty and equality, as well as the well-being that naturally follows from it, will insensibly lead to this desirable revolution."[18] Such statements are so odd, so seemingly self-contradictory, that they raise the question of whether this eighteenth-century writer was using the words in a sense wholly different from the one they bear in the early twenty-first century. How could a foreign government that insisted on imposing its "domination" on a population that saw it as illegitimate (what "infidels" really meant to the Egyptians) claim to be providing guarantees of "liberty and equality" to each Egyptian. What did "liberty" mean to the savant?

Clearly, it did not imply national self-determination. In this pre-Wilsonian world, a foreign empire could provide liberty and equality to individuals in another state. It did so by removing the despots that once ruled that state and allying with the local middle strata. The French assumed that popular sovereignty did not imply national self-determination, but rather was a value that could be achieved within an imperial framework. The fiction of sibling republics, each modeled on the Directory, only lightly papered over the dominance of the elder sibling, Paris. Egypt, too, had its Directory or Divan. But it was not the government of Egypt. It was the gov-

ernment of the French Republic of Egypt. The public, moreover, might not immediately recognize its own salvation from tyranny. The savant seems to be putting
forward an early version of the much later Marxist "false consciousness" argument.
The French had liberated the Egyptians, but the latter were unable to recognize it,
blinded as they were by "fanaticism." They could, however, be accustomed to French
rule, at which point they would suddenly recognize the gift they had been given.

Not all the French gave in to the blandishments of terror and arbitrary rule.
Bernoyer watched in horror as the "liberation" of Egypt revealed itself as a harsh
military occupation aimed at taxing the country to pay for its conquest. How the
similar looting of Italy had escaped his notice is hard to explain. The carts full of
treasure from liberated Rome had rolled into Paris for months. Bernoyer reported
how distasteful he found it to be sent out to a poverty-stricken village of mud huts
to demand further extractions. When the village headman proved unable to secure
them, the French bastinadoed him (beat the soles of his feet). The designer of the
uniforms for the new French camel corps fulminated against the way General d'Ar-
magnac summarily executed rebels captured after the abortive popular rebellion in
Cairo of October 1798. He insisted that these were not criminals duly executed, but
victims: "I refer as victim to any person whom one causes to die without judgment."[19] Among the most prominent concerns of the generation that made the revolution had been to end *lettres de cachet* and other royal practices involving arbitrary
commands and arrests.[20] As a partisan of Rousseau and Voltaire, it deeply pained
Bernoyer to see the French army employing the technologies of rule typical of the ancien régime. Worse, he worried that Bonaparte was going native. "What mortified us
most," he remarks, "was that Bonaparte used the same methods as the Mamluks."[21]
Bernoyer's sentiments made a swift odyssey from exhilaration and Enlightenment
hope for a revived Egyptian nation to a sullen realization that the French had themselves been transformed into Oriental despots.

The French misadventure in Egypt lasted only three years. Marked by repeated
local revolts and by Ottoman invasions, it finally fell to a joint Anglo-Ottoman invasion force in 1801. The last French commander, Menou, had more than fulfilled
Bernoyer's worst fears, insofar as he both converted to Islam and adopted an iron-
fist strategy for ruling the Egyptians. The Egyptian Directory or Divan was swept
away by the new Ottoman viceroy, its members loudly proclaiming that they had
been coerced into collaborating with the infidel. One of its more prominent members, the Muslim clergyman and historian, Abd al-Rahman al-Jabarti, wrote a
scathing account of the French occupation, presumably in part to rehabilitate himself as a good Ottoman subject. The only real administrative practice instituted by
the French that survived them was their division of Cairo into eight sectors.

GLADSTONE AND EGYPT

Let us turn to our second instance of imperial intervention. The Egyptian crisis of 1881–1882 is among the best examples of liberal imperialism. Both French and British politicians and diplomats urged intervention, for a set of shifting reasons. Among the developments that provoked the greatest alarm in Paris and London was the establishment of an Egyptian parliament in the fall of 1881, after over a year of agitation by aggrieved landlords and other taxpayers. Egypt was deeply in debt to the French and British bondholders and governments, and per capita debt servicing by Egyptians was the highest in the world at that time. Since parliaments typically control budgets, many Egyptians saw the new legislature as a brake on profligate spending and borrowing. Some 50 percent of the Egyptian budget was dedicated to debt servicing, however, and French and British diplomats reasoned that if parliament itself overspent its half of the budget, Egypt might begin being unable to meet its financial obligations.[22]

The French thus put enormous pressure on the new president of the cabinet, the conservative Ottoman Sharif Pasha, to swear to abide by "international agreements." The stately language actually referred to debt servicing. He acquiesced, probably in part because he had nothing but contempt for Egyptian "peasants" and had no desire to share key powers with a nativist legislature. Egypt at this time was ruled by an Ottoman-Egyptian elite oriented in part to Istanbul, but the majority of the subjects was Arabic-speaking Egyptians who had largely been excluded from political power. The parliament was a vehicle for the power of the Egyptian urban and rural middle strata. As the French and British foresaw, the new legislature immediately began insisting that it control the budget. In response, the French and British governments issued a "joint note" in which they stressed their support for the Ottoman viceroy, Khedive Tawfiq. This note implicitly supported the Egyptian executive's claim to control finances.

The Egyptian reformists of late 1881 clearly desired to reduce the perquisites of the foreigners in their country. They engaged in a politics of nativist symbolism and xenophobia. In October of 1881, a French newspaper editor insulted the Prophet Muhammad, provoking such an angry public reaction that he was forced to flee the country. Peasants in the countryside began refusing to repay usurious debts to Greek and other European moneylenders. One provincial consul wrote, "business transactions between natives and foreigners are affected." The jobs of the 1,300 extremely well-paid European civil servants in the Egyptian bureaucracy were increasingly insecure. Auckland Colvin, the British comptroller serving in the Egyptian cabinet to oversee the repayment of Egyptian debts (working for something called the Franco-British "Dual Control"), defended the interests of the European hangers-on. He sent dispatches to the *Pall Mall Gazette* in which he put his own alarmist interpretation on Egyptian developments. That newspaper was the favorite of Prime Minister Gladstone and other members of the British elite. The convergence of big finance, of expatriate commerce, and of international news, contributed to drumming up a war fever in Britain. In their dispatches, both Colvin and the British consul, Sir Edward Malet, explicitly expressed their anxiety that the new parliament would overspend its half of the budget, making it impossible for the government to designate the full other half for debt servicing.

Political changes in France in late fall of 1881 brought a less belligerent government to power, so that increasingly the onus for stopping the unwelcome outbreak of democracy in Egypt fell upon the British. There were French and British representatives on the Egyptian cabinet at that time, in the odd way of informal colonialism. The British comptroller Colvin came to represent the interests of British merchants and officials in Egypt. When a group of Ottoman-Egyptian officers plotted a coup against the new, more democratic government in February 1882 and were thwarted, the issue arose of what to do with the conspirators. Treating them leniently, as Ottoman viceroy Tawfiq inclined to do, would send the signal that the reformist parliament and cabinet members were in fact illegitimate and had unjustly provoked the authoritarian officers. The cabinet was increasingly dominated by reformists like al-Barudi and the popular minister of war, Gen. Ahmad `Urabi, and they wanted the mutineers sent to harsh exile in the Sudan. On May 25, 1882, the British and French presented yet another joint note to the viceroy, demanding that the rebellious officers be merely sent out of the country for a year, and that the reformist al-Barudi be dismissed, along with Gen. `Urabi. The note was underlined by the appearance of British gunboats in the harbor of Alexandria. Egyptian crowds came out into the streets and gave such support to `Urabi that Viceroy Tawfiq felt he had no choice but to reinstate him.

A turning point occurred on June 11, 1882, when a riot broke out in Alexandria between Egyptians and Europeans.[23] Mobs, angry about the insults heaped on `Urabi Pasha and European interference in Egyptian affairs, as well as about high taxes in part provoked by European loans, set upon Greeks, Italians, British, and French in the country's major port city. It was a Sunday, and many Europeans had left the city. The ones who remained were exposed, but were well armed. Europeans sniped at the crowds, killing hundreds. Perhaps fifty Europeans died. The Egyptian government responded slowly to the disturbances, only restoring order that night. The English-language press reported the riots as a massacre of Christians by Muslim mobs, who had been whipped up by dangerous officers like `Urabi. (In fact, like most urban riots, it had local roots. There is no evidence of `Urabi wanting such disorder.) The correspondent for the *London Times* was a British merchant with heavy investments in

Alexandria, and the American ambassador suspected him of deliberately distorting the facts of the case to create a war hysteria back in Great Britain. The Ottomans had sent a negotiator, Dervish Pasha, to attempt to reduce tensions between the Egyptian reformists and the Ottoman viceroy. He "reported on attempts by European Consuls to heighten tension in Egypt by distributing handbills among the Christian population encouraging them to flee Egypt." Some 50,000 terrified Europeans immediately streamed out of the country (there had been 90,000 expatriates in this country of about 8 million). This exodus itself was seen by European consuls and merchants as an affront to European power in the country, and it placed in danger remaining European property and investments.

Later historians, with the notable exception of Alexander Schölch, played down the degree to which British policy makers rather stridently insisted on regular debt servicing by Egypt and so added to the crisis. The way in which British investors and merchants of large property had become a subsidiary Egyptian elite in their own right (and with their own interests) has often also been overlooked. The rhetoric of Egyptian disorder and the supposed threat of a military coup, often instanced by the British war camp (Hartington on the cabinet and Dilke, under-secretary of the foreign office) as a reason for intervention, was overdrawn. The Egyptian government intervened to restore order to Alexandria in reasonably good time, and the state continued to function normally in June. The British were not, as Robinson and Gallagher once suggested, "sucked into" Egypt by "instability." The British and the French contributed significantly by their gunboat diplomacy to the creation of what instability there was.

Schölch demonstrated that European consuls and merchants residing in Egypt, anxious about the security of their property, used their contacts in the British press and the foreign office to create an impression that the Egyptian government was falling apart and that the lives of tens of thousands of expatriate Europeans were in dire danger. In fact, there were only two significant anti-European riots in June, in Alexandria and in Banha, and in both instances government troops came in to protect the Europeans the same day.

Afaf Marsot and the late John S. Galbraith argued that Gladstone was not very interested in Egypt and was willing to cede Near East policy to the Admiralty and to cabinet members like Hartington who were both consumed by it and in favor of war.[24] Gladstone did not even bother to attend some of the more important cabinet meetings held on the Egypt crisis, and was barely consulted about the Admiralty's plans to bombard Alexandria (which it did on July 11, setting in motion the ultimate British invasion and occupation of Egypt). It is possible that Gladstone's commitment to keeping the empire from expanding was blunted by the brouhaha over the June 11 riots in Alexandria, since he had made his career earlier on by defending Balkan Christians from what he called Ottoman atrocities. As I wrote in my book,

"The prospect of saving the rest of the world is the chief inducement for a liberal to become an imperialist, and the European and Egyptian crowds unwittingly offered the liberal government that stimulus in June."

It was even alleged by the war party that British ships in Alexandria harbor were endangered by the Urabist revolutionaries in June, which seems by any measure a gross exaggeration. This rhetorical move is also key to liberal imperialism, that is, the depiction of the enemy as an aggressor with the ability to harm the powerful West, even when the enemy is patently weak and under siege from that West.

After the July 11 British bombardment of Alexandria, which caused massive fires that gutted the once beautiful port, and provoked extensive looting and the flight of much of the population, Egypt was pushed into a revolutionary situation. Viceroy Tawfiq remained in Alexandria, protected by the British troops that landed there. But much of the rest of the country gave its allegiance to an ad hoc and hastily called National Congress, made up of parliamentarians and other notables who met in Cairo and declared Tawfiq deposed on grounds of treason. Far from being a military coup, as the British depicted it, this "common-law" government was determinedly civilian and overruled General `Urabi on a number of occasions—most fatefully when it foolishly ordered him to try to make a stand at Tel el-Kabir outside Cairo. He thought them unwise in their strategy, but obeyed. There is also some evidence of the beginnings of a social revolution in July and August, as the Ottoman elite fled the country to Istanbul, and peasants invaded and occupied the ownerless estates. The revolutionary government in Cairo even formally decided to divide the abandoned haciendas among the peasants.

The British invaded in August, and Sir Garnet Wolseley inflicted a decisive defeat on `Urabi's army at Tel-el-Kabir. The doggerel of imperialist balladeer William Topaz McGonagall sums up the attitude of British jingoists:

> 'Twas on the 13th day of September, in the year of 1882,
> Which Arabi and his rebel horde long will rue;
> Because Sir Garnet Wolseley and his brave little band
> Fought and conquered them on Kebir land.
>
> He marched upon the enemy with his gallant band
> O'er the wild and lonely desert sand,
> And attacked them before daylight,
> And in twenty minutes he put them to flight.[25]

`Urabi's army is characterized, not as the military wing of an indigenous Egyptian movement for democracy, but as a "rebel horde." The lush Nile Valley is reduced to "wild and lonely desert sand." Back in the real world, the British put Tawfiq back on his throne as viceroy and subjected the country to British imperial rule at the top through the Ottoman-Egyptian bureaucracy, which they left in place. They permanently prorogued the democratically elected Chamber of Deputies and its constitution, returning Egypt to despotism. In the early twentieth century, they allowed a Duma-style consultative assembly to meet, but gave it no legislative power. Imperialist historian Bernard Lewis praised this castrated chamber as a "model" for the rest of the Middle East, graciously proffered by the enlightened British, mendaciously obscuring the British abolition of the feisty, elected Chamber of Delegates of 1881.[26]

THE U.S. WAR IN IRAQ

Some of the politicians who backed the U.S. war against Iraq were genuinely appalled at the virtual genocides committed by Saddam Hussein, or seriously worried about the prospect of the Iraqi Baathists developing nuclear weapons, and made the case on grounds of human rights and international norms. The Bush administration and its supporters, and especially the neoconservative camp, however, often appealed as well to the rhetoric of empire. Despite the rationales articulated by Bush administration spokesmen and by influential advisers—including terrorism, weapons of mass destruction, and human rights—the war had another, more important, and less openly stated aim. The aim of the American war in Iraq—as articulated by Richard Perle, Paul Wolfowitz, and other neoconservative defense intellectuals—was to change the pillars of U.S. policy in the Middle East.[27] For many Bush administration figures, one key lesson of September 11 was the need to abandon the alliance with oil giant Saudi Arabia. The United States needed as an ally a major petroleum producer in the Persian Gulf that could offer military and naval bases, could moderate the price of petroleum in favor of the West, and could serve as a springboard for growing U.S. influence in the region. The United States had lost Iran, which played many of these roles, to the Khomeinist revolution of 1979. It had attempted to replace Iran with Iraq and Saudi Arabia, and this substitution, while problematic in some ways, had seemed to succeed in the last decade of the cold war. The Iraqi invasion of Kuwait, however, necessitated not only abandoning the Iraq alliance but developing a policy of "dual containment" against Iraq and Iran.

The United States was thus left, in the 1990s, with a Saudi alliance in the Gulf. While the extreme political and religious conservatism of the Saudi elite had seemed an asset to U.S. elites during the Cold War and had been used against the Soviet Union in Afghanistan, it seemed increasingly undesirable as radical Islamism emerged as a threat to the global status quo in the course of the 1990s. Islamist revolts threatened Algeria, Egypt, and Israel's hold on the Occupied Territories, as well as having succeeded in instituting an anti-American government in Afghanistan in the form of the Taliban. Behind the scenes, the U.S. Agency for International Development and other arms of the U.S. government often found themselves in competition with Saudi-financed projects in places like Bangladesh, with the Saudis pushing radical Islam and hyperpatriarchy. Rumors swirled of Saudi wealth flowing to the Algerian and other radical Islamists.

September 11 convinced the American nationalists—whether assertive realists such as Dick Cheney and Donald Rumsfeld or neoconservatives such as Paul Wolfowitz, Douglas Feith, and Richard Perle—that the Saudi alliance was no longer tenable. On the one hand, the puritan Wahhabi form of Islam spread by Saudi influence and oil wealth seemed to them deeply implicated in the spread of radical anti-American ideas and the formation of groups like al-Qaeda. On the other, the U.S. attempt to base troops at Prince Sultan air base and elsewhere in the kingdom had enraged Islamists, who saw this move as a desecration of what they considered the holy land (the sacred cities of Mecca and Medina are in Saudi Arabia). The American nationalists began considering a thoroughgoing reconfiguration of the U.S. posture in the Gulf. By overthrowing the Baath party and putting a new, democratic government into power in Iraq, the United States would acquire a new oil ally. Iraq's potential for daily oil production could equal that of Saudi Arabia in the long term, and so it could play the role of helping keep petroleum affordable for the industrialized West. Strategically, it overlooked the Gulf and provided excellent strategic basing for U.S. troops. Its population was thought to be largely secular, and so it might provide a much better model for the sort of Middle East the United States now wished to create than the authoritarian monarchy of Saudi Arabia with its alliance with Wahhabism.

The neoconservatives dreamed that a U.S.-installed Iraqi regime would replace Saudi Arabia and would begin a democratic revolution throughout the Middle East, recalling events in Eastern Europe after the fall of the Soviet Union. The plan as stated was fraught with obvious flaws. Iraq, an ethnically diverse country that had labored under thirty-five years of brutal dictatorship, was an unlikely flag bearer of democratization. Moreover, the process in Eastern Europe has produced Milosevic's Serbia and Kuchma's Ukraine, as well as Poland and the Czech Republic. The hawks appear to have believed, incorrectly, that Iraq's petroleum-producing capacity might be able to offset Saudi influence over the oil markets. And, although Iraqis, Wolfowitz said, "don't bring the sensitivity of having the holy cities of Islam being on their territory," he apparently did not then know about the Shiite shrine cities of Najaf and Karbala. The hawks had been convinced by their client, Ahmad Chalabi, head of the expatriate Iraqi National Congress, that Iraq's Shiites were secular and would embrace America and democracy. The realists in the Bush administration, such as Dick Cheney and Donald Rumsfeld, were less interested in democracy and were perfectly happy to hand Iraq over to a new strongman.

The real reason for the war on Iraq was therefore to replace Saudi Arabia as an oil ally with Iraq, to marginalize Riyadh and combat the alleged effects of its Wahhabi proselytizing, and to create new "secular" Shiite allies in the region who might prove useful in combating Khomeinism in Iran and the Lebanese Hizbullah. For the neoconservatives in particular, this strategic move was calculated to weaken those regional states that opposed Ariel Sharon's expansionism and to ensure that he could proceed with his annexation of much of the West Bank. It is difficult to see in what way the new policy actually addressed the challenge of September 11, insofar as it was unconnected to al-Qaeda, the fight against which was put on a back burner while the vast U.S. military machine concentrated on Iraq.

As Fred Cooper suggests in this volume, the United States and Britain put themselves in a position in Iraq analogous to that of the late European colonial powers of, say, the 1950s or 1960s, which were preparing their colonies for independence. Like the European colonial powers after World War II, the Anglo-American coalition adopted a developmentalist rhetoric, arguing that the purpose of their rule in Iraq was social progress in preparation for independence.

As it happened, the Iraqi Shiites were much less secular in orientation that the United States assumed.[28] The Shiite slums of East Baghdad, with a population of over 2 million, teemed with poor youngsters who idolized the Sadr family, which in turn was committed to establishing an Iran-style theocracy. The movement was now led by the young firebrand Muqtada al-Sadr, who began demanding a withdrawal of U.S. troops in April 2003, as soon as the war ended. The organized Shiite parties, such as the al-Da`wa al-Islamiyyah, the Supreme Council for Islamic Revolution in Iraq, and the Iraqi Hizbullah, also aimed at the creation of some sort of Islamic state. Many Shiites were secular in mindset, and the Communist Party at one time had a substantial following, but it had been devastated by Baath persecution, undertaken at the behest of the United States. The secular Shiites, especially strong in Basra, had no viable political vehicle in the immediate aftermath of the U.S. invasion.

Ironically, Wolfowitz visited Najaf and Karbala in the second half of July, and inadvertently set off a riot in Najaf. U.S. marines increased their security for his visit, which came a day after Muqtada's fiery sermon calling for the establishment of a shadow government and popular Shiite militia. The increased security raised fears among Sadrists that the United States planned to arrest him (which is after all what Saddam would have done). The rumor of such an attempted arrest provoked demonstrations by thousands of Sadrists late on a Saturday, after Wolfowitz had left. They were repeated on Sunday, until the crowds were convinced that Muqtada had not been bothered. Only a few weeks later, a huge truck bomb went off in Najaf, assassinating SCIRI leader Ayatollah Muhammad Baqir al-Hakim, one of the few hardline Shiite clerics who had been willing pragmatically to cooperate with the Americans.

U.S. rule in Iraq after the war underwent three basic phases, each with parallels to past U.S. nation building. Initially, retired general Jay Garner was made head of the Office of Reconstruction and Humanitarian Aid, and was hoping to put Iraq on an even keel within six months and go home. This plan would have entailed putting Ahmad Chalabi and the Iraqi National Congress in charge of the Iraqi bureaucracy, supported by his militia. It resembled the policy toward France after the Allied victory in 1945, where the government was handed over to the Free French. This policy was favored by Cheney and Rumsfeld. Garner was quickly sidelined in a Washington power struggle that remains obscure, but before he went out of office in early May, he appointed seven Iraqi politicians to a governing council, including Chalabi and his allies. They were intended to call a national congress in July of 2003 to pick an Iraqi government.

Garner's successor, appointed May 6, was L. Paul Bremer III, a career State Department official and former ambassador to the Netherlands who had gone to work for Henry Kissinger's risk assessment company. At first (phase 2A), Bremer intended to rule Iraq himself by fiat for two or three years. He disbanded the Iraqi army altogether, put off reinstituting the ministries, and attempted to sideline the Garner-appointed governing council. Bremer appears to have disliked Ahmad Chalabi and to have implemented a State Department policy of attempting to marginalize him, despite working for the Department of Defense, where Chalabi had warm supporters. On the other hand, Chalabi appears to have been the major voice arguing for disbanding the Baath army, seeing it as a threat to his eventually coming to power. The initial Bremer plan resembled postwar Japan, with Bremer playing MacArthur. He initially did not plan to have an Interim Governing Council or early elections. Bremer's somewhat high-handed project was derailed by the rise of a low-intensity insurgency in the center-north part of the country, where Sunni Arabs predominated, as well as by the emergence of Shiite populist movements that staged recurring if somewhat small demonstrations. Bremer quickly concluded that he could not hope to rule Iraq by fiat for years, after all. He therefore modified his plan, appointing an Interim Governing Council on July 13 (phase 2B), in hopes of gaining some legitimacy for his Coalition Provisional Authority by gaining Iraqi allies. They were, in short, intended to play the Japanese emperor to Bremer's MacArthur. His twenty-five-member IGC, however, was dominated by expatriate politicians who had little local popularity, and by independents who had been in the country under

Saddam but had no grass-roots organization. The IGC was deeply divided, including a majority of Shiites along with Sunni Arabs and Kurds from all over the country, and found itself able to make few executive decisions beyond appointing heads of ministries. Since it was directly appointed by Bremer, it lacked popular legitimacy or true representativeness, and so failed to take the Iraq seat at the United Nations or to garner much public support. Bremer envisaged that the IGC would appoint heads of ministries, then decide on how to select delegates to a constitutional convention that would draft a new constitution, oversee the writing of the constitution, conduct a census, and ultimately proceed toward general elections in 2005.

In the summer of 2003, Bremer's Coalition Provisional Authority disregarded the 1907 Hague Regulations and the 1949 Geneva Convention on occupied territories, which forbid the occupying power to alter the laws or social structure of the occupied territory. The CPA announced that a kind of shock therapy would be applied to the Iraqi economy, which would be completely thrown open to foreign investment. Foreign companies would be allowed to buy any Iraqi concern without regulation, and would be allowed immediately to repatriate all profits. The CPA also began attempting to sell off twelve major state-owned Iraqi industries. Likewise, a flat income tax of 15 percent was set for Iraqis beginning in 2004. The flat tax, which is highly regressive and benefits the wealthy disproportionately, has been a favorite project of the American right for some time. Unable to implement it in the United States, laissez-faire advocates delighted in imposing it imperially on formerly Arab socialist Iraq. These actions in the economic sphere were among the clearest examples of U.S. imperialism, insofar as they went well beyond what international law allowed an occupying authority to do and aimed at reshaping Iraq's quasi-socialist economy in free-market mode. Bremer appears to have had in mind the "shock therapy" applied in post-Soviet Poland, a modest success, though similar policies were applied in Russia to disastrous effect. The practical effect of these American-imposed economic rules (against which many members of the IGC protested) was muted by the lack of security in 2003, which discouraged much foreign investment in Iraq.

The third phase of U.S. rule in Iraq began in early November, when Paul Bremer suddenly flew back to Washington for consultations with President George W. Bush and National Security Adviser Condoleezza Rice. The plan for two or three years of direct U.S. administration of Iraq had collapsed in the face of a growing Sunni Arab insurgency and the inability of the IGC to agree on how to select the drafters of a new constitution. The Kurds and Sunni Arabs tended to want the drafters to be appointed by the IGC, so as to ensure representation of their ethnic groups. In contrast, Grand Ayatollah Ali Sistani, chief Shiite religious authority, had given a ruling or fatwa on June 28 demanding that the drafters of the constitution represent the sovereign Iraqi people and be elected on a one-person, one-vote basis. In Shiite Islam, laypersons are required to follow the rulings of leading Shiite jurists on subsidiary matters related to Islamic law. The Shiites on the Interim Governing Council insisted on following this ruling, thus making it impossible for the IGC to reach a consensus.

On his return to Iraq, Bremer negotiated a new timetable with the IGC, announced on November 15. He gave up on having a new constitution written any time soon. The agreement specified that the IGC would draft a "basic law" that would govern elections. The elections would not be general. Rather, the American-appointed provincial councils and the IGC would select delegates who would in turn elect a transitional parliament, by May 31, 2004. The most prominent Kurdish leaders protested that the plan made no provision for the emergence of a consolidated Kurdish superprovince in the north, which they favored. (Kurds speak an Indo-European language rather than Arabic, though Iraqi Kurds are bilingual, and they have long sought greater autonomy from Baghdad.) Grand Ayatollah Ali Sistani again protested, insisting on general elections. This time the Americans and the IGC defied the Shiite leader, insisting that there was no time to prepare for general elections so soon. The IGC members had little in the way of grassroots support, and might have fared poorly in such an open election, but could hope to be returned to office by their own appointees. The United States opposed one-person, one-vote elections in the spring of 2004 for fear that Islamist radicals, Arab nationalists, and Baath remnants might be returned. The United States maintained that general elections would eventually be held, in 2005. Like St. Augustine in his youth, the Bush administration prayed for virtue, but "not yet." This third phase of the U.S. occupation most resembled the Afghanistan model, with the appointed provincial councils substituting for the (stage-managed) Loya Jirga that elected President Hamid Karzai in July of 2002. It implied an abandonment of any hope that the United States could directly reshape Iraqi society on the basis of laissez-faire capitalism and civil administration. There were, then, three different models in less than eight months, with the Washington infighting reinforced by the problem the United States had in getting control of the security situation. As an experiment in rehabilitated empire, the Iraq case faltered badly in its first year.

In removing the Baath regime and eliminating constraints on Iraqi Islamism, the United States unleashed a new political force in the Gulf: not the upsurge of civic organization and democratic sentiment fantasized by American neoconservatives, but the aspirations of Iraqi Shiites to build an Islamic republic. That result was an entirely predictable consequence of the past thirty years of political conflict between the Shiites and the Baathist regime, and American policy analysts have expected a different result only by neglecting that history. To be sure, the dreams of a Shiite

Islamic republic in Baghdad may be unrealistic: a plurality of the country is Sunni, and some proportion of the 14 million Shiites is secularist. In the months after the Anglo-American invasion, however, the religious Shiite parties demonstrated the clearest organizational skills and established political momentum. The Islamists are likely to be a powerful enough group in parliament that they may block the sort of close American-Iraqi cooperation that the neoconservatives had hoped for. The spectacle of Wolfowitz's party heading out of Najaf just before the outbreak of a major demonstration of 10,000 angry Sadrists, inadvertently provoked by the Americans, may prove an apt symbol for the American adventure in Iraq.

The main stated goals of the U.S. invasion of Iraq proved far more difficult to accomplish than its proponents envisioned. Baathist Iraq posed no serious danger to the West, either as a producer of weapons of mass destruction or as a purveyor of terror. Despite President Bush's repeated claims, there were no significant links between the secular, Arab nationalist Baath and the radical Islamist al-Qaeda terrorist organization. There also turned out to be no nuclear weapons program and possibly no serious chemical or biological weapons programs or stockpiles after the mid-1990s. Far from finally defeating Khomeinism, U.S. policy has given it millions of liberated Iraqi allies. Kurdish demands for a consolidated Kurdish "canton" and for a very loose federalism in Iraq may also threaten the peaceful evolution of a new state. The Iraqi Interim Governing Council declined to recognize Israel, citing Iraq's membership in the Arab League and lack of genuine progress toward a Palestinian state. Saudi Arabia will continue to be the most influential oil state, because of its impressive ability to be a swing producer (it can produce as much as 11 million barrels a day, but could survive economically on 7 million barrels a day; only an average of 76 million barrels a day are produced worldwide). Al-Qaeda and allied terrorist threats were not countered by the invasion of Iraq, and it is possible that they will have been given a new field to play on.

Theorists of the 2003 war against Iraq by the Bush administration such as Paul Wolfowitz emphasized three reasons for the campaign: the Iraqi weapons of mass destruction programs and stockpiles, the threat of terrorism emanating from Saddam Hussein's regime, and the atrocities of the Baath regime against the Iraqi people. These justifications for war resonated with the two earlier instances of imperial intervention in the Middle East discussed above. The French alleged that the Mamluks were oppressing French merchants and interfering in their Mediterranean commerce, harming France. The British hawks maintained that the `Urabi movement threatened the safety and property of the 90,000 expatriate Europeans in Egypt at that time, as well as the security of British vessels in Alexandria harbor. In both these previous episodes, the rulers were depicted as despots depopulating their countries and oppressing their people. The Mamluk regime in Egypt was in fact oppressive, especially to urban residents, who were badly overtaxed, though the burden was more bearable for the peasants. The `Urabi movement represented a demand by the Egyptian middle strata for more representative modes of governance and lower taxes, challenging the overtaxation imposed by heavy European debt-servicing demands. The charge that the movement was no more than a military junta oppressing the legitimate Ottoman viceroy was among the more monstrous lies in the history of liberal imperialism. In contrast, the charges against Saddam Hussein's regime of massive human rights violations were if anything understated, since it seems increasingly clear that it killed several hundred thousand Iraqi citizens during its thirty-five years in power. Still, for most of the Bush administration figures that sought an Iraq war, issues other than Iraqi human rights loomed largest.

The French intervention in Egypt proved to be an unmitigated disaster. The French inability to gain naval control in the Mediterranean gave the British fleet the ability to sink the French squadron, stranding Bonaparte and his army. The French were unable to break out through Ottoman Syria by taking Acre (Akka) on the Syrian coast, because the British navy intercepted their shipments of heavy artillery by sea from Alexandria. The French military faced attrition from popular uprisings and local diseases, and could not hope to stand for long against Ottoman and joint Ottoman-British military attacks aimed at expelling them from Egypt. Bonaparte slipped out of the country after only a year, hiding the catastrophe from the public and managing to come to power. In 1801 the French soldiers surrendered and gained passage back to France on British vessels, on condition that they not ever fight British troops. The British ruled Egypt directly for four decades, but in the end they were weakened by World War I and proved unable to stand against the popular political mobilization achieved by the Wafd party after the war.

The age of direct imperialism gradually gave way after World War II to much less direct forms of political domination. The war deeply harmed the liberal European economies, making it harder for them to shoulder the financial burdens of empire or to justify it to their weary publics. The Fascist approach to colonialism, and Fascist domination of Europeans, undermined the glib moral justifications given for it in liberal societies (the Dutch public, having felt the Nazi jackboot, found it difficult to continue ruling Indonesia by main force). The social mobilization of the subject populations, including a rise of literacy, urbanization, mass media, political parties, and, often, some industrialization, made them increasingly difficult to rule directly. The rise of indigenous bourgeoisies of significant wealth in the colonies often led to the formation of political cliques eager for self-rule and increasingly unwilling to collaborate with the foreigners. The cold war frightened even paternalistic Washington politicians such as Eisenhower into supporting decolonization, lest French and British repression in Africa and Asia make Communism popular among increasingly resentful colonial subjects. The threat of Soviet intervention also made the industrialized democracies of the West less prone to military adventurism beyond carefully defined spheres of influence.

The U.S. hawks grouped in the Project for a New American Century hoped that the end of the cold war had revived the prospects for empire. The Iraq War was a stalking horse for a series of planned occupations. The answers of influential neoconservative thinker Bill Kristol to the questions of journalist David Corn are instructive here:

> CORN: Do we have 450,000 troops for each country of the axis of evil to occupy all three?
> KRISTOL: We should have. We should have. Exactly. A hundred and fifty thousand troops for each of the three countries is about perfect. That's the size of the army, about 450. And those three regimes need to be changed.
> CORN: And you're for a tax hike to support this, right?
> KRISTOL: I would gladly have a tax hike to get rid of those three regimes.[29]

In fact, the low-intensity guerrilla war staged by Sunni Arabs in the center-north of Iraq, the political mobilization of the Shiites by religious parties, the demands of the Kurds for more autonomy, and the inability of the appointed Interim Governing Council to reach consensus on any of the major issues facing post-Saddam Iraq made it increasingly difficult for the Americans to envision attempting directly to rule and shape Iraq for any length of time. Although the Bush administration initially hoped that Paul Bremer would rule Iraq virtually by fiat for two or three years, after only six months it threw in the towel. The institution of a caretaker Iraqi government on June 28, 2004, with elections planned for January 2005, was an admission that the United States could not mount a direct imperial administration of a major country in the global South in the twenty-first century. With so many U.S. troops mired for so long in a Mesopotamian quagmire, an incipient neoconservative campaign for further wars, this time against Iran and Syria, lost steam. One proponent of aggression against Iran in the Pentagon came under scrutiny by the Federal Bureau of Investigation for possible espionage for Israel. The collapse of the case for the Iraq war, based on Iraq's putative weapons of mass destruction programs and supposed links to al-Qaeda, seriously damaged the rhetorical legitimacy of empire among a significant portion of the American public. The alienation of the main U.S. allies, who opposed unilateral revival of direct imperialism, revealed its costs when the United States failed to find significant international financial or military support for the occupation beyond the government of Tony Blair in the United Kingdom.

The chaotic and mismanaged aftermath of the Iraq war and the clear resentment of Iraqis at being occupied once again put empire in bad odor. The hawkish realists and neoconservatives had demonstrated that in a unipolar world, dominated by a hyperpower, wars of naked empire could be launched again. But the sort of difficulties faced by the late imperial powers after World War II still bedeviled any such adventures, particularly given the political mobilization of the masses and the leveling effects of guerrilla campaigns by asymmetrical cells against much more powerful and sophisticated armies. Regime change is easy, now. Regime creation, in accordance with the desires of the imperial power, remains as difficult as ever. A return to "softer" and less financially and politically costly means of foreign domination in Washington seems likely, much to the chagrin of the hawks. Theirs was likely a detour, rather than a keynote, of the early twenty-first century.

7. LAW AND LEGITIMATION IN EMPIRE

CAGLAR KEYDER

I

The background history on which I am basing the following speculations is the experience of the Ottoman Empire with constitutionalism during the period before World War I. For about five centuries, the empire had operated on the basis of a legal pluralism ultimately dominated by the Islamic element. Empires are distinguished by differentiation into distinct groupings—societies with their own rules of cohesion, networks, solidarities—and pluralism is an essential element of empire. Since there is no pretension to homogeneity and no natural borders (the idea of empire connotes a sense of unceasing expansion), each conquest brings a new community into the jurisdiction of an empire. In this context legal pluralism indicates that there is recognition by the imperial center that distinct communities will remain intact as relatively autonomous entities, and that the autonomy of their legal regime is an essential component of their survival. For the Ottomans communities were mostly defined on the basis of confessional separation. This was realistic, in the sense that in a relatively locally based social and economic existence, marriages and other significant transactions occurred within the community, networks of the quotidian were built on the basis of religious practice, and the vocabulary of communal solidarity derived mostly from the discourse of the divine. Law of the communities, as distinct from the law of the empire, was directed precisely at upholding the rules of intracommunity social conduct.

There was a large number of constituent communities in the Ottoman Empire, including regions, provinces, tribal units, and most famously the *millet*.[1] Most of these units were corporate entities to some extent, relatively autonomous in most of their internal affairs. Millets were not territorially identified; they signified personal status of their members, regardless of their location. They operated their own educational institutions and levied their own internal taxes. Most importantly, they were in charge of their community's legal regime in most matters of civil law, such as marriage, inheritance, and intracommunity matters of debt and contract. The communities were structured around their churches such that the hierarchy which produced a patriarch or a chief rabbi also provided a legitimate interlocutor with whom the Ottoman rulers could interact in matters concerning the religious community.

In addition to the laws of the communities, there was also state law issued by the imperial center.[2] This corresponded to a civic law valid for the entire population in matters such as security, property in land and taxes, but also to the Roman *jus gentium*, because intercommunity matters would obviously fall within its jurisdiction. Hence, it was possible to talk about the coexistence of two differentiated conceptions of order working at two different levels: a tradition-based community order and a state-based civic order, but both ultimately secured by the imperial authority.

The Ottoman age of reforms changed all this.[3] The need for centralization had already been felt, in response to the growing independence of the provincial notables, the *ayan*, during the previous century. Starting in the 1830s, under pressure from Europe, and in an attempt at self-defense, Ottoman bureaucrats undertook administrative and legal reforms designed to launch a new form of modern state. Foremost in their mind was gaining legitimacy in the interstate arena in order to forestall the Great Powers' predatory appetite. The modernization of the state along the lines of the modern western blueprint would earn them a place in the concert of Europe, a goal that was achieved with the Crimean War and the Paris treaty of 1856. While a sort of success was granted the Ottoman bureaucrats on this score, the internal dimensions of the reform were much more problematic. Based on the prototype of the centralized modern state invented in the West, the reformers had envisioned an empire that would be transformed into a single legal space, where the subjects would become citizens directly in relationship with the administrative center, without any mediation by communities. In a series of legislation culminating in the Constitution of 1876, modernization from above was largely achieved and, legally, the empire had been transformed into a single political space. I will call this transformation of a differentiated and layered political order into an homogeneous space *constitutionalism*.[4]

Constitutionalism meant that the segmented societal order would come under the jurisdiction of an expanding civic order, which itself would now be justified on the basis of modern notions of formal equality and individual rights. During the entire period of state modernization, reception of western law continued and the empire progressed toward a constitutional entity, emulating a modern nation-state. The desire to modernize the state, and thus to reduce the autonomy of the communities, without being able to substitute a new basis for loyalty and solidarity, spelled its demise. The new unified legal space led to inequality and polarization, and to social tensions that could not be contained. Eventually, nationalist movements emerging out of the former millets, and ultimately the Great War, brought about the empire's dismantlement. Just before the end, an activist faction of the ruling elite had become the governing party, and was transformed in the direction of Turkish nationalism. Its leaders embarked on a project of turning the old empire into a new version of itself, with a clear hierarchical vision and a supremacist blueprint, dominated by one of the ethnic elements in the mix. This project led to much chaos and human suffering.

II

In the absence of schools and media and communications, law is the major formal medium of interaction between subject and sovereign in an empire; hence, law plays a paramount role in the legitimation of empire. Imperial law in the Ottoman Empire, as opposed to the law of the communities, was state law aiming at state control, and it sought to gain legitimacy more from its formal consistency and rationality than through acceptance because it was the result of some deliberative process. The Ottoman empire was a bureaucratic empire which in its administration had recourse to a corps of officials selected and promoted according to merit, organized in the rational manner of a bureaucracy.[5] Imperial law was their primary tool. Imperial state law, however, left the lifeworld to be regulated by the traditional practice of the communities. Nonetheless, excesses of the communities could be appealed, and courts could be used as a check against the exploitative tendencies of local potentates. Hence, there was a layered legitimation: for most cases arising out of everyday concerns, subjects were confronted with their community orders. Imperial law had its own designated sphere, or was brought in as a review mechanism; but it did not bear the full weight of legitimating the social order. [6]

Pace Weber, in modern nation-states where there is a direct relationship of the citizens with the state, the consistency and procedure-boundedness of state actions, as well as the transparency and calculability of court decisions, are supposed to provide for the legitimacy of legal-rational authority. This legal-rational legitimacy, however, is generally supplemented by some degree of nationalism, the ideology of nation as community. In addition, a deliberative process of democracy may cement the relationship between the state and the citizen: politics in the nation-state may introduce substantive changes in the script and transform the norms on which procedural legality is based. Because laws can change in response to substantive demands articulated through the political process, legitimacy is also based on the availability of these channels, and not only on consistent legality. Traditional and even bureaucratic empires, however, are not open to such political dynamics. Their populations cannot be construed as communities, and democratic deliberation is not a feature of their political process. Instead, legitimation works through the division of the legal field into two distinct levels of law: law at the imperial level which is formal, and perhaps rational, and law at the community level with a strong substantive component, which serves to sustain the community.

One accommodation of this substantive working of the law in the Ottoman case was the autonomy granted to different groups, especially, but not exclusively (e.g., in the case of tribes) on the basis of religion. The millet system allowed for legal autonomy in the case of family law and intracommunity matters. Such legal autonomy served to preserve "community" in the sense that law could be used to maintain relations that would uphold the established balances within the group. For this to be achieved, law had to function in a substantive manner, not unlike Weber's ideal-type construct of *kadi* justice. According to Weber's conception, the kadi renders judgments "in terms of concrete ethical or other practical valuations":[7] the kadi is concerned with the consequences of his judgments from the perspective of stability of the social order within the community. Hence, kadi justice is substantive rather than formal in its orientation. Within preconstitutional empires, all community law is kadi justice, for it is oriented precisely to maintain the community vis-à-vis both the other communities and the overarching framework of the empire. Even when state law has to be translated to the local level, where it applies to matters regulated by the state, e.g., property, kadi justice may introduce interpretations that are based on a certain conception of community and social order.

There was also an indirect consequence of this autonomy that allowed communities to institute mechanisms of welfare and solidarity, in order to materially protect their members from various risks. These ranged from mosque- or church-centered charity to more formal mechanisms of *waqf*, which was a particularly well-developed institution in the Ottoman context, for Muslims and Christians alike. Guilds served a similar purpose for urban craftsmen. These traditional welfare instruments had to function in environments where they could be protected from formal stipulations and from the incursions of market rationality; in other words, legal autonomy was important because of the symbiosis between community-maintaining institutions and their substantive accommodation.

This balance between the imperial state and community organization, between the formal law of the empire and the substantive orientation of community institutions, was destroyed by constitutionalism. Constitutionalism committed the empire to regard all subjects as equal in their dealings with the state. By creating a single legal space, by granting all subjects the same law, it took away the substantive autonomy granted to ethnic groups, geographical and administrative units, tribes, and millets. The layered form of legitimacy enjoyed by imperial power was disbanded in favor of modern legality—formal and rational law with universal jurisdiction, in front of which every citizen was promised to be equal.

The constitutive elements of the new era were a series of legislations starting with the 1838 free-trade agreement, which outlawed trade monopolies that had been the most effective instruments in the political regulation of the economy. The *Tanzimat* reforms in the following year abolished collective obligations and privileges, instituted individual and equal obligations, and initiated the route toward rule of law and unified citizenship. A new criminal law in 1840, a reform decree in 1856, a nationality law in 1869, the codification of the *shari'a* in the 1870s, and the unification of the appeal process of the various criminal courts followed. The Constitution of 1876 and its repeal by the sultan did not much influence this trend.

Constitutionalism, which effectively "modernized" the empire but also brought its end, was initiated by the state elite: state-making modernizers from above had as their objective the maximization of control and the building of efficient and effective state mechanisms. The construction of a modern state allowed them to participate alongside other representatives of modern states in interstate or suprastate forums. At the same time, the Ottoman state elite were under European pressure to choose the constitutional path. It may be argued that there was a collusion of interests here: while formal law and liberalism, implying the restriction of the Ottoman state's capacities of intervention, facilitated the incorporation of the empire into the expanding realm of European capitalism, they also allowed the state elite to import the European model of the modern state and overhaul the administrative blueprint of the empire.[8]

Once the process of reform was initiated, its constituency from below also became effective. Intensified interaction between communities, demands for a uniformity of legal and administrative regulation, calls for predictability and calculability are the expected outcomes of "modernization." The actors in the vanguard of this modernization were the trans-millet bourgeoisies, those who had formed supra-millet networks, the *évolués,* and the cosmopolitans. They would be the prime beneficiaries of a universalization of legal arrangements.

Constitutionalism invalidated the older division between state and community, thus making it necessary that new sources of legitimacy be discovered that would operate both at the material and the discursive levels. At the discursive level, the new principle was found in Ottomanism, *Osmanlicilik,* an imperial patriotism, claiming an imagined community made up of all the subjects of the empire, regardless of religion, language, and ethnicity.[9] Ottomanism was made concrete in the opening of all administrative ranks to non-Muslim citizens of the empire, and in the gradual development of a religiously and ethnically integrated imperial elite. This is reflected well not only in the composition of the standing bureaucracy, but also in the Parliament of 1877, which was perhaps unique in the history of multiethnic empires in terms of its diversity: there were 77 Muslim, 44 Christian, and 4 Jewish deputies.[10] Muslims included Turks, Arabs, Kurds, Tatars, and Albanians; Christians included Greeks and Armenians of different sects. The Parliament could also be seen as an attempt to introduce representational, if not fully democratic, legitimacy by allowing deliberation and debate in the making of the new laws. The freedom of deliberation enjoyed by the deputies, however, lasted only a brief period, to be replaced by the autocratic rule of Abdulhamit. This rule did not reverse Ottomanist "multiculturalism": ethnically diverse Muslims and non-Muslims continued to be well represented in both central and provincial Ottoman administration.[11] New educational opportunities and career experiences continued to mold a unified Ottoman elite, who indeed shared the common perspective of Ottomanism.

At the level of the social and economic everyday life of the masses, however, a quite different story was unfolding, with considerably less benign implications. In the less fluid society prior to the nineteenth century, populations had lived in isolated villages or well-defined and residentially segregated neighborhoods in cities; daily life was mainly conducted within communities. The 1838 trade treaty robbed the state of its principal protectionist capacity. Import and export taxes became minimal, and as exports increased competition over the use of land grew intense. There were new lands opening for export agriculture where capitalist relations defined new relations in space and supplanted traditional peasant societies.[12] Old forms of possession and property became subject to a new regime of ownership where competition for land as commodity intensified. After the 1858 legislation on land, peasants with traditional rights of tenure found themselves toiling on private property; transhumant tribes were forced to confront newly arrived owners and fight for territory they had considered theirs by custom. Land had become valuable as trade escaped the earlier restrictions the Ottoman state had imposed in typical provisionist impulse.[13] Greater trade volumes undermined guilds in urban areas. A unified legal system that did not permit the protection of communities suddenly opened up economic life to operation under new rules. These are the reasons why Ottomanism remained an elite ideology whose appeal could not be widened among masses who "saw their own interest not in strengthening the power and increasing the intervention of the central government, but in maintaining the rights of the communities and strengthening the administrative autonomy of the provinces."[14]

The empire had opened up to trade while the state lost its ability to protect its population and to compensate for the social and economic impact of commodification and the ensuing division of labor. The substantive capability enjoyed by the communities had previously accommodated an adequate framework for the self-protection of the society. Welfare institutions could be set up when communities maintained legal autonomy. But legal unification now curtailed the operation of the communities based on a substantive logic; processes of modernization weakened the lateral mechanisms of solidarity operating within communities and left the stage open for the expansion of the self-regulated market. Since the imperial state, which had relinquished a good part of its fiscal prerogatives to a foreign consortium (the Public Debt Administration), did not have the capacity to institute social policy at a supra-community level, the population was left unprotected against the polarizing and excluding operation of the market.[15]

From 1838 until World War I the Ottoman realms were incorporated into the world market at a rapid pace: by the end of the period 15 percent of the output was being exported.[16] Indebtedness and consequent bankruptcy of the state had made resistance in economic policy matters to impositions by transnational capital improbable. The social implication of this incorporation was that there developed an extremely unbalanced ethnic topography. Most of the groups who benefited from the growing incorporation were Christians and Jews who had enjoyed a small initial advantage in terms of linguistic affinity or networks already in place. Greeks in particular but also Armenians and Jews became "market-dominant minorities" occupying privileged intermediary positions in the economic nexus with Europe.[17] This is not to say, of course, that all Greeks or Armenians, each of whose millets made up perhaps one-tenth of the Ottoman population, became rich merchants; but rich merchants, bankers, professionals, and later manufacturers were disproportionately Christians and Jews.

As the pace of economic change accelerated those who benefited from new market opportunities started to settle in cities and the social schismosis between different ethnic groups came also to be reflected in the human geography of the empire. Schools and community organization, patterns of consumption and levels of modernization of material culture and lifestyles, were increasingly growing apart. This divergence was exacerbated by cultural, educational, and missionary activities, which gradually came to awaken ethnic consciousness among the Christian and Jewish populations. Against this background of the embourgeoisement of a segment of the Christian population, Muslims became conscious of their rapid relative decline and increasingly resentful.

Within the Christian and ethnically distinct Muslim populations, the social upheaval experienced through the new range of activities led to the rise of a new mercantile class which came to rival the established grandees of the communities. The corporate units of communities had functioned on the basis of social hierarchies underwritten by church organization or traditional elite domination. When new activities emerged that yielded greater returns both economically and increasingly in social terms, binding their beneficiaries to the masses in new networks, the status of the traditional elites suffered. The division between the old and the new was manifest in the willingness of the new groups to opt for separatist nationalism, as against the old establishment elites who were content to extend credence to the chances of success of Ottomanism.

The social upheaval led to a similar challenge on the Muslim imperial elite, contributing to the success of the Young Turks who were the activist and radical faction of the Ottoman ruling cadres.[18] They had attended schools that formed the elite for imperial service, and they initially remained committed to the Ottomanist ideal. While nationalism had made important inroads within the Greek and Armenian communities, and separatism was a credible platform among various Balkan populations, Turks came to nationalism only after the 1908 revolution. After the Young Turks, now incarnated as the Committee of Union and Progress (CUP), succeeded in reinstating the constitution and reopening the Parliament in 1908, elected deputies, again with a composition reflecting the proportion of ethnic groups in the population, started legislating with remarkable sophistication and seriousness of purpose. At first the CUP remained committed to the goal of modernizing the empire as a multiethnic unit: a unitary and secular modern state. Not only the Parliament but the cabinet as well reflected the promise of a multiethnic empire.

The benign phase of the constitutional government ended, however, after a series of military reversals in the Balkans; the accelerating pace of wars allowed the Turkish nationalists to win the debate and sway the ruling party. After 1912 the CUP abandoned the project of devising an imperial patriotism; they instead decided to impose a Turkish supremacist nationalism on the territory they still controlled. This was the final phase of the empire. Since the early nineteenth century, the empire had gone from its classical incarnation to its constitutional version, and finally to its ethnic supremacist and belligerent phase.

At the time of constitutionalizing the Austro-Hungarian Empire, there was an attempt to think through the alternative of a political system based on the relative autonomy of different groups. How could there be a modern legal order that conserved some autonomy for definable communities? Could there be an "organic citizenship" where communities would remain as some intermediary order and continue to function as the vessels of substantive concerns?[19] This, of course, was counterposed to "atomic citizenship" in the French mode. Otto Bauer and Karl Renner insisted that state and nation had to be thought as separate entities, and that there should be no necessary identity between them. Renner further argued that it was possible to divide citizenship into levels of nation and state. Individuals would thus have a layered allegiance, to their nations and to their (imperial) state. Federalism based on territorial separation could be one option; but this prescription would not apply to the case of geographically dispersed ethnic groups, such as Jews in the Habsburg Empire, or Greeks, Armenians, or Jews (or any of the Muslim ethnic groups except the Arabs) in the Ottoman, who had no territorial identification.

There was no thinking in the Ottoman Empire about adapting various autonomies and the millet organization to the constitutional period. Neither the legal and political substance nor the formal operation of organic citizenship in a constitutional empire had been thought through.[20] Nonetheless, the option of organic citizenship, however vaguely formulated, became the principal platform of a political party during the short period of electoral competition before the war.[21] A faction among the Young Turks declared themselves to be in favor of decentralization and devolution, and contested the elections in 1912 as the Liberal Union (known as the Entente Libérale). They drew support from among the non-Muslim and non-Turkish elements in the population who still had faith in the empire but wanted to retain community autonomy, and from Turks who were suspicious of the CUP's activist centralism and militant secularism. The centralists, however, emerged as the winner of a suspect election, and Ottomanism was buried as an ideology retrospectively described as naive. The atomized citizenship model not only had the advantage of logical simplicity, but it also maximized state control by creating a unified space; it comforted state actors by promising to eradicate intermediary levels of affiliation. This was the prescription that the CUP found to its liking, for, during the six years until the final dismantlement of the empire in 1918, they would rule with naked coercion and thuggery, attempting to replace constitutional equality and rule of law with ethnic nationalism and dictatorship. The Turkish nation-state traces its lineage to this laying of the groundwork for an ethnically exclusionary centralism.

III

In the rest of this article I would like to talk about the onset of globalization and the recent period of American assertiveness, employing the vocabulary of imperial constitutionalization and its aftermath. If we follow world-systems usage in defining the world order that prevailed before the period of multilateral governance of globalization as hegemony, we may argue that stable hegemony and the classical period of empire are similar. The hegemon, in establishing a *jus gentium*, determines the central legal and institutional order to reign as a civic framework, a basic law of nations, and expects compliance. Like various communities in the empire and Ottoman millets, nation-states have autonomy in their internal affairs; there is pressure on them to rationalize, harmonize, and assimilate their legal systems insofar as these legal systems encroach on *inter*national dealings, but there is general agreement that the internal practice of law finding may be substantive given "national interest."[22] In the high period of American hegemony, this national interest was identified with the imperatives of welfare and development that justified a fair amount of autonomy and legal idiosyncrasy. The division between the overarching legal structure of the empire (formal administrative law) and the particular arrangements of communities (millet-based substantive law), finds its parallel in the Westphalian contours of hegemony with its division between national and international law.

If hegemony was the form of empire during the golden age of post–World War II capitalism, globalization after the 1970s ushered in a constitutionalism. Globalization undermined the balances constructed by hegemony and necessitated a universal law, along with the relative erosion of layered citizenship. Nation-states, whose status paralleled the communities of empire, lost their autonomy as the networks of governance embraced all communities. A unification of the legal field was gradually imposed, thus effectively depriving nation-states of legal autonomy.

As in the case of Ottoman constitutionalism, globalization was primarily a strategy imposed from above. The literature makes much of globalization from below, which provided the ground-level transformative pressure, creating constituencies for constitutionalization. Ground-level transformations amount to the intensification of commerce and social and cultural interaction among nations, conducted independently of the regulation implicit in national and international law. Similar to the individuals from different millets who were brought into closer contact with the modernization of the economy and everyday life in the empire, citizens of different nations in the age of globalization formed new boundary transgressing networks and found themselves requiring new rules of engagement that could bypass the supervision of the states. But, it cannot be forgotten that the fields of intensified interaction, such as global markets, media, communications and transportation, along with the rules and standards and the dispute-resolution mechanisms permitting such interaction, have to be—and were—deliberately constructed. As in the history of nation-states, in the history of the emergent global field as well, the rules of ownership and the rules of exchange had to be constituted by law. The law governing globalization was imposed from above, but, as befits the constitutional stage, it was also autonomized in a large number of multilateral institutions such as the World Trade Organization, the various agreements on intellectual property, and rules and standards on media and communications.

In the Ottoman Empire constitutional reform started from above, as a state impulse, but was embraced by the trans-millet elites within the communities. At the end of the twentieth century too the initial impetus for globalization of law came from the hegemonic state. More precisely, the hegemonic state was mostly acting on behalf of transnationalizing economic interests when it took on the role of imposing on recalcitrant nation-states a set of common rules. These new rules, to be accepted by all nation-states, represented an increasing juridification of transnational life within the parameters of a unified legal field. Maximalist proponents of globalization wanted the new constitutionalism to create a truly universal legal field—with no concession to localisms. Human-rights discourse, deriving its strength from a modernist faith in individual autonomy, represents the boldest attempt at the universalization of civil codes, the inner sanctum of local difference.[23] Human-rights discourse derives its normative strength from the ideal of individual autonomy, which also underlay the constitutionalist prescription of "atomized citizenship." Atomized citizenship within the nation-state offered the new community of the nation as the vessel within which such individual autonomy could be cushioned. Atomized citizenship in the empire proved to be more difficult to accommodate when the mediate communities concurrently lost the ability to proffer the accustomed communal protection. Universalism in the globalized world is similarly difficult when the protection that was provided by nation-states erodes under the pressure of the extending market.

The thinking on cosmopolitan citizenship[24] in an emerging global polity, with its emphasis on individual rights, closely adheres to the format of citizenship in the nation-state, without confronting the problem that the emerging global unit exhibits a major deficiency by not being able to offer a legitimating ideology parallel to nationalism in the nation-state. Optimists argue that the constituencies for the local and the particular are now much weaker; liberal modernization has in fact won, and the only detractors are the old and threatened political elites. They claim that individuals are reflexive and empowered;[25] that millets are no longer consequential, nationalism has in fact been superseded. Thus, there is no need to worry about organic citizenship; what we do have to worry about is the good and proper functioning of constitutionalism. This claim professes a faith in the Weberian argument of legal-rational legitimacy, now for the sake of a global authority, that constitutionalism in itself would be sufficient to legitimate the new order.

Constitutional reform from above is represented by all the multilateral institutions and agreements that regulate security and the economy, environment and crime, that nation-states are compelled to subscribe to. Globalizing elites within nations, whether their interests are material or ideal, are the natural constituencies whose intentions coincide with the project imposed from above, and who provide the internal pressure on their states to comply with the external imposition. At the same time, however, the masses find their lifeworld under attack by all the new rules, and the solidarities they relied on for protecting their societies eroding. The unified legal field at the global level has broken down all barriers to commodification and has forced nation-states to carry out massive deregulation, thus making it very difficult to continue with the old practices of provisionism—in the form of monopolies, subsidies, price supports, and simple favoritism in contracts. The widening commodification of the elements of daily life and its necessities (a good example is the much discussed case of the privatization of water) has followed upon the end of provisionism. The new legal field has also imaginatively deepened commodification by extending the scope of the powerful category of intellectual property—arguably the most important form of property for the constitution of a global field of exchange. Perhaps the most impressive success of the agreements for the World Trade Organization has been the imposition of stringent intellectual property rules on states, protecting patents and copyright, as a precondition of membership in the WTO.[26] This extension of private property to what used to be considered as commons (such as in the case of seeds), and to necessities (as in the case of medical drugs), and its extremely skewed ownership distribution are principal elements of an intensifying resentment. The new rules prohibit the mediation of a local authority in their application; in other words, they seek to maintain a high standard of formality, with no possibility of appeal to contextual and substantive difference. The formal application of these rules in greatly unequal contexts obviously leads to even more aggravated inequality. The greater awareness of inequality and vast difference, produced through the indiscriminate application of formal rules, creates an unprecedented consciousness of polarization.[27]

At the same time there has been more direct and damaging impact on the capacities of states to counteract the emerging polarization. States have also been compelled to opt for austerity and renege on many of their promises to protect society, especially in those areas of the world that have been most adversely affected. The most important proximate reason for this has been the debt trap, which has obliged states in the global South to use their revenues for servicing their external debt obligations. Even without debt, however, globalization is perceived as requiring states to enter into a contest to attract transnational capital, leading them to reduce taxes. The decline in state revenues deprives them of resources with which to compensate for the polarization caused by the operation of the new rules. It is only a small minority of the states that still maintain the fiscal capacity for sustaining the programs associated with social rights of citizenship. This inability to continue to fund a society-protecting welfare state is the principal determinant of the eroding legitimacy of states.

Globalization, or the constitutionalization of the American empire, has created a polarized world where the objectified rules of property and exchange lead to social upheaval, threaten established order, and cause inequality and polarization. The erosion of the autonomy of the nation-state implies that intervention to protect the society from these outcomes, for example through redistribution or guaranteed levels of income, is increasingly difficult. Is there any way in which this seemingly inevitable prognosis for strife and crisis of legitimation, can be avoided?

There is an optimist's answer to this question, which argues that the protection and substantive maintenance provided by communities (or nation-states under American hegemony) may potentially be offered by the higher-level polity. As described above, this alternative was not on the agenda in the Ottoman case, except through a rudimentary thinking on organic citizenship. During the short history of globalization, however, the political struggle that finds expression in social forums, in the workings of innumerable ad hoc and organized resistance groups at local and transnational levels, and in the movement protesting "corporate globalization" that was initiated in Seattle, may prove effective in taming transnational capital some-what, to achieve a degree of "regulation" on the otherwise savage workings of un-regulated markets. Thus, there have been gains, notably, in the matter of intellectual property and environment, and promising beginnings of a discussion on labor standards. These gains result out of politics conducted mainly within civil society, where the opposing sides are local and transnational movements and multilateral institutions (in most cases the WTO) that originally represented transnational cap-ital. In other words, a political field has emerged that sidelines the nation-states, within which bargains may be made and new rules negotiated. It might thus be pos-sible to accommodate new demands of substantive (ethical) nature and to refor-malize the rules on the basis of these demands. This may be seen as the birth of a new global governance that may evolve into the authority of a set of interlocking multilateral institutions, offset by social movements of various provenance, and which may thus legitimate the new order through democratic deliberation.

Such a pacific scenario of gradual social democratization overlaps with the pro-jections of a Kautskyian universe where transnational capitalists have devised ways of peaceful coexistence, and do not mobilize their respective states to wage struggles for markets on their behalf.[28] In fact, it is not clear which respective states these might be in cases of complicated ownership patterns of the largest transnational corporations. Global capital represents a complex intertwining of national capitals; hence, it is not difficult to envisage a more or less unified transnational capital agreeing that competition and conflict would not be along national divisions. These are the defining elements of a multilateral order: a Kautskyian field of global capi-tal, and a globalized legal order existing via networks of institutions and courts which function independently of the states that have brought them into being. The legitimation of such a multilateral global order may work through the republican citizenship of various levels of social and political movements that extract social-democratizing concessions from transnational capital and thus transform the rules grounding the operation of these institutions. This process may in time be comple-mented by some version of "cosmopolitan democracy," perhaps including a parlia-mentary body as representative as the Ottoman assembly.

IV

Under the harsh light of realism cast by America's new imperial project, this attractive vision now seems like a fairy tale. The problem is that the entire multilateralist equation is designed to bypass the states and state actors; and, in particular, to marginalize and transcend the hegemonic state. It may well be that global capital is Kautskyian in the sense of preferring a juridification of the playing field in which pacific competition is the rule; this, however, does not guarantee that states accept the passive role accorded them by this arrangement. There is, in addition, the problem of time: the tensions implicit in a juridified globalization may well take their toll before social-democratic legitimation has a chance to prove itself—with the result that security, the premier rhetorical prop of the imperial state, gains ascendancy over market and material progress.

It is evident that law is made by the state but attains an autonomy in its functioning. This is what juridification means, where the legal field, in its complex composition made up of scholars, commentators, lawyers, and the judiciary, has its own mode of operation, acceptable methods of argumentation, and hierarchy of legislators, interpreters, and practicioners.[29] Once laws are made, they become the object of interpretation within the functioning of this legal field. The same situation prevails supranationally. Constitutionalism at the global level has brought into existence networks of multilateral institutions that all operate in the juridical manner. In other words, like the legal system in the modern state, global courts and other mechanisms of dispute resolution, such as the WTO, as well as treaties and agreements, attain an autonomy from their makers.[30] Neither the hegemonic power, nor any other state may exercise sovereignty over them. As they gain more permanence, their traditions become more entrenched, and their personnel grow more confident. In other words, juridification of the governance of the global order, which is what we mean by multilateralism, translates to the emergence of networks of dispersed authority, independent of the hegemonic or otherwise powers that established it. As one result of this juridification, the hegemonic power finds itself to have made laws only to see them gain autonomy and lose instrumentality. From the point of view of transnational capital and the globalized corporate bourgeoisie, this is as it should be: the more the emerging legal structure gains autonomy from states, the more predictable it will be. For the political actors of the hegemonic state, however, this is a novel situation. Having unleashed globalization, they will have created the very institutions which, in their multilateral autonomy, will no longer require their progenitors. Constitutionalism, or the juridification of rules, diminishes the space that politics controls. This is why it is consistently offered as a prescription to irresponsible political rulers of all the other countries. The hegemonic power feels, however, that the same prescription unacceptably restricts its ability to function.

We may interpret the change in American behavior since 9/11 as a reaction to increasing autonomization of the new constitutional order. The unilateralist Committee of Union and Progress (CUP) in the last years of the Ottoman Empire also turned away from constitutionalism because juridification had created a situation where the population was polarized and millets could no longer operate in the previous mode to contribute to the legitimation of the imperial order. Perhaps Ottomanism and the workings of the Parliament, along with the new imperial insitutions, could eventually provide the grounds within which a new order could be negotiated. We will never know: not only because wars intervened, but also because any development in that direction was truncated by CUP's unilateral assertion of state power based on the privileging of the perceived interests of the dominant ethnic element. The CUP had come to power following a coup d'état, and consolidated its power by rigging the 1912 election. They then entered the war on the German side and hastily started to engage in ethnic cleansing—dismantling constitutionalism in the name of Turkish-nationalist politics.

The American state exhibits a similar frustration with juridification and multilateralism—but now played out on a world scale. Washington's rhetoric of national interest is perhaps not new, but its newfound intensity since 9/11 strikes the world as a departure. With the war in Iraq, conducted in the absence of United Nations approval, the break with multilateralism became even more obvious. There is also indication that the United States wants to extricate itself from, and even actively undermine, all transnational institutions that it cannot unilaterally control, unless these institutions accord special status to American nationals. The message is that henceforward there would be a postconstitutional order representing the preferences of the state actors of the hegemonic power.[31] By opting for unilateralism American state actors not only actively sabotage the complex network of multilateral institutions, but they also declare themselves to be autonomous of the interests of what would seem to be the dominant forces in the economic sphere: the globalized transnational corporate bourgeoisie.

If it is not simply a short interlude within the longer trend toward multilateral globalization, the question of how this new imperialism may legitimate itself becomes pertinent. As argued above, multilateralism as the form of global governance does have the potential to produce a democratic dialogue among the parties of various interests to impact on the constitutional order. How could the hegemon expect to legitimate the unilateral destruction of the constitutional order? One positive perspective on this destruction could be to see this attempt at undermining the constitutional order as a Polanyian reflex against the market and liberal rules—a return to the substantive at a higher level. Prompted by an increasing pitch of reactions fueled by the ravages of the market, the hegemon decides to override the rules. Interwar empires (German and Japanese) arose as part of the impulse to counteract the liberal market and protect society. Similarly, the state actors of the CUP during the last days of the Ottoman Empire might have argued that they had to give up constitutionalism in order to protect the downtrodden and majority element in the empire. Mutatis mutandis, the new American empire could attempt to gain legitimacy, in the country and in the world, by claiming to repair the damage (unemployment, worsening income distribution) of liberal globalization, by overriding the neoliberal strictures of the previous era. But, the benign register is difficult to detect in the arguments or the intentions of the American political elite. Instead, having tried constitutionalism, the American state may be advancing in a direction of a less benign domination where the millets will enjoy much less autonomy than in the preglobalization days of hegemony, and where they will be differentially treated according to their relationships with the master nation. Of course, this is precisely the kind of transformation that the CUP attempted to impose on the Ottoman millets, with disastrous consequence.

The trajectory of the last century of the Ottoman Empire was from a differentiated and layered system of millets to constitutionalism and finally to the imposition of national supremacy; the trajectory of the world system of the last several decades has been from a system of hegemony with nation-states to multilateral globalization, and finally to the beginnings of an imposition of a unilateral empire. In both cases, it was the imperial (and hegemonic) states that promoted constitutionalism (multilateralism) and the ground-level construction of new networks that could not be contained either within millet or national communities that required it. Similarly, it was the state officials in the empire and the hegemonic state who decided that constitutionalism implied loss of control, and a new form of governance was needed. For the Ottomans the experiment ended with a rump state and isolation.

PART III

MODELS OF POWER

8. IMPERIALISM OR COLONIALISM?
FROM WINDHOEK TO WASHINGTON,
BY WAY OF BASRA[1]

GEORGE STEINMETZ

We have no desire to dominate, no ambitions of *empire*.

—George W. Bush, State of the Union address, January 2004[2]

America is, so to speak, the greater island that could administer and guarantee the balance of the rest of the world.

—Carl Schmitt, 1955[3]

The United States now arrogates to itself the option of making or breaking regimes around the world. . . . the way for a country to get itself defined as a threat is to defy Washington on a matter that it declares vital. . . . Does this sound like an imperial stance to you?

—James B. Rule, 2004[4]

The developing American form of empire . . . is solely an empire of bases, not of territories, and these bases now encircle the earth.

—Chalmers Johnson, 2004[5]

I. BEYOND DISAVOWAL? ON EMBRACING EMPIRE

During the past four years we have seen an abrupt reversal of the fortunes of the "declinist school of analysis" of U.S. power. This school insisted that American global hegemony was almost exhausted due to "imperial overstretch" and the decline of the U.S. share of overall world production.[6] Almost simultaneously we saw the emergence of the thesis of the diminishing importance of the nation-state, according to which, in Habermas's words, "the external sovereignty of states" in general has become "an anachronism."[7] Michael Hardt and Antonio Negri drew out the logical consequence of these arguments, painting the contemporary world as a decentralized network of criss-crossing partial sovereignties. One of Hardt and Negri's most original contributions was their paradoxical attempt to wrest the term *empire* away from its ages-old association with the idea of the state. They reassociated Empire (now capitalized) with the centerless, deterritorialized global capitalist system itself.[8]

Since 2001, however, these predictions of the end of state-centered geopolitics, American hegemony, and state-centered imperialism have themselves taken on something of a gilded historical patina. The extent to which Hardt and Negri's *Empire* was conditioned by the historical conditions of its own production has become evident, canceling out much of its exhortative futurology. These knowledge conditions were historically specific to the 1990s, and more generally to the deceptively *informal* character of American empire since the early nineteenth century. During the decade after the fall of the Berlin Wall, the United States moved farther and farther ahead of the rest of the world militarily, and with the decline of the Russian counterweight, it became a seemingly unprecedented *hyperpower*.[9] This does not mean that the United States became invincible or that it was now able to turn its every policy whim into reality.[10] The salient point is that the degree of unipolarity—the military gap between the United States and its closest contenders—is unprecedented in modern global history, surpassing even British hegemony in the mid-nineteenth century.[11] The United States has over two million military and civilian Department of Defense personnel deployed worldwide, along with another two million of their dependents, constituting an unprecedented "empire of bases." American economic supremacy is not as absolute as during the first decades after 1945, but it is still remarkable. Even today, U.S. absolute and per capita production levels continue to match or even exceed those of the European Union, despite the latter's larger population.[12]

Yet despite this unipolarity, American foreign policy tended to follow established patterns during the 1990s under Presidents Bush Sr. and Clinton, and even began to move in the direction of more multilateral overseas interventions. The Clinton administration publicly expressed regret for U.S. support for earlier military coups in Iran and Guatemala.[13] Treasure Secretary Lawrence Summers referred to the United States in 1998 as the "first nonimperialist superpower."[14] Moreover, the same apparent reluctance to fully embrace America's lone-superpower status was evident during the administration of Bush Sr., which continued to adhere to the cold war premises of containment, deterrence, and working through international organizations like the United Nations and NATO.[15] Bush Sr. explicitly disavowed the program of "lone superpower" U.S. hegemony set out in the Pentagon's "Defense Planning Guidance for the Fiscal Years 1994–1999" and signed in 1992 by Paul Wolfowitz.[16]

Since the 2000 election, of course, it is precisely these ideas that have become the official basis of U.S. foreign policy.[17] Commentators have pointed out that the move toward full-scale unilateralism was already well under way during the latter years of the Clinton administration.[18] Thus it seems that we are not talking about a difference between the Republican and Democratic parties so much as a historical transition in the model of international governance (and of domestic governance and regulation as well) that transcends the political party differences.[19] The peculiar characteristics of the period from 1989 until at least the mid-1990s therefore represent the first element of the sociology of knowledge about (American) empire during the 1990s. Hardt and Negri's *Empire* was not the only book to be confounded by it. World-system theorists, who tend to derive politics from economics, deduced from the lack or weakness of American foreign interventions in this period that the United States was also falling behind economically.[20] The world-systems theorists' prediction was that the United States would be replaced by a new hegemon or that there would be a devolution of the entire capitalist "core" (that is, the rich countries of the global North) into forms of protectionism and (neo)colonialism. The evidence for these predictions is weak at best, in light of NAFTA and other antiprotectionist measures of the 1990s. Globalization theories were correct about the relentless dissolution of boundaries in this period but often overlooked the role of the U.S. state in promoting this "openness."

The second aspect of American power that seems continually to generate the mirage of its own disappearance is its informal, universalistic, and euphemistic form, which most recently has operated in the register of human rights.[21] As Carl Schmitt pointed out more than half a century ago, American power (first in the "Western Hemisphere" and later in the world as a whole) does not typically annex and permanently occupy foreign lands—with the important exceptions of the westward expansion of the continental state, Hawai'i, and the colonies created from the spoils of the Spanish-American War. Instead, U.S. control usually operates through indirect political and economic influence, support for friendly local regimes, and seemingly universalistic rules of exclusion from the community of "decent" nations—the exclusion of violators of free trade, freedom of movement, and more recently human rights. This approach seems to apply an equal standard to the entire world, in contrast to the earlier European colonial rules of exclusion directed against non-Christian or racialized Others, or the legal rule of difference that was applied internally within the United States to African Americans. In this respect, there is continuity between the 1990s and the past four years. Both the "multilateral" interventions of the Clinton era and Bush's "unilateral" wars have been framed as interventions against the new barbarians—the *nonindividualistic* "Asiatic societies" and "tribal cultures of Africa" (Habermas), the morally burdened, disorderly, nonliberal, and *nondecent* peoples (Rawls)—while tolerantly offering them the opportunity to achieve or to regain their inherent status as equals.[22]

Whatever the deeper levels of continuity in American policy, the past four years have seen an unmistakable reassertion of U.S. military and economic power, and this has been accompanied by an embrace of the idea of "American empire" across the political spectrum.[23] Of course, the United States has been repeatedly described as an empire since at least the 1950s, starting with the writings of Carl Schmitt,

William Appleman Williams, and Williams's followers within the "Open Door" school of diplomatic history, among others.[24] Another wave of books analyzing the United States as empire appeared in the early 1970s with the apotheosis of the Vietnam War and the antiwar movement.[25] But agreement on this description of American policy has been far from universal. As W.A. Williams observed in 1980, "the words *empire* and *imperialism* enjoy no easy hospitality in the minds and hearts of most contemporary Americans."[26] Indeed, many defenders of the current Bush administration's global "grand strategy" (including Bush himself—see the epigraph to this section) vehemently reject the trope of empire as an official description of their program.[27] Nevertheless, the claim made by writers like W.A. Williams and Michael Ignatieff that the United States is "an empire . . . without consciousness of itself as such" no longer rings true.[28]

The language of empire is not only contested but also famously ambiguous. The extreme level of terminological slippage and confusion is illustrated by a well-known discussion of the topic by Arthur Schlesinger Jr. from the mid-1980s. Here Schlesinger seemed unable to decide whether to describe the United States as constituting an "informal empire," a "quasi-empire," or, "from the viewpoint of the great empires of history . . . *no empire at all*."[29] The shifting from "empire" to "imperial" and from "imperialism" to "colonialism" in Schlesinger's essay is not unusual in this literature. Raymond Williams acknowledged that words like "imperialism" are inherently disputed, but he also insisted that these "historical and contemporary variations of meaning" pointed to "real processes which have to be studied in their own terms." Tellingly, Williams's main example of such instability of meaning was "American imperialism" itself. The *direct* political control of dependencies from a controlling center seemed to be less salient in the American case, Williams noted, and yet "the primarily economic reference" of imperialism to a system of "external investment and the penetration and control of markets and sources of raw materials" was, he thought, "still exact."[30] What Williams neglected was the range of less direct technologies of control of peripheries from a center, which I will argue is the defining characteristic of imperialism, as well as the distinctively political and ideological motives driving imperialism.

The varying usages of the imperial terminology do more than merely index changing states of world affairs. The *discourse* of empire is also part of the very object we need to analyze if we want to understand what modern empire is and how the United States relates to this category. Social theorists nowadays tend to agree that social life is inextricably a matter of discourse as well as material processes (of production, domination, exploitation, etc.)[31] The depiction of the United States as an empire within some corners of academe and the foreign-policy establishment is not just an epiphenomenal counterpart to more substantial political developments; instead, it is a *per-*

formative bid to make visible what was often historically hidden or euphemized as democracy, free trade, and human rights. Carl Schmitt suggested that the universalizing rather than exclusionary frame was an inherent aspect of U.S. imperial power all along, or at least since the 1820s. W.A. Williams argued similarly that the United States had long pursued a mainly noncolonial or even *anticolonial* imperialism, seeking the advantages of the market openness epitomized by the "Open Door" policy in China at the end of the nineteenth century.[32] One question we need to ask is what difference it might make for U.S. overseas interventions to be openly described as empire.

This leads me to the other questions that I will address in this essay. The unconcealed language of empire is not the only discursive practice that is constitutive of empire.[33] We also need to investigate the ceremonial trappings of U.S. power, the practices and scattered signifiers that give American life its increasingly imperial flavor. On the one hand there is the militarization of the culture in ways reflective of empire: civilians driving Humvees, the navy welcoming almost 8,000 civilians aboard its vessels for publicity purposes in a single year, universities and high schools (under the "No Child Left Behind" Act) being compelled to admit military recruiters or risk losing federal funds, and the enrollment of 500,000 high school students in the Junior Reserve Officer Training Corps of the army, navy, and air force.[34] The "Freedom Tower" planned to replace The World Trade Center in Lower Manhattan evokes, in the words of one critic, "ancient obelisks, blown up to a preposterous scale and clad in *heavy* sheaths of reinforced glass—an ideal symbol for an empire enthralled with its own power."[35] But imperialism is not only about militarism, and this survey would also have to include the flocking of overseas students to American universities from all over the world, which recalls the mass immigration to the imperial Roman homeland. Similarly, the influx of luxury goods (60 percent of the world's beluga caviar comes into the U.S., for example) recalls Anthony Pagden's comment about traditional empires offering "the lure of luxury, opulence."[36] We should also ask how empires like the current U.S. have appropriated earlier imperial practices and adapted them to their own purposes.[37] A final question concerns the diffusion of practices and identities from the imperial core to the dominated periphery and in the opposite direction—the contemporary analogue to Cooper and Stoler's "reverberations between colony and metropole."[38]

Rather than engaging in an *affirmative* inquiry into the lessons *for* American empire, this way of posing the problem emphasizes a *critical* investigation of the lessons that are learned *by* empires and of the ways established "metropolitan" practices are implanted into imperial borderlands. By asking what determines the variable forms of empire, and what, if anything, is distinctive about contemporary American imperialism, we may be able to learn historical and theoretical lessons of our own.

Even a cursory examination of the popular and theoretical language of empire presents us with several tasks. Clear analytical definitions (of empire, imperialism, colonialism, etc.) are needed, even while we recognize that they are necessarily historical and overdetermined by their "folk" meanings and that actual historical empires pursue mixed strategies (e.g., the mid-19th-century British empire, which engaged in colonization in India and "free trade imperialism" in China and Latin America). My definitional effort in the first part of this paper is undertaken in light of the eternal paradox of an American foreign policy that observers have long described as imperial while agreeing that it differs in some fundamental way from classical empires and from modern forms of European colonialism. As a historian of German colonialism, I am confronted by a parallel set of paradoxes connected to a state (the Bismarckian one) that described itself as an empire long before embarking on a career of explicit overseas colonialism. Drawing on the U.S. and German examples, I will specify four basic forms of empire. The last three of them occur in both modern and nonmodern forms; I am concerned with their specifically modern guises. The adjective *modern* is used here in a strictly chronological sense, indexing the period from the latter eighteenth century to the present. The adjective *nonmodern* encompasses both the early modern and the premodern, and it avoids the connotations of underdevelopment that modernization theory attached to "tradition."

There are four types of empire, the first three territorial, the fourth nonterritorial (in ways specified below):

1. classical (or nonmodern) territorial, land-based empires;
2. modern territorial empires;
3. colonial empires; and
4. imperialism, a system of control of far-flung areas without territorial annexation.

These forms are real (not ideal) conceptual types, but that does not mean that they always exist in a pure or isolated form. I will return to this point in a moment. One implication of these definitions is that the United States and Germany have both been imperial in differing ways throughout much of the past two centuries.

In the second part of the paper I will contrast the German and American forms of empire, focusing on four sorts of imperial relationship:

1. combinations of imperialism and colonialism (or other approaches to empire);
2. relations between a particular state, region, and the world system;
3. imagined relations between past and present empires;
4. core-periphery reverberations, and the new American form of imperialism.[39]

II. FOUR TYPES OF EMPIRE: HISTORICAL DEFINITIONS

The overarching category in this discussion is *empire* itself; colonialism and imperialism can be defined as subcategories of empire. Empire referred initially to large, land-based agrarian political systems; Rome was the European prototype. These empires were militarized and perpetually expansive. They were characterized by the subjection of a multiplicity of peoples to a single supreme power. One result of the conquest and incorporation of far-flung peoples was that nonmodern empires were inherently multinational (or as we would say today, multicultural), even if this was often combined with a universalizing ideology (the cult of the emperor, Islam, Christianity, etc.). Examples of multiethnic empire, after Rome, include the Habsburgs, the Romanovs, and the Ottomans.[40] Despite their vaunted multinationalism, historians of nonmodern empires also emphasize the ways in which peripheral populations or elites were sometimes integrated into the core culture, losing their distinctive ethnic identities in the process. The Ottoman Janissaries, an elite corps in the Ottoman army, were recruited from the Balkans and elsewhere as children and raised within official Islam. Traditional empires also combined militarization with various activities intended to stabilize and pacify geopolitical relations. This combination of aggressive expansion and attempted stabilization may appear contradictory, but is essential to Schmitt's concept of a Nomos or regulating principle for international relations, which does not necessarily preclude warfare among the parties encompassed within a geopolitical Nomos, but specifies the form that warfare should take. The peoples incorporated into empires were offered promises of peace and prosperity while typically being compelled to yield tribute to the center.[41]

Modern territorial empires, the second type, retain many of the features of traditional ones: the combined emphasis on stabilized peace and military strength, ceaseless territorial expansion, and multiculturalism overlaid with a universalizing ideology. Some modern empires officially encouraged emperor worship, including Napoleonic France and the Germany of Kaiser Wilhelm (see Figure 1) and Hitler.[42] By the 19th century the Habsburg "Empire" was no longer growing, but it had a history of earlier expansiveness, a token of which was preserved in its ethnic diversity. Bismarck's unified Germany called itself an empire before there was any indication of its overseas colonizing career. But there were recurrent episodes of dynamic, militarized expansion both in Prussia and its German successor state, from the eighteenth-century partition of Poland (1772–1795) through to Hitler's bid for a European-scale "Third Empire." The forging of the unified German state between 1864 and 1871 was a violent process of territorial conquest, starting with the annexation of Holstein from Denmark in 1864; then the Prussian annexation of Hanover and several other states in the Austro-Prussian war of 1866 (which allowed the eastern and western parts of Prussia to become contiguous by integrating Hanover and several other states and also to form the Prussian-dominated North German Federation); and finally the occupation of Alsace-Lorraine in 1871. This relentless process of conquering and integrating new lands resembled the westward continental extension of the United States during the same period. A new process of contiguous expansion began in 1938 with the *Anschluss* of Austria and Sudetenland, followed by western Czechoslovakia and Poland. Prussia/Germany's repeated bouts of continental annexation were interrupted by periods of relative stasis during which the fruits of conquest were assimilated into the overarching state structure.

Germany was officially called an empire because it united various formerly independent states under the aegis of the Prussian king, now called the German Kaiser (Caesar). Of course neither an emperor nor a monarchy is a necessary element of land-based empire. Rome acquired most of its extended empire while it was a republic, and the United States has been a nonfeudal republic since independence.[43]

FIGURE 1: "The People of the German Colonies pay Homage to the Kaiser," cover of the German colonial journal *Kolonie und Heimat* (volume 6, no. 28, edition A, 1913)

With its Polish, Alsatian, and other linguistic minorities, the Bismarckian empire was also certainly multinational—though not to the extent of its Austrian-Hungarian or Russian neighbors. Wilhelm Riehl observed in the middle of the nineteenth century that there was "a Protestant Germany and a Catholic Germany,"[44] and for the most part, these groups were still distributed into separate states after 1871. Whereas most European states in 1900 continued to reflect the legacy of the non-imperial Nomos (in Carl Schmitt's sense) of the *jus publicum Europaeum* that was created in 1648, which operated under the *motto cujus regio, ejus religio,* Bismarckian Germany exhibited a comparatively high level of religious division. Indeed, the German Empire's religious constitution—its Protestant cultural and political dominance combined with a sizable Catholic minority (36 percent) and a small Jewish minority (2 percent)—most closely resembled that of the nineteenth-century United States.[45]

Both classical and modern land-based empires are characterized by territorial expansion, but they are also defined by their magnetic pull and radiating influence on people beyond their official borders. As Pagden emphasizes, empires are places to which people migrate: Germany changed after the 1880s from a land of emigration to one of immigration.[46] Just as the United States has become the global center of gravity for a myriad of processes taking place beyond its own borders—ranging from filmmaking and the Internet to the legal processing of human-rights cases and reparation claims by *overseas* victims against *overseas* perpetrators[47]—imperial Germany became something of a regional model and center of attention for central and eastern Europe. This imperial radiance can be distinguished from the *deliberate* exercise of influence outside national borders, which is more characteristic of imperialism, and colonialism (although the boundaries between these practices are blurry).

A third form of territorial empire is *colonialism,* which involves the occupation and annexation of regions beyond the global core and the seizure of foreign sovereignty. The initial goal driving colonialization is often economic exploitation and trade. *Modern* (as opposed to *early modern*) colonialism is structured around legal and ideological practices that insist on the inferiority and inequality of the colonized, that is, by a "rule of difference" (Partha Chatterjee). Modern colonial states often had dualistic legal codes in which native legal disputes were processed by indigenous authorities, or according to a European rendering of indigenous law. Crimes that were considered serious or those pitting Europeans against natives were adjudicated within the colonizers' own legal system. In other colonies there was a unified legal code with native testimony being granted less weight than colonizers' claims.[48] This systematic differentiation was often (but not always) organized around signifiers of "race." Colonizers seemed to require such an institutional declaration of the inferiority of their colonized subjects in order to legitimate their own presence in the colony, both to themselves and to their constituencies back home (legitimacy in the eyes of colonized subjects was generally a nonissue). Whenever this overarching binarism began to erode, as in the late phase of German colonialism in Qingdao and in some of the British and French West African colonies in the middle of the twentieth century, colonial states were already turning into something noncolonial or postcolonial—or into mixed systems.[49]

Modern colonialism also needs to be distinguished from the *early modern* variant. The colonies that arose during the nineteenth century were defined by their emphasis on the problem of specifying and stabilizing the culture and conduct of the colonized—that is, by the practices that came to be called native policy (*Eingeborenenpolitik* in German).[50] As one prominent German colonial journal, *Die deutschen Kolonien,* stated on its masthead, "colonial policy is, above all, native policy." To understand what native policy was we have to recall that the populations that were conquered and colonized in the nineteenth century were almost always *already* familiar with their conquerors prior to annexation, due to the legions of European explorers, missionaries, and merchants who swarmed the globe. This meant that prospective colonial subjects were believed to be capable of strategically manipulating the codes of the colonizer. The perceived instability of the colonized—expressed in ubiquitous European discourses of lying, cheating, trickery, and mimicry—defined native policy as the modern colonial state's central task, specifically, as an effort to stabilize the colonized by urging them to adhere to a single, constant definition of their own culture. Although the quest for markets and raw materials was certainly a leading motive in the *acquisition* of many colonies during the late nineteenth century, the problem of native regulation became paramount once these regimes were up and running, often overshadowing immediate economic considerations.[51] By contrast, early modern colonialism did not confront populations that were already familiar with their colonizers, and as a result it was less centrally focused on the problem of (precolonial) mimicry. It is doubtful that native policies (or earlier analogues to native policy) were structurally central to early modern colonialism.

This attempted stabilization took place within the assumptions of the rule of difference, which meant that full-scale assimilation was out of bounds.[52] The desire to regulate native culture also meant that colonialism could not tolerate incommensurable, uncodified difference. Modern colonialism was torn between an impetus to *commensurate* and *codify* the colonized Other and a simultaneous pressure to keep the colonized from becoming so similar to the colonizer that the latter would have to acknowledge the arbitrariness of his suzerainty.

A related difference between modern and early modern colonialism concerns the rule of difference itself. Early modern colonizers had less difficulty justifying their overseas conquests, both because the foreign Other was seen as "heathen" and because discourses of equality and democracy were less developed. At the same time, Christianity allowed for the possibility of genuinely assimilatory policies in early modern colonies. The enfolding of indigenous Americans into the church was not nonsensical or off limits to a Bartolomé de Las Casas. As Todorov observes, missionaries like Las Casas were remarkably unobservant ethnographers precisely because they believed that Native Americans were potential Christians.[53] By the eighteenth century, discourses of the rights of man, "noble savagery," and the rumblings of abolitionism jostled with biological racism, such that no single metacode dominated European representations of the colonized or precolonized Other. It became necessary to justify colonial conquest in terms other than Christian ones, but it was unclear just what those terms would be. However tautological and circular it may seem, resisting assimilation was one way of insisting on and reinforcing the inferiority of the colonized and justifying their conquest and domination.

We can also draw a general distinction between early modern and modern colonialism in the area of cultural and carnal mixing. The early modern Portuguese coastal colonies of Goa and Macao were characterized by extensive cultural and "racial" mixing, as were Dutch Indonesia and the frontiers of the Cape Colony through the eighteenth century.[54] The governments of old and new colonies both turned against such mixing, however, with the racial bar falling harshly at the end of the nineteenth century. The *intimate* implications of the rule of difference are expressed most powerfully in colonial fiction. Romances between colonizer and colonized became increasingly ill fated, and even catastrophic, over time. Whereas the mixed couple in Heinrich von Kleist's *Bethrothal in St. Domingo* (1811) is destroyed by a racism whose source is at least partly external to the two lovers, the couples in Friedrich Gerstäcker's *Tahiti* (1885) or Somerset Maugham's Samoan tale "The Pool" (1953) come to a catastrophic end due to *internalized* racism on the part of the European husbands and a seemingly inexorable slipping back into an uncivilized native nature on the part of their Polynesian wives.[55]

The assumption of inherent native inferiority that is built into the sinews of the modern colonial state generally precluded the creation of loose federations in which the colonies are allowed to govern themselves, along the lines of some antique empires and modern imperialist systems. While it is true that the French thought that they could preserve the French empire after 1945 through just such a federated structure, as Fred Cooper has pointed out, this plan pointed forcibly away from colonialism and toward some different imperial form.[56]

This definition of colonialism calls into question many polemical and metaphorical uses of the term. Wherever conquered subject populations are offered the same citizenship rights as conquerors in exchange for their assimilation into the ruling culture, we should probably not speak of colonialism. The activities of the U.S. occupation forces in Iraq and their specific technologies have often been reminiscent of European colonialisms. Many news media initially described Ambassador Paul Bremer as the "governor" of Iraq, a term redolent of colonialism, while Tariq Ali referred to the "recolonization" of Iraq.[57] But the United States has long perceived greater advantages in informal and indirect imperialism as opposed to direct colonial governance. The explicitly colonial American moment at the end of the nineteenth century is an exception to this rule. As Wesley Clark pointed out in a critique of the neoconservative celebration of the idea of American empire, "Americans tended, on the whole, to be 'leavers,' not colonizers" during the twentieth century.[58] At the end of 2003 it appeared that the U.S. occupation of Iraq might be prolonged due to resistance and a lack of planning for the postwar period, but at the time of writing, elections have been held and an Iraqi constitution has been drafted. The intention never was to subject Iraq to direct colonial-style rule. Nonetheless, the United States will try to guarantee the friendliness of the "autonomous" regime, and tens of thousands of U.S. troops are certain to remain in Iraq as a partial infringement of Iraqi sovereignty and to assure that the neoliberal utopia does not revert to state socialism.

This brings us to the fourth, *nonterritorial* form of empire, modern *imperialism*. Like colonialism, imperialism is driven by goals of economic exploitation and trade, and also by security concerns that are linked indirectly to economic motives. Modern imperialist powers like the United States intervene at will to depose regimes or to install new ones, but they then depart or recede into the background, leaving behind a military base, an advisor, or an ambassador. They typically show little interest in micromanaging local conditions and ostensibly respect the autonomy of the peripheral state, intervening only when conditions become unstable.[59] Of course there is a continuum rather than a sharp dichotomy between a colonialism that smashes native sovereignty and governs in its stead and an imperialism that respects foreign sovereignty except in emergencies. Many regions within modern colonies were governed by "indirect rule," and as Jürgen Osterhammel cogently argues, that category can itself be subdivided into varying degrees of directness, with the Princely States of British India at one pole and appointed tribal leaders (chiefs) at the other extreme. The key point, however, is that even the indirectly ruled regions or groups were ultimately subordinate to, and fitted into, an overarching colonial state.[60]

Imperialism is also an overall political orientation on the part of Great Powers toward the global political system. As Jürgen Osterhammel points out, great powers often *combined* colonialism and imperialism, but the latter is "in some respects a more comprehensive" strategy. For example, imperialism may treat colonies "not just ends in themselves, but also [as] pawns in global power games." Imperialism is "planned and carried out by chanceries, foreign ministries, and ministries of war, colonialism by special colonial authorities and 'men on the spot.'"[61] Thus the German Foreign Office and navy authorities decided to loosen Germany's grip on the Qingdao colony in the years leading up to World War I for global military-strategic—i.e., *imperialist*—reasons, to the great chagrin of colonialist circles in and outside the colony (see below).

In order to specify imperialism more precisely we need to distinguish between the acquisition of *territory* and the authoritative political ordering of *space*. The latter refers to the creation of what Carl Schmitt called a Nomos or global division of space and spheres of influence (*Großraüme* or "large spaces") within which states extend their control outside their proper boundaries. Schmitt noted with respect to the Monroe Doctrine, which declared that the United States would not allow any foreign power to intervene in the Western Hemisiphere, that "every true empire around the world has claimed such a sphere of spatial sovereignty beyond its borders." The 1939 Panama Declaration "forbade warring states from undertaking hostile acts within a specified *security zone*" and effectively "extended *Großraum* thinking over the free sea." U.S. empire since 1945 has not been oriented toward laying claim to territory but rather to a total "domination of sea and air" in the interest of a freer movement of capital, commodities, and people and the stabilization of conditions within the Nomos.[62] The dense web of U.S. military installations in more than 140 countries does not contradict this claim, since these are usually located *within* the sovereign territory of other states and do not claim sovereignty over indigenous inhabitants of those bases.[63] Other mechanisms of exerting control include setting conditions for loans or foreign investment and granting or withholding diplomatic recognition.

Imperialism is thus distinctly modern (again in the chronological sense). Its origins can be seen above all in the early modern Portuguese empire, although the Hanseatic League and the mercantile Italian city-states (Genoa and Venice above all) represent earlier, less global, precursors. Whereas the Spanish empire in America and Asia was oriented toward the creation of permanent colonies and had a "clearly enunciated policy of *conquista y reducción*," the early Portuguese empire in Asia and Africa was primarily imperialist—a sort of early modern version of the contemporary American empire of bases. Since "profitable trade" was Portugal's main goal, there were no plans, initially, "for founding a territorial empire by force of arms." Although the Portuguese network of bases did eventually become militarized, taking the form of *fortalezas,* "each of which had a military force," and *feitorias,* which were also strongholds (*casas fortes*), there was no pretension of exercising "sovereignty in theory nor hegemony in practice" over the indigenous societies that surrounded them.[64] Like contemporary American imperialism, however, the Portuguese intervened to prop up friendly non-European governments, as when they helped the Ethiopian Emperor Geladewos repel an Ottoman-backed Muslim invasion in the 1540s.[65] Although the African continent was not the primary target of Portuguese imperial efforts, it was here that they created a string of coastal forts and enclaves along the northern and Atlantic coasts during the fifteenth century, as well as a number of slave-based plantation economies on islands like Madeira, the Azores, and Cape Verde.[66] Slaves for these insular mini-colonies and, somewhat later, for Portuguese Brazil and the Spanish colonies in America, were assembled at slaving bases like São Tomé and Fernando Pó.[67] For the most part, Portugal emphasized trade rather than colonization. The Portuguese also set up *prazos* along the banks of the Zambezi river starting in the sixteenth century. These were land estates that engaged in plantation agriculture and mining, and traded gold and (especially after 1800) slaves. The prazos were sometimes heavily fortified, but they did not try to conquer the surrounding areas or even to restructure the indgenous political or religious systems of the Africans (*colonos*) living within their jurisdiction, and thus were more like bases than colonies. The prazos gradually escaped from Portuguese royal control and became Africanized (and Indianized) culturally and "racially" as their overlords lost contact with Europeans and intermarried with Africans and the Goanese, who dominated prazero society by 1789. The leading historian of the prazos describes them as a "precolonial institution."[68] Only in the later nineteenth century did the Portuguese begin to extend direct, formal colonial rule over all of Mozambique.[69] Similarly in Angola, Portuguese settlement and systematic conquest of the hinterlands did not begin until the end of the nineteenth century, in the context of the European scramble for Africa and the abolition of the slave trade (which happened only in 1878 for Angola); effective control was finally established after 1920. Before that Portuguese settlement was concentrated on the Angolan littoral, mainly at Luanda and Benguela, and the settlers' and soldiers', main contact with the interior involved slave trading and raiding.[70] The only genuine Portuguese colony in the early modern era other than Brazil was Sri Lanka, most of which was under Portuguese control by 1619. By 1658, however, the Portuguese were replaced as the colonial rulers of Sri Lanka by the Dutch.[71]

The best known imperialist power, and the one that gave rise to the most systematic theoretical reflection on the concept, was nineteenth-century Great Britain. Immanuel Wallerstein and his students have argued that imperialism was characteristic of periods in which the world system is dominated by a hegemon oriented toward opening up markets to trade rather than protecting exclusive trade routes between nationally controlled colonies and specific countries in the core.[72] The modus operandi of an imperialist hegemon is illustrated by the violent British efforts in the nineteenth century to force China to accept missionaries and the opium trade. Britain (and France) infringed on the Chinese state's sovereignty but did not try to smash it or to take over the government of China.[73] Nor did Britain monopolize the trading and other rights that were wrested from China in the Treaties of Nanjing (1842) and Tianjin (1858), but shared them with the other powers.

The British example illustrates that colonialism and imperialism overlapped in time and did not follow a unilinear historical sequence. The early modern founding of colonies in the New World was followed by a relative abstinence from new colonization in the mid-19th century (with a few important exceptions like India); in the late nineteenth century Britain joined in the general scramble for colonies. Individual trading factories or revictualing stations with little claim on their hinterlands were now transformed into fully colonial states, as in the cases of Mozambique and Angola. Conversely, the United States' involvement in Puerto Rico after 1898 was initially colonial but gradually became more imperialist, as the inhabitants gained U.S. citizenship (1917) and the right to elect their own governors (1947).

Although the Wallersteinian thesis can partly account for the alternating emphasis on colonialism and imperialism in different eras, it ignores the fact that the two approaches were often pursued simultaneously by the same core powers. As we have already seen, a combination of both strategies was characteristic of Portugal, which governed Sri Lanka directly while sticking to the coastlines in the rest of Africa and Asia, and of imperial Germany and the United States after 1900. The next section will investigate these complications and hybrid forms of empire using the examples of imperial Germany and imperial America.

III. COMPLICATIONS OF EMPIRE: GERMANY AND AMERICA COMPARED

(1) HYBRID IMPERIAL FORMATIONS

Imperial Germany and the United States both combined all three of the *modern* forms of empire between 1870 and 1945. The United States pursued an *imperialist* open-door policy in China at the same time as its *colonial* conquest of Puerto Rico and the Philippines (see Julian Go, this volume). But colonialism remained a secondary arrow in the American imperial quiver, even after 1900. Since the early cold war, the United States has turned against colonialism, pursuing different imperialist nonterritorial strategies.

In contrast to the United States, Germany was more involved in colonialism than imperialism between 1884 and 1900. After the turn of the century, however, Germany increasingly focused on influencing noncolonized parts of the global periphery by less direct means, including the policies that contemporaries called "cultural

imperialism." The government began funding programs to spread German influence in places where they had colonial projects, like China, and where they had
none, such as Latin America and the Ottoman Empire.[74] Imperial Germany's engagement in China before 1914 demonstrates that the overlapping of colonial and
imperialist approaches was not without tension. Prussia had pursued something
akin to the American open-door policy in China starting in the 1860s.[75] But in 1897
Germany departed from this approach by invading the coastal village of Qingdao in
Shandong province and forcing China to lease the territory the Germans called
"Kiautschou" (Jiaozhou) for ninety-nine years. The existing settlements on Jiaozhou Bay were razed and the city of Qingdao (Tsingtao) was erected in a segrega-
tionist colonial style, with separate European and Chinese districts and different
legal systems for the two populations. The Germans began almost immediately to
extend their military power into the surrounding province, occupying villages and
undermining the authority of local Chinese officials. All relevant branches of the
German metropolitan government, from the legation in Beijing to the navy secretary and the kaiser in Berlin, supported this aggressive approach. As the wife of the
German envoy to Beijing wrote in 1897, "Whatever the Chinese might have been in
the past, today they are nothing but dirty barbarians who need a European master
and not a European ambassador, and the sooner the better!"[76]

Beginning around 1904, however, influential parties within the German state began to argue that Germany should try to win China as an ally, given the kaiser's increasing isolation within Europe in the buildup to World War I. Around the same
time, theorists of "cultural imperialism" began to suggest that Germany would be
better able to counter American and British influence in China through scientific,
medical, and educational assistance rather than military bullying. A concrete instan-
tiation of this revisionist program was the Qingdao German-Chinese University,
which opened in 1909. Its curriculum combined German/European and Chinese
material, and there was a mixture of German and Chinese professors. The Chinese
state helped finance the school, and the Chinese Educational Ministry posted a permanent representative there. The governor of Qingdao, Oskar von Truppel, tried to
torpedo this project, arguing that the colonizers would be making a colonial "category mistake" (*Begriffsverwirrung*) if they granted the Chinese equal status in the
university administration.[77] The Chinese, he insisted, were not the Germans' partners, but rather "our charges [*Schutzgenossen*], our subjects."[78] Von Truppel was overruled, however, and he was dismissed from his post as governor soon afterward. In
many other instances after 1904, imperialist motives trumped colonial ones, gradually undermining the rule of difference and hence the colony's self-justification.

In Southwest Africa and Samoa, by contrast, an informal system of German influence was transformed into explicit colonialism after 1884 and 1900, respectively.

Bismarck initially hoped to run Southwest Africa on the cheap by delegating its government to a chartered trading company and letting indigenous polities continue to govern themselves.[79] Berlin was gradually drawn into a more direct, colonial-style regulation of the indigenous populations in both regions. A colonial state replaced the chartered company in Southwest Africa, and its staff quickly expanded along with the colonial army. The colonial government finally officially acknowledged that it was involved in "native policy" after the genocidal war against the Ovaherero in 1904, and it began issuing regulations that aimed to smash and completely restructure the social organization and culture of the surviving Ovaherero. The imperialist indirectness of the Germans' activities in the mid-1880s had given way to explicit colonialism.

A similar shift occurred in Samoa. The first German attempt to exercise direct political control over Samoa was a government headed by Eugen Brandeis, a former Bavarian cavalry officer, in 1887–1888. During the next decade, through 1899, consuls from Germany, Britain, and the United States acted as advisors to the Samoan king, along with a foreign "president" in charge of the main European settlement at Apia. In 1899 Samoa was partitioned between Germany and the United States, and the two powers began to govern their respective parts of the island chain as proper colonies.[80]

(2) Relations Between a Particular State, a Region, and the World System

Before 1914 Germany and the United States had roughly equal amounts of power in the world system. Both countries had been overshadowed geopolitically by Britain during the middle decades of the nineteenth century, and both had begun to challenge that hegemony. As it became impossible for the two states to engage in further contiguous land-based expansion, and as British hegemony began to decline, they both began to annex overseas colonies. After its three foundational wars, Bismarckian Germany continued to play by the rules of the Westphalian system, in which national rather broader regional boundaries defined the limits of proper state activity, at least within Europe. Nazi Germany then revived land-based expansive imperialism inside Europe, for the first time since Napoleon. Germany's *recent* relations to eastern Europe have occasionally taken on an imperialist quality, as with the Kohl government's diplomatic recognition of Croatian and Slovenian secession in 1991 (triggering the dissolution of Yugoslavia), which was defended with reference to democratic self-determination.[81]

After 1945 the United States assumed the role of hegemon within the world system; its status as a hyperpower has become even more pronounced since the faltering of the Soviet/Russian counterweight. The fact that a country like Germany (or a supernational entity like the EU) is still able to exercise some control within its regional *Großraum* does not contradict this claim. After all, the United States (like other European powers) was also subject to British hegemony during the nineteenth century; Britain claimed to be "the representative of all the West," including the United States, in dealings with China, for example.[82] The United States succeeded in creating a sphere of imperialist influence in the Western Hemisphere following the Latin American wars of independence, but in cases like the struggle over the Oregon Territory Britain was able to contain U.S. ambitions even in its own backyard.[83] A hegemon typically focuses its interventions on spaces that are not included within such secondary regional *Großraüme,* but it may also oversee and manage the local hegemonies of regional powers. Thus Germany, while powerful within Europe, has long been a crucial staging area for U.S. military interventions and is the country with the largest number of extraterritorial U.S. military personnel in the world—199,950 military and Department of Defense civilian employees and their dependents in September 2003, a larger U.S. military presence than in all of East Asia and the Pacific combined.[84]

The American rise to preeminence has been accompanied by a worldwide abandonment of colonialism. The United States played a direct role in this process by opposing European colonialism just as competition with the USSR for the allegiances of the Third World intensified.[85]

(3) IMAGINED RELATIONS BETWEEN PAST AND PRESENT EMPIRES

We can also ask how empires are shaped by "traditions"—including inherited discourses (through the determinations I have called "precoloniality")—and how, via "spectral comparisons," empires borrow from or disavow their own imagined imperial pasts.[86] Like other European empires, Germany drew frequently on the Roman register. Indeed, the German Empire that was created in 1871 described itself as a successor to the "Holy Roman Empire of the German Nation"—which was itself the putative heir of the original Roman Empire. The German emperor was called the Kaiser, that is, Caesar. With the construction of the Brandenburg Gate in Berlin in the years 1788–1791, Prussia patterned itself not only on Athens—the gate was modeled after the ceremonial entrance to the Acropolis—but also on Rome: atop the gate was the *Quadriga* with its horse-drawn chariot, and the chariot was driven by Irene, the Greek goddess of peace, who was changed into Victoria, Roman goddess of victory, after the German victory over Napoleon. But the most explicit and full-scale Romanism came with the Third Reich. Hearing Wagner's "Rienzi" (1842) supposedly transformed Hitler's worldview, inspiring him to emulate the Roman patriot Cola di Rienzo.[87] Albert Speer was directed by Hitler to redesign Berlin along monumental Roman lines, using materials that would eventually deteriorate into proper, lasting ruins as in Rome. Hitler envisioned the future city as a "global capital" comparable only to "ancient Egypt, Babylon, and Rome" and planned to rename it "Germania."[88] Hitler designed Roman-style standards that were carried by the Nazis in their parades.

American imperialist culture also relies on classical Roman practices and semiotics. Anthony Pagden reminds us that the United States "is ruled from a city that was built to replicate, as far as possible, parts of Ancient Rome" and that "no other modern nation is governed from a building called the Capitol."[89] Others, like Niall Ferguson, have attempted to hector the United States into a more explicitly colonial approach by evoking an idealized memory of British imperialism. The vexed historical legacy of America's own anticolonial past stands in some tension with these attempts at a revitalized Roman tradition.

(4) Core-Periphery Reverberations, and the New American Form of Imperialism

Empire thus involves, among other things, a relationship of political domination between a core state and one or more peripheries. To understand empire's effects we need to ask first about the transfer (or "transculturation") of practices from center to margin. These flows have produced both profound connections and important differences between domestic and peripheral forms of political domination. In the German case, domestic ideologies—above all, precolonial representations of the to-be-colonized—decisively shaped colonial native policy. Class struggles among representatives of the splintered German elite—the nobility, the bourgeoisie, and the university-educated middle class—were transposed into the colonial state and fought out there in a different register, namely, in the register of contending claims to superior *ethnographic acuity*.[90] Material practices and objects were also shipped out to the German colonies, such as monuments, architectural styles, and prefabricated "tropical houses" (*Tropenhäuser*). The *backflow* of German colonial practices and images to imperial Germany was less pronounced than comparable lines of transmission from the British colonial empire to the UK. But the generic European colonial periphery influenced pre-1918 German culture in manifold ways, from the shops selling *Colonialwaren* (colonial goods) to the proliferation of literary fantasies and racial ideologies about the Orient, Africa, and America.[91] The 1907 "Hottentot election" in Germany was the result of the emperor's dissolution of the parliament (*Reichstag*) after the majority, including the Social Democratic Party (SPD), voted to refuse further funding to conduct the genocidal war against the Khoikhoi/Nama peoples of Southwest Africa. The SPD lost 38 of its 81 seats in the Reichstag as a result. The distant colonial war thus may have contributed to the genesis of World War I by breaking the Socialists' previous momentum toward an absolute majority.

A distinctive aspect of current U.S. imperialism is the way it exports well-established *neoliberal* approaches to governance and *post-Fordist* patterns of "flexible specialization" from the domestic and "economic" spheres into overseas military and imperialist practice, while simultaneously threatening certain key features of "domestic" post-Fordism.[92] The U.S. military increasingly models itself on a post-Fordist firm surrounded by a network of small parts producers delivering custom batches at a moment's notice. The post-Fordist emphasis on shorter, more specialized, computerized production lines is echoed in the turn to smaller, lighter, more flexible military formations with land, air, and sea capacities; precision-guided "smart bombs;" computerized battlefields; and other elements of what has been called the "new American way of war."[93] The post-Fordist emphasis on niche markets is paralleled in American efforts to discourage the European Union from creating an autonomous army and to encourage individual NATO members "to concentrate on carving out 'niche' capabilities that will complement U.S. power rather than potentially challenge it."[94] Post-Fordist "just-in-time production" is mirrored by what could be called "just-in-time" political coalitions and alliances, like the one cobbled together by the United States on the eve of the 2003 war in Iraq. Tim Mitchell's interpretation of the relations between oil and U.S. foreign policy suggests that the war in Iraq is part of a larger historical trend toward *financialization* or rentier capitalism—another core element of post-Fordism.[95] This geopolitical model originated within the "private economy" and the economic think tanks.

Post-Fordist neoliberalism is expressed most sharply in the privatization of military services. In 2004, there were "as many as 20,000 private contractors operating in Iraq," outside of any system of rules or regulations.[96] Entire U.S. overseas military bases are being run by private military companies. For example, Kellogg Brown & Root, a Halliburton subsidiary, built Camp Bondsteel in Kosovo and maintains every aspect of life there except for performing military duties.[97] Early modern European colonial regimes also relied on private armies, but the more relevant contrast is with the *modern* colonial period of the late nineteenth and early- to mid-twentieth centuries, in which the (colonial) state assumed most military obligations (even if soldiers were usually recruited among the colonized). During the Fordist era (the mid-1950s to the mid-1970s, for the U.S.) it was still politically possible to criticize close relations between the military and private industry as an unnatural "military-industrial complex." Now such imbrication is considered normal.

As military imperialism becomes more flexible, imperial political life in what since September 11, 2001, has been called "the homeland" has tended to become more authoritarian, generating a sharpening set of contradictions within the overall mode of regulation. The emerging social formation is no longer characterized by ever-increasing openness, as in the 1990s, but instead seems to be moving toward a strange combination of market liberalism and sociopolitical closure, an authoritatrian post-Fordism.[98] But even the openness of markets is threatened by the intensification of domestic security measures, curtailments on civil liberties, and restrictions on international flows of people and products. For example, the Pentagon's new regional command for the defense of North America, created in 2002, demanded "that all significant foreign acquisitions of American companies be subjected to a national security review."[99] It remains to be seen whether these countervailing trends can be reconciled in a way that permits a prolonged period of capital accumulation and profitability.[100]

A related other question is whether the United States is simply following in the footsteps of Portuguese, Dutch, and British imperialism, or whether these elements of privatization and authoritarianism are part of a historically novel form of empire. On the one hand, various American imperialist institutions seem historically familiar. The "status of forces agreement" that the United States negotiates with each "ostensibly independent 'host' nation" for the legal treatment of its forces is a contemporary version of the extraterritoriality agreements forced on China by the Great Powers in the nineteenth century.[101] In terms of its global reach, the network of U.S. military bases recalls the nineteenth-century British network, which stretched from the Falkland Islands (Malvinas) to Port Edward (Weihaiwei). Nor is there a qualitative difference in the overall orientation of the two empires. Both were driven first and foremost by profits, but also engaged in all manner of political interventions beyond the boundaries of their bases, overthrowing and supporting regimes, arming and disarming, advising and extending loans. Aside from the lack of interest in colonies in the case of the contemporary United States, and the post-Fordist/neoliberal contours of regulatory policy, the main difference seems to be one of quantity rather than quality. As Niall Ferguson points out, "Britain's share of total world output was 8 per cent" in 1913; the equivalent figure for the US in 1998 was 22 percent." Nor did Britain ever enjoy the same "lead over her imperial rivals" in terms of military expenditures.[102] The sheer scale of U.S. dominance matters, both for the forms of empire and for the forms of anti-imperialism that are continuously (re)generated.

CONCLUSION: LESSONS AGAINST EMPIRE

I asked at the beginning of this chapter what difference it might make for the United States to embrace an imperial self-description. The answer, I think, depends on whether this is part of a critical self-analysis, an examination of America's imperialist role, which would inevitably bring with it a critique of imperialist self-deception. For even if imperialism does not necessarily entail a politics of ontological division between humans in the core and the periphery, it generates a belief among its citizens in the justification of interventions that deprive the rest of the world of autonomy and the right to radical difference. Analyzing the conditions that produce this imperialist consciousness amounts to a criticism of those same conditions.[103] This is obviously not the same as "embracing" America's imperial role. But while it is often asserted that the left assumes that the United States is imperialist, there is little consensus yet on what a critical anti-imperialism might mean in this day and age.

This is related to the question of lessons about (or *against*) empire as opposed to lessons *for* empire.[104] The rejection of lessons *for* empire is not just a normative argument but also an analytic one, based on characteristic ontological features of social life. Society is an "open system" in the sense that social events are typically overdetermined by a multiplicity of causal structures rather than being produced by a single mechanism (as in the ideal production of an effect in a scientific laboratory experiment) or by a constantly recurring cluster of causes. The openness of the social means that we will never attain the positivist grail of the "constant conjunction of events." Although we may be able to *explain* events such as the nineteenth-century European scramble for colonies *retroductively,* we will never be able to predict such events except by lucky chance. As a result, the only kind of affirmative lesson we would ever be able to give to empire, even if we were so inclined, would be to prescribe policies for it, like those who drew up the plans for the recent U.S. invasion of Iraq. But the outcome would be just as difficult to foresee. A preferable way of avoiding having one's work functionalized for empire, to avoid the "ear of the prince," is to try to create accounts that are ontologically and epistemologically adequate to the processual, conjunctural, contingent nature of social life, and hence irreducible to simple policy statements.[105]

9. WHO COUNTS?
IMPERIAL AND CORPORATE STRUCTURES OF GOVERNANCE, DECOLONIZATION AND LIMITED LIABILITY

JOHN D. KELLY

In our world there are politics of mass and count, individual and group. Basic political relationships determine who counts, who is counted, and who is accounted to. New structures of account remake the world, economically and politically. Is the United States an empire? Should it be? Are there alternatives to empires and nation-states? I will reconsider these questions in terms of relationships of count and mass, counting and accounting.

The denunciation of a U.S. empire is old, especially from the Left. As a fantasy of the Republican Party it is newer. Under George W. Bush, after 9/11, it has become as fashionable on the Right as it has long been on the Left to determine that the United States is an empire, but the Right also declares that it should be empire. This makes "empire" and "imperialism" no more impressive to me as a tool for illuminating description, let alone critique. Some things can be illuminated about U.S. power by describing the United States as an empire: mainly, that its actions have significant global consequences. If you really want to, you can call the United States a commercial empire, perhaps, or some other new kind, with a broader definition of "empire" or "imperial," perhaps one that makes any political hegemony imperial. Signs are flexible. Definitions vary. It is not simply an error of fact to declare the United States an empire, as when Chalmers Johnson relies on the concept of "informal empire," or Susan Sontag declares that we are witnessing the transition from republic to empire. It is a question rather of our critical judgment in the refining of our tools and our choices of tasks. I am more interested in showing what is occluded, blocked from view, covered up, if we look for the modalities of American power, and look more generally for this era's social and political order, under the sign of empire.

I seek to describe some contradictions particular to the world after decolonization, the world of nation-states, the UN world we now live in, in contrast to some of the contradictions in political and social organization characteristic of the now collapsed European colonial empires. Obviously I cannot hope to be exhaustive, but will seek instead to be illustrative, raising questions especially about the real modalities of economic and political power, now. This essay begins with a preliminary philological and historical issue: when and why did the British decide that they had a British Empire? It then asks what was occluded by British self-conceptions of empire on a Roman model. One answer, in short, is the rise of joint-stock companies in the early history of European colonial empires. Drawing on but revising Thorstein Veblen's theory of capitalism, I will suggest the centrality of these emerging corporations in the institutional history of capitalism, and the rise of finance to domination of production. But I will focus more on consideration of the significance of joint-stock institutions of governance for colonial societies. In early European colonies, joint-stock company projects turned government into an ongoing enterprise to be accounted for as such, accounted to a privileged audience to whom alone, but to whom absolutely, the governors were indebted and bound. Decolonization then involved consequential institutional transformations. First the corporations and then the "nation-states" achieved a formal, legal status of limited liability.

Diagnosis of the United States as an informal, virtual, or new sort of empire will lead one to prescribe more decolonization, ratifying and ramifying the structures of limited liability. Here you will get something different. Criticism of the moral vectors of self-determination and the nation-state reveals different contradictions in the era of U.S. hegemony. It suggests different quests for remedy. The world needs means that don't amount to sabotage (in Veblen's terms). The world needs means by which its excluded people can overcome the limited liabilities of both corporations and nation-states and intervene in policy making, to count and be counted in the actual reckonings of entitled general interest and general will.

EMPIRE, BRITISH, AND EMPIRE, ROMAN

Who decided that the British had an empire? When? What was at stake in the depiction? These are good, preliminary philological questions for anyone asking, philosophically or otherwise, whether the United States is or should be an empire. The British Empire was more than one among peers: by 1900, the British Empire had created, attracted, and captured roughly half the capital invested on the planet. No other political entity, European or otherwise, was close to this kind of dominance of global finance, before 1900 or since, until the situation of the United States at the conclusion of World War II.[1] (And Jomo K.S. is right that we should attend to the dynamics of capital as we discuss the dynamics of empires—*see chapter 16, this volume.*) The apex of the British Empire was, not coincidentally, also the apex of the first transnationalization of European finance, the first high-tide mark for extra-domestic capital investment. As economist Dani Rodrik and others have shown, despite all rhetoric about unprecedented globalization, extradomestic investment as a percentage of all capital investments has only recently and slightly surpassed the ratio of the European colonial world. Now, half the world's investment capital transits through the U.S. financial markets, en route to almost everywhere. But whether we are wise to declare the existence of an American empire akin to the British Empire depends, in part, on how wise the British were to declare the existence of a British Empire on the model of the Roman Empire.

As Max Weber famously argued, ideal types make description possible. Many Shakespeare scholars have perused his corpus, especially *The Tempest,* in hope of finding a critique of empire there despite Shakespeare's historical position at the very nascence of European colonization projects. In *The Tempest* scholars can find Arial and Caliban already slyly civil and stolidly sullen, fairly or unfairly enslaved, perhaps deserving, and perhaps capable, of liberation. But one doesn't find a "British Empire" in Shakespeare, or any sustained analysis of a nation conquering, possessing, or ruling other nations. The *OED* finds a use of *British Empire* as early as Shakespeare's day, in a 1604 petition to the king. But the first high-water mark is much later for British recognition of a "British Empire": it is in the 1760s, especially in celebration of victories in the Seven Years' War, especially victories over France in both North America and India. Then one gets titles such as Goldsmith's 1768 *The Present State of the British Empire in Europe, America, Africa and Asia, containing a concise account of our possessions in every part of the globe.* Thus, on the one hand, the British Empire comes into being along with global or planetary reckoning by the British. And on the other hand, it is accompanied with the thrill of world-level military success. The Seven Years' War could equally, or possibly more justly, have been named the First World War, especially given the breadth of location of its significant contests. The British made much, on the eve of disaster in North America, of their triumphs in North America. And a primary way this self-admiration was expressed was by comparison of Britons with Romans. Wolfe, the victor in Quebec, was repeatedly sculpted as a Roman conqueror, much as Clive and William Jones came to be depicted as Roman soldier and statesman in toga after India had replaced lost America as the imperial centerpiece.[2] We can compare, here, the French revolutionaries who chose to wear togas, noted with interest by Karl Marx in the famous opening of *The 18th Brumaire.* In a fashion more sustained and no less bizarre, the British found a means to understand and measure their colonizing capitalist empire by way of upstaging the Romans.

Shakespeare and others had already been dramatizing British kings and Roman emperors, in much the same historical and tragic genres. Conceptions of a British Empire grew up in a milieu of controversial comparative evaluations of ancients and moderns, at least from Francis Bacon onward. But in those debates, it was not until the nineteenth century that the moderns did not begin on the defensive, facing the Renaissance question of whether they measured up to things and intellects ancient. To give Britain a history in the Roman mold became the herculean task of an extraordinary lineage of intellectuals, engaging the likes of Hume and Macaulay. But in 1776, timing being everything, the genre of history writing itself was redefined by another historian of Rome, Edward Gibbon, whose advice about decline and fall of empires was timely indeed.[3]

The United States is now taking the European colonial empires and especially the British Empire as a paradigm of something. Certainly we have no shortage of experts on the British Empire (notably Niall Ferguson) announcing its lessons, and thereby some inevitabilities and fatalities that empire is bound to mean for the United States. But before I get to the argument that the era of decolonization has made the world situation profoundly different, it is worth noting that the very idea of a British Empire was not simply a neutral and necessary description of something. The British found it useful to imagine a British Empire because they wanted to measure themselves with and against Rome. Being Rome, being like Rome, being the next Rome, even being greater than Rome was what finding oneself in a British Empire was all about.[4] Marx argued that the banners and battle cries of the past were paradoxically necessary to the project of building the future, that the French republicans needed Roman togas to build a new republic. The British imperials had more sustained use for them, to style themselves recurrently as the lawgivers. We need to wonder, then, what American Republicans want with worn-out British togas—it is certainly not the look, given John Ashcroft's insistence on curtains to hide the toga-clad statue of justice. And we should wonder what was occluded by the conclusion that the British conquests, colonizations, and other global enterprises from the seventeenth through the early twentieth centuries were a "British Empire."

STANDARD AVERAGE EUROPEAN, OR, COUNT, MASS, AND CAPITALISM

The languages of modern Europe share significant grammatical features, linguist Benjamin Lee Whorf has argued, among them the domination of events by things in the "terms of cosmic scope of reference" (events are types of things, things are not types of events), and enormous structural elaboration of the potential to distinguish things by count versus mass. Space and even time become virtual substances with a form, countable in formal units, hours, minutes, feet, miles, of time and space, making Newtonian space-time intuitive, and the idea that the formal units made or changed the substantive mass less intuitive. Depiction of things in what Whorf termed SAE or "standard average European" languages could routinely avail itself of "the measure phrase," a noun of count or form connected to a noun defining mass or substance: a pile of sand, a cup of coffee, a ream of paper, a pound of flesh. The measure phrase is extended aggressively in the SAE languages: a piece of paper, a pair of scissors, a pair of pants. In situations of identification the mass nouns usually need the count nouns for references to succeed: one can speak of a lake (of water) but more rarely of a water. Whorf speculated that the grammar developed with capitalism, or, as he would put it, "modern business," driven by the needs to specify units to facilitate the expanding logic of exchange and its accounting at various levels. Things come in countable quantities, with specifiable form and content.[5]

Efforts recur to find intrinsic connections between capitalism and democracy, whether as critical as Marx of bourgeois political process or as celebratory as Francis Fukuyama's "end of history" argument.[6] My own view is far from Fukuyama's. If the Nazis had gotten a little farther in their heavy-water physics, we would (if we were not dead) be discussing flimsy neo-Hegelian depictions of the Third Reich, rather than the nation-state, as the end of history. But I think that a count-and-mass, measure-phrase grammatical capacity is a condition of possibility for most varieties of both capitalism and democracy, and that much can be gained by tracking the connections made and unmade between the two in the development of the massings and countings of people. This is precisely what doesn't happen if we Romanize the history of British hegemony too far, and allow imperialism's shadow to block from view a few new things under the sun. The Romans, like the British, had contracts, civil courts, lawgivers, commodities, and various forms of commoditization of labor, including free labor. I will leave it to specialists whether the Romans had any conception of labor as a substance measurable in units of time rather than task or product, and thus the allegedly catalytic time-based versus task-based wage form. In any case the British fetishized the commodity and commoditized themselves more extensively.[7] But I want to exit the efforts to build up to all of capitalism from the commodity and its secrets, and connect the potentia of count and mass to a different institution that developed with and largely within the British Empire: the joint-stock company, the corporation, the firm.

Some but not all European colonial ventures were organized as joint-stock companies, mercantile groups constituted as bodies politic and corporate that financed themselves by selling "shares" that entitled their buyers to shares of anticipated profits. Joint-stock companies were particularly popular with the British crown, which issued many royal charters for joint-stock companies until Adam Smith's advice to quit the practice was taken to heart in the early nineteenth century. The Dutch East Indies Company and several French companies were also significant forces in colonial history—but my point is only that the long, complex early history of the joint-stock company is largely ensconced in the history of European colonization, not that it is the cause of European colonization or the only major form taken by it. As Weber argued about the development of capitalism and the state, more generally, the causal nexus is by no means unidirectional. Developments in company governance and colonial government were densely intertwined at many, but not all, sites in the European empires, as early as the Mayflower Compact in 1620 (a proposed charter to constitute "a civil Body Politick" sent by misplaced colonists for approval by their king, modeled on company charters, celebrated in later centuries as a deliberately drafted constitution for self-government, and possibly the first one). But as commercial enterprises, the joint-stock companies of the new world (with the exception of the Hudson Bay Company) were not generally as successful, long-lived, expansive, or politically central as those of many old-world colonies, a pattern that merits more attention than it can receive here.[8] The point, here, is simply that the first versions of these other leviathans, the first large-scale joint-stock companies, emerged at some important sites of European empire.

In 1833, T.B. Macaulay vividly recognized the strangeness of these new, other leviathans, when he took the measure of the British East India Company and urged legal reforms:

> the transformation of the Company from a trading body, which possessed some sovereign prerogatives for the purposes of trade, into a sovereign body, the trade of which was auxiliary to its sovereignty, was effected by degrees and under disguise. . . . The existence of such a body as this gigantic corporation, this political monster of two natures, subject in one hemisphere, sovereign in another, had never been contemplated by the legislators or judges of former ages.
>
> It is true that the power of the Company is an anomaly in politics. It is strange, very strange, that a joint-stock society of traders—a society the shares of which are daily passed from hand to hand . . . should be intrusted with the sovereignty of a larger population, the disposal of a larger clear revenue, the command of a larger army, than are under the direct management of the Executive Government of the United Kingdom. But what constitution can we give to our Indian empire which shall not be strange, which shall not be anomalous?[9]

The problem was political constitution under circumstances characterized by leviathan mercantile companies. Macaulay was right to call the situation "unparalleled in the history of the world." He knew that the ancients could not solve his problems, and I doubt we can solve them even with general theories of "modernity" or "governmentality," which can tend to focus on what is intrinsic to the means and neglect the particular institutional structures that order the means to particular ends (as in a theory of bureaucracy in general). I want to examine the significance of these colonial capitalist institutions, these joint-stock companies, for other developments in so-called governmentality,[10] and I will rely on American theorist Thorstein Veblen, not Marx, to suggest a critical theory of capitalism centered on the increasingly complex and significant institution of the joint-stock company.

Thorstein Veblen, in 1919, announced the arrival of a new order he called "postmodern," an economy nothing like the one envisioned by Adam Smith.[11] Marx could lampoon Moneybags buying labor power for the wages of labor, but he had a personified capitalist meeting and bargaining with the individual laborer in a physical market. Veblen calls "the modern point of view" the ethical normalization of a world in which people bargain over things and live by way of transactions with producers at similar scale to themselves, the butcher and the baker of Adam Smith's paradigms. Very different is the situation of the worker employed by a firm so large he or she cannot name its owners, and the situation of a consumer surrounded by commodities the prices, styles, and availability of which are set by mechanisms so vastly beyond the consumer that the offers are mainly take-it-or-leave-it. In this corporate order, the calculation of price and supply on the part of the firm is only a small fraction of all its strategic calculation. Industrial (especially engineering) calculation of the possible and viable is only the beginning of corporate planning of when and where and how to produce what. Moneybags as a captain of industry, an actual producer of goods, was long since hegemonized, in fact colonized, by financiers dominating financial markets, who will as happily not produce and even sabotage the production of others if that is where the greater profit will lie. Veblen pushed his image of a new kind of capitalism very far in its operating logic from the symmetric relationships presumed in most conceptions of exchange. And he developed a scathing appreciation and critique of the newest political ideas of his time: Wilsonian "self-determination" and its strangely uncoordinate partner, the idea of "development" of the economies of backward countries. But before we go on we have to return to what Macaulay understood and Veblen did not: the origin of the joint-stock companies so central to finance-dominated capitalism, capitalism beyond mere circulation of commodities. Veblen shared with Marx, Hobson, Lenin, et al. the illusion that the imperial, colonial world came last in the history of capital, the final frontier. But joint-stock companies are creatures of European colonialism. The capacity of management to make decisions about the lifeworld of productive activity in generalized financial terms begins there, under colonial conditions and at the core of colonial relationships. Even in their present form, in the logic of their count and mass, and more precisely in the logic of who does, and does not, count, and what does and does not get taken into account, they still bear the mark of the "political monsters" that were their forbears.

In joint-stock reckoning one group of people, the shareholders, own the enterprise, and they employ another group, the management, to contract with, control, and manipulate other people, both workers and consumers (and recursively, other whole firms), in a fashion that meets the interests of the shareholders. More rococo elaborations now abound in our financial world. Recursively, the management of companies can acquire whole other companies as well as contract with them. Not only are the identities of shareholders in flux as they buy and sell shares, resetting their value each time, but also, these distant, evanescent figures are no longer necessarily actual people. A very large volume of the shares of stock in the companies are owned not by individuals but by other incorporated entities, such as the insurance companies and pension funds that competitively seek the best return on their collected premiums, and mutual funds that simply manage being an owner better than individual owners generally can (and might thus invest also on behalf of an insurance company or pension fund). Few or none of these elaborations were imaginable at the outset of "stock markets," and a more complete treatment of the development of company counting and accounting would need, at minimum, a history of both measurement techniques and examination of other relevant institutional histories, notably a history of taxation.[12] But the recursive layering, technical developments, and institutional complexities have not displaced the core organizing vector, the sharp binary between owners and others, in fact colonially descended—what has come to be typed as the distinction in rights between the shareholders and the stakeholders. No matter how far abstracted, mediated, and otherwise distanced the shareholders get from any actual transaction of a priced, consumable commodity, their rights still organize the logic of the system. The lifeworld can grow entirely dependent on commodities, or more especially a locality can become entirely economically dependent on a particular enterprise, e.g., a company town, a monocrop region, without gaining equivalent or countervalent claims of right. No matter how high the stakes for the stakeholders, the enterprise is constituted for the sake of the shareholders. Management actually dominates the institutional agency of these companies; economist John Kenneth Galbraith argued that management routinely replaces maximum return for shareholders with maximum growth of the enterprise as their real operating goal. This surely varies historically and by industry. But the mandate to serve the owners, and the kinds of license it provides, does not. The mandate to operate exclusively in consideration of the shareholders' imputed economic interests frees the agency of management, licensing any necessary ruthlessness in dealing with mere stakeholders.

Stakeholders managed in the interests of shareholders, shareholders almost entirely removed from social and political relationship with stakeholders: this core institutional logic of joint-stock companies is not merely similar to the constitution of governance of the European empires. The European empires developed a form of nation and nationalism in the position of the shareholders quite distinct from the "deep horizontal comradeship" and symmetries internal and external characteristic of later liberalisms, and reified by Benedict Anderson.[13] In what Corrigan and Sayer, in *The Great Arch,* characterized as a succession of cultural revolutions, the people who constituted "the nation" in England expanded from the barons signing the Magna Carta, to the aristocracy, to men with a certain standing expressed in property, even to universal adult suffrage. But until very late in the history of these empires, the idea of equality of nations was abstract and unlikely at best, and hierarchies of peoples internal and external were both real and consequential. At the core of the empire the individual sovereign of divine right gave way to a group that ruled by way of election. Most histories of democracy neglect the entwinement of systems for count and account in state governance with histories of direction of joint-stock enterprise, despite the fact that these modalities were closely intertwined, especially in England. As Barney Cohn used to argue, there wasn't an East India Company faction in the British government of the eighteenth and nineteenth century so much as a replication in company and government politics of the same parties and factions. While some deep roots of deep horizontality for citizenship lay in memories of Greek and Roman politics, others perhaps as consequential lie in the governance of the first great companies, where the sheer symmetry of the shares was less refutable by any distinction of moral or ethnic qualities, where their fungibility belied any historical, identitarian definition of their virtue, power, or basis of claim of right. The will of the shareholders was as countable as the performance of management was accountable. The duty of management to the shareholders was clear and their performance starkly auditable, the rights of the shareholders impeccably established, and the ethical foundation of the power of management over peoples governed, as in India, was clearly delimited by the priority of service to shareholders. The sovereign space of exception appeared to lose all moral hazard in this structure, delimited by duty that positively required both creative violence and imposition of constraining rules on the governed. Joint-stock company projects turned government into an ongoing enterprise, to be accounted for as such, to a privileged audience to whom alone, but to whom absolutely, the governors were indebted and bound.[14] Far more thoroughly than any concept of "civilizing mission," the needs and constitutional right of the shareholders justified and could even be argued to mandate the otherwise exceptional impositions of government in colonial conditions.

In short, far from imperialism being a late phase of capitalism, the building of a British Empire depended in large part on innovations in economic institutional order, especially the joint-stock company, that became central to the rise of capitalism as we know it. The entwined rise of European colonizations and joint-stock leviathans led eventually to colonization of almost everything by institutions of finance. The question need not be how a global periphery was reshaped by a European center. We might also ask what happened to the visible ethnic hierarchies that were the stuff of imperial lifeworlds, in the realms of all stakeholders, when the corporate form sublimed and joint-stock companies were no longer, so exclusively, owned in one nation and operating in others. And we might wonder how these other leviathans, born as bodies politic and corporate, and active in the business of governance, sovereignty, and the state, were eventually disentangled from the world of sovereign responsibility.

LARGE, INVISIBLE HANDS

Macaulay's 1833 speech explaining the new charter for the British East India Company was occasioned by a specific crisis within the operating logic of the British Empire. The doctrines of political economy, especially as extracted from the *Wealth of Nations,* were having greater impact in the nineteenth century than the eighteenth. Smith's polemic against the East India Company monopoly was much debated. And the critique of monopoly also had guns and sails, in the form of practically unstoppable illegal trade. The Company's directors complained of the burdens of government of India, especially defense, without the real profits of monopoly. The solution was to end the monopoly and disentwine company from the burdens of sovereignty. While the East India Company was the centerpiece, the larger question was basic. Across the empire, companies were severed from British imperial government. From chartered partners in royal sovereignty, the companies were demoted to regulated enterprises under government supervision.[15]

The reforms of the 1830s are fascinating, the institutionalization in many domains of what Veblen called "the modern point of view," the image of society made by trucking and bartering individuals. The abolition of slavery was as much a dismantling of an original colonial capitalist institution as was the intercission of company and government in India. Macaulay argued fiercely for the propriety of a new form of Company government for India, actually, and the reforms he led did not so much sever company and government as sever the company into a mercantile enterprise reporting only to its shareholders and a separated sovereign Company bureaucracy reporting only to the crown. But he saw a need for a functionally appropriate continuing relationship between the two parts, and one that would serve the truest interests of the Indian stakeholders in company enterprise: so he put the government and people of India into debt to the newly independent trading company. This way, he argued, the company would have a continuing interest in the welfare of the people of India, since they could not pay back their debt if their economy further declined. The disciplinary propriety of debt for impoverished governments and peoples is no new idea.

The abolition of company monopolies and direct sovereignties, or conversely the institution of "Crown rule" throughout the empire was ratified after the so-called Mutiny in India in 1857, for which the continuing company bureaucracy was scapegoat. The principle that joint-stock companies, with their private interests, should not be partners in government, and with it the various conceptions and legal enactments of their limited liability, was precisely what made their hands invisible in continuing economic planning, and what sublimed the rights of shareholders over stakeholders. Redress of corporate abuses was a matter for the regulatory apparatuses of government. But what principle of justice guaranteed government in the public interest? Whose appeals, where, counted for what?

SELF-DETERMINATION, OR, DECOLONIZATION ON THE AMERICAN PLAN

What is really wonderful about self-determination, especially in the nation-state form, is that it seems to make the nation so shareholder-like. Occasionally one runs into politicians (e.g., Ross Perot) who go so far as to collapse the levels entirely, declare that they are running for CEO, with the citizens as the shareholders or even the board of directors. But the vulgar extremes are not the main connection between the institutional logics of the nation-state and its predecessors in political institutional design, the European colonial empires and the joint-stock companies.

We can enter into these relationships via historical narrative and its actual dialogics as easily, probably more easily, than we can via comparing ideal types, abstractions about who gets to be counted, and who gets to be a counter, and which amassed wills count for what, things or people, means or ends. Narrative is easier: Woodrow Wilson faced a dilemma as World War I raged, considering the national interest of the United States and whether to enter a European war. His administration was not particularly keen on seeing either side win and sought a commanding height from which to win the peace rather than the war. His advisor Colonel House organized a body of intellectuals and set it to advise the president on what to seek as the outcome of the war—it might have been the closest thing to an actual intellectual vanguard ever to directly influence world history, regardless the alacrity with which Lenin and his Party, Wilson's contemporaries, also made their plans and raised their banners. What Wilson's intellectuals determined, as the American goal for a world peace, was a world league roughly kindred with the perpetual peace plans that preceded it, like the others hoping to replace a balance of power with a congress of symmetries and equality. But Wilson's league was to be of nations, not states, in its conception, every sovereign present symmetric with the others in the dependence of its right and power to govern on its representation of the will of its people. In all but name, the nation-state was born.[16]

How then do we calibrate this with the continuing history of joint stock, its means and ends? Veblen can help us again. In comparison: Karl Marx and Antonio Gramsci did most of their intellectual work in the aftermath of failed political enterprises. For each, the treatise was second place to praxis. For Veblen, the vast success of his first, most innocent book, his neoevolutionary but highly ironic treatment of "the leisure class," made him a public intellectual from the outset, but one in search of his party and cause. Veblen was anti-anti-Bolshevik, for peace and against war, and above all deeply skeptical of the politics of vested interest, his name for the kind of structure of manipulation that organized the persistent steering of state policy down the roads built by corporate planners. Unlike other democratic socialists, notably H.G. Wells, who coined a phrase when he described World War I as a "war to end all wars," Veblen was deeply suspicious of the motives and cognizant of the consequences when capitalist empires attacked each other. Like Wells he was rueful years later when reconsidering his wartime political acts. But for Veblen the dilemma was not supporting the British at war but whether to aid and support the Americans planning peace. Veblen participated in House's planning enterprise. Regardless of his later disappointment in the outcome, which he thought reshaped the world not nearly enough, Veblen's interventions into the American interventions into world political institutional order make fascinating reading. Two of his planning papers survive, one about how to reckon memberships of colonial territories in a League of Nations, and the other an acerbic, trenchant, and prescient critique of the new conception of what the European colonies need, something the House crowd was calling "development."[17]

As Veblen summarized it, "self help" was the favored political solution of the liberal order. Under the conditions of the new order, capitalism dominated by large firms and financial markets, self help was bootless. (*Bootless* was one of Veblen's favorite words.) Veblen was far more skeptical, and more accurate, in his estimation of the political and economic future of the world's poor than were his Marxist contemporaries. "Development" was clearly going to be a disaster for people on the world's periphery, where it would primarily mean the maximal export of natural resources at minimum cost. But leaving the world's poorest nations in the political hands of their colonizers would not mitigate the damage, since they too would sponsor "development," but via a cronyism respecting the vested interests of their own particular friends and partners (one can think in fact of Haliburton) that does not lessen the exploitation via development, but simply makes it less efficient. In a

world in which scientific engineering was vital and was locked down by the proprietary rights of the something-for-nothing "shareholders,"[18] the only thing worse
than being exploited, for people with nothing but labor or labor and land, was not
being exploited. To keep the major enterprises of the new order out would be to lose
access to all the crystallized knowledge that they monopolized, in the one area
where patents and charters still generated monopolies. And if a colonial master
would be worse than no help, little could be expected, either, from the "self help" of
a local, national state, no matter how free or democratic, since the vested interests of
the capitalist centers could not, under most foreseeable circumstances, be coerced by
such limited sovereignties. Still, in sum, Veblen argued for a specific economic policy
for Wilson's new world order, the best possible under contemporary conditions. Since
all particular political mediators were likely to be the tools of equally particular vested
interests, Veblen argued that the United States should seek general agreements on tariffs and trade, the ruthless replacement of all bilateral trade arrangements with multilateral trading rules: not to end the predatory practices of the vested interests, but
merely to render their economic activities most efficient.

Thus for his own reasons Veblen argued for things that already were, or would
soon be cornerstones of U.S. economic policy: open doors and limited liabilities,
multilateralism and freedom especially for corporate enterprise. He had no illusions,
though, about its potential to deliver prosperity to the abjected and downtrodden,
and even less about the prospects of what became Wilson's centerpiece, and later a
battle cry of the Roosevelts and a cornerstone of the UN: self-determination. What
politics required was not only formal freedom but also substantive leverage. To confront vested interests one had to overcome their tactics, and there lay the deepest political problem, the politics of what Veblen flamboyantly called sabotage.

SABOTAGE, TERRORISM, AND LIMITED LIABILITY

Inside and outside the United States, political observers angry at U.S. deployments
of economic, diplomatic, and military power exclusively in American self-interest
have resorted to depicting the United States as an empire. The underlying politics
here is largely about shame, as if the United States, having long agreed that the European empires were evil, would then desist from its worst interventive practices.
Then the world could finally truly decolonize. The logic is that of decolonization itself: that if, somehow, the unwarranted domination of nations by other nations
could be prevented, then we would really have something.

But if the redecolonization of Iraq is telling us anything, it is that there is no solution to contemporary political predicaments expressible in the form of the proper
rules for U.S., or European, or even NGO intervention into the politics of "failing"

states.[19] The question is not the rules for "our" intervention into "their" politics but their intervention into ours. So, what exactly are the rules, for the intervention of the world's poor into the governance of the United States, or the policy making of the world's major corporations?

It is extremely hard for "them" to get "our" attention. In Monrovia, capital of Liberia, on July 21, 2003, a desperate crowd got global attention, momentarily, by staging a macabre demonstration of their despair. Trapped by encroaching militias, refused help by the U.S. embassy, and calling for U.S. protection, the refugees piled up dead bodies next to an embassy wall emblazoned with the American seal. The nameless mortar victims disconnected from kin and clan formed a mass of bare death; it took several hours for world media to settle on a count of eighteen for the piled dead. "The group demanded to know why Washington has not sent troops," the Associated Press reported. "'We're dying here,' screamed some in the crowd, as two American servicemen in camouflage watched from behind bulletproof glass. One man held up a hastily scrawled sign: 'Today G. Bush kill Liberia people.'"

"Today G. Bush kill Liberia people." On the day of this anti-funeral, this confrontational massing of bare death, George W. Bush did speak to the media about events in Liberia. Bush said, "We are concerned about our people in Liberia. We're continuing to monitor the situation very closely. We're working with the United Nations to affect policy necessary to get the cease-fire back in place." On behalf of the UN, Kofi Annan openly called for immediate U.S. military intervention, invoked the prospect of mass death, and argued that immediate action could prevent tragedy, avert another mass destruction in Africa. But Bush was crystal clear on his limited liability. His concern was "our people in Liberia," as every action of the U.S. embassy demonstrated. And if Africa is the recurring opposite of Iraq, the site of tragic nonintervention, its own exceptions are sobering. The United States did not do well, or do good, in Somalia, and the local resentment built precisely when it became clear that the Americans focused most on "our people," and had absolutely no intention of staying, let alone taking over.

Teaching the United States to be, or not to be an empire will not solve the increasing violence of our world. Nor will that violence be more than ameliorated by the best rules for U.S., NGO, European, or other intervention or nonintervention into political tragedies. To Veblen the core problematic lay in the asymmetry between the actions of what Veblen called vested interests, and the kinds of sabotage that had to be resorted to when subaltern, abjected people confronted vested interests. For example, consider the political limits Veblen saw as tragically inevitable in labor unions. The unions' main tactic, the strike, is a form of sabotage, a refusal to produce, even a deliberate intervention to prevent any production at a given work site (the substantive violence sometimes behind the ritualized picket line). The problem with strikes as the central political tool is twofold: first, the intrinsically negative character of the intervention, but second, and more subtle, its borrowed and shamefaced quality. Deliberate manipulation of the process of production is the core business of management, constantly vigilant for better ways to undermine rivals and coerce better deals out of exchange partners. Veblen, with a romantic streak favoring the virtues of the heroic engineer, emphasized the deliberate restriction of production to only the most favorable terms, and thought that a plenitude could follow if engineers were set free. His critique of the labor union and his concept of sabotage can be sustained without the whole romance, though. The hardest thing for the labor union is that what it does is fully visible, and obviously destructive, and often not even legal, while the forms of sabotage that management relies upon are rarely visible or obvious, however destructive (rare is the Microsoft that openly makes its browser free when confronted by a rival in Netscape). Above all, what corporations do in their own self-interest is almost always impeccably legal and even honorable, because they are assiduous in pursuit of the interests of the shareholders.

This is no brief for so-called terrorism. I seek, rather, a description of the conditions that produce its logic, the conditions of possibility for new wars that can turn peacekeepers into sorcerer's apprentices. The self-protections of limited liability entities, including both corporations and nation-states, are mostly already built in, rarely visible, and easily morally defended when they have to be visible. Gestures to anticipate or answer the needs of the world's poor are understood neither as primary duties nor as prudential deals benefiting both parties, but rather as actions outside self-interest, as charity, as gifts, as donations, putting recipients into debt. Citizens and shareholders react with weariness when the needy ask for more, and with honest outrage when the abject aren't satisfied or grateful for what has already been given. Efforts to take direct action against agencies of self-serving limited liability often take the form of open, deliberate, and visible sabotage. And the means to stop sabotage are by themselves also purely negative.

The Liberian anti-funeral has spurred something in my analysis, but it has not brought Liberians peace or security, nor even entrance into the U.S. embassy. Above all what counts, and is now counted in U.S. newspapers, is deaths of Americans. During the Vietnam War the U.S. military embarrassed itself with lopsided casualty reports, which were either fraudulent or evidence of appalling numbers of Vietnamese dead for each American casualty. Much better then not to record the consequences of American military deployment for the Iraqis, especially the civilians. It is extraordinary that the United States even carried this refusal to count to the dead, uniformed military of the army they sought to engage; this refusal to count is a direct violation of the Geneva Conventions. But then, it was equally extraordinary how that Iraqi army melted away, rather than engaging the Americans back, leaving behind the empty uniforms. But the sign of the times is the other side of the extremity in U.S. reckoning: U.S. fascination with the U.S. war dead. Dead Iraqis need not even be counted, let alone individualized. But the names, pictures, life histories, and interviewed relatives of U.S. war dead are routinely and recurrently news, a virtually sacred story that can be renewed every day. Not bare life or death, the most explosive stuff of U.S. national politics, they are a tale full of sound and fury, but signifying what?

RESCUING POLITICS FROM THE NATION-STATE

I am aware that this essay realizes Veblen's goal of avoiding "undue precision." I won't finish by addressing loose ends, missing complexities, or more parts of world history. Nor will I try to round out thin or one-sided portrayals. Instead, with apologies to historian Prasenjit Duara, and with respect for his call to rescue history from the nation,[20] I will try for something more useful: a positive political vector. If the question cannot be simply whether the United States is to be or not to be an empire, and if sabotage is forestalled—immoral, and also bootless—even though it has a logic and point, then what? If we believe that the United States acts too imperially, then we can be comforted by the notion that some successor of ours will live the dream of a decolonized world, full of self-determining nation-states. To the degree that we already live the limits of self-determination, and some of us a lot more than others, what then might we hope for? And work for?

The Gandhian call was to hope and work for something higher than independence: interdependence. The literature on globalization shows that this is what we already have, like it or not. But limited liability is the bad faith of the American dream. Foreign aid appears a charity, a gift; the poor appear to demand a handout, to be unable to recognize and handle debt the way a moral agent should. The Gandhian road, further, was to call not for human rights but for human duties, from which rights would follow like water from a spring. There is of course sense in this. If an insurance company, to be licensed to operate anywhere on the planet, had to be responsible for overseeing improvement in health care for some segment of the planet, the people of that segment would have more grounds to expect something (especially if the license reviews were a competition with real risk to the companies' licenses). But of course, we have to wonder what it would take for such a regulation becoming real, and that would be an insurance industry willing to cooperate because it feared worse. If Aetna's continuing existence depended on improvement in life expectancy in Bangladesh that would be very good news for people in

Bangladesh, but as a nation-state Bangladesh could never have leverage to move Aetna, the insurance industry or any branch of any major industry to make the rights of Bangladeshis connect directly to the duties of the company. It would take a much larger entity than a Bangladesh.

Against the image that our problem is nation-states exerting dominating influence beyond their legal boundaries, then, we find the opposite problem: the absence of any means to collect real political will beyond the level of the nation-state, especially will to renegotiate on behalf of stakeholders with the deliberately invisible shareholders. In his paper for this conference, Frederick Cooper speaks of the recent fashion to expect the demise of the nation-state; with this I am reminded of the impatience of many critical voices with the idea of organizing a political party. But perhaps the idea of the political party as the modern prince, the foremost tool for political change, is not so much outdated as boxed in by the greatest trick of the limited liabilities. Perhaps what the world needs is global-level political parties, sort of like NGOs but, again, less shamefaced, because they could be clearer, more open, and more legitimate in representational foundation. One reform well within the grasp of the world's poorest nation-states could readily begin them: election, rather than appointment, of delegates to the United Nations. Imagine a United States having to negotiate, not military intervention with a recalcitrant France, but tariffs with a global Green party, representing not only Bangladesh but also 136 other states. (More likely, the United States would have to deal with a global neoliberal party— but the global party would still have to deliver something to maintain its constituent support.)

I am not predicting such a turn in world politics. The pressures to sabotage such a system would be extreme, with so many local and global interests threatened. I am merely pointing at what would be neither empire, nor self-determination, in hopes that politics can be rescued from both of them. Absent an alternative, we will continue to live in a world of increasingly visible sabotage against the ongoing, invisible limits intrinsic to our global public culture, which bottles up "stakeholder" political will in the limited horizons of nation and state, while leaving the other leviathans free roaming and growing, far less transformed from their colonial roots, and far less limited in their ambitions than their liabilities.

In Mogadishu, the U.S. military destroyed its local position and ended many American and Somali lives in order to recover the body of a single dead U.S. soldier. In Monrovia, the United States would not touch the mangle of the anti-funeral. They called in an NGO to carry off the dead and do something "appropriate" with the bodies. Counting and accounting will always be central in the routines and rituals of capitalism and democracy. Botched accountings, whether in Mogadishu or

Florida, will always matter. But the starkest sign of the current extremity of American power is the sharpness of the line it draws between who must and must not be counted, recognized, individualized, rendered human and rightful. No system has ever been more extreme in its distinctions between who does and does not count than the form of capitalist democracy currently practiced by the Republican-led Americans. In their dreams it can dress up in the togas of imperial lawgivers.

10. EMPIRE AND IMITATION

SHELDON POLLOCK

The invitation to think about the new American empire and historical experience raises a number of important and hard questions especially for students of the non-modern non-West.[1] I will address just three in this essay, and only in a very schematic (and unavoidably reductive) manner. The first concerns historical knowledge itself, a problem that can only be registered and not resolved, except insofar as registering goes some way to resolving it. The second has to do with comparative history of the empire form, whether such a thing is even possible, and if so, what it might look like. Connected to this is the last and most difficult question: Can such a history, assuming it is possible, help us find our political way forward between the Scylla of the American empire and the Charybdis of the order of nation-states, its one apparent alternative? Can it point us toward some different, non-coercive mode of global power-culture, some cosmopolity perhaps, which might appear less hopelessly utopian if history could show that some people somewhere may once have lived in something like it?

I

Contemporary discussions of the lessons past empires may have for present ones make several assumptions that must come as a surprise to anyone who has followed the debates on historical knowledge over the past few decades. One is that we really can acquire true knowledge of history; another is that this knowledge is useful to us, that we will benefit by acting upon its truth. Since its recent near-death experience—having been reduced to mere storytelling by literary critics and to sheer ideology by philosophers, and this after long and cruel neglect by social science—history hasn't had it so good in a generation.[2]

The contradictions in the critique of historical knowledge were never very far beneath the surface. Hayden White could reduce history writing to tropes (metaphor, metonymy, and so on) and modes of emplotment (romance, tragedy, and the like), yet he never seemed much worried that the truth of the history he wrote of the rhetoric of history writing might be undermined by its own rhetoricity. Edward Said could praise Hayden White and still believe that he, too, was writing factuality and not fictionality when writing the history of orientalism. Subaltern historians need historical truth—they're not novelists, after all—and Ranajit Guha undoubtedly believed he was seeking the truth about the history of elementary aspects of peasant insurgency even when arguing that "ideological neutrality" is a myth "central to liberal historiography." It's not clear how anyone could actually subscribe to these critiques—*andere Schichten, andere Geschichten,* different tropes for different folks— and still imply, as everyone most certainly implied, that the history they were offering was true. The problem here was not bad faith; it was overlooking the contradictions rather than looking them in the eye and showing us how to live with them. And this recognition, that objectivity resides, if it resides anywhere, in the open acknowledgment of our untranscendable subjectivity, seems the one way to exorcise the ghost of metaphysics that philosophical hermeneutics finds haunting all historicism.[3]

The question whether we can know the truth of history is compounded by another concerning the relationship between knowledge and action, especially historical knowledge and political action. Even supposing we somehow come to grasp the real lessons of the past, what enables us to act on them, let alone guarantees that we will act responsibly? It has often seemed to me far easier to argue that it isn't those who forget the past who are condemned to repeat it, but, on the contrary, those—in Ayodhya, Belfast, Jerusalem, Kosovo, or Washington—who remember it. And this makes it clear that we have not made much progress in understanding the advantages and disadvantages of history for life.

Yet somehow all these worrisome problems have suddenly disappeared and once again scholars are invited to offer truths from yesterday relevant to the dilemmas of today. The problem, an Indian colleague once said to me, is not that American thinkers are so quick to take up new theories, but that they are so quick to drop them. But that may not be a bad thing in the present instance. The literary and philosophical critique of historical knowledge was an interesting trip to a dead end. And as for acting on such knowledge, people have learned and will continue to learn lessons from history without needing historians to teach them. In fact, one thing a comparative history of empire demonstrates is that it is only by looking at past empires that people have learned how to be imperial at all, since empire is a cultural practice and not some natural state. Moreover, the very project of learning, or unlearning, the lessons of empire—including the project of this book—forms part of a history of imitation of the sort I examine in what follows. We needn't any longer bemoan the impossibility of knowing the past or learning from it. What we do need are new pasts to know, with their potentially new lessons.

Yet, even if we can agree to forget that historical truth isn't available to us and may not be advantageous for life anyway, and are emboldened to proceed with a consideration of past empires, we are still not in the clear. What exactly is this unit of analysis, "empire"? What historical eras of empire are meaningful to the present, and why those? The concept of empire is notoriously vague, and the major works on the topic over the past fifty years haven't done much to lessen the imprecision epitomized in the standard dictionary definition, "supreme and extensive political dominion."[4] After all, what constitutes "dominion," and how dominant does it have to be—and how extensive is extensive enough and how supreme supreme enough—for dominion to count as empire? The term has become so elastic that scholars can speak, without qualification, of a Swedish or a Maratha empire in the seventeenth century, a Tibetan or a Wari empire a millennium earlier.

Nor is it by any means obvious, if we ask how deep in the past to go to learn the lessons of empire, that we can provide a coherent answer. Many believe the lessons of modern European empires, like that of the British in India, are pertinent to the contemporary United States. But what about the lessons of a modern Eurasian empire like the Soviet Union in Central Asia, or of an East Asian empire like that of the Chinese in Tibet, or of an early-modern European empire like that of the Portuguese, or of an early-modern South Asian empire like that of Vijayanagara . . . and so on back to the Neo-Assyrian? What disqualifies any of these from providing object lessons, and why? How narrow must the time frame be to permit inferences to be drawn, and what value, if any, can be attributed to inferences drawn from wider ones?

Comparisons across huge expanses of time are problematic, because of course things do change. Capitalism entered history, so did Enlightenment rationality and the Rights of Man; modernity with its novel ideas of the sovereign state, territoriality, development, and the like; and not least, unprecedented technologies of war. Undoubtedly all this has enabled new empires to actualize things old empires could only dream of, and to dream of new things to actualize (although no one yet seems to have charted precisely how such elements of newness have modified the very notion of empire over time). While all this may readily be admitted, it is arguable that something of the idea and practice of empire has remained stable over the long term, with earlier ideas and practices sedimenting in later embodiments successively. After all, the very talk of "American empire" presupposes a readiness to slot it into some longer lineage—and perhaps even a cognitive necessity of doing so. But it's not only this kind of sedimentation that speaks in favor of a deeper history lesson. So does the possibility of learning, from a potentially radically different imperial past, other lessons in the service of a radically different future.

That there were such different imperial pasts, real inflexions in the imitative process, is part of what I try to show in what follows, despite the conceptual difficulties that stand in the way. One of these has already been alluded to, the problematic category "empire" itself, which requires discursive prudence and careful distinctions, between say overseas empire and state-as-empire, or between external and internal colonialism. Another is the conceptual apriorism the term carries. For good reasons, which are made even better once we grasp the history of imitation, the Roman Empire has long been the archetype in the West for thinking about empire as such. But the problem with archetypes is that they tend to prestructure perception and to prevent us from even seeing what may be different about other, nonarchetypal kinds of extensive power-culture formations, with their other, potentially redeemable legacies.[5] You can't compare empires let alone learn their lessons if you don't know what counts as empire, or if all that does count is what was done by whoever did as the Romans did.

So with respect to the unit of analysis and historical depth, as with historical truth and the uses of history for life, I adopt here a purely pragmatic approach. You do what you can do and take what you can get—no guarantees, no absolutes, no boundaries.

II

As a category of analysis empire may be vague, but in a number of the most important political formations in southern Eurasia from about 500 B.C.E. to the coming of colonialism and beyond, empire can be said to have formed a coherent category of practice.[6] This is so precisely because the empire form was continuously re-created through historical imitation, a process that seems to have run along two axes: vertically in time (through historical memory), and horizontally across space (perhaps through what archaeologists have named peer-polity interaction).[7] The vertical and horizontal course of imperial imitation could be plotted among a range of embodiments: the Achaemenid version in Iran beginning around 500 B.C.E. (followed by the Sasanid from the early third century C.E., and perhaps the Ghaznavid of eleventh-century Afghanistan); the Hellenic-Macedonian (followed by Byzantine); the Roman (followed by the Carolingian and Ottonian; the overseas imperial version of the early modern era, Dutch-English-French-Portuguese-Spanish, and twentieth-century Fascist); the Maurya version in India (followed by the Kushana, and Gupta, and perhaps also the Khmer of Angkor in Southeast Asia). Other empires were joined in other networks of vertical and horizontal linkages: the Central- and Inner-Asian version, for example, connected the Xiongnu, Turkic, Uighur, Mongol, and ultimately Mughal, Safavid, and Ottoman polities.

Historical imitation as such is a widespread, even central, social and political dynamic, though little systematic attention has been paid to it. We don't get very far trying to explain it from an externalist perspective like that of Marx, for whom political actors seem nothing but con artists who "anxiously conjure up the spirits of the past," using "time-honored disguise and borrowed language." Marx may well have been aiming here, as Sartre believed, at a "difficult synthesis of intention and result" and offering a new theory of human action, but this seems never to have been elaborated by Marx or anyone else. Modern sociological theory might be said in part to begin—if Emile Durkheim begins it—with questioning the very place of imitation in motivating social action, since it was contra Gabriel Tarde's notion of imitation in the case of suicide that Durkheim offered his theory based on group characteristics. But imitation has remained an element in this theory; it has been used for example to explain the presence of similar bureaucratic structures in varied national settings ("institutional isomorphism").[8] From within the subjective horizon of premodern actors, with their different mimetic standards and logics of organization, such behavior might be thought of as a kind of ethnotheory of practice: there are certain things you must do to become an imperial person.

Recent scholarship has carefully explored the imitative nature of the new-world European empires, which, descending from visions of imperial antiquity attempted "to perpetuate the traditions and the values of the empires of the ancient world."[9] But it is important to note that the traditions in question, Hellenic and Roman, themselves derived from notions of empire that arose across southern Eurasia in the latter half of the first millennium B.C.E, when a new model of polity first came into being that envisioned governance as essentially and necessarily translocal rather than local. The originators of the model were the Achaemenids (c. 550–330 B.C.E), whose political world-empire, the first in history, was beheld by their contemporaries with astonishment (in 440 B.C.E Herodotus marveled at Xerxes' intention to "extend the Persian territory as far as God's heaven reaches"). The imperial lineage that began with the Achaemenids includes both European and Indian imitators: on the one hand, Alexander the Great (356–323 B.C.E), regarded by recent scholars as the last of the Achaemenids, followed eventually by Rome of the Principate (27 B.C.E–c. 425 C.E.); on the other, the Mauryas (c. 320–150 B.C.E), followed eventually by the imperial Guptas (c. 320–550 C.E.).

There has no doubt been actual convergence in the development of the empire form across time and space because of the imitative dynamic of empire building, just as there has been convergence in the nation form through the imitative dynamic of nation building. Yet if the repertory of ways of being imperial has had a certain regularity, the imitative process itself has never been rigidly rectilinear and homogeneous. For one thing, we can identify some mixing across lineages of imperial emulation. Thus in India the Mughals adopted from their Hindu predecessors not only components of symbolic authority but also specific practices of rule, whereas the British started out by imitating the Mughals before going Roman.[10] For another, and far more significant than these kinds of fusion, stark differences can be demonstrated in the Indian and western forms of imperial imitation. Empire makers in the two worlds made a very varied selection from the imperial toolbox first assembled by the Achaemenids.

This may hardly seem like news in itself, but scholars tend to think of premodern empire in far more undifferentiated terms. Some trace the very roots of the form itself to a new conception, in the so-called Axial age, of the relation between the political order and "the higher transcendental order," which is accordingly supposed to be co-present with the development of empire.[11] Less clearly expressed but still common is the assumption that early Eurasian empires, emerging out of this putative causal matrix of a transcendental breakthrough, were all basically alike as culture-power formations: in respect of territorial infinitude, the "extreme centralization" of the political structure, or the "absolute power" and divinization of the emperor.[12] This assumption is, I believe, incorrect in the case of India, as a comparative analysis of the early empire form can show. Several components of such an analysis have already been suggested: ideas about imperial space; modes of rule; and religion, specifically the role of a universal God. An additional and especially salient diagnostic is communication, in particular imperial language, which may be taken as representative of cultural practices more generally. (Political economy is omitted only because insufficient data are available for pre-Mughal empire in India.) A comparison of Indian and western empire according to these criteria demonstrates how significant deviation from the standard model was.

Around 519 B.C.E. the Achaemenid emperor Darius invented a new form of imperial communication, the monumental inscription, that would become a standard feature of the empire form reproduced across Eurasia for centuries. Ashoka, third of the Maurya kings of India, imitated the royal idiom of the Achaemenid records when introducing the epigraphical habit into India around 260 B.C.E. The cultivation of an imperial language was still a long way off in both worlds, and linguistic pluralism reigned: Darius like his successors issued inscriptions in Persian, Akkadian, and Elamite, whereas Aramaic, which is entirely unrelated to Persian, served as an important language of state. Ashoka employed a demotic register of Middle Indian, which he had no more interest in promoting as an imperial literary idiom than Darius had in the case of Old Persian. Cultural homogeneity, at least in communication, appears to have been a matter of equal indifference to both.

Measured by our three other criteria, however, Ashoka's empire radically modified the received Achaemenid model. First, in terms of territoriality, the Persians had sought power as far as power could be sought; theoretically there was no limit to empire. For Ashoka, power may have been conceived of as "extending to the horizons," as for all subsequent Indian overlords, but that was the horizon of subcontinental space. The apparent paradox of such limited universality is one of several that marked Indian empire. Second, governance for the Achaemenids was characterized by administrative uniformity regulated everywhere by Persian aristocrats, the "dominant ethno-class."[13] And thus it is unsurprising that ancestry and ethnicity were repeatedly celebrated by the Achaemenids in their royal documents. For Maurya India, except perhaps in core areas where members of the imperial family ruled, the political order cannot be characterized as an ethnically restricted and bureaucratically homogeneous patrimonial state. Ashoka never once mentions his lineage, and ethnicity as a political value finds no place in his conceptual scheme. A political ideal of encouraging local rule—of "uprooting" but then "restoring" local power elites—that would be reaffirmed for centuries to come was likely already in play. The element of violence in the exercise of political power in early India should not be minimized, to be sure. But where else in the ancient world, or in the modern world for that matter, has any agent of state violence ever declared in public the remorse Ashoka expressed over the "one hundred and fifty thousand persons carried away captive, the one hundred thousand slain, the many times that number who died," in a record issued expressly to dissuade his sons and great-grandsons from ever "thinking of new conquest" by arms? Our last diagnostic reveals equally great divergence. The Achaemenids regarded their vast empire as having come to them thanks to the once narrowly tribal and now transcendent deity, Ahuramazda, the "Wise Lord." "By the grace of Ahuramazda am I king," Darius proclaimed. "Ahuramazda has granted me the kingdom." The assumption that a religious plan—promoting a universalist Buddhism—underpinned Ashoka's quasi-universal empire has rightly been discarded in contemporary scholarship, and the new consensus emphasizes the political-moral over the religious (let alone sectarian) nature of the doctrine of *dhamma* (*dharma*). Even had Ashoka been following a more strictly religious plan, he betrayed no sense whatever of having divine guidance in doing so.

Subsequent inheritors of the model first elaborated by the Achaemenids were Rome of the Principate and the polity of the imperial Guptas. Again, important parallels testify to the model's reality, and important variations to its adaptability. When in 14 C.E. Divine Augustus proclaimed his "achievements," "by which he brought the circle of the lands under the empire of the Roman people"—this from his last testament carved on his Tiber-side tomb—he was imitating Alexander (and ultimately Darius), just as it was in imitation of Ashoka (and in the last instance Darius) that around 375 C.E. Samudragupta, "the great king of kings . . . who has no adversary equal to him on earth, whose fame is tasted by the waters of the four oceans," proclaimed his conquests on a victory pillar set up on the banks of the

Ganges. The novel element in both cases is not where or what they spoke but how they spoke.

The imperial Romans and the Guptas alike fostered a new literary language, for the former, one invented at the end of the First Punic War (240 B.C.E.) when Rome achieved hegemony in the western Mediterranean; for the latter, one invented around the beginning of the Common Era, with stimulus from the courts of the Indo-Scythians and Kushanas, new power seekers who had immigrated into the subcontinent from west and central Asia. From that point on, cultural homogeneity in terms of literary language would become a core practice of empire—indeed, empire's *compañera,* as the first Castilian grammarian Nebrija famously put it to Queen Isabella in 1492—and a key mechanism of transculturation. But all this unfolded in completely different ways in the two worlds. Compulsion and reductivism, or so I have argued, characterized the spread of Latinity (if more as imperial process than policy), whereas volition and pluralism can be seen in the spread of Sanskrit culture. In the western empire, the local languages of continental Europe and North Africa, from Celtic to Punic, attained no literary existence and eventually perished. When in the first century Pliny wrote that Italy was "chosen by the power of the gods . . . to gather together the scattered realms . . . [and] unite the discordant wild tongues of so many peoples into a common speech so they might understand each other, and to give civilization [*humanitas*] to mankind, in short to become the homeland of every people in the entire world," he was describing a cultural-political project that would have been incomprehensible to his contemporaries in India. Sanskrit was voluntarily cultivated across southern Asia, and it was through the mediation of Sanskrit that local languages from the Deccan to Java first achieved literacy, eventually to emerge as cultural-political competitors of Sanskrit as the age of empire waned with the start of the "vernacular millennium" around 1000 C.E.[14]

The two empire forms also differed profoundly according to our other analytic criteria. Territorially, the Guptas represented themselves as universal sovereigns— they achieved a "conquest of all the earth," after all—but with two important qualifications. Like Ashoka's, theirs was a finite universalism, which recognized Bharata Varsha, "the Land of Bharata" (a new conceptual space developed in the early centuries C.E.) as constituting the limits within which political power made sense: "It is only in the Land of Bharata that the logic of legitimate force [*dandaniti*] pertains," says a medieval Sanskrit text on statecraft, adding, "and this logic is something to be studied by Indian people of all four social orders in the present and the future as it was in the past."[15] Yet, this geobody was not *emplaced,* so to speak, but could be and was moved all across southern Asia as far as Champa in today's south Vietnam: holy

Ganges Rivers, golden Mount Merus, and legendary Fields of the Kurus (where the *Bhagavad Gita* is set) began to appear everywhere (including elsewhere in India itself). People in tenth-century Angkor or Java could see themselves as living, not in some overseas extension of India, but inside "an Indian world."[16] The impulse here was captured perfectly by Xuanzang, the Chinese Buddhist pilgrim who visited India in the seventh century: "People of distant places with diverse customs generally designate the land that they admire as 'India.'" By contrast, in Roman imperial space a single *urbs* (city) lay at the heart of the *orbis terrarum* (circle of lands), with a *limes*, or frontier (often a very hard, walled, frontier) around its edges. In governance, the Guptas continued the old pattern noted earlier of incorporation of local elites; Samudragupta "favored all the kings . . . by releasing them after capture," in order to rule their own domains in subservience to him. Roman imperial governance meant bureaucrats and a military apparatus spread over endless territory, the selective award of citizenship as a device of elite cooptation, the ubiquity and homogeneity of Roman law. Indeed, this last component serves as a synecdoche of *imperium* and offers another strong contrast with precolonial *rajya* of South and Southeast Asia, where law remained largely local, as no doubt did actual rule.

A last distinction, and the most arresting when measured against orientalist presuppositions, pertains to religion. In early India, kings may have been endowed with a numinous aura, embodying as they did portions of the deity, according to conventional political theology. But they never became the center of divine cults as such; on the contrary, they were often celebrated as the most devout worshippers (like Samudragupta himself, *paramo bhagavatah,* the "great devotee of Vishnu"). The supreme deity, for its part, was hardly interested in political outcomes at all—it never directly granted heavenly mandates or awarded parcels of land like celestial real-estate agents elsewhere—and most certainly was never identified with the god of a political ethnic group. In fact, before the early modern period, peoples in South Asia cannot even be said to have formed ethnic groups at all, as modern social science understands these and with which the history of Europe abounds: communities of common descent with shared memories and horizontal solidarities. It's therefore unsurprising that no Indian ruler or people claimed anywhere at any time that God had chosen them or given them a land or provided them guidance or enabled them to conquer other peoples or lands. In the Roman thought world, belief in the providential nature of the *imperium,* as something universal and willed by the gods, is widely attested at least from the end of the third century B.C.E. When on the eve of the birth of the Principate Cicero wrote that it was "by the will of the gods that we have overcome all peoples and nations," he was expressing an idea long resonant in the minds of Romans—and one that again would have been unintelligible to contemporary political thinkers in India. It also found its complement in the imperial cult of the divine emperor.[17]

Empire makers in post-Gupta India and in post-Roman Europe would adopt many features of these two different imperial styles. Other contributors to this book describe in their own ways how in respect to territoriality, governance, communication, and religion, the Christian empires down to the modern period were often characterized by universalism, centralization, homogeneity, and singularity. In India, patterns set by the Maurya and Guptas continued to be reproduced by later rulers, if only in aspiration and imagination as the actualization of empire became less frequent. Governance over the Indian geobody, for example, could increasingly be asserted by multiple overlords simultaneously; all of them were *chakravartis*, those who "turn the wheel" of universal power over the world. This world would continue to be thought of as the "imperial field" (*chakravarti-kshetra*)—even in the absence of a unified empire—that was coterminus with the "Land of Bharata." Such multiple universal polities, no less than the multiple Indias mentioned earlier, were not mutually exclusive nor was their coexistence seen as illogical or unreal. Indian political life simply allowed for a different logic and alternative reality.

A thousand years later, many of these political values found their final reembodiment in the last imperial polities of precolonial India, the Vijayanagara *rajya* (c. 1336–1565) and the Mughal *saltanat* (c. 1526–1858). With respect to visions of territoriality and modes of governance this meant the limited universalism and layered sovereignty of ancient stamp. With respect to culture and communication Vijayanagara (for the most part ruled by Kannada- or Tulu-speaking kings) evinced a pluralism that acknowledged the realities of the new vernacularization of South Asia, publishing records in all the southern regional languages (as well as occasionally in the old imperial language of Sanskrit) and patronizing literature in all these idioms. Among the Mughals, a comparable nonethnic cosmopolitanism prevailed: as language of court and state the Mughals adopted Persian, which was foreign to them (they were originally speakers of Chaghatay Turkish). With respect to religion Vijayanagara observed a policy of support for all spiritual orders, Shaiva, Vaishnava, and Jaina, and certainly tolerated Islam as well (permitting a mosque to be built in the core of the capital city). The Mughals too maintained the careful "social balance" of a multiculturalism *avant la lettre,* such that in 1600 Badayuni, a Mughal court historian, could describe India as a place where "no one interferes with another's business, so that every one can do just as he pleases." This was not to last, however. When a century later the anomalous attempt was made to absolutize this older model—to the extent that Aurangzeb could call the "main pillar of government" the collecting of information about its people—the empire began to crumble.[18]

III

It would be going too far to reduce all imperial practice in the West to the territorial universalism, dynamic centralism, compulsory culture, ethnocentricity, and certitude of divine superintendence inherited from Rome and, in part, ultimately from Persepolis. As they continually learned lessons from the past, European empires oscillated between remaking the world in one image and attempting to conserve difference under an imperial umbrella. And various mechanisms were developed, dual monarchy, indirect rule, and so on, which were meant to address the general imperial problem of how to rule large and differentiated dominions at acceptable cost with acceptable levels of conflict.[19] Nonetheless, a set of convictions continued to be shared across many imperial formations: that power had to be extended as far as power could be extended; that metropolitan culture was in the end the single sustainable culture; that differences in language, law, and belief could and often should be planed away; that given peoples had political destinies as imperial peoples; and that a universal god mandated the extension of their empire and was to be worshipped everywhere their empire went. With their program of *colonisation de l'imaginaire* in Mexico and the conviction embodied in the dynastic device of their founder, the Holy Roman emperor Frederick III (AEIOU, *Austria Est Imperare Orbi Universo,* that is, "Everything on earth is subject to Austria"), the Habsburgs no less than their near contemporaries the Mughals were learning lessons from the past—if from a very different past.[20]

The new American empire no doubt differs too, and dramatically, not only from the Roman prototype, but even from Rome's more recent Spanish or French or British descendents, first and foremost in respect to its mode of actual dominion. Various equivocations represent this as consensual, informal, or virtual empire, or empire by invitation, though it seems rather more coercive, formal, actual, and gate-crashing given that the United States has troops stationed in more than 140 countries to ensure that its 5 percent of the world's population may continue to consume 30 percent of the world's resources.[21] We're also told that republics don't make good empires, and that American imperial ambitions have always been constrained by American isolationism.[22] Yet again, in other respects, continuities link the American empire form with past imperial practices. In its drive to monopolize authority it has eviscerated many other forms of supranational global power; witness the almost complete abasement of the UN over the Iraq war. Manifestations of America's assertive universalism in terms of political ideology, culture, and religion are ready to hand. The *National Security Strategy of the United States of America* (2002) acknowledges only one "sustainable model for national success: freedom, democracy, and free enterprise" to now exist in the world (though bringing "the hope of democracy, development, free markets, and free trade to every corner of the world" will occur only as permitted by "the union of our values and our national interests"). This state discourse is intertwined with a political theology of apocalyptic Christianity, where history is the unfolding of a divine process ("the loving god behind all of life and all of history" as the 2003 State of the Union address puts it)—a theology pervasive in American life and that, especially in the form of Christian Zionism, it would be unwise to view as mere opportunism on the part of the governing elite.[23] And complexly intertwined, too, with more diffuse processes of cultural homogenization.[24]

As the United States becomes gradually more at ease with such continuities and settles into the lethal embrace of empire, the convictions of old-style imperial practice increasingly shape policy recommendations. With respect to governance, only one political path is open to the non-West, toward U.S.-style liberal democracy, imposed from outside and top-down, no matter what the local costs. "It will take time to educate and train a modernizing and liberal elite," reads a recent Hoover Institution publication on Iraq. "Eventually, patronage through tribe and kin will have to be stamped out in favor of an educational and bureaucratic meritocracy."[25] It's an old logic of western empire: truly successful dominion lies not in exercising direct coercive power over them as in turning them into us: Roman citizens, Christians, constitutional parliamentarians.

The model for imitation much recommended these days to U.S. policy makers is the British Empire in India. (The British colonialists themselves, especially after the 1857 Rebellion, had learned how to be imperial by studying Rome, a referent ubiquitous in British discourse of the Victorian era.).[26] The truly great British achievement to be emulated by America, we're now being told, lies in the political sphere: the implantation of parliamentary democracy. "Few scholars dare acknowledge"— again the Hoover publication speaks—"that, for all the problems, British rule did in fact make India's modern democracy possible. What are we to make of the fact that one of the key British rationalizations for empire turned out, in large measure, to be true?"

Here is not the place, nor have I the competence, to analyze the history of democracy in India; but some assumptions in the above account may be questioned. For one, we cannot be certain that British imperialism was the necessary precondition for the birth of Indian democracy, and that it could never have arisen autonomously. Leave aside the fallacy that post hoc must be propter hoc, and the disregarding of the role of the nationalist movement in India and its search for common rules.[27] Inconvenient enough is the corollary of this logic: that British imperialism would have to be credited as well with creating the military dictatorships of Pakistan and Burma, and the state of continuous nationalist war in the region since 1947. A second unstated assumption is that actually existing Indian democracy is in fact good for India. We can't of course know whether it's an improvement over forms of governance that might have developed out of traditions of Indian statecraft and polity of the sort mentioned above. But we do know that western-style democracy has been no unalloyed benefit. It has been inseparable from violence, and it has brought to power—perhaps even created—the BJP (Indian People's Party), which many observers feel justified in regarding as a Hindu Falange.[28] Yet perhaps the most astonishing, even imperial, myopia here lies in the belief that the people of Iraq or anywhere else should aspire to a national politics of the sort now on offer in the United States, which produced an illegitimate and mendacious presidency capable of waging an illegal and immoral war.

Whether the most recent episode of American imperialism is following some necessary logic, continuing a longer-term historical pattern (as several chapters in this book argue forcefully), or is instead the responsibility of a particularly reckless and bizarre ruling clique, I won't hazard to guess; scholars of empire and imperialism, like scholars of history generally, are always debating structure versus agency.[29] What is clear is that the new empire poses a grave threat to world peace and must be resisted everywhere it manifests itself: in its attempt to weaken all autonomous institutions (while creating various submissive groupings like the vaguely evangelical "coalition of the willing"); to raise ever higher its own *limes* to keep out the new barbarians, transnational migrants; to generate ever more constrictive forms of universalization authorizing only preapproved forms of power and culture.

At the same time, resistance to empire does not necessarily entail accepting the dichotomous thinking that appeals to the sovereignty of the nation-state, though many who offer multinational alternatives to empire seem strangely unmoved by nationalism's demonstrated menace. The nation-state is as much a historical fossil as coercive empire. Viewed from the long history of empire, its life has been, not only nasty and brutish and short, but entirely anomalous.

For postnationalists there seems to be no other alternative than a new cosmopolitan order of culture-power. There has been much talk of this ideal recently, indeed of some new kind of empire replacing the failed empires of old. Discussion has not always been marked by a satisfactory appraisal of where we are now and how we get from here to there.[30] Yet some elements of the current visions can provide bearings on a compass for where we might head. After all, we need to learn not just negative lessons, about the inevitability of resistance to empire, for example, but positive lessons for a cosmopolitan politics. Part of what I always find lacking here are grounds for hope of the sort that utopia derives from once-existent *topoi*, those real places and real practices of the past that show how malleable are the supposed iron laws—ethnicity, "linguism," nationhood, and the like—of culture and power. What if we could assure ourselves that there once were people who inhabited a conceptual universe not so dissimilar from cosmopolis, however paradoxical modernity has made such a habitation seem? A universe of imperial centers without peripheries, because the center could be everywhere in general and nowhere in particular; of peoples without ethnicities—a real "multitude" instead of ethnicized and nationalized subjects—whose movements were never stopped by frontiers; of a universalism that knew its limits and did not stand in fatal contradiction with either cultural or political particularisms?

Of course empire is not just a matter of ideas about space, rule, culture, or god. It's also "robbery with violence, aggravated murder on a great scale, and men going at it blind." But as Marlow goes on to say in Conrad's classic text, "The conquest of the earth, which mostly means the taking it away from those who have a different complexion or slightly flatter noses than ourselves, is not a pretty thing when you look into it too much. What redeems it is the idea only. An idea at the back of it; not a sentimental pretence but an idea; and an unselfish belief in the idea—something you can set up, and bow down before, and offer a sacrifice to."[31] The history of empire in the West has usually been a history of imitating certain of these supposedly redeeming ideas, of territorial totality, governmental centralization, cultural uniformity, and the providence of a political god. Yet other models have existed, like the Sanskritic cosmopolitanism of Bharata Varsha and the Islamic cosmopolitanism of Al-Hind, which suggest however faintly some alternatives. These are no doubt anomalies—like India itself, "the strangest of all possible anomalies," in Macaulay's unintentional tribute. But anomalies are not fantasies, and these can be shown to have been lived realities in the past of the nonmodern non-West. And this new past might point toward the possibility of a new future, a kind of Empire that might finally end the numbingly repeated imitations of empire.

11. CHINA'S AGRARIAN EMPIRE: A DIFFERENT KIND OF EMPIRE, A DIFFERENT KIND OF LESSON*

R. BIN WONG

The Chinese empire has figured modestly, if at all, in recent comparisons of empires being made within academia or the more public pronouncements about "empire" and U.S. foreign policy. At first glance this seems a bit strange since no part of the world has had more experience with empire than China. On closer examination, however, it becomes clear that the reconstitution of empire in East Asia from Roman times, through the period of Mongol domination, and past the era of Ottoman grandeur makes the case of Chinese empire a difficult one to locate comparatively. To be sure, those of us who have spent most of our time studying the Chinese past haven't been all that helpful. When we venture out of our periods of expertise we usually move into other times in Chinese history or to other areas in East Asia and occasionally in Europe, almost never to other empires. For both specialist and generalist alike, the Chinese empire's ill-fitting presence in a taxonomy of empires can be glimpsed by noting its failure to obey the standard life course options of empire.

The Chinese empire neither divided into separate sovereign states in the manner of an Austro-Hungarian or Ottoman empire, nor did it set free what some regard as its colonies in the manner typical of both European and the Japanese empires. Nor was the Chinese empire part of the pattern of imitation that Sheldon Pollock locates for many other Eurasian empires such as Rome and Persia. This is not to say that Chinese political practices were not influenced by outside factors. The empire's relationship to steppe peoples repeatedly affected its political developments; the military power of forces from the steppes contributed to the destruction of some dynasties and at least as importantly led crucial reunification efforts.[1] More pacific influences also mattered deeply. The movement and penetration of Buddhism into Chinese society at elite and popular levels has left lasting imprints on Chinese culture and politics. Yet, even if the Chinese agrarian empire was hardly closed and isolated as various westerners from the Enlightenment forward have imagined, the Chinese imperial experience does not meet most of our expectations about empires more generally; it fits comfortably neither in the land-based empires of Eurasia nor the maritime empires of European powers. While all of those empires have now left the world historical stage, the Chinese empire in some senses at least still exists, transformed into a territorial state that since the early nineteenth century has grappled with political challenges increasingly different from those that it had faced over the previous two millennia. Its contemporary political structure, which includes "autonomous regions" subject to different governance principles and procedures than those applied to most of the country, strike many observers as odd, yet it is certainly part of the legacy of an agrarian empire reformulated as a national state. But of interest in this volume is not primarily how China became the only agrarian empire to be largely reconstituted as a territorial state that has survived into the twenty-first century. Instead, we focus in this volume on lessons of empire more generally. Here, the Chinese empire offers lessons about how leaders of an empire succeeded in extending rule over many millions of people and much territory for a very long time. I will suggest that the difficulties of sustaining agrarian empire in Chinese history and the kinds of solutions, or at least the general sensibilities behind them, which met those challenges, offer a useful perspective on some factors affecting how durable American power will prove to be in the coming decades.

FROM AGRARIAN EMPIRE TO NATIONAL STATE

Earlier generations of historians were routinely impressed by the continuity of China's imperial political system. More recent scholarship has chipped away at that solid consensus, at an extreme by arguing that the term *China* is a modern invention and didn't exist historically. This vantage point encourages us to realize that the agrarian empire was not simply composed of a large and unchanging government ruling a single and homogenous people over more than two millennia. But by focusing exclusively on either temporal discontinuities or spatial variations in the extent of empire, we can easily miss the distinctiveness of a Chinese political tradition that built up a set of political texts and formulated a range of policies that collectively defined strategies of good government for a sizable part of Eurasia. The ideas and institutions of this empire were neither constant over time nor uniform through space, but they did enable a changing repertoire of visions and actions through which political leaders reconstituted and reproduced empire over many centuries. These principles and institutions also served as models for fourteenth-century Koreans, fifteenth-century Vietnamese, the Manchus preceding their mid-seventeenth-century conquest of the Ming empire, and the eighteenth-century

Ryūkyū kingdom which was incorporated under Japan in the late nineteenth century as Okinawa prefecture.[2]

The existence of a rich repertoire of political ideas and institutional forms doesn't mean, of course, that the leaders within each, let alone across all, Chinese dynasties made the same choices or achieved the same results. In general there was a trend toward increasing size and complexity of the bureaucracy with an oscillation of centralizing and decentralizing tendencies over the two millennia of imperial history. The territorial extent of empire also varied. Moments of dynastic collapse in the third and tenth centuries were followed by protracted periods of divided rule. Indeed, over a period of more than three centuries following the collapse of the Tang dynasty during the first decade of the tenth century, there appeared a set of states governing the former territories of the Tang dynasty that formed a multistate system of sorts. Some of these states, like Korea, Vietnam, and the Ryūkyū kingdom in later centuries, adopted some political principles and practices of the agrarian empire to varying degrees. Confucian ideas and institutions could thrive outside the agrarian empire. Moreover, they were by themselves inadequate to maintain or even re-create empire after it had collapsed. It was the Mongols who, as a by-product of their march toward a vast world empire reaching far beyond the borders of any Chinese empire, defeated the leaders of regimes forming a multistate system. The destruction of these competitors and the subsequent withdrawal of the Mongols from China created the opportunity for military leaders within China to reconsolidate rule along some of the spatial dimensions of earlier Chinese dynasties.

The Chinese agrarian empire also persisted because it was not weakened from within by the emergence of regional power holders who built up their resource bases from an expanding commercial economy. In many parts of Eurasia the expansion of markets and the creation of new concentrations of commercial wealth transformed politics significantly. In both Europe and Japan, rich merchants formed groups who exercised a variety of influences over political authorities initially at the municipal level and later, as territorial states were built, at the level of central governments. In the Ottoman Empire, by way of contrast, commercial expansions included the formation of merchant elites who promoted regional bases of power. In China, merchant groups also formed along with long-distance trade and increased market activity after 1500. Key features of the economic expansion broadly resembled those in Europe, but without similar political consequences. The political economy of agrarian empire absorbed commercial expansion without allowing, let alone promoting, increased political power for merchants. In part, the lack of political power follows from the government's decision in the late fourteenth century to tax lightly and rely largely on agrarian rather than commercial revenues, thereby avoiding the need to negotiate frequently with merchants to meet state fiscal needs. The ideal of limited extraction was not always pursued faithfully, but merchants certainly did not develop the capacities to negotiate with officials and influence political structures and decision making as their counterparts did in many other settings.[3]

There are still other reasons why an imperial political form continued to be viable in China for a much longer period of time than elsewhere in the world. By the sixteenth century, the Chinese state had a well-established bureaucratic system staffed by individuals, most of whom had passed civil-service examinations in order to qualify for government posts. Rules prohibited an official from serving in his natal province and efforts were made to limit the spread of informal networks of official influence that would hamper the effectiveness of administrative oversight. Official performance was routinely evaluated for reward and punishment; bureaucratic career mobility depended on those evaluations as officials were rotated frequently to mitigate opportunities for them to form relationships from which they would personally and illicitly profit if immorally inclined. Officials did, however, seek to protect the material interests of their jurisdictions, aiming in particular to promote the security of peasant livelihoods. This meant, especially in the eighteenth century, official efforts to transfer resources to poorer frontier regions inhabited by both Han Chinese and different minority peoples in order to help them develop economic bases more similar to those of more prosperous interior areas. While not able to raise peripheries to the same standards of living as those enjoyed in ecologically and geographically more favored places, political priorities on promoting the material capacities of poorer areas made the idea of exploiting the resources of these areas for the benefit of wealthier core areas very difficult to conceive.

Direct bureaucratic rule over a vast agrarian empire was a remarkable political achievement to sustain for many centuries, but it was also, by today's standards, a very limited one. The vertically integrated civilian bureaucracy responsible for the day-to-day governing of society was in absolute terms the world's largest, but given the vast territorial size of the empire and its large population, more than 1,300 county-level units and some 250–300 million people in the second half of the eighteenth century, officials lacked a widespread bureaucratic capacity to penetrate routinely below the county level in order to do much that affected people's daily lives beyond collecting taxes and maintaining social order. In the most densely populated and commercially developed areas such abilities did emerge in the eighteenth and nineteenth centuries, but did not become the general norm throughout the empire. Officials did routinely hire staffs to help them with their duties and also worked with local elites to create institutions of local order such as granaries and schools; they expected these elites to contribute funds to repair temples, roads, and bridges and to help organize and manage tasks like dredging of river beds and reinforcing water dikes. They could expect this kind of help because local people with wealth, whether from land or commerce, were often part of families in which education was taken seriously and they or members of their families had educations that exposed them to the same kinds of Confucian precepts that animated official approaches to rule as strategies to sustain local social order. As a result, from 1500 to 1900, the agrarian empire was ruled by a combination of direct and indirect forms of rule in which the indirect and informal were clearly subordinated to the direct and formal.[4]

Cultural norms mattered more generally. Not only was there an elite culture shared by officials and locally important people across the Han parts of the empire with well over 90 percent of the total population, but there was also a common set of ideas that officials and elites jointly promoted among the general population. These Confucian ideas were often joined to particular social practices, such as those associated with weddings and funerals, as well as more general social relationships, such as those among various family members and between common people and their superiors. Officials and members of the local elite both promoted these ideas in a variety of ways. In the eighteenth century, a lecture system was implemented across the empire with regular lectures delivered by either officials or elites on particular social or ethical themes, a kind of sermon without a pulpit or religious institutional forms more generally. The promotion of Confucian-inspired practices to form the core of proper behavior was supplemented by more direct government engagement with popular forms of religious belief and practice.

Chinese worshipped at temples a variety of deities with Buddhist and Taoist origins. Deities sometimes had locally specific functions, like a deity believed to watch over sailors, while others were more generally associated with female fertility, material prosperity, and the like. The government beginning in the tenth and eleventh centuries engaged in a sophisticated kind of regulation of religious devotion. Officials maintained a list of deities, the worship of which they deemed acceptable and a far smaller list of deities that at times they worried about. The latter list was composed of those deities associated with millenarian visions that charismatic religious leaders could use to mobilize armies of true believers dedicated to overcoming the present world to prepare for a new and better future. Failing to make either list of deities were any number that occupied a kind of gray area of being neither officially endorsed nor proscribed. Thus, in practice officials allowed a considerable variety of popular religious practices as they expanded the list of officially recognized deities to include ones that people had found particularly efficacious.[5]

Several features of the late imperial Chinese state's approach to religious practice and popular culture more generally bear highlighting for what they tell us about the nature of imperial rule. First, officials care about what people believe and worship because certain practices are definitely associated with promoting social order and others are as strongly identified with threatening social order; at the same time many religious practices are simply tolerated in practice even if not acknowledged in principle. Second, the Confucian ideas and practices promoted politically among the common people by officials and elites as a means to ensure social order are tied to a larger set of Confucian cultural beliefs that officials and elites share; there is not, in other words, the same kind of dramatic divide between local cultures and the more cosmopolitan aristocratic culture that is often drawn for early modern Europe. Third, considerable cultural diversity lies outside the Confucian template of belief and practice without forming distinctive and competing clusters of belief; indeed, a syncretism between ideas having initially Confucian, Buddhist, and Taoist origins created varied compounds at both the elite and popular levels of culture from the fourteenth century forward.

The Manchus who proclaimed their Qing dynasty in 1644 pursued strategies of rule over the vast majority of the empire's population that they learned from earlier Chinese dynasties. They also learned from previous inner Asian dynasties in China to make efforts to sustain themselves as a distinct political elite, and they succeeded through an institutional separation of themselves from the larger population. At the same time they increasingly spoke Chinese, as they shared some foods and many cultural practices with the Han Chinese majority. The Manchu emperors specifically were tutored in the Confucian classics and expressed, especially in the eighteenth century, commitments to a Confucian agenda for achieving domestic social order through intensive efforts to promote social welfare and Confucian beliefs and rituals, efforts more active indeed than those of their Ming dynasty predecessors.[6] In addition they added new inner Asian domains over which the previous dynasty had no claim.[7] In these regions there was little or no effort to promote the cultural or material agenda used for most of the empire's population. The Manchu emperors engaged Mongols, Tibetans, and others on the steppe through a political and religious language of authority and faith that drew upon symbols and imagery harkening back several centuries to the Jurchens and Mongols, as well as Tibetan Buddhist beliefs shared by many subject to Qing rule who lived beyond the pale of Confucian acculturation. These areas were one of two kinds of areas in which the states following the Qing dynasty's collapse in 1911 faced particular challenges. The other problematic areas were those that had fallen under some other power's nineteenth- and twentieth-century colonial rule; these have had varied postcolonial experiences. Hong Kong and Macau have moved from colonial status under a European power to incorporation within the People's Republic. Taiwan, which was governed for fifty years as a Japanese colony has not been made part of the People's Republic, in large measure (and with admittedly some simplification) because the U.S. government decided in late June 1950 to move its Seventh Fleet into the waters separating the

Nationalists fleeing the mainland from Communist pursuit. This naval action was only one element of a far larger set of actions taken by the U.S. government after 1945 to assert American power in East Asia that include the occupation of Japan and the division of Korea. From the vantage point of the longer-term transformation of what had been the Chinese agrarian empire, the inclusion or exclusion of areas that had once been part of the empire have depended on the actions of other powers on its peripheries. These relations were far different from those within which most other agrarian empires had been enmeshed at an earlier time when they divided into separate states, the Chinese case resembling partially the Russian situation. The combined comparison of the roles of the domestic and foreign relations of different agrarian empires may prove a way to bring the Chinese case more readily into a taxonomy of empires.

A brief examination of the inner Asian areas of the Qing empire that often became troubling to postimperial governments suggests a kind of artificiality to the distinction of "domestic" and "foreign," certainly historically and possibly for more recent times as well. These areas were those parts of the Qing empire where the cultural components of political integration had been lacking. The Manchu rulers of the Qing dynasty had actively promoted a Confucian agenda of rule across the sedentary portions of their empire but relied upon other strategies among the peoples of inner Asia over whom they also established authority relations. Basic to the ritual and symbolic legitimacy the Manchus claimed among many of their subjects across inner Asia was their shared faith in Tibetan Buddhism and the Manchu emperor's patronage of the Dalai Lama. The Manchus built upon relations between earlier Tibetan Buddhist religious orders and the Mongols who ruled China between the mid-thirteenth and mid-fourteenth centuries. The Mongol patronage of a particular sect helped to secure its power within Tibet as the Mongol rulers received from this sect recognition as universal Buddhist rulers. The Manchus gained a similar kind of legitimacy among inner Asian peoples for their support of the Dalai Lama. Were these relations with Tibetans, Mongolians, and Uighurs, to name some of the most prominent non-Han groups of inner Asia, "domestic" or "foreign" for the Qing empire? They were not managed through the same bureaucracy that governed the vast majority of the empire's population. Nor were they handled through the same ministry responsible for diplomatic relations with clearly foreign regimes, including those in Korea, Vietnam, and the Ryūkyū kingdom. The issue of whether Tibet was part of the Qing empire or not in terms of a "domestic/foreign" binary only became pressing when other imperial powers began seeking residence and trading privileges with the area in the late nineteenth century.

When the British and Russian empires sought relations with Tibet in the late nineteenth and early twentieth centuries, the status of the Dalai Lama's government became increasingly ambiguous. Would the British make an agreement subordinating Tibet in a manner similar to what they had already done in Nepal, would the Russians instead gain a greater presence, would Tibetans themselves forge an alliance with Mongol groups to resist outside pressures more effectively, or would the Qing government make persuasive before a new set of political actors in the region their prior relationship as one of sovereign authority? None of those possibilities in fact materialized. Instead Tibet, without any regional allies, asserted its independence at the same time as the Republic of China claimed Tibet. The Republic of China after 1912 believed itself to be the ruling successor to the territories previously governed by the Qing dynasty. With governance becoming increasingly defined by criteria that accorded with western ideas about sovereignty, the first postimperial Chinese regimes made claims to sovereignty without any capacity to enforce them. But the claims mattered for they formed a key part of the political context for later Communist military offensives to incorporate Tibet into the People's Republic as an "autonomous region."

The pressure of foreign relations with western powers also reconfigured the diplomatic logic, rituals, and institutions of Chinese relations with other parts of East Asia by the time that Tibet had developed an ambiguous status in the late nineteenth century. In the case of Korea, which had for centuries maintained a tributary relationship with the agrarian empire, this relationship was redeployed to fend off Japanese political pressures in the 1870s and 1880s as the Qing government sought to sign diplomatic treaties between Korea and European powers in the hopes of creating some political defense against increasing Japanese encroachment. These efforts proved ineffective when several years later the Japanese fought the Qing military in Korea and ended up taking over the country as a colony in the early twentieth century. Well before that process had been completed, the Qing government had learned that its logic of tributary relations did not square well with the western dichotomy of domestic and foreign when it sought to persuade Robert Hart, the British official in charge of the Imperial Maritime Customs Administration (a Sino-foreign bureaucracy collecting foreign-trade taxes on behalf of the Qing state at low rates congenial to merchants), that the administration should also collect taxes in Korea because that country was part of the Qing tributary system. Hart wanted to know if Korea was part of the Qing empire or if it was a separate country—only if it were part of the empire's domestic territory did extending the administration seem appropriate; otherwise a separate administration would have to be established.

Beyond the Qing empire the pressure of western expansion on diplomatic relations in East Asia can be seen in the transformation of the Ryūkyū kingdom from a tributary state of both the Qing empire and the Tokugawa shogunate into Okinawa prefecture under the Meiji state. British interest in establishing a presence at a port in the Ryūkyū kingdom was followed by American queries that were part of Commodore Perry's "opening" of Japan regarding the status of the Ryūkyūs; the Japanese assured the Americans that these islands were most definitely part of Japan, that the government collected taxes and allowed trade with the Qing empire to take place from the area.[8] The need to define political relations with areas on a state's peripheries in terms understood by western powers was basic to the late-nineteenth-century creation of domestic rule and foreign relations in East Asian politics.

The ability of western powers to impose through military superiority their diplomatic conventions of international relations in the nineteenth century forced the Qing empire and other Asian governments that remained independent to develop abilities to negotiate according to the concepts and sensibilities advocated by Europeans and Americans. These efforts to learn a new discourse of foreign relations became joined to efforts at forging new institutions to transform governments more generally toward political forms developed in the West. For the first time in their histories, Chinese, Japanese, and Korean leaders had to learn to compete politically with governments from beyond the East Asian region who possessed capacities for generating wealth and power beyond any they had ever seen. With varying degrees of success, East Asian governments adopted western ideas and institutions. These translation exercises have been the conventional focus of much study of East Asian politics in the late nineteenth century. While studies devoted to such topics tell us much about what was "new" in the period, they usually fail to explain how older concerns and practices either persisted or became transformed. In the Chinese case such concerns included how to rule territories that the Manchus had brought under their empire. While the governments that immediately succeeded the Qing dynasty lacked the institutionalized capacities to rule the inner Asian portions of the former Qing empire, they quickly took up the language of "nation" and "sovereignty" to claim rhetorically these territories. Several decades later, the Communists would proclaim in the mid-twentieth century their rule over most of the inner Asian dominions of the Qing empire using the language of territorial sovereignty and a national state ruling several nationalities. Yet, the actual working relationships between the central government and these former imperial peripheries were not made institutionally uniform with those defined for the rest of the country.

The presence of the "autonomous region" nomenclature today in the People's Republic affirms the persistence of political relationships in China that don't fit the standard mold of domestic policies despite clear claims of sovereignty being expressed by the Chinese state and in large measure affirmed by foreign governments, if not all foreigners more generally. China is certainly not unique in having institutional variations to incorporate anomalous areas. Here and elsewhere, we can look to the history of how national states were constructed to understand features that don't fit patterns of uniform rule. The stark contrast between problems and strategies of rule in autonomous regions and those present in the rest of China suggest two different lessons about the legacy of empire in China which in turn may inform our more general concerns about empire and global political relations today.

First, today's China is the only country that in large measure occupies the territory of a previous agrarian empire. Such a postimperial outcome was by no means necessary. But the possibilities were more likely here than in other empires. Key among the enabling conditions was the late imperial state's promotion of common cultural practices that helped to create a shared social identity that persisted amidst political fragmentation. Instead of distinct groups within a former empire seeking to build their own states or struggle for autonomy from governments that succeeded imperial states, Chinese political leaders and elites mainly shared a broad belief in a Chinese nation spanning the people and territory of the former Qing empire. Competing political forces generally pursued a common goal of subordinating other social identities and political agendas to create a unified Chinese state and nation. Moreover, the kinds of state and nation envisioned and pursued first by the Nationalist government and after 1949 by the Communists drew upon traits of the late imperial system.[9] The ideal state worked through a vertically integrated bureaucracy that could command obedience when needed and elicit support and acceptance at all other times. The Communist state in particular also fused politics and culture and made Communist ideology a hegemonic discourse to replace Confucian categories. The Communists have sometimes shown more anxious concern over issues of orthodoxy than their late imperial predecessors, which likely follows at least in part from their greater capacities to monitor people's expression of beliefs. At other times, however, the Communist state has had moments of toleration for diverse cultural practices, including popular religious ones that continued beliefs linked to those common in the late empire.

Second, appeals to a culturally or racially defined nationalism based at least in part on earlier political formulations of proper cultural practices were difficult to apply to people who were never subject to the earlier appeals. For both them and for those who had lived under other states' colonial government for some period of time, distinct political institutions and different mixes of political appeals had to be blended to promote government authority. These have generally included efforts to acknowledge and accommodate local and regional interests, at least economic and material ones. In the past decade under the influence of capitalist sensibilities about the use of natural resources, this has begun to change and the exploitation of peripheries to serve the more populated interior has gathered some political momentum, but certainly through the early 1980s the poor peripheries, including Tibet and Xinjiang, as well as those areas with larger proportions of ethnic Han, received resources directed by the center to the peripheries in an effort to promote economic development. This strategy resembles the approach that late imperial Chinese governments took toward governing their peripheries and achieving empire-wide integration. Under the Manchus, eighteenth-century officials encouraged migration to frontiers, transferred resources to these regions, and sought to develop their agrarian economies. The Qing state understood the success of its imperial project depended on the prosperity of all those it ruled. Central government officials retained a belief in an ancient Chinese political maxim that the people rebel when they are harshly treated and denied the abilities to maintain basic subsistence. Of course the differences in the late imperial and post-1949 situations tend to obscure these similarities from our view, which are further occluded by the preference of many contemporary specialists to understand what the Communist state does in terms of similarities to other Communist states rather than in a historical perspective.[10]

What does this brief review of some traits of Chinese empire relevant to the survival and transformation of China as a territorial state in the twentieth century suggest we ponder when considering the usefulness of "empire" as a notion to understand global political relations today? For much of the past half millennium, when Chinese states have had the capacities to rule large stretches of territory, they have relied on a mixture of ideological appeals and recognition of material interests to anchor their authority. Coercion periodically mattered, but the durability of empire is hard to imagine without repeated acts of persuasion and negotiation along the way. In general Chinese governments have made more efforts to make clear the importance of the material interests of peripheries and relied more on shared beliefs in their cores. Over time, in China, as the rest of the world, coercive capacities for states have dramatically grown, so that the threat of force has come to occupy a far more salient place than it did in the past. Historically, China's empire like that of many other large agrarian land empires relied relatively little on brute force. But where other agrarian empires typically divided their subjects into distinct groups and often delegated authority over the groups to elites within each, the Manchus and their Han predecessors of the Ming dynasty (1368–1643) ruled the overwhelming majority of their millions of subjects under the same kind of bureaucratic administration. The priority placed on vertically integrated rule by a civil-service bureaucracy was unusual, not merely among empires but among any states before the nineteenth century and no doubt is partially responsible for the Chinese empire's longevity.

The mix of interests, beliefs, and coercion that define relations within countries and between them has always been varied and China's experiences are obviously only one part of a much larger set of possibilities. They remind us how ill fitting the model of the world's political organization in terms of sovereign national states asserting authority over their subjects while observing principles of diplomatic equality with each other has been, even in the era it was supposed to hold. In general, politically weaker places have been subject to the imposition of power over them, coercively or not, and had their interests compromised by these relations, or at least the interests of the majority of people living in such places. The world has been far too large a space across which to implement the institutions of democratic decision making and a politics in which voices are heard equally. The challenge remains of imagining and pursuing strategies to increase political participation and make people's passions and interests count in some meaningful way. The case of the Chinese empire, in particular its final half millennium, suggests to me that we might ponder the implications of a political system that sustained its rule by recognizing the material interests of its weaker and more peripheral areas at the same time as it promoted a set of beliefs that were hegemonic but open to a diversity of practices and beliefs that lay outside its template.

The strength and durability of the Chinese empire may well have depended on some recognition of its limitations and the core's interest in the material success of its peripheries. China's transformation into a territorial state and its failure to match the ideals and institutions viewed as normative for national states today obscures how the logic and dynamics of Chinese agrarian empire persisted for centuries not as a static monolith but a complex and changing system that yielded both problems and possibilities for political leaders who followed in the twentieth century. For the shared concerns of the essays in this volume, thinking about how the leaders of the Chinese empire managed to sustain a stable and open system for centuries suggests lessons that could well inform our thinking about the notion of an American empire. The leaders of agrarian empire in China achieved their successes without any of the ideas about democracy and modern political ideals so many people in the world today believe in deeply. Yet, they managed to recognize that their subjects had interests that they had to address at the same time as they sought to persuade them to accept certain beliefs and practices—such an agenda for imperial rule could be a "lesson."

To imagine an American empire somewhat similar or broadly parallel to the late imperial Chinese empire, we might look for American leaders rethinking the logic of negotiations between political actors over interests and beliefs in ways that allowed those in subordinate positions to gain greater voice and encouraged those in positions of superiority to take the measure of their limitations and promoted a rethinking of what their interests are in places geographically distant but politically central to their exercise of power. To the extent that this mind experiment strains our imaginations, we can appreciate how different the strategies of empire in Chinese history have been from the political principles and practices that are articulated and pursued in today's world.

12. IMPERIAL POWER AND ITS LIMITS: AMERICA'S COLONIAL EMPIRE IN THE EARLY TWENTIETH CENTURY[1]

JULIAN GO

When the United States first occupied Afghanistan and Iraq, more than a few commentators responded affirmatively. Their idea was that the world *needs* an American empire.[2] Some of these commentators have accordingly pointed to the British colonial empire as a model. "Afghanistan and other troubled lands," declares Max Boot, "today cry out for the enlightened foreign administration once provided by self-confident Englishmen in jodhpurs and pith helmets."[3] Others have been more skeptical of the British comparison and instead emphasize America's uniqueness. They stress America's capacity for creating a new kind of empire—an exceptional empire that bears little relationship to European empires before: "America's empire is not like empires of times past, built on colonies, conquest and the white man's burden.[. . .] The 21st century imperium is a new invention in the annals of political science, an empire lite, a global hegemony whose grace notes are free markets, human rights and democracy."[4]

The problem with these claims is that they elide America's own imperial past. The United States has long had its own empire. Beginning in the late nineteenth century, it temporarily occupied Cuba and then seized Puerto Rico from Spain as a permanent colony. It also went across to the Pacific to take Guam, the Philippines and, further still, the Islamic "Moro" provinces in the southern part of the Philippine archipelago. Around the same time, the United States took the eastern islands of Samoa. This was an empire that spanned the globe. It encompassed millions of imperial subjects. It paralleled and ideologically rivaled that of England's (do we forget that Kipling's infamous poem, "The White Man's Burden," was written for the United States after the Spanish-American War, not for Kipling's British compatriots?). And it was an empire in which the notion of an "empire lite"—an exceptional empire spreading American liberty and democracy—was first forged.

Perhaps when we consider questions of American empire today, we need not look at the British example or presume that "empire lite" is somehow novel. Perhaps we need only scrutinize America's own imperial past. Such an examination would then shed better light on America's imperial present, as well as its possible futures. It would remind us that the United States has always been an empire like any other, even as it has always fashioned its empire as exceptional. It would also reveal the multiple and often contradictory ways in which the United States has exercised its imperial power, while finally disclosing the limits which those exercises in power faced.

A NEW EMPIRE

A brief season of war has deeply changed our thought and has altered, it may be permanently, the conditions of our national life. We cannot return to the point whence we set out. The scenes, the stage itself upon which we act, are changed. We have left the continent which has hitherto been our only field of action and have gone out upon the seas . . . and we cannot live or act apart.

—WOODROW WILSON, 1898[5]

Wilson was undoubtedly prescient in his views of American power in the aftermath of the Spanish-American War of 1898. By the Treaty of Paris with Spain, the United States obtained Puerto Rico, the Philippines, and Guam as colonies, and it seized the eastern part of the Samoan islands thereafter. These acquisitions manifested a continuation of America's prior expansionist practices on the North American continent. But they also marked a novel departure for the United States.

On the one hand, long before Wilson portended America's novel imperial future, the United States had been extending its control over new territories and peoples on the western frontier. That extension served as a precedent for ruling the overseas territories and their inhabitants in several respects. When the United States Congress debated the annexation of the Philippines, for example, many legislators justified annexation by making equations between Filipinos and Native Americans.[6] When the Supreme Court declared in 1901 that the new "wards" in the overseas territories were not deserving of full citizenship, it too made reference to Native American groups. Furthermore, when American colonial authorities later talked about "civilizing" overseas colonial subjects, they conjured recent attempts at home to make Native Americans "conform to the 'white man's ways.'"[7] But in several respects, the acquisition of Puerto Rico, the Philippines, Guam, and Samoa also marked an important departure.

For this we must keep in mind that America's prior westward expansion had had at least two distinguishing features. First, it had followed the prototypical pattern of settler colonialism. Westward expansion had been prefigured or accompanied by white settlers, and the settlers in turn expropriated the land for themselves while expelling and displacing native populations. When not exterminating them, the government forced them onto reservations.[8] Second, westward expansion eventually brought the full integration of the newly settled territories into the federal system. This was premised upon the Northwest Ordinance that declared that newly ceded lands should be "settled and formed into distinct republican States, which shall then become members of the Federal Union and have the same rights of sovereignty, freedom, and independence, as the other States."[9] Thus, as the U.S. federal government had extended into territories of the western frontier, it established transitional governments designed to pave the way towards statehood. Accordingly, these territories (which included Hawaii) were known as "incorporated" territories.[10]

The annexation of Puerto Rico, Guam, the Philippines, and Samoa deviated from this overarching pattern. First, it did not involve settlement, expropriation, or the expulsion of native inhabitants. There was a notorious absence of white settlers and local populations remained in place. Justice Brown of the Supreme Court thus pointed out the difference between the new "possessions" and the contiguous territory of the west by stressing that the latter was "inhabited only by people of the same race [e.g., settlers], or by scattered bodies of native Indians," while the former contained peoples who represented "differences of race, habits, laws and customs."[11] The result was that, with the new colonies, American officials had to directly rule millions of inhabitants. The new empire in this sense was less about settler colonialism than it was about "administrative colonialism"—viz., "the establishment and maintenance, for an extended time, of rule over alien people that is separate from and subordinate to the ruling power."[12]

The related difference was that the new overseas possessions demanded novel juridical and political categories. Through a series of Supreme Court decisions in 1901, the new possessions became categorized as "unincorporated" territories. This was a new legal invention, designed to match the novelty that the overseas territories posed. Essentially it was a warrant for the United States to declare sovereignty over new territories and peoples without having to grant them equal standing. It meant that the new overseas territories were subject to the full sovereignty of the United States but, unlike incorporated territories like New Mexico or Hawaii, they would not necessarily become equal states in the Union. The question of future political status was deferred, left up to Congressional choice, and the inhabitants of the territories were not granted the full protection of the American constitution. As the popular cartoon character Mr. Dooley put it, in reaction to the Supreme Court decisions: "Th' supreme court has decided th' constitution don't folow th' flag."[13]

The novelty of the new empire was not lost on observers such as William

Willoughby, an economist turned administrator in Puerto Rico. Willoughby stressed that while U.S. expansion prior to 1898 had been marked by the "settlement by emigrants from the old territory and the consequent extension . . . of American institutions," the acquisition of Puerto Rico, Guam, Samoa, and the Philippines marked "an entirely new phase in the expansion of the United States and to a certain extent representing a direct breaking with precedent." Prior acquisitions were based on the idea that the acquired territories would eventually enter the Union, enjoying "full equality with the other States" and "possessing the same political rights and privileges." But the new acquisitions meant that

> the United States was for the first time confronted with the possibility, if not the certainty, that for an indefinite time to come the territory under its sovereignty would have to be divided into two classes having a different political status; the one constituting the United States proper and enjoying full political rights and privileges, and the other dependent territory in subordination to the former and having its form of government and the rights of its inhabitants determined for it.[14]

Simply put, by seizing Puerto Rico, Guam, the Philippines, and Samoa, the United States had become a formal overseas colonial empire just like its European counterparts.[15] "The United States," Willoughby stated bluntly, "has definitely entered the class of nations holding and governing over-seas colonial possessions."[16]

IMPERIAL VISIONS AND THE FORGING OF EXCEPTIONALISM

While the United States became an overseas colonial empire, its emergence as a new empire posed pressing issues of self-conception and national identity. What exactly was the new empire about? And what did overseas empire mean for the United States? Pro-expansionists resolved these questions with relative ease. According to Theodore Roosevelt, for example, the new empire was merely the realization of America's manifest destiny. "In the year 1898," Roosevelt declared in 1900, "the United States finished the work begun over a century before by the backwoodsman, and drove the Spaniard outright from the western world."[17] According to others, the issue was a bit more complex, but it nonetheless came down to something similar. The new empire may or may not have been an expression of America's manifest destiny, but at the very least it was a logical necessity.

This view was most strongly advanced by Bernard Moses (who later served in the Philippines) and Woodrow Wilson (then a professor at Princeton whom colonial officials often cited). Both contended that the new empire was the necessary outcome of the overwhelming forces of globalism and the reality of racial hierarchy. Moses claimed that because of "modern means of communication" and the ever-present "commercial motive," the world was becoming one. Thus, any notion that the "lesser races" could proceed through history in an autonomous way—that is, without intervention by the "superior races"—was simply "utopian." Supposedly, the "superior races" were bound to empire.[18] Wilson stated similarly that advances in technology and European political and commercial expansion had served to create a "new world order." In the new order, "no nation can live any longer to itself," and the West would necessarily dominate the East: "The East is to be opened and transformed, whether we will it or no; the standards of the West are to be imposed upon it."[19] Empire was a fact not to be wished away. Neither, then, was the fact of an emergent American empire.

This discourse is suggestive of a history that repeats itself. Just as proponents of American imperialism today argue that American empire is a necessary outcome of America's privileged power, so too did expansions after 1898 argue that America's new empire was inevitable. But the parallel between past and current discourses of empire is even more remarkable than that. For example, when proponents of America's new empire pondered what kind of empire the United States should become, they turned to the British. The idea was that the United States, land of Anglo-Saxons, should model its empire after England's. In fact, scholars such as Franklin Giddings asserted that Americans and Britons should form a joint Anglo-Saxon empire, fending off the Chinese and Slavs. He also took Kipling's urgings seriously, claiming that together Britons and North Americans should use empire to civilize the world. As members of the "Teutonic races," the United States and England were to be "coworkers in the tasks of civilization."[20] John Burgess, Giddings's colleague at Columbia, added to the chorus: "the teutonic races are instructed . . . with the mission of conducting the political civilization of the modern world."[21]

These racialized calls fed an emerging process of imperial mimicry and interimperial isomorphism. While Niall Ferguson has recently suggested that the United States should copy the British in their globally civilizing endeavors, such imitation was already performed by pro-expansionists in the wake of 1898.[22] American policy makers and colonial officials dutifully scoured papers and books on the British imperial experience, seeking models and maps for how to conduct colonial governance. After Elihu Root was appointed by President McKinley to head the Department of War and thereby take charge of overseas colonies, the first thing Root did was "make out a list of a great number of books which cover in detail both the practice and the principles of many forms of colonial government under the English law." His stated goal was "to take the lesson we could get from the colonial policy of other countries, especially Great Britain."[23] Administrator Cameron Forbes spent his journey from San Francisco to Manila pouring over Europe's colonial record; while some of the officials who administered the Islamic provinces of the Philippines visited London's colonial office to find inspiration in the British rule of

Malaya.[24] On the homefront, a veritable publishing machine emerged to aid this labor of emulation. Enterprising academics and authors produced countless books on the European empires. Universities added courses on the history of European imperialism to their registers. One academic, Alleyne Ireland, even proposed that a new academic department be formed at the University of Chicago in order to train Americans in the paths and pitfalls of colonial administration. His model was the British colonial service.[25]

Still, there was a critical hitch to this process of emulation. Nationalist pride soon took precedence. Scholars, statesmen, and officials looked to the British Empire for guidance; they also agreed upon the idea of a racially underpinned civilizing mission. But they nonetheless differentiated America's new empire from England's, proposing that the United States was better suited for taking up the imperial mantle. After reviewing the history of British colonialism in Asia and Africa, Bernard Moses claimed that British colonialism had been "reckless and tyrannical," failing to meet up to the civilizing ideal. According to Moses, England's own history of monarchy had been the culprit, instilling in the British a conservative attitude that extended to their colonial practices. But the United States was special. Because it had had a unique nonfeudal and nonmonarchical history, Americans were endowed with a political wisdom and a liberal character unmatched by any other. Thus, only the United States would be able to construct a "wise and beneficent [sic] governmental authority over a rude people" and offer its imperial subjects an "impulse and guidance toward the attainment of a higher form of life and larger liberty."[26] Woodrow Wilson added that while imperialism and its civilizing mission was inevitable, the United States was to play a special role in the process: "a leading part" in civilizing the world. Since the United States had had the privilege of cultivating a perfect liberal democracy, it alone had the "peculiar duty to moderate the process [of imperialism] in the interests of liberty; to impart to the peoples thus driven out upon the road of change . . . our principles of self-help; teach them order and self-control; impart to them . . . the drill and habit of law and obedience."[27]

The exceptionalist paradigm for America's empire was thus born. The United States would join its European counterparts in forming a presumably enlightened empire, but its imperial mission was distinct. Rather than ruling overseas colonies for centuries as the British had been doing, and rather than ruling in a "reckless" and "tyrannical" manner, the United States would use colonialism as a mechanism for spreading the gospel of American liberal democracy. "The territories we have obtained from Spain," exclaimed President McKinley, "are ours not to exploit, but to develop, to civilize, to educate, and train in the science of self-government." So added Bernard Moses: "If America has any mission outside of her continental limits, it is not to preserve among less developed peoples such institutions and customs as make for bondage and social stagnation, but to put in their place the ideas that have made for freedom, and the laws by which this nation has been enabled to preserve its freedom."[28]

The vision was simple enough. It was also remarkably resonant with discourses on American empire today: the United States would use its power benevolently, taking on the task of transforming, uplifting, and democratizing foreign peoples. As Elihu Root summarized: "the obligations correlative to this great power are of the highest character. . . . [I]t is our unquestioned duty to make the interests of the people over whom we assert sovereignty the first and controlling consideration in all legislation and administration which concerns them, and to give them, to the greatest possible extent, individual freedom, self-government in accordance with their capacity, just and equal laws, and opportunity for education, for profitable industry, and for development in civilization."[29] With the birth of America's imperial exceptionalism in 1898 came the first articulation of "empire lite."

MANIFEST EXCEPTIONALISM

The plan to use colonial control as a mechanism for transforming colonial subjects and training them in self-government was not a ruse. When devising colonial rule for Puerto Rico and the Philippines, the first officials drew upon the exceptionalist theme and gave the tutelary ideal a palpable manifestation. Indeed, having noted that the British Empire had been too "reckless and tyrannical," policy makers and officials dismissed it as a guide for colonial government in Puerto Rico and the Philippines. They instead proclaimed a mission of "democratic tutelage" and "political education." Puerto Ricans and Filipinos would be given American-styled elections, local governments, and national assemblies so that, under the "strong and guiding hand" of American officials at the apex of the colonial state, they could learn the ways and means of American-styled self-government. Colonial subjects would vote, hold office, and help to formulate legislation, while American officials would give them "object lessons."[30] As William Willoughby explained: "It is not merely that such a [colonial] government will furnish greater advantage in the way of more and better schools, roads and public works of all kinds, greater care of matters relating to public health and the like . . . it will [also] serve as an instrument of instruction constantly at work training the habits, methods of thought and ideals of the people."[31]

Colonial state building in Puerto Rico and the Philippines followed from the plan. The military rulers who first administered the colonies immediately set up local governments and held elections to staff them. This was to be, as one military official put it, a "sort of kindergarten" in democracy, initiating the process of teaching the people "our best American thought and methods."[32] Subsequent civilian administrators continued in the effort. In both Puerto Rico and the Philippines, they set up tutelary colonial states that gave extensive participation in the government to the colonized. They instituted ballot systems designed to teach the "sanctity of the ballot" and, making equations between the colonized elite and the corrupt "bosses" of immigrant machines at home, they used a range of techniques drawn from the Progressive movement to discipline the colonized into the ways of liberal democratic governance. Participation in the government by locals below, with supervision by American officials on high, was key. It would "constitute a valuable means of educating and instructing the local officials in the art of government and administration, by pointing out errors [and] encouraging higher ideals."[33] The overarching idea was that as Puerto Ricans and Filipinos learned their "lessons," American control would devolve, and the colonized would eventually receive full self-government.[34]

Of course, the tutelary project, manifesting as it did the American colonialists' sense of exceptionalism, faced various criticisms from their imperial counterparts. British observers, such as Mrs. Campbell Dauncey, found the idea of teaching self-government to Filipinos ridiculous. An expatriate living in Manila, she recorded in her journal:

> The [American] Ideal is this you see, that every people in the world should have self-government and equal rights. This means, when reduced from windy oratory to common-sense, that they consider these Malay half-breeds to be capable . . . of understanding the motives, and profiting by the institutions which it has taken the highest white races two or three thousand years to evolve. [. . .] When I come to think of it, America with this funny little possession of hers is like a mother with her first child, who . . . tries to bring it up on some fad of her own because it is so much more precious and more wonderful than any other child any one else ever had.[35]

But the American officials stood firm. In fact, to the project of "practical political education" they hitched a range of other projects. One was public education. The authorities in both colonies constructed extensive public school systems such that, by 1930, funds devoted to public schooling in both colonies trumped expenses for public health, policing, and infrastructure-construction. The idea was to provide technical skills and civics training so that the "ignorant and credulous masses" would come to "know their rights" and exercise them as liberal democratic subjects.[36] The other major program was economic development. The officials constructed extensive public-works systems, built central banking facilities offering flexible credit, and tried to reduce existing trade barriers between the metropole and colony. Of course, such measures in part benefited American capital, but in the officials' view, they were critical for civilizational growth. Predating modernization theories of democratization later proposed in the 1950s, officials argued that economic development stimulated by American capital would undo the putatively medieval social conditions in the two colonies and stimulate sociopolitical development. With "Yankee capital," claimed Governor Taft in the Philippines, would come the "moral improvement and the education of the people," promoting "Yankee ingenuity, Yankee enterprise, and Yankee freedom."[37] Tutelage, transformation, and hence "empire lite" was thus more than an abstract ideal. In Puerto Rico and the Philippines it was reality.

SAMOA, GUAM, AND THE "MORO" PROVINCE: THE LIMITS OF TUTELAGE

The policy of democratic tutelage in Puerto Rico and the Philippines might not be surprising to some observers. Doesn't the United States have a unique set of liberal anticolonial values and traditions that would naturally give shape to its imperial endeavors? This has been a common stance to take when discussing American empire.[38] The problem with it is simple: it fails to account for what went on in other parts of America's imperial sphere. In fact, the colonial regimes in Samoa and Guam brushed the tutelage strategy aside and instead opted for a much less ambitious approach to governance—an approach exactly of the European mold. Colonial authorities in Samoa, for example, structured the government so as to keep Samoan "customs" intact rather than to eradicate and replace them. They divided Samoa into different districts corresponding to what they took to be the "ancient" sociopolitical divisions. Then, rather than holding elections to staff the administrative apparatus, they appointed hereditary native chiefs. Here the expressed model was not tutelage but indirect rule in British Fiji—a form of rule, as one colonial official put it, that would be maintained "without interfering with the deeply rooted customs of the people or wounding their susceptibilities in any way."[39]

Authorities in Guam structured their colonial regime similarly. Guam did not have hereditary chiefs, but under Spanish rule it had had native district officials known as *gobernadorcillos* (or "little governors"). The gobernadorcillos were typically the leading elite of the island, and the first American governors did not alter the system. They kept the preexisting positions intact without elaboration, merely reappointing the gobernadorcillos as "commissioners." Thus, unlike the political system in the Philippines or Puerto Rico, local leaders were not chosen through American-styled elections. There was no talk of "political education" at all. Rather, preservation was the goal.[40] This was much to the dismay of the inhabitants, who soon became critical of the autocratic character of colonial administration. In 1910, the governor of Guam discovered that the following anonymous handbill had been circulating among the Chamorros:

Salam! Salam!
I'm the Governor of Guam,
I'm glorious and great,
I'm a pampered potentate,
So I am.
I run things as I please
Get down on your knees,
I'm the ruler of the tightest little island in the seas,
That's me.
Those who do not like me,
I shut up or send away,
I'm a wonder and I know it,
Of the thirty-third degree.
Behold! Behold!
I'm fearless and I'm bold.
I'm the government, the law;
Kings refer to me with awe,
So I'm told.[41]

Why the difference in policy? Rather than America's distinct traditions and values, the answer lies in a larger principle of empires everywhere. Empire was never a simple reflection of a single function or interest, and imperial domains did not always have equal standing. Empire is a complex formation: some parts of it are slated for some purposes, while other parts for very different ones. In the American empire, Guam and Samoa were supposed to serve a distinct function indeed. They were seized primarily as coaling and naval stations to facilitate America's rising naval power in the Pacific and, accordingly, both Guam and Samoa were put into the hands of the United States Navy Department. This meant that colonial authorities were also naval commanders and, in turn, their foremost concern was stability and order. Preservation became the rule for colonial rule: policies aimed at transformation or change would do little else than disrupt "indigenous" systems and pose a threat to naval imperatives. Fittingly, when calls later surfaced from some circles in Washington to have Congress replace naval administration with civilian rule, the Roosevelt administration urged the navy to do all it could to prevent Congressional action. "If left alone Congress will probably do nothing about providing a form of government for the Islands," wrote the White House to the navy secretary, "the inactivity of Congress must be deemed to be an approval of the continuance of the existing government. It is very desirable that this should be so."[42]

The imperatives of naval rule also impeded other developmental projects. Rather than pursuing economic-cum-civilizational growth, for example, the naval authorities prevented landholdings deemed traditional from being sold without their permission. They also closed off the islands to traders so as to prevent islanders from becoming dependent upon external economic forces and to impede disruptions to what the authorities took to be traditional ways of life. Authorities took the same approach to public education. While the government funded one or two public schools, neither Guam nor Samoa saw the kind of educational program carried out in the Philippines and Puerto Rico. Funds devoted to education in Samoa were next to nothing; and in Guam, they took up a sparse 17 percent of the budget. To boot, the curriculum was severely restricted. While schoolchildren in the Philippines and Puerto Rico were given civics classes, students in Guam only learned "habits of cleanliness" and, at most, English. "It is not the intention," wrote the governor, "to carry the instruction of the mass much beyond that."[43]

Still, naval imperatives were not the only factors that limited the reach of tutelage in the empire. Indeed, American authorities brushed the tutelary project aside even in some parts of the Philippines, where naval administration had not been established. Specifically, they brushed it aside when dealing with the Islamic "Moros" in the southern regions of the archipelago (Mindanao, Sulu, and Palawan), a group whose numbers reached close to 300,000. Here, colonial discourses of race, ethnicity, and "development" were key. When devising government for these provinces, the American authorities made haste to contend that the Moros by their religion were fundamentally distinct from the "Christian tribes" of the islands. They also argued that the Moros had been left unpenetrated by Spain and that they were of a distinct "civilizational" stage of development. While the Christianized Filipinos had been subjected to Spanish influence, and while the Filipino elite had had some amount of education, the Moros were but a band of "wild" and "savage" tribes. Authorities saw them as akin to "the best North American Indians—[such] as the Nez Perce and Northern Cheyenne."[44] Also important, in the Americans' view, was the fact that the Moros were plagued by internal wars and were geographically dispersed over an extended territory. The first American authorities had a difficult time discerning bounded units of sovereignty in the provinces, much less locate "traditional" lines of authority and leadership. At issue here was not so much a "clash of civilizations" as it was the particularity, and arguable inadequacy, of the Americans' understandings.

A special approach to ruling the Moros followed. First, American authorities placed the provinces of Mindanao, Sulu, and Palawan into the hands of a governing department relatively autonomous from the tutelary regime in other parts of the Philippines. These "special provinces" thus formed a colonial state within a colonial state.[45] Second, military commanders were put in charge, many of whom were drawn from the "Indian wars" at home. In turn, the military commanders extended control through a series of treaties and, when necessary, through the violent suppression of resistance. The end result was that American authorities ruled through collaboration with Moro leaders, at least when and where they could discern who they were (often confusing, for instance, "Sultans" and local "datus"). In all, the idea was not to "civilize" but to keep intact—or as it was, reconstruct—the Moros' political system as best the Americans could perceive it.[46] At most, the authorities tried to curb some of the more "barbarous practices" of the Moros (such as debt relationships the Americans classified as slavery), but democratic tutelage or political education was never the goal. As one officer summarized in 1909: "We have not yet built up a state nor reached the mass of the people in any general uplifting movement. . . . The mailed fist is the first law of the land—peace would be impossible without the actual presence of troops—for this country is neither ready nor has it ever known any other form of government."[47]

So much for the exceptional and uniquely democratizing force of the American empire. So much, too, for appeals to America's anticolonial and liberal values. True, the Americans had articulated a lofty goal: they claimed they would use colonial occupation to teach, train, and transform. But due to the contingencies of occupation on the ground, the distinct functions of colonial control, and the epistemic violence of the colonizers' classificatory schemes, American authorities ultimately created an internally differentiated imperial archipelago of multiple ruling strategies that together belied the singular exceptionalist vision.[48]

THE TENSIONS OF TUTELAGE

This is not to say that just because tutelage was actualized in Puerto Rico and in the "civilized" parts of the Philippines it went untroubled. Even in these colonies, events and contingencies on the ground brought tensions to bear. To be sure, in the Philippines, not all of America's imperial subjects responded positively to the Americans' designs. Revolutionaries in Luzon took up arms against American occupation and inhabitants of other provinces joined in as well. The result was a protracted war that cost no less than 400,000 Filipino lives. America's benevolence was thus predicated upon violence. Ballot boxes and elections were imposed through guns and bullets. The irony was not lost on anti-imperialists at home. "It appears, gentlemen," quipped Williams Jennings Bryan, soon after news of the Philippine war reached the States, "that our destiny is not as manifest as it was two weeks ago."[49]

The Philippine-American war gave tutelage a troubled tone, and not only because of its horrific violence. For even as the war waned, the threat of a renewed uprising remained ever present, and Filipino elites did not hesitate to use the threat against their American mentors. In turn, the American authorities were taught a lesson in humility. They came to realize, however inchoately, that their colonial power depended less upon their own benevolent designs than upon the power that the colonized were willing to grant them. A politics of patronage and concession followed. Whenever the Americans proceeded too swiftly or openly against the elites' entrenched positions, the elite in turn conjured the specter of revolution, and the Americans had to retract.[50] In the end, the American authorities could not discipline and democratize as much as they had initially hoped.

To make matters worse, the American authorities on the ground did not obtain the necessary legislation from Congress at home. They had initially hoped for economic policies that would help fund developmental projects but Congress, working from its own interests, failed to enact them. This too fed the politics of patronage and concession. To fund their developmental projects in the absence of proper Congressional legislation, American authorities had to enact new taxation policies that depended upon the cooperation of the Filipino elite. In exchange for that cooperation, the Americans ended up perpetuating rather than undermining the elites' traditional political power.[51] The result was the creation of what Benedict Anderson has called "cacique democracy."[52] The Americans had proclaimed to undermine and replace local sociopolitical structures with liberal democracy, but the troubles of tutelage meant that they had to sustain them.

Even in Puerto Rico, where the people did not resist American sovereignty, the tutelage project ran into trouble. This time the trouble had to do with translation. On the one hand, the Americans announced and enacted the project of teaching the people "self-government" and "democracy." On the other, the Puerto Rican elite prior to American occupation had already constructed their own distinct meanings of the categories. The elite had equated democracy with *autonomía,* which in turn meant the unrestrained power of the political elite and single-party rule. Democracy as *autonomía* meant that the party that best represented the people should take the reigns of the state and dole out patronage as party leaders saw fit, regardless of formal legal codes. This was not the kind of democratic self-government that the Americans had hoped to impart, and so they stood befuddled as the Puerto Rican elites accepted tutelary rule but then used the colonial state *not* as a "school of politics" to be disciplined into the Americans' preferred forms of democratic government but rather as a site to cultivate their own patronage-based party power. The result was that the policy of political education was subverted by what the Americans called "political corruption"—practices marking an excess of meaning that went uncontained by the Americans' categorical scheme.

For their part, the Puerto Rican elite had little sense that they were doing anything wrong. Hadn't the American authorities stated that tutelary rule would bring "self-government"? And didn't self-government mean democracy as *autonomía*, hence single-party rule and patronage? Of course, the Americans, insistent upon giving lessons in what democracy "really" meant, took measures to uproot the elites' corrupt practices. They centralized the state as never before. But this merely created an additional problem. In equal measure to the Americans' so-called educating measures, the elite responded with an indignation unprecedented. Seeing in the centralized colonial state evidence of a promise betrayed, they soon became disillusioned with tutelary occupation. In fact, while they had initially accepted tutelage on their own cultural terms, and while they had therefore responded positively to it, many began demanding something that they had not demanded from Spain (or from the United States) previously: national independence.[53] These unprecedented calls for independence set the basis for various "terrorist" activities against the United States in later decades.

To be clear, these troubles of tutelary rule had little to do with a lack of will on the part of the Americans, much less a failure to emulate British models. In many ways, the United States and its agents had done what they could to realize their grandiose goals. Nor did the tensions lie in an unrealized "empire lite." At the time, and in the Americans' own views, the new empire was as liberal and benign as it could be. The problem is much more general, even as it is much more straightforward. Simply put, empire is never made by imperialists alone. While current commentators insist that all it takes for imperial success are willing rather than reluctant imperialists, or the right imperial models imported from across the Atlantic, empire is always a matter of ruler *and* ruled, colonizer *and* colonized. And those who are ruled are not always if ever malleable to the fancies of those who make the rules.[54]

In the end, what began as an ambitious attempt to fashion a distinctly benevolent tutelary empire wound up as an empire like any other—an empire marked by strategies of accommodation and concession forged on the cheap and on the spot; an empire plagued with problems of (mis)translation and local resistance, unexpected indignance and unforeseen violence on both sides. Woodrow Wilson was thus correct. The Americans at the turn of the twentieth century had indeed "gone out upon the seas" to extend America's ostensibly exceptional power. But what they found there, and what Wilson did not foresee, was the limit of power's reach.

PART IV

EMPIRES AS INTERNATIONAL ACTORS

13. IMPERIAL AND COLONIAL ENCOUNTERS: SOME COMPARATIVE REFLECTIONS

SANJAY SUBRAHMANYAM

At the moment, as a putative citizen of the global republic of letters, I suspect I have less than one vote.

—PARTHA CHATTERJEE, 2003

The deliberations at the meeting in New York on "Lessons of Empire" from which the present volume has emerged left a large number of questions open, including—not surprisingly—questions of prognosis, of how the interstate political system would evolve in the decades to come. But then, historians, social scientists, and other "professionals" have never been particularly good at crystal-ball gazing. In the Spain of Philip II, a young woman called Lucrecia de León often proved better at predicting the direction of political events through her dreams than the hardened professionals who surrounded and advised the Habsburg monarch. Few in the early 1920s, and least of all men like Winston Churchill, would have been willing to predict an early dismantling of the British Empire, though many did undoubtedly scent that the United States was a power on the rise, if only it could set aside its isolationism and provincialism. But the New York meeting also left open some fundamental questions of definition and of characterization with respect to the present and recent past. It is to these questions that this brief essay turns, although it shall, alas, not entirely resist the temptation to engage in some crystal-ball gazing of its own.

Less than two decades ago, it was rather fashionable to compare the Soviet Union to an "empire," and even an "evil empire." One of the ideologues who fashioned U.S. foreign policy in those years, Edward N. Luttwak, put his knowledge of classical empires to good use in those circumstances, comparing the declining Roman Empire to the Soviets, and arguing that similar factors were in operation in the two cases. At that time too (as the conference organizers stated), much of the "public debate tended to use empire as a metaphor, for unlimited power for a state to act arbitrarily," and it was unusual in academic circles at least to speak of the United States as an empire (even though political posters in places like India routinely castigated U.S. imperialism). But others thought of the Soviet Union rather literally as an empire, with a Russian core, conquered territories to the east and south, and a fringe of tributary states in Eastern Europe. To be sure, the emperor could come from Georgia or Ukraine, but the dominant culture was seen as Russian, Cyrillic was being imposed where the Arabo-Persian script had once flourished, and it was argued that a single state religion (communism) was imposed where once a diversity of beliefs were to be found. The belief was, as with Luttwak, that this imperial superstructure would crumble soon enough, and—as one cartoonist saw it—the great matrioshka doll of the Soviet Union would be broken open to have the component parts running helter-skelter. In the event, he proved right, but whether this was from ideological wishful thinking, or from hard analysis, is a different matter.

The disappearance of the Soviet Union has meant that the United States no longer has a counterpart—an Ernst Stavro Blofeld to pair with James Bond—onto which it can project the imperial role, keeping for itself the nobler task of defending freedoms, the Charter of Human Rights, and open markets. The Manichaean world order having broken, some in the United States today seem determined to transform it into a version of the Soviet Union, and the Bush administration has taken on the old Soviet mantle in many respects, though it does not see its role as being defined by a territorially contiguous zone. If the United States is an empire, it is undoubtedly one of a new type, for reasons that I shall set out below. Its theory of suzerainty does not correspond exactly to the old notions of layered sovereignty; but the United States today clearly does not recognize that other states possess sovereignty as an inalienable right. In a similar vein, the broad thrust of much recent American internal legislation, as well as of American actions in an international sphere, is to deny the validity of universal human rights even as an idea. A single American life is clearly worth multiple lives of citizens of some other country, according to a graded calculus. In this world, the United States and its citizens are also seen as possessing superior rights to other individuals. Those who wish to accede to these superior rights are invited to become Americans, as the best means of safeguarding themselves as individuals, although this may itself not be a guarantee (if, for example, one is a naturalized Arab American born in Yemen). Since 1950, the United States, like the Soviet Union, frequently acted in a way that was in contradiction with its own declared principles as part of the normal exercise of statecraft. Today, what is significant is that the declared principles are themselves so extreme, and so based on an assumption of the monopoly of moral authority (whether on the part of Christian fundamentalists or Straussian neoconservatives), that one can only hope that they can or will never be implemented, or in other words, that they will be tempered by pragmatism.

The use of a millenarian vocabulary in some of these statements has of course not passed unnoticed, including such ideas as "the end of history," which themselves have clear eschatological echoes. So, whatever is new, it is also clear that there is something here that is old, where the ghosts of political orders past still haunt the imaginations of both actors and spectators. Now, the past few decades have seen no lessening in the intensity of debates and discussions concerning the place of empires in the early modern and modern worlds. These debates have if anything been aggravated, and at times grown more confused in their conceptual terms, partly because of the advent of the current known as "postcolonial studies," in which historians of India have played a quite significant part. Three issues seem to be central in these debates, and I shall address each of them in turn, in the hope of allowing a possible dialogue to emerge between historians of different parts of the world (and more particularly Latin America and South Asia) who work on the period between the late fifteenth and the mid-nineteenth centuries. The three issues that I shall consider in turn are as follows:

- The *synchronic* problem, namely, how to reconcile the very different trajectories followed by societies in Asia and America, in the face of European empire-building projects.
- The *diachronic* problem, namely, the conceptual relationship between the empires of the early modern period (say, 1450–1750) and those of the later period, which is sometimes read as a shorthand for the relationship between the Iberian empires and those of France and Great Britain.
- The issue of the complex passage from empires to nation-states, and the consequent reflection on the "modernity" or "archaism" of empires themselves as a political form.

But before entering into them, it may be useful to look, if only briefly, at two recent and contrasting books that address the question of empires. The first is a relatively brief essay of some two hundred pages by Anthony Pagden, *Peoples and Empires: Europeans and the Rest of the World, from Antiquity to the Present*;[1] the second, a collective enterprise that is over five hundred pages long that is the outcome of a conference, and simply entitled *Empires*.[2] In the first of these works, Pagden begins by attempting to define what an empire is, noting that "today, the word is generally used as a term of abuse, although one that is often tinged with nostalgia." Eventually preferring a description to a rigorous definition, he nevertheless notes that from the time of Tacitus, anyone who alluded to "empire" usually had in mind an allusion "as much to its size as to its sovereignty, and ultimately it would be size which separated empires from mere kingdoms and principalities." Pagden goes on to note that "because they have been large and relentlessly expansive, empires have also embraced peoples who have held a wide variety of different customs and beliefs, and often spoken an equally large number of different languages."[3] We are thus already edging somewhat closer to a definition, and this is confirmed by the statement that "because of their size and sheer diversity, most empires have in time become cosmopolitan societies," structures of political authority in which rulers "have generally tolerated diversity [but] . . . have also inevitably transformed the peoples whom they have brought together."[4] The key elements can now be brought together in a sort of definition: an empire is a large sovereign state, which is relentlessly expansive, embraces a wide variety of different customs and beliefs, and peoples who practice a vast array of languages; the imperial society tends to be cosmopolitan and the political system is tolerant of diversity, even if "empires have [also] severely limited the freedoms of some peoples."[5]

Pagden's purpose here is to permit a broad and inclusive notion of what the category of "empire" means, one that can allow him to run the gamut from Alexander the Great and the Romans, through the Safavids and Ottomans, to the Habsburgs, and as far as Queen Victoria. The editors of the second volume chose however to limit their temporal ambit in order to explicitly exclude empires from the eighteenth, nineteenth, and twentieth centuries. While stating that they considered the division between the "early" empires, such as the Achaemenids, the Satavahanas, the Assyrians, or classical Rome, and the empires of the sixteenth and seventeenth centuries to be artificial, and noting their "scepticism concerning the intellectual legitimacy of this divide,"[6] they nevertheless preferred to reiterate that the Iberian empires (which are represented by several contributions, including one by the present author) of the sixteenth and seventeenth centuries were quite distinct from the British or the French empires of the eighteenth and nineteenth centuries. I shall return to this problem briefly below, in discussing the problem of the "colonial empire," which is usually schematized as a particular type of empire that is fundamentally characterized by exploitative economic relations between an imperial core and a subject periphery. An empire may possess all the characteristics set out by Pagden, and yet not be structured in a fashion that permits systematic unequal exchange, or tributary economic flows towards the imperial center. In this respect, the Iberian experience in sixteenth- and seventeenth-century America and Asia was obviously quite markedly different. From the second quarter of the sixteenth century, massive tribute in the form of precious metals flowed into the Habsburg imperial center from its American possessions, first through dethesaurization and then through the exploitation of mines. The structure of empire, whether in New Spain or the Peruvian viceroyalty, remained deeply dependent on raising resources through systems of forced labor or corvée, and also in the case of some areas, on plantation systems that exploited slave labor. Whether one looks at the Spanish or the Portuguese possessions in America therefore, it is clear that their relationship to Iberia was a dependent and tributary one in economic terms. This did not mean of course that locally implanted elites—and even some descendants of Native Americans—did not also benefit. Nor did it mean that the net effects of these tributary flows were necessarily positive for the Iberian economies, where they produced inflation, the social redistribution of wealth, but not necessarily high rates of growth either in agriculture or artisanal production. Yet the contrast in the relationship with Asia at the very same period was striking. Trade on the Cape Route for the Portuguese was essentially a balanced, bilateral trade, with bullion and other goods being sent out to Asia, in order to purchase pepper, spices, indigo, and textiles. The financial resources raised through fiscal means in Asia by the Portuguese *Estado da Índia* did not constitute a veritable surplus that allowed the state to finance intercontinental trade on a tributary basis, and it is difficult to talk of systematic "unrequited flows" from Asia to Iberia in this period. Even the Spanish presence in the Philippines did not permit the exaction of a net tribute that was sufficient to allow even a small proportion of trade between Manila and Acapulco to be financed thereby. Both Portuguese and Spaniards undoubtedly had imperial ambitions in Asia in this period. But the notion of empire that existed was based on ideas of extensive dominion and layered sovereignty (an emperor being a "king over kings"), rather than a "colonial empire" in the classic British or French sense. Obviously, this does not exclude the possibility of relatively restricted and classic comparisons, such as between the Jesuits in Peru and China, or the workings of city councils in Goa and Bahia. But such comparisons must take into account that the Jesuits in China—however glamorous they may appear as individuals—were minor players in both a political and strictly missionary sense, pretty much at the mercy of the Chinese imperial system, while those in the Peruvian viceroyalty were not.

Thus, the synchronic problem of "empire" poses itself directly when one attempts to think through the Asian and American cases in the same movement. For the moment when the Iberian colonial empires are being established, and take root, in America, is a moment of relative political impasse in Asia. Rather than the Spaniards or the Portuguese, the great territorial expanses are in the hands of the Ottomans, the Mughals, and the Ming and Ching dynasties in China. Far from being subject as passive victims to the imperial drive of the Iberians, these other powers often powerfully repulse them, and even if not, limit the extent to which the Spaniards and Portuguese can gain footholds in Asia. Now, the same synchronic problem poses itself in a reverse sense when one turns to the nineteenth century. For the great moment of decolonization in America, and of retreat for the Spanish empire, is equally the moment when first the East India Company and then the British

Crown extend their control over India and some parts of Southeast Asia and West Asia. The conquest of India begins in the 1740s and 1750s, accelerates around 1800, and is finally consolidated after the bloody events of 1857–58, when a major peasant and urban rebellion over much of northern India is brutally suppressed. This is rather difficult to explain, if one assumes like Joseph Schumpeter (in his "Zur Soziologie der Imperialismen" of 1918), that empires were themselves archaic political forms, representing the carryover of atavistic impulses from an earlier era. Here then is what Schumpeter wrote, in a classic passage:

> Modern Imperialism is one of the heirlooms of the absolute monarchical state. The "inner logic" of capitalism would have never evolved it. Its sources come from the policy of the princes and the customs of a pre-capitalist milieu. But even export monopoly is not imperialism and it would never have developed to imperialism in the hands of the pacific bourgeoisie. This happened only because the war machine, its social atmosphere, and the martial will were inherited and because a martially oriented class (i.e., the nobility) maintained itself in a ruling position with which of all the varied interests of the bourgeoisie the martial ones could ally themselves. This alliance keeps alive fighting instincts and ideas of domination. It led to social relations which perhaps ultimately are to be explained by relations of production but not by the productive relations of capitalism alone.[7]

If this is the case, Britain, which is usually seen as the paragon of nineteenth-century industrial modernity, appears to be the laggard in comparison to the far more politically advanced Iberian world. In any event, leaving Schumpeter aside, the comparison of the Latin American and Asian cases can only lead to deep synchronic embarrassment of one or the other kind. This is a problem that the gurus of postcolonial studies do not appear to have posed when suggesting that this category be transferred to Latin America from India. For, in any normal sense of the term, the postcolonial in much of Latin America must refer to the latter half of the nineteenth century, rather than to the events and processes after World War II.

This leads us logically to considering the other major issue that we have set out at the outset, namely the diachronic relationship between the Iberian empires of the early modern period, and the British and French (and to an extent Dutch and Belgian) empires of the nineteenth and twentieth centuries. The common assumption here (shared by the editors, if not the contributors, of *Empires*), is that a radical break occurs somewhere in the eighteenth century, and that the "modern empires" that exist after this date have a different character than those of the "early modern" period. This break may be seen as primarily ideological in nature (post-Enlightenment empires being presumably different from their precursors), or primarily functional in character. A problem immediately arises though with respect to both the Portuguese and Spanish empires, since they in fact survived into the post-1800 period, and in the case of the Portuguese, was conserved until as late as the 1970s. The usual response to this problem is to state that the Iberian empires in fact reinvented themselves in the course of the nineteenth and twentieth centuries, leading to what has been termed the "second" and the "third" Portuguese empires, for example. For instance, this conception is clearly (if implicitly) present in a rather well-known work, namely W.G. Clarence-Smith's *The Third Portuguese Empire, 1825–1975: A Study in Economic Imperialism* (1985); this "third empire" is hence assumed to have been reinvented after the Napoleonic wars, to have been somewhat modern in character, and also to have been conceived within the context of a form of "economic imperialism." Yet, to state the contrast so baldly between early modern and modern empires may be somewhat abusive, and in fact may even mean that the historian is participating in the Whiggish view of history put out by apologists of the British and French empires in the nineteenth century. For, whatever the institutional and conceptual continuities between Iberian and northern European empires, it was characteristic enough for British historians, administrators, and travelers (from Richard Burton to F.C. Danvers) to insist that their imperial *mission civilisatrice* had nothing to do with the half-breed empires of the "dagoes." An etymological dictionary informs us, incidentally, that the word "dago comes from the Spanish given name Diego. It is nautical in origin and originally referred to Spanish or Portuguese sailors on English or American ships. This usage dates to the 1830s. The meaning eventually broadened to include anyone from southern Europe, before narrowing again and restricting usage to Italians."[8]

The issue of the nature of continuities (or the lack thereof) between the early modern and modern empires is brought starkly into focus if we consider the history of a particularly long-lived empire, namely that of the Ottomans. Emerging as a petty polity on the eastern fringes of a declining Byzantium in the early fourteenth century, the Ottoman Empire truly came into its own only in the fifteenth century, after having suffered a severe defeat at the hands of the Central Asian conqueror Timur (d. 1405). It is thus possible to talk of a first phase of uncertain emergence lasting a century, and then a second phase of a century and a half, taking us from the time of Mehmed the Conqueror (in the mid-fifteenth century) to the close of the sixteenth century and the reign of Murad III (1574–1595). These three centuries to 1600 are taken then to constitute the "classical period" in Ottoman history, followed by a phase which was once described as that of "Ottoman decline," but which is now more generously termed "a period of transition," leading first to eighteenth-century "decentralization," and then to the "radical westernization reforms" of the nineteenth century, culminating in imperial dissolution after World War I. Now the Ottomans have a curious place in the comparative history of empires. As Halil Inalcik and Donald Quataert, editors of the two-volume work, *An Economic and Social History of the Ottoman Empire,* state in their general introduction, "it can be said, without exaggeration, that the Ottoman superpower in the East substantially contributed to the shaping of modern Europe," but the same authors also note that from the eighteenth century, the study of the Ottomans is largely one of "a traditional Muslim society trying to determine to what extent it should follow European ways."[9] This still leaves open the question of how the Ottomans compare to the Spanish Habsburgs in the sixteenth and seventeenth centuries from the viewpoint of comparative imperial history. The parallels are clear in terms of the characteristics laid out by Pagden: elite cosmopolitanism, a multilingual culture, the protection of a certain sort of cultural diversity in the two cases, even if the Ottoman Sultans were aggressive Sunni Muslims and the Habsburgs aggressive Catholics. But certain stark differences also emerge. In the first place, the Ottoman Empire was almost entirely a contiguous state, which did not have separated territories with the exception of a few islands in the Mediterranean. Secondly, and this is a related point, the Ottoman state was during the greater part of its career not a state with a Turkish core and a non-Turkish periphery that was subordinate to it. Anatolia and Rumelia did not systematically exploit and draw in resources from the outlying territories, in the sense that Castile drew resources from its American territories. Further, the two empires witnessed contrasting processes of acculturation. If, as Serge Gruzinski and others have shown in works like *The Conquest of Mexico*[10] the Spanish empire in the Americas was a case of the *colonisation de l'imaginaire,* no such conquest of minds took place in Ottoman Hungary or Iraq. There was no attempt at a comprehensive program of the top-down imposition of an Ottoman *Leitkultur,* whether in the Balkans, Iraq, or the Maghreb, even if we are aware that some forcible conversion to Islam did take place.

In this sense, the Ottoman Empire seems to stand apart from other empires, which were based either on programs of economic exploitation, or cultural homogenization, or both. Even if sixteenth-century observers often compared Charles V to Süleyman the Lawgiver, the empires that the two presided over were in fact fundamentally different. And no matter what measures of reform the Ottomans attempted in the nineteenth century, these were simply not designed to make their structure conform to something like the Habsburg or, after the accession of Philip V in 1700, Spanish Bourbon model. True, the slogan of the *Tanzimat* reforms of the years 1839–76 was centralization and westernization, but this was paradoxically meant to transform the Ottoman Empire into a sort of sprawling unitary state, rather than into a colonial empire in the European style.

In this sense, the true heirs of the Spanish Habsburgs and Bourbons in the matter of empire may well have been the British in the late eighteenth century. Recent historiography, such as P.J. Cain and A.G. Hopkins's two-volume work, *British Imperialism,* admits that too much has been made of the "modernity" of the nineteenth-century British Empire and prefers to see long-term continuities in terms of the "gentlemanly capitalists" who presided over that empire.[11] In a similar vein, C.A. Bayly in his *Imperial Meridian* has written of the British Empire between 1800 and 1840 not in terms of its precocious modernity, which was imposed over a set of traditional societies elsewhere, but rather as a set of "proconsular despotisms," which in fact "complemented features of a revivified conservative régime at home."[12] While Bayly agrees with Vincent Harlow's work *The Founding of the Second British Empire, 1763–1793*,[13] in perceiving a "Second British Empire" that emerged in particular after 1783 and the loss of the American colonies, he nevertheless argues that one cannot see British developments as sui generis in character, as exceptionalist historians have usually argued. The parallels with the empire of the Habsburgs are equally brought out, when Bayly notes that he "would agree with Hopkins and Cain that the economic value of empire to Britain continued to lie much more in its contribution to finance and services than to the emerging industrial economy."[14]

This view implicitly poses a challenge to the dogma of the mainstream of postcolonial studies, which sees Europe as a *deus ex machina*, and thus takes a curiously old-fashioned view of "modernity," which is seen as first a European monopoly, and then a European export to its peripheries, which in turn explains the emergence of the nation-state from within the residue of empire. Without wishing to impose a teleology on the transition (which, like all historical processes, was surely contingent), it could be argued that at least four distinct trajectories of the formation of nation-states can be detected in the past two centuries. The first case, the classic one, is of the coalition of smaller contiguous polities to form a nation-state, as with Italy or Germany in the nineteenth century. A second possibility is the fragmentation of a multiethnic structure—the empire—into national polities that claim a more or less unitary internal ethnicity and linguistic structure. Such a model may fit rather diverse instances, from that of Ireland, Malaysia, or Mexico, to that of Turkey, though we should naturally be cautious in assuming that "ethnicity" is itself a natural category. The third possible trajectory is the case of the nation-state that is itself also the imperial center, as in the instances of Spain, Portugal, the Netherlands, and Britain, and where national identity is produced simultaneously with empire rather than after it. The fourth and final case, often treated as exceptional, is where the nation-state continues to possess many key imperial features: multiethnicity, a variety of languages, a certain degree of cosmopolitanism, as well as large scale. Instances from the twentieth century can be found, ranging from the Soviet Union and China, to India, with the United States being a limiting case. Thus, just as we cannot assume a single imperial model in the early modern world (as the contrast between Habsburgs and Ottomans shows), we cannot assume a single mode of transition between the world of empires and that of nation-states. From an Indian viewpoint, the national boundaries between Chile, Peru, Argentina, Bolivia, Colombia, and Venezuela make little sense, for what separates these countries is certainly not more significant than what separates the states of the Republic of India. And if the Peruvian may detest the Argentine, the Tamil nurses his own negative stereotypes of the Bengali.

To conclude, the purpose of this brief and rather disparate reflection has been to reopen a certain number of assumptions and to question some pieces of conventional wisdom, with regard to the empires of the early modern period—and especially those with an Iberian center. It provides far fewer answers than the questions that it asks, but it is based on the belief that the facile acceptance of fashionable slogans such as "postcolonial studies" is no substitute for posing the difficult problems that a connected history of the early modern and modern worlds summons up. Nor will it do however, to throw the baby out with the bathwater, and insist on jettisoning categories such as "imperialism" and "colonialism." If our discussion has demonstrated one thing, it is that all empires were not colonial empires, nor were they necessarily based on similar economic and cultural logics. This does not require us to jettison the concept of empire, only to employ it with greater caution and precision. Similarly, while the economic exploitation of the colonies by the metropolis does not sum up the totality of relations between the two, and while it certainly does not rule out the possibility of various forms of internal exploitation (for example, of slaves by free settlers), it is difficult to justify a vision of the viceroyalties of Mexico or Peru, or of the colony of Brazil, where these political structures are treated as similar to Tokugawa Japan or the kingdom of France. The tyrannies imposed by "political correctness" are of course many; and one of them is to feel that one is obliged to be "politically incorrect" even at the risk of abandoning common sense.

Where does this leave us with respect to our point of departure, namely the possible "lessons" that the history of past empires might hold for the future trajectory of the United States? Is the United States really in the process of becoming an empire? To some the question appears moot, for the view has been defended that the United States has long been an empire, in one of two senses. The first argument would refer to consistent American expansion to the west and southwest from the time of the Lewis and Clark Expedition of 1803–1806, the subjugation and destruction of Native American populations and polities, and the overall politics of the making of the new contours of the continental American polity over the course of the nineteenth century. There is certainly some justice to this argument, though the appropriate comparison then might be to China in Sinkiang and Turkestan, or to the Brazilian *bandeirantes,* rather than to the seaborne empires that we have referred to above. In this sense, the United States had however more or less ceased to be an empire by the twentieth century, just as Brazil had ceased to be one, by "incorporating" territories into the body of the nation. A second, and quite distinct, argument, refers to U.S. ambitions overseas, whether in the Philippines, or in territories such as Guam, Puerto Rico, Samoa, and so on. Here, it would seem to me that the significance of these territories (the brief episode of the Philippines excluded) is not substantial enough to warrant the use of the term *empire*. With regard to more recent episodes, I would hence continue to hold the view that the U.S. conception of its role in territories in West Asia which it has recently conquered, whether singly or jointly, does not appear to be one of long-lasting direct occupation. Both Afghanistan and Iraq seem to suggest this. Rather, it corresponds to the idea of creating client-states, with a level of sovereignty that is less than total, in a form of "tutelage" or "indirect rule." In turn, it may be argued that even if the number of such client-states continues to grow in the years to come, it will still not constitute an empire. Nor is it clear that these regimes are in fact totally different from client-states that the United States has had in the past, such as Iran under the Shah, or Chile under Pinochet.

To my mind, the real significance of recent developments lies not here, but in the transformations that are being wrought in the institutional basis of the American polity and political culture itself. A culture of intolerance and xenophobia has quite rapidly come to dominate the United States, not merely in respect of the Muslim world (where it is evident), but with respect to other "foreigners" too. The ideal today, it seems, in the imaginary of the Patriot Act, is the American who does not travel, who does not possess a passport, and who remains locked in the self-sufficient world of the United States. A recent example of a celebration of such "American-ness" is the film *Lost in Translation,* directed by Sofia Coppola, where audiences are asked to view with sympathy the dilemma of two ill-adjusted and self-pitying Americans who are "lost" in Japan, because they have not taken the elementary precaution of learning anything about the place. Despite its crude racist humor (the Japanese are apparently all Lilliputians), this film has broadly received laudatory reviews (and several Golden Globe and Oscar nominations and awards) in even the "liberal" American media, which chooses to ignore its xenophobia and collective cultural narcissism. In a similar vein, it is commonplace for newscasters of even mainstream networks such as CNN to refer today to the Franco-German relationship as "the axis of weasel," while even more violent language may be found on cable channels like Fox News. Such xenophobia provides a fertile ground for the propagation of legislation making the arbitrary detention of non-Americans (or the cancellation of their flights, or their deportation to their "countries of origin") culturally and politically acceptable, but it cannot be thought to provide a lasting basis for the economic prosperity of the country. For, in the course of the twentieth century, one of the mainstays of American economic growth was the drain of human capital from other parts of the world to the United States, as skilled workers who had been trained elsewhere transferred their skills, when in their twenties or thereafter, to the American marketplace. It is this move that the new xenophobia has called into question, though it remains to be seen whether any of the other high-wage islands in the world, such as the European Union, are capable of profiting from the conjuncture.

Are there self-correcting mechanisms that will ensure that the move described above proves temporary, as was the case with McCarthyism, or the earlier "Red Scare"? This is where the new international and interstate environment may have a significant role to play. For there is little doubt that the relationship between domestic and international politics cuts both ways, and that it is not only the changing nature of imperial centers that has in the past impacted on "peripheries." Thus, even if the United States is not an empire, the vision of its unlimited power with regard to all actual or potential adversaries—both today and in the foreseeable future—seems destined to produce a form of hubris that is quite unlike what obtained in the bipolar context of the 1950s. This augurs well neither for those who live in the United States, nor for those of us who have "less than one vote" in the new global republic of letters.

14. WAYS OF REMEMBERING THE *MAINE*: LESSONS OF 1898 IN SPAIN AND CUBA[1]

CHRISTOPHER SCHMIDT-NOWARA

While preparing the conference that occasioned this volume, many of the participants apparently turned to Niall Ferguson's new book, *Empire,* as a crucial reference point, myself included. So ubiquitous was his book in our papers that Stephen Howe quipped that if Ferguson did not exist then we would need to invent him. Shortly after the conference, Hollywood followed with a film that echoed aspects of Ferguson's historical narrative: *Master and Commander: The Far Side of the World. Master and Commander* is based on two of Patrick O'Brian's novels and set aboard a ship of the Royal Navy during the Napoleonic wars. The filmmakers, in combining the two novels, decided to switch the evasive foe of Captain Jack Aubrey and his crew from a U.S. frigate to a French one. As with Ferguson's book, nostalgia for an imagined British world order and the temptation to compare, or collapse, empires past and present have proven irresistible. Writing in the *New Yorker,* Anthony Lane sighed in yearning tones: "What the novels leave us with, and what emerges more fitfully from this film, as if in shafts of sunlight, is the growing realization that, although our existence is indisputably safer, softer, cleaner, and more dependable than the lives led by Captain Aubrey and his men, theirs were in some immeasurable way *better*—richer in possibility, and more regularly entrancing to the eye and spirit alike." In the *New York Times,* A.O. Scott uncharacteristically growled: "'Master and Commander' hums with humor, passion and life. It makes you wish Napoleon were still around, so we— that is, I mean, the British Empire—could beat him all over again."[2]

It would seem that American readers, reviewers, and filmgoers are practicing the "imitation" that Sheldon Pollock sees as central to the construction of empires. One aspect of this process is diachronic, establishing temporal continuity between empires past and present. A foreign-policy expert voiced this tendency aptly in a review of Simon Schama's *A History of Britain* when he referred to Great Britain as the "previous superpower." Moreover, Ferguson clearly appeals to the synchronic emulation of the predecessor by spelling out a series of historical lessons for the United States to follow, something Lane and Scott coyly hint at as well.[3]

However, one might ask if instead of imitation and emulation we are witnessing dissimulation. In other words, in re-creating the era of British hegemony as a place and time where the fears and fantasies of the current crisis can be confronted and potentially resolved, are advocates of imitation silencing what many would consider to be the United States' own imperial past? Several of the contributors to this book ask similar questions. Julian Go's chapter addresses the subject of how the United States governed its Caribbean and Pacific possessions after the short war with Spain in 1898, surely important precedents for the present situation. John Kelly calls our attention to the long-range impact of Alfred Thayer Mahan, one of the foreign-policy and military gurus of the war with Spain and its aftermath.

To add to this exploration of the silences amid the busy discussion and imitation of empire, I related to the conference participants an anecdote about a piece of New York trivia with which I frequently quiz my students at Fordham University's Lincoln Center campus. About half the students at the undergraduate college commute; many arrive at Fordham via the Columbus Circle subway stop. There at the southwest entrance to Central Park is a huge monument topped by gilded statues (see

FIGURE 1

figure 1), competing for attention with other memorials to nations, empires, and capitalism, including an increasingly overshadowed statue of Columbus, the Trump Tower, and most recently, the Time Warner towers. The life of the park buzzes around it, as people sit and take in the scene, drink coffee, play music, and rendezvous with friends. Those of us at Fordham see it every day. "What is it?" I ask them. Almost none have answered correctly in five years: it is the monument to the *Maine*, the battleship that exploded in Havana harbor in 1898, precipitating the declaration of war between Spain and the United States.[4]

Though apparently forgotten now, the monument gained the attention of leading boosters, businessmen, and politicians at the time, flush from the acquisition of three former Spanish colonies—Puerto Rico, the Philippines, and Guam—and hegemony in a fourth, Cuba. For instance, William Randolph Hearst, perhaps the most notorious proponent of war against Spain, directed the fund-raising for the monument. As in our day, pundits spoke of the United States after the events of 1898 as a new empire, perhaps the inheritor to its Anglo-Saxon parent, the British Empire. Certainly, the monument to the *Maine* is replete with images of liberty, martyrdom, and empire. One façade is inscribed with the following dedication:

> To
> The Freemen
> Who Died in the
> War with Spain
> That Others
> Might be Free

Columbia Triumphant crowns the monument, bearing not only the laurel branch of victory but also the fasces, a reference to the Roman Empire and its symbols of power. Other figures in the monument represent Peace, Courage, and Fortitude, while the statue of a young boy symbolizes the young nation, Cuba. Indeed, at the monument's unveiling in 1913, former president William Taft referred to this image when he said that, "Cuba is our foster child."[5] (See figure 2.)

This tutelage extended beyond the former Spanish colonies "liberated" in 1898. In the early twentieth century, the United States would also intervene in the Dominican Republic, Haiti, Nicaragua, and Panama. These events and the interests that structured them were not identical to the current actions in Iraq and Afghanistan, but the two moments are by no means incomparable. In fact, there is one link in

FIGURE 2

particular that leads directly from 1898 to the present as Robin Blackburn noted in our discussions: Guantánamo naval base at the eastern end of Cuba, a legal and political no-place that the current administration has found invaluable in its borderless war against terrorism. Despite the fact that the news media report regularly on Guantánamo—about military tribunals, interrogation methods, suicide attempts, and criminal investigations of translators and clerics—it is the British Empire that has apparently captured the public imagination concerning the present moment.

However, historians, intellectuals, and publics in two other countries continue to think about what the *Maine* has left in its wake; in Spain and Cuba the lessons of 1898 form the core of contemporary national histories and ways of thinking about empires past and present. These memories are not necessarily more truthful than American reckonings, or lack thereof, of 1898—they too are shaped by local political, cultural, and institutional interests. However, the ways in which Cubans and Spaniards remember the *Maine* suggest that the lessons of empire are closer for Americans than the far side of the world. In particular, they demonstrate that the tensions inherent in American "nation building" in Iraq and Afghanistan have precedents in Cuba, where patriots had their own visions of the state and the nation. They also indicate that U.S. rivalries with Western Europe—suddenly even more complicated after the devastating attacks in Madrid and London in 2004 and 2005—are long-lived, complex, and always intertwined with Europe's own tortuous imperial histories.

TOWARD 1898: AN EMPIRE FORETOLD

On October 10th, 2003, President Bush announced a tightening of the travel ban to Cuba; he also made known that Secretary of State Colin Powell and Housing and Urban Development Secretary Mel Martínez would spearhead a plan for "Cuba's transition from Stalinist rule to a free and open society." The announcement was carefully timed: "The President made his remarks on the 135th anniversary of the beginning of the Cuban revolt against Spanish colonial rule. 'Today, the struggle for freedom continues—it hasn't ended—in cities and towns of that beautiful island, in Castro's prisons and in the heart of every Cuban patriot,' Mr. Bush said."[6]

On October 10th, 1868, Cuban patriots took up arms against the Spanish colonial state, beginning what would be a thirty-year struggle for independence. Along with Puerto Rico, Cuba was the sole American colony that remained to Spain after the Spanish American revolutions had led to independence in the 1810s and 1820s from Argentina to Mexico. Throughout the nineteenth century, Spain clung tenaciously to its Caribbean possessions, sources of revenue for the metropolitan treasury and of fortunes for planters, entrepreneurs, and merchants. Cuba became the largest slave society in Spanish American history during this period, importing hundreds of thousands of African slaves to work on plantations that made the island the world's biggest producer of cane sugar by the middle of the nineteenth century. Because of this dynamic and productive sugar complex, Spain delayed as long as possible in abolishing slavery, finally doing so in Puerto Rico in 1873 and in Cuba in 1886. Only Brazil abolished slavery later, in 1888.[7]

In defending this rich colony, Spain had to contend not only with challenges from Cuban patriots but also from the United States.

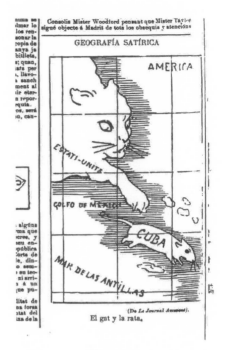

FIGURE 3

Filibusters tried to invade the island in the 1840s and 1850s, hoping to annex another slave state to buttress the South. The U.S. government also proposed buying Cuba from Spain at midcentury. More seriously, however, U.S. politicians, since independence, considered themselves to be the ultimate arbiters of Cuba's fate, not unlike President Bush in the twenty-first century. The military intervention in 1898, supposedly triggered by the explosion of the *Maine,* had figured into the American political imagination for a century at that point. In the later nineteenth century, such an intervention seemed more likely as the United States exercised increasing economic leverage in Cuba, not so much via direct investment but by the absorption of Cuban sugar. By the end of the century, virtually the entire Cuban sugar crop was destined for the United States.[8]

Spaniards and Cubans alike were well aware of U.S ambitions and its growing economic weight (see figure 3).[9] They actively compared the realities of Spain's actual colonial rule to the possibilities of a U.S. takeover. For Spaniards, their defeat would lead not only to the loss of Cuba but also to the rise of U.S. hegemony throughout the Americas. This was a nineteenth-century "clash of civilizations," between the Latin race and the Anglo-Saxon, Catholics and Protestants.[10] Some Spanish commentators believed that this fundamental antagonism made it improbable that Cuba would become part of the United States. In the judgment of a leading contemporary economist:

> Regarding a union with the United States, it is highly unlikely. Everyone who knows that country knows that the sweet, soft, generous, and indolent character of our islanders contrasts notably with the severe, tenacious, enterprising character of the Yankees. Language, habits, customs, religion, relations, and sympathies all link our islanders to Spain and separate them from the United States.

But not all Spaniards were so confident. One prominent diplomat and journalist foresaw an American juggernaut: "Alas! if [the United States] were to possess Cuba, everything would change. Her soldiers, acclimatized in Havana's barracks, would no longer be decimated by the heat. . . . Triumph will be swift in coming. We repeat again, alas! for the Spanish American Republics the day Cuba ceases to be Spanish!"[11]

Patriotic Cubans, in contrast, were intrigued by the United States; some hoped to imitate it, others to become part of it. For example, Cubans who studied at Jesuit universities in the United States at midcentury returned with a passion for baseball. They loved not only the sport, but also its potential for defining a new culture that would distinguish Cuba from Spain. Others favored what they considered to be the American model of political decentralization. If Cuba were to remain part of the Spanish empire, perhaps it could achieve greater self-rule, like a state in the North American republic, or like Canada under British rule.

However, many Cubans shared the preoccupations of their Spanish counterparts about the profound difference with the United States, even while disagreeing vehemently over the justice of Spanish rule. For a committed patriot and revolutionary like José Martí, the United States was not a model to be emulated or joined, but one to be avoided at all costs. The United States was not Cuba's potential ally but its implacable foe. Martí had joined the fight for Cuban independence as a young man in the 1870s. He spent the rest of his life (he died in combat against Spanish troops in 1895) working to organize political and military forces dedicated to Cuban independence. Much of that time was spent in exile in the United States, primarily in New York City.

Not unlike the Spanish defenders of colonialism in Cuba, Martí represented the United States as an essentially antagonistic culture. The United States was the land of Jim Crow, lynching, and obsession with profit. These were not the values that Cubans were fighting for in Martí's view. Rather, he hoped to unify all Cubans regardless of race or origin into a fraternal national community, a potent message in a society with large numbers of immigrants and people recently emancipated from slavery. Martí warned his compatriots, and other Latin Americans, of the threat from the North and urged them to defend their values and cultures against the impending invasions:

The conceited villager believes the entire world to be his village. Provided that he can be mayor, or humiliate the rival who stole his sweetheart, or add to the savings in his strong-box, he considers the universal order good, unaware of those giants with seven-league boots who can crush him underfoot. . . . What remains of the village in America must rouse itself. These are not the times for sleeping in a nightcap, but with weapons for a pillow, like the warriors of Juan de Castellanos—weapons of the mind, which conquer all others. Barri-cades of ideas are worth more than barricades of stone.[12]

AFTER 1898: REMEMBERING EMPIRES, REDEEMING NATIONS

As Martí feared, the United States eventually intervened in Cuba, during the final war for independence begun in 1895.[13] If American boosters spoke of sacrifice, tri-umph, and liberation—while also intimating an indefinite tutelage—and emulated the symbols of earlier empires, Spanish and Cuban responses were quite different. In their own ways, Spaniards and Cubans saw 1898 as a moment of national failure. For Spaniards, defeat by the United States and the loss of Cuba were profound hu-miliations that revealed the country's failure to modernize. For Cubans, 1898 marked the fateful event augured by Martí; after thirty years of planning and armed strug-gle, Cubans found their quest for independence gravely compromised by "those giants with seven-league boots." Nonetheless, these histories of failure and compro-mise have given way to histories of redemption and renewal. The events of 1898 have continued to loom large in Cuban and Spanish national histories, but how they figure has changed dramatically.

For most of the twentieth century, Spanish intellectuals saw in 1898 decisive proof of their country's backwardness, as well as of Anglo-Saxon perfidy (see figure 4).[14] This bitter denunciation—which began with the brilliant group of intellectuals known as the Generation of '98 (Miguel de Unamuno, Pío Baroja, Azorín, Antonio Machado among others)—shaped visions of modern Spanish history for genera-tions. From the right, the Franco regime (1939–1975) and Spanish conservatives held that foreign ideologies like liberalism and socialism had forced Spain to devi-ate from its authentic Catholic history; these imports had eroded Spain's peculiar virtues, weakened the nation's moral fiber, and led it into the debacle of 1898. From the left, both foreign and national, the failure of liberalism—as well as related fail-ures, such as the failure of industrialization—in the nineteenth century explained not only the "Disaster" of 1898 but also the overthrow of democracy in the 1920s and 1930s.[15]

Two processes, however, turned the tide in how Spaniards remembered 1898 and the history of empire. First, how historians comprehend and write about the events leading to 1898 has changed dramatically. Immediately after 1898, most scholars

FIGURE 4

and commentators dismissed Spain's efforts at colonial rule in the Caribbean as hapless and doomed to failure, essentially confusing the causes of imperial defeat with the consequences. However, new research on Spanish colonialism and capitalism in the nineteenth century has shown that the remaining colonies were cornerstones of Spain's uneven transition to modernity.

For instance, research in notarial archives in different regions of Spain revealed that leading economic actors accumulated their initial fortunes in the colonies through banking, commerce, or various aspects of the massive slave and sugar economy of nineteenth-century Cuba and Puerto Rico. Even Spaniards who had never traveled to Cuba or the Philippines invested heavily there (especially in Cuba) or depended on the protected colonial markets as safe havens for their agricultural products, manufactures, and merchant fleets. Moreover, hundreds of thousands of Spaniards migrated to the Caribbean colonies over the course of the century, a stream unstopped by the military defeat of 1898. Little by little, historians throughout Spain's diverse regions were finding that Spanish rule in the Caribbean and Pacific was complex and dynamic, more complicated than the dismissive images associated with the Disaster of 1898. In other words, if Spain were less archaic than the Generation of '98 and other critics insisted, then perhaps historians had to draw new lessons.[16]

Second, the cycle of commemorations that Spain witnessed in the 1990s forced intense reflections, official and spontaneous, on the histories of Spanish empire *and* imperial defeat. The official commemorations of 1992 were practically elephantine in their scale: they included state expenditures on academic conferences and publications, the Seville Expo dedicated to the 500th anniversary of Columbus's first voyage, the Barcelona Olympics, and Madrid's status as Cultural Capital of Europe. However, for anyone who visited Spain regularly during that decade it was immediately apparent that 1492, despite official sponsorship, took a back seat in the public imagination to 1898.[17]

The revisionist scholarship on colonialism and Spanish modernity played some role in this surge of interest in 1898, but there were larger processes at play that historians were just beginning to understand in their full dimensions. Several factors shaped this process of remembrance but we might point to two in particular: first, as the Spanish economy took off in the latter part of the twentieth century, firms began to invest heavily in Latin America, not least in Cuba. Indeed, the Spanish presence in Cuba is immediately tangible to any visitor to Havana, be it in the form of prominent hotels or the brightly illuminated Spanish embassy on the Malecón. Second, the human toll of the Spanish war against Cuban patriots was horrendous. Not only did Spanish forces carry out deadly counterinsurgency tactics aimed principally at the Cuban agrarian population but the Spanish side also suffered huge losses, approximately 50,000 deaths, mostly from diseases such as yellow fever. Thousands of Spanish troops would also die in colonial campaigns in Morocco in the early twentieth century. In other words, the human cost to Spaniards themselves in the defense of Cuba, and later in other wars, has left both vivid memories of 1898 and a deep distrust of foreign military interventions.[18]

Not surprisingly then, Cuba, place of Spanish fortunes and Spanish graves, figured most prominently in this process of remembering. Many Spanish commentators curiously revived the language of nineteenth-century colonialism when discussing the triangular relation between Spain, Cuba, and the United States at the end of the twentieth century. In doing so, Spaniards cast themselves as the defenders of Cuban independence against the imperial pretensions of the United States, a most ironic role reversal. For example, one of the periodic resurgences of American revanchism toward the Castro regime came right in the midst of Spanish recollections of the events leading to 1898. The Helms-Burton Act, passed by the U.S. Congress, would empower the United States government to take legal action against foreign firms that invested in Cuba, a measure that directly threatened the Spanish businesses with an ever-growing presence in the island. In an editorial in *El País* speaking out against the threat, the author, consciously or not, relapsed into the language of empire. Not only was the title, "The Cuban Question," straight out of the past but the demand that Spain defend Cuba because it was "la España ultramarina" (overseas Spain) had a decidedly archaic ring to it. The language of empire was recast, curiously in the idiom of anti-imperialism.[19]

The vigor of the denunciation and the affirmation of Spain and Cuba's lasting bonds, not just economic but more importantly, cultural, indicated a quite different attitude towards 1898 in Spain at the end of the twentieth century. After 1898, historians, pundits, and intellectuals from left to right saw the "Disaster" as confirmation of Spain's failure to compete with modern nation-states like the United States. While dynamic "Anglo-Saxon" nations scrambled to expand their empires, Spain was imploding, a victim of its inability to break free of the past. In contrast, by the end of the twentieth century, historians painted a more complex picture of Spanish modernity and colonialism. Moreover, in the mass media, commentators sounded a generally euphoric note about Spain's progress over the last one hundred years; once a pariah, it was now in the western European mainstream. Spain's history was not as aberrant as the Generation of '98, the Franco regime, and scores of historians foreign and national proclaimed for most of the twentieth century.

While in Spain, a sense of national redemption has come through a peaceful transition to democracy after Franco's death in 1975, the growth of Spanish capitalism, and the opening of the country's intellectual life, in Cuba, revolution has transformed memories and renderings of 1898. U.S. forces occupied Cuba after quickly defeating Spain in 1898. In a process that resonates with contemporary events in Iraq, political and military leaders debated with increasing pessimism a transfer of power to a Cuban government. Though the occupiers very loudly expressed their doubt about Cubans' capacity to govern themselves, their hands were tied by the Teller Amendment, written into the congressional authorization for war in 1898 as a guarantee of Cuban independence after the U.S. intervention. In a first step, the occupation regime called municipal elections that limited the franchise to men over the age of twenty-one; property and literacy requirements were also imposed. By so restricting the franchise, the United States hoped to form a government of the wealthy classes friendly to the occupation. However, supporters of independence and U.S. withdrawal were victorious, forcing reconsideration on how the transfer of power would be put into effect as Cubans prepared to draft a constitution.

American officials were gloomy. General Leonard Wood, the occupation governor, wrote to Senator Orville Platt that "The men whom I hoped to see take leadership have been forced into the background by the absolutely irresponsible and unreliable element. . . . The only fear in Cuba to-day [*sic*] is not that we shall stay, but that we shall leave too soon. The elements desiring our immediate departure are the men whose only capacity will be demonstrated as a capacity for destroying all hopes for the future."[20] Platt and his fellow senators responded to these dire predictions. Though they stopped short of overriding the Teller Amendment, they attached a new amendment named after Senator Platt to the 1901 Cuban constitution that guaranteed a role for the United States in preserving public order in Cuba and protection against foreign debt or intervention. That the Platt Amendment expressed doubt about Cubans' capacity for self-government was explicit. Senator Albert Beveridge said, "The welfare of the Cuban people . . . was still open to attack from another enemy at their weakest point. That point was within and that enemy themselves."[21]

The Platt Amendment was a source of great resentment in independent Cuba; it also shaped the nature of Cuban politics by giving the United States a recognized role in the preservation of public order and prosperity. For example, Cuban parties would stage uprisings, hoping to precipitate a U.S. intervention and the reshuffling of political office. Cubans felt, and used, the American presence in other ways as well. North American firms invested heavily in the resurrected sugar industry and other sectors of the economy. Protestant missionaries flocked to the island, as did tourists. Many Cuban nationalists came to feel that Martí's omen was borne out: the United States after 1898 not only intervened in the politics and economy of the island but also threatened to extinguish the national culture. The regime created by the 1901 constitution became known in Cuban historiography as the *neo-república,* not to be confused with the true republic; as in Spain, 1898 was a moment of national defeat.

In contrast to the language of liberation etched in stone at Columbus Circle, many Cubans remembered the U.S. intervention as the origin of a new form of domination and subjugation. The title of a midcentury essay by a leading historian expressed this sense of indignation: *Cuba Does Not Owe Its Independence to the United States.*[22] Cubans had liberated themselves from Spain, only to have true sovereignty headed off by the United States in 1898. However, Cubans did not suffer defeat passively; revolutionary movements fought not only to restructure the Cuban state and society but also to reshape Cuba's relation with the United States. For example, the revolution of 1933 that overthrew the dictatorship of Gerardo Machado took as its slogan "Cuba for the Cubans," directed not only against U.S. preeminence but also against foreign immigration and investment in the economy. Though the United States impeded the most radical nationalists from taking power, it had to agree to abrogate the Platt Amendment.

The U.S. checked the radical impulses of Cuban revolutionaries in 1933 but failed utterly to do so in 1959. Cubans immediately cast the revolution as the redemption for 1898's strange defeat. Louis A. Pérez Jr. has demonstrated in detail the linkages that many Cubans, including Fidel Castro, drew between 1898 and 1959: Castro was the heir of great patriotic leaders like Martí and Calixto García, while the rebels of the Sierra Maestra were latter-day *mambises* (the term for Cuban rebels in the nineteenth century). Speaking soon after victory, Castro announced: "This time the revolution will not be thwarted. . . . This time, fortunately for Cuba, the revolution will be consummated. It will not be like the war of 1895, when the Americans arrived and made themselves masters of the country." This narration of the past century-plus of national history—a story of renewal and liberation—remains paradigmatic to this day.[23]

CONCLUSION

Thus, in Cuba as in Spain, 1898 continues to shape historical memories and the political imagination. What began for both countries as an unparalleled disaster that provoked agonizing soul searching now works as the pivot in histories of national redemption. Memories of 1898 not only define national histories but also histories of empire: Cubans see the revolution of 1959 as a blow against the Yankee imperialism of 1898, while Spaniards have used their own language of empire in the service of anti-imperialism, protesting U.S. policies towards Cuba and, more recently, almost universally opposing the war in Iraq.

Indeed, Spanish voters, in the aftermath of the terrible massacre in Madrid, castigated the conservative Partido Popular (PP) for its support for the United States and the United Kingdom in Iraq, returning to parliamentary predominance the Partido Socialista (PSOE), whose leader took a fervently anti-war stance. José Luis Rodríguez Zapatero immediately withdrew Spanish troops from Iraq; he also affirmed Madrid's commitment to Paris and Berlin in international affairs, breaking his predecessor's brief alliance with Washington and London. Critics in the United States have portrayed the PSOE's victory as a triumph for al-Qaeda, which sought to punish the PP, and as a resounding defeat for the Bush administration. For instance, the conservative columnist David Brooks asked, "What is the Spanish word for appeasement?" Another contributor to the *New York Times* asserted, "It must be said: Spanish voters have allowed a small band of terrorists to dictate the outcome of their national elections."[24] While it would be impossible to deny the impact of March 11th on the 2004 election, these events did not take place in an historical vacuum. Spaniards deeply distrust foreign wars and what could be perceived as imperial aggrandizement because of their own histories of war with subject peoples and their tormented memories of imperial collapse.[25]

I do not mean to say that Cubans and Spaniards remember 1898 and its after-math more accurately or truthfully than do Americans—in both countries diverse interests and accretions of knowledge shape the memories and uses of the past. Nor do I seek to represent Cubans and Spaniards as selfless victims and critics of U.S. ag-gression: In 1898, many Cuban elites welcomed the U.S. intervention, collaborated with the occupying regime, and continued to emulate aspects of North American culture. During the war with Cuban forces between 1895 and 1898, the Spanish po-litical and military leadership fought a brutal counterinsurgency (including the first widespread use of concentration camps) that cost thousands of civilian casualties and helped to precipitate the U.S. invasion. Rather, I dwell on these histories because they offer pertinent lessons of empire applicable to the tensions in the international order among the United States, Europe, and postcolonial nation-states: First, from these perspectives, the talk of American empire is not novel but venerable, long pre-dating the climactic moment of 1898, or 2003. Second, Cuban histories and memo-ries of 1898 raise questions (good to ask if not to accept uncritically) about the United States' commitment to national sovereignty and democracy in the aftermath of invasion and occupation. Finally, Spanish responses to 1898, especially in the im-mediate flush of March 11th, provoke reflection on the human cost of foreign ad-ventures in the metropolis itself and the political will of the electorate to support empire.

The events of 1898 play little part in American discussions of empire; rather, the era of British global hegemony is the stuff of imperial reckonings. The logic of anal-ogy and imitation shapes this move: that the United States is the lone superpower of the twenty-first century has led historians and others to search out a similar histor-ical situation from which to draw lessons. Moreover, the United States seems to be following the tracks of the British through the Middle East and Central Asia in at-tempting to redraw the global order. However, the detention of hundreds of Taliban and al-Qaeda prisoners at Guantánamo naval base in Cuba indicates that the United States is far from undertaking a novel or unprecedented venture that can be compre-hended only through analogy. Contemporary U.S. ambitions are diachronic not only with the "previous superpower" but also with earlier moments of American warfare and conquest. Contemplating the actions and ambitions of Cecil Rhodes, not to mention Jack Aubrey, is instructive. But the events and people enshrined in metal and stone at the entrance to Central Park can remind us that it was not only the British Empire that sought to liberate peoples by conquering them, wrestled with the dilemmas of subject populations with their own visions of liberation, or in-spired the anger and wrath of Western European rivals burdened by their own his-tories of empire and decolonization.

15. AGRICULTURE, INDUSTRY, EMPIRE, AND AMERICA*

CRAIG N. MURPHY

It saddens Jonathan Schell that after September 11th the United States embarked on the path toward "universal empire" that has been temporarily opened by the country's unexpected military predominance after the cold war.[1] Many students of international relations understand the imperial motivation as ubiquitous across the territory and history of settled human societies. Yet, the material, economic ground of empire—settled agriculture—is no longer the primary foundation of human societies. Modern industry is. Even before the information age, industrialism, and, in particular, capitalist industrialism has had its own expansionist logic that in some ways contradicts and, in other ways, reinforces the logic of empire. The American imperial strategy often ignores the impact of the logic of industrialism, while presuming that the ends served by the American variant of the industrial system are universally accepted. The current U.S. administration does not consider the possibility that the triumph of capitalist industrialism may be incompatible with American predominance. We may be in an epochal transition, one as significant as the transition that gave us "governments" and "international systems" as a response to the agricultural revolution, but the new American empire at the beginning of the twenty-first century is not the similar political solution to the economic revolution that began at the opening of the nineteenth century.

THE NEW AMERICAN EMPIRE AND EMPIRE'S CONSTANT LOGIC

The great strength (and, no doubt, also the great weakness) of international relations relative to the other social sciences is its yearning to take a global perspective on the human condition, a view across space and across time.[2] As a result, there would be relatively wide agreement among students of international relations about the set of cases to which the current push toward universal empire is a part.[3] This set includes all those cases when a militarily preponderant state has been able to expand far beyond its original borders. In each case, an important goal of the expanding state was simply self-defense, security. Military preponderance just assured that security could be served by expansion.

For most of human history (or, more accurately, prehistory), if the typically small-scale societies of gather-hunters or herders came into conflict with one another, they could resolve the conflict by movement. Migration, not war was the basic stuff of prehistoric "international relations."[4]

With settled agriculture, with the agricultural revolution (which was not an abrupt, rapid change, but something extending over scores of centuries), the opportunity costs of migration became excessive, while the likeliness of conflict between societies increased. Networks of relatively prosperous, settled societies created a niche for parasitic communities whose mode of "production" was raiding. To use an appropriate word in its original, Norse, sense, these "Viking" societies, these raiders (the first of which predated the Norse by thousands of years) created the security dilemma that drives so much of the analysis of international relations "realists." Realists argue that all states have essentially the same motivations. As Hans J. Morgenthau put it, "The struggle for power is ubiquitous in time and space."[5] Place one raiding society in a system of peaceful, agricultural communities, and the logic of self-defense (and of alliances to assure collective self-defense against raiders and any allies they develop among militarized settled communities) will assure that every settled society becomes militarized in order to survive.[6]

One step further and we have arrived at the standard "realist" argument that the best way to achieve defense against possible raiders is for your society to dominate all others: the urge to universal empire is a constant. This is the logic of "empire," the push toward universal domination resting, ultimately, on military force; the goal is a universal "empire" as distinct from, perhaps, a global "hegemony" of the ideas of a leading nation or social strata. Of course, this security-based, abstract logic of empire differs from the actual "logic in use," the complicated ideologies motivating the expansion of real-world states. Moreover, throughout history, the number of real-world states that appear to have pursued universal empire is small. Yet, international-relations realists would argue that the goal only seems to be rare because it is so rare that a society has such a preponderance of force that universal empire is anything more than a chimera. Why, after attack from the raiders of al-Qaeda is the Bush administration pursuing something that looks like universal empire? Because, given the unprecedented relative preponderance of American military power in the decade after the collapse of the Soviet Union, the United States thinks it can, and American policy makers see an open path toward that kind of supremacy. There are other similarities between the current American push for universal empire and the larger world historical pattern.

Even within just the "old world" of Eurasia and Africa, no attempt to achieve universal empire has ever been successful. With rare exceptions, the most that any government achieved for more than a generation was supremacy over one of the old world's population lobes. There have been empires of the South (India), the East (China), and the West (Persia, Rome). The current U.S. empire is a lineal descendent of the empires of the West.

The new U.S. empire shares one advantage of its immediate western predecessors. After the Columbian conquest, the competing empires of Atlantic Europe used the living and mineral wealth of the Americas that came so easily to hand (largely due to the virulence of old-world diseases on Native Americans), to create unprecedented domains that crossed the traditional old-world lines. For nearly two centuries, an island on Europe's northwest corner ruled the empire of the South. Maintaining ties to the wealth and power originating in India became a central goal of the expansionist nineteenth-century British Empire, the closest global approximation to universal empire, so far. Similarly, the United States' agricultural and mineral abundance, especially in comparison to other wealthy industrial societies, contributes to its global supremacy.

Finally, the problems of internal governance of empires recur. Charles Tilly and S. E. Finer have made us aware of the degree to which the state, or to use Finer's simpler term "government,"[7] was a consequence of "international relations," in particular of the dominance of warrior castes in settled societies who promise protection from foreign warriors. "Government" can take many forms and, paradoxically perhaps, empire grows well in republican soil. Warriors who represent the people can more easily amass resources than those who rely on coercion at home can. Yet, western theorists at least, have long feared that the maintenance and extension of empire may turn "Conciliar" polities into "Palace/Forum polities: the Greek tyrants, the 'perpetual dictatorships' conferred upon Sulla and Julius Caesar . . . Napoleon . . . Stalin."[8] Thus, commentators today worry about the xenophobic populism and the restrictions on civil liberties marshaled to support the limitless "war on terrorism" that Schell, and others, see as the public face of the new American quest for universal empire.

THE QUEST FOR EMPIRE AND THE LOGIC OF INDUSTRY

For all these similarities, we would be misguided to rely on the pattern that goes back to Egypt's First Dynasty to explain the trajectory of the new American empire. Industrialism has transformed human life as significantly as settled agriculture did.

The most dramatic shift is the more than tenfold, step-wise increase in human population: the demographic transition that began in the late eighteenth century and will be completed in the late twenty-first century. Population explosions and later stabilizations track the diffusion of the factory system and its products from Europe around the world.[9]

We should not be surprised at this since the common promise of the two key elements of the industrial system—machine production and a global division of labor—is material abundance. That abundance should allow the human community to grow. Harnessing tools to nonliving sources of power (the essence of the "machine" for Babbage or Marx), allowed those tools to produce much more. Increasing the technical division of labor across all workers and machines, extending the logic of Adam Smith's pin factory to the whole world of work, promised even greater efficiencies.

These, then, are the elements of the industrial system: Most goods are produced by *machines,* by tools that are linked to nonliving sources of power.[10] Machines create what John A. Hobson called, "a new economy of force and knowledge."[11] The "force," as Charles Babbage opined, reflected, "the most singular advantages we derive from machinery . . . the check which it affords against the inattention, the idleness, or the knavery of human agents."[12] The men who controlled the machines could control the workers who served them, including by introducing new *technologies* to produce more from less. That is where the "economy of . . . knowledge" comes in: The new ease with which new technology could be introduced by the machines' controllers created a new impetus for a constantly innovating *science.*

Self-reinforcing processes creating more goods by enthralling more and more workers to machines and continuously developing technology and science could be set in motion by a range of different forces. The profit motive was only one. It has been equally possible to have industrial systems based on the command of governments bent on increasing the technical division of labor across all the workers under their control. Conceivably, even an economy of affection, a "traditional" redistributive economy could establish a complex technical division of labor that benefits from the productive advantages of the machine. Karl Polanyi hints at this possibility[13] and Gandhi, whose views about industrialization are often caricatured, was opposed only to machines meant to "enrich the few at the expense of the many" and hoped for a democratically controlled economy that would invest in, "the heavy machinery of public utility that cannot be undertaken by human labour."[14]

Of course, industrialism actually rode in on the horse of capitalism, which Marx and Engels correctly understood as having its own logic of expansion at least as strong as the realist concerns that compel settled agricultural societies to seek security through dominance. Yet, it may be even more important to recognize that any society that attempts to achieve the benefits Adam Smith promises will, in fact, be expansionist. "The Division of Labour" (and, hence, the expansion of wealth), Smith told us, "is limited by the Extent of the Market," by the extent of the world united under a single economic system.[15] To pursue economic growth—whether by the macroeconomic policies of the welfare state, by the "development" policies of the Third World, or even under the heavy hand of a command economy—in the long run, means establishing larger and larger economic societies, and, ultimately, a single global economy.

Yet, unlike the logic of empire, the Smithian, or liberal, logic does not require military force. The Smithian teleology points toward a global hegemony of liberal ideas. The school of analysis that international relations calls "functionalist" provides visions of an achieved cosmopolitan world in which the technical division of labor has become universal, and the problem of "government" is no longer one of coercion or military defense. Instead, men and women would come increasingly to rely on democratic procedures to reach agreement on the "one best way" to work collectively as our scientific and technical knowledge changes.[16]

Arguably, international-relations "functionalism" and the schools of analysis that have developed from it have provided a more accurate picture of the real work of international affairs over the last 200 years than "realism" has. Functionalists can explain the integration of industrializing states including Germany, Italy, and the United States.[17] The functionalist argument illuminates the unification of Europe over the last half-century, and the even more difficult to explain processes that led to a relatively integrated and peaceful Europe in the late nineteenth century. And functionalism fits well with other, empirically strong, arguments of liberal international relations, including those that explain why formally democratic states rarely go to war with one another, an argument that goes back to Smith's contemporary, Immanuel Kant.

Liberal international relations argues that the republican governments that are the most likely to promote the Smithian logic can easily find grounds for peaceful relations with one another. There may be reasons for liberal societies to pursue imperial projects against illiberal societies—for a United States to attempt to conquer an Iraq—but there is no compelling reason for a liberal state to act imperiously toward another liberal society.

This is why predictions of the behavior of the militarily predominant United States based on the traditional logic of empire, alone, are likely to be wrong. Yes, the Bush administration and its predecessors, at least as far back as Reagan, have been pulled toward the pole of empire by the security logic and their military predominance. Nonetheless, the United States is also the major champion of liberal globalization, pulled toward the Kantian pole of international law and the transnationalization of municipal law. The U.S. government helps create networks of institutions that bind the American state and its citizens into relationships that transform states with republican polities into what Karl Deutsch called a "pluralistic security community," an international society with compatible, but not identical, elite values and predictable and responsive patterns of government to government interaction.[18] The fact that the United States and Western Europe are part of such a community, and that major EU states are not simply American vassals, should help contextualize the original disagreement over the recent war in Iraq. It certainly should help explain why it may be possible to mend fences and develop a multilateral approach now.

If the liberal logic at times pulls a militarily dominant United States toward the pole of empire, the lacunae in that logic help pull other liberal societies toward the logic of empire. In *International Organization and Industrial Change: Global Governance since 1850*,[19] and a group of related papers, I argued that economic globalization has taken place through a step-wise process that partially reflects the kind of Smithian and Kantian logic elaborated by generations of liberal internationalists. Yet, post–industrial revolution globalization also reflects social processes to which liberals tend to be blind, especially various recurrent forms of opposition to the liberal vision. For the politics of empire, the most significant form of opposition has been, and will continue to be, from industrial societies that do not embrace liberal capitalism. That is the threat that the Axis posed to Britain and the United States; it is the threat posed by the old Soviet system and by Communist Party–ruled China, at least before it headed down its capitalist path.

This opposition also is what unites the disparate set of countries that George W. Bush calls "the Axis of Evil." Islamist Iran, the tyrannical command economy of Iraq, and the oddly similar, if supposedly "Leninist," regime in North Korea all embrace the industrial system. With nuclear weapons, each of the regimes might have been able to avoid incorporation into a world of *liberal capitalist* industrialism. At the extreme, Iran, at least, might present an industrial model that could be a viable, expanding alternative to liberal capitalism.

More significantly, capitalist China, which certainly does capitalism differently than the United States and the European Union do, might also become a threat, in the way that the (capitalist) fascist alliance eventually threatened Britain and the United States. Nonetheless, the history of that conflict may be instructive and may indicate how easy it may be to integrate China into a liberal capitalist world. Recall that the problem with Italy, Germany, and Japan was not their rejection of domestic liberal political institutions. Nor was it even their "imperialism" in Africa or Asia. In fact, as Nehru argued in his brilliant contemporary analysis of the origins of World War II, a key part of the *political* background both of the actual appeasement policy of Britain's conservative government, and of the failure to use the League to counter moves in Manchuria and Ethiopia, was the continuing sympathy that many reactionary British policy makers had for the racist ideology underlying fascism.[20] The ultimate problem with the fascist states was their direct attacks on other European countries and on the United States. A China with restricted military ambitions could fit within an American empire.

Of course, the possible alternatives posed by the various members of the "Axis of Evil" does not necessarily makes these regimes logical targets for imperial conquest by the United States, but it does explain why champions of liberal globalization would be concerned about these states. More significantly, it points to a general reason why states and private elites outside the United States might, at times, welcome manifestations of an American itch for universal empire. The United States, as the holder of most of the coercive means at the disposal of those who champion liberal capitalist industrialism, is the one "indispensable power," even if this was not exactly Madeleine Albright's meaning when she began promoting the phrase.

In a similar way, at the end of the nineteenth century, Britain looked like the indispensable power to advocates of capitalist industrialism in many parts of the world. Supporters of the empire could be found in the United States, in the "white

FIGURE 1. An 1886 supplement to *The Graphic* promotes the Imperial Federation League, which argued that the growth of the British Empire must lead to a federation of equals, united to protect common interests.

dominions," in the smaller states of Europe, and even among native trading associations along the West African coast, or in the house of a Gujarati attorney who would later break the British hold on the empire of the South. The British "liberal imperialists" understood the value of British predominance in the same way that Albright and many members of the Bush administration do. They hoped for the rapid development of independent democratic nations (with the franchise perhaps temporarily restricted by race) in the white dominions. These would later be joined by the "less-advanced" peoples of India, the Arab world, etc. All would unite in a world of liberal economies and democratic harmony with the United States, the European republics, the "advanced" nations of Latin America, and perhaps even an increasingly liberal Germany.

One of the failures of the British Empire, like so many of the modern empires of the West, was its inability to treat its colonized as equals. Victorian Britain failed to open the imperial elite to include the ethnoclasses that ruled in Britain's name in other parts of the world. Saul could become a Roman, and could bring Rome the ideology that would allow it to rule the West for centuries. Gandhi could no more become British than Amilcar Cabral could fully become Portuguese. That made one man available to destroy the most powerful of the descendants of Rome, while the other destroyed the oldest.

Of course, this is a general problem of all empires: how to balance incorporation (which, in a system regarding itself as democratic, could be read as an eventual promise of equality) and the differentiation that serves the unequal access to power, in all its forms, which is at the heart of the imperial enterprise. Race need not be the only basis for making such distinctions. Portugal tried to maintain the boundary through a legal system by which, in theory, anyone could become assimilated and, hence, "civilized." Yet, when it came down to the brass tacks of assigning the most qualified government-trained agronomist in many years, no one objected to a black man, Cabral, wishing to work in an insignificant job in Guinea, a job he was attracted to by the radical political commitments he had developed in the racially divided metropole.[21]

Late in life, Susan Strange, who often argued that the Achilles' heel of the U.S. empire might be its inability extend "citizenship" to elites in other nations, seemed to suggest that training in and somewhat slavish adherence to particular economic and military doctrines might eventually be used to establish the essential credentials. Leo Panitch has made the point more concretely:

> It is certainly the case that there are citizens and semi-citizens of the U.S. empire as Susan Strange once put it; a Canadian cannot avoid noticing this. . . . Canadians who work in the Canadian Defence Department—and, I would add, in the Canadian Finance Department—who walk the streets of Ottawa but have a degree of influence on American foreign

policy and economic policy are semi-citizens of the American empire. It is a type of empire which has penetrated other sovereign nation-states and which, in turn, does indeed include them in decision-making . . . except at a clear moment of crisis.[22]

Yet, the partisans of empire in the "indispensable" United States, especially the United States of the Bush-era Republicans, may suffer from a problem similar to that faced by the Portuguese in the mid-twentieth century. William Robinson and Jerry Harris argue, persuasively, that the social groups promoting and largely governing the increasingly integrated global economy are merging into a single transnational capitalist class.[23] Nonetheless, this class is not the constituency of the holders of force within the global order. George W. Bush's core constituents remain largely white, Calvinist and/or fundamentalist Christian, unilateralist, suspicious of non-Americans and even of those nonwhite Americans who fail to assimilate completely into a narrow set of cultural norms.[24] The cultural narrowness of that base may prove the undoing of the post–September 11th American imperial venture. It is one reason to be less fearful that today's xenophobic populism and restrictions on civil liberties will be with us far into the future.

INDUSTRY AND WORLD ORDER

From a longer historical perspective, the failures of Britain and the United States to carry out what might be called the "liberal capitalist imperial project" should not be surprising. If the industrial revolution represents a break as significant as the agricultural revolution, and if it took more than a thousand years for the characteristic governance forms of that era (the state [Finer's "government"] and "international systems") to emerge, we should hardly expect the characteristic forms of the industrial age to have developed in just two centuries.

Yet, others might argue, science and technology have given us a very different world than the one marked by the agricultural revolution. Time (along with space) has been compressed, accelerated, as a consequence of our abilities to reach out to the ends of the earth. The current American empire is connected with a shift in industrial capitalism that relies upon the transformations of technology that have made the world smaller: we live in a world that is closer to the Smithian vision of a global factory than anything that has come before. The vast, inexpensive bandwidth of modern communication allows coordination of production across continents. Inexpensive jets move ever-heavier goods from point to point anywhere across the globe, and, increasingly, profit comes from the sale of "information," "commodities" that flow through the instantaneous and less-and-less costly channels of communication themselves.

The information-age economy has, seemingly, solved some of the conflicts in the "Fordist" world of the mid-twentieth century. In those days, workers in the privileged parts of the world could only be satisfied by the system of mass production *and* mass *consumption*; they had to be paid, the way Ford had pioneered—paid enough to afford the products that they made. In the (semi) "post-Fordist" world, much larger unit profits can come from producing commodities in parts of the global factory where workers could never imagine owning the cars, shirts, and shoes they construct for the privileged societies that entered the industrial world earlier. And working people in those privileged societies remain quiescent, in part because *their* mass consumption remains, in part because they know their own jobs might be the next to be shipped abroad.

Of course, a layer of Fordism remains. The manufacturing sector of South Korea became a site for effective labor campaigns and the mass consumption to which labor's victories contributed has been part of that country's economic "miracle." Yet, high "noncompetitive" Korean wages lead Korean capitalists to search for other, non-Fordist, workers abroad, and the anxieties felt by working men and women in the industrial core have been transferred to Koreans as well.

Is post-Fordism, then, a sustainable economic system and the objective correlative of the new American empire? I think not. It simply shifts the set of conflicts that are most troubling to the maintenance of capitalist industrialism. It pits working people in the First World against those in the Third. In that sense, its logic is the same as that of late-nineteenth-century imperialism, at least as understood by Hobson.[25] To sustain the nineteenth-century version, even the "indispensable" British, including the liberal promoters of an imperialism that envisioned the universal triumph of democracy, supported military adventures that secured the Third World's profits of firms closely tied to those who dominated the state. I fear that there is nothing fundamentally new in the Bush administration's policies.

My hunch is that the "utopian" visions of Gandhi and of functionalists like Mary Parker Follett, the early-twentieth-century business and social theorist who thought it possible to gain democratic agreement on when to employ new technologies,[26] may have more staying power than the twenty-first-century American empire. The Smithian vision rests on assumptions about human motivation developed in a particular time and a particular place under very specific conditions. As Indian psychologist and social theorist Ashis Nandy writes, while almost all of us want physical and emotional security and to be able to follow a calling, material abundance and the continuous invention of new things are irrelevant to those needs.[27] They are as irrelevant as the magical cornucopias imagined by state-legitimating fertility cults of ancient agricultural societies. Conflicts linked to the industrial systems that liberals regularly ignore, most of them also ignored here, will shape the future world order more significantly than the restricted vision guiding today's ephemeral American empire. These include conflicts over the democratic control of technological innovation, over the periodic destruction of traditional social solidarities that capitalist industrialism demands, over the value of fundamentally different cultures, and over the right relationship between humanity and the rest of the living world.

16. IMPERIALISM IS ALIVE AND WELL: GLOBALIZATION AND EAST ASIA AFTER SEPTEMBER 11

JOMO K.S.

It must be a sign of the times we live in that a contemporary conference on the "Lessons of Empire" has so little consideration of recent economic theories of modern or capitalist imperialism. A century ago, there was a lively debate about contemporary imperialism principally associated with the English liberal John Hobson. Although he changed his view of imperialism over time, in his classic book on the subject, Hobson found imperialism objectionable for at least two main reasons. First, he believed that imperialism was the consequence of the emergence of oligopolistic or monopolistic power due to the concentration of capital, which negated the liberal ideal of competitive capitalism. Second, he believed that the international expansionism associated with imperialism was due to the undue political influence of such powerful monopolies, violating liberal democratic ideals.

Lenin was to draw upon Hobson and Rudolf Hilferding's analysis of contemporary finance capital, involving an alliance of banks with industrial monopolies, to make a trenchant argument for what later became the Third International's objection to the national loyalties of the social democrats of the Second International. In doing so, following Marx, he argued that the inherent tendencies in capitalism toward concentration and centralization meant that Hobson's imperialism was a consequence of the evolution of capitalism, rather than an aberration, as suggested by Hobson.

Later, Lenin went on to argue that imperialism implied that while the immediate task of struggle in capitalist economies was socialism, the struggle against imperialism for national liberation was the priority in the colonies and semicolonies. This struggle for national liberation would involve anticolonial multiclass alliances. As is well known, the economist Joseph Schumpeter later argued that imperialism was in fact a precapitalist atavism that would disappear with the fuller development of capitalism.

The contemporary context for discussion of imperialism and empire is remarkably different. In some respects, post–World War II imperialism has been significantly different from the prewar colonial empires. While elements of continuity have been captured by the slogan "neocolonialism," aspects of discontinuity were recognized by early uses of the term "postcolonialism."

After all, postwar U.S. hegemony began with Bretton Woods, the cold war, and the Marshall Plan, rather than "gunboat diplomacy" or its contemporary and later equivalents. The long record of U.S. military and other interventions abroad for over two centuries, and direct U.S. colonialism since the Spanish-American War does not in itself negate the many novel aspects of U.S. hegemony, which also changed over time. And recent attempts to rethink contemporary imperialism on more postmodern and postcolonial lines, e.g., in terms of "network hegemony" and transnational corporate collusion, should not obscure the changing realities of U.S. hegemony, especially after the end of the cold war.

Nineteenth-century English liberalism espoused both economic and political liberalism. Hobson invoked liberalism to oppose the oligopolistic economic implications and political influence of monopolies who represented the negation of liberalism in both senses. Hence, from such a liberal perspective, it would be consistent to promote both economic and political liberalism. The problem with most—though not all—contemporary economic neoliberals is that they insist on laissez-faire economic conditions while not opposing the emergence, consolidation, and influence of oligopolistic modern corporations, often by their emphasis on private-property rights. Hence, contemporary economic neoliberals can be described as inconsistent, contradictory, and even opportunistic from such a liberal perspective.

Some economic neoliberals are not political liberals, although recent political discourse has generally tended to associate economic liberalism with political liberalism. Many would insist on rolling back the role, power, and influence of the state in both economic and political senses. However, many of the institutions promoting economic liberalism have not insisted on liberal political institutions and processes, claiming that political interference would be beyond their mandates. Not surprisingly then, economic liberalism has been imposed in a variety of illiberal conditions, often enhancing foreign corporate economic interests. However, illiberal political conditions are not necessary for contemporary economic imperialism, and may well be the less preferred political option. After all, imperialism with consent, or Gramscian hegemony, is generally thought to be far less costly and problematic than contemporary colonialism.

The recent revival of interest in empire and imperialism has been prompted by recent developments. It arises after the apparent victory of the West in the cold war and the apparent demise of existing state socialisms. This political triumph is often linked to the rise of so-called neoliberal economic ideology including a benign, if not enthusiastic attitude towards economic liberalization, including its transnational or cross-border component termed globalization, which the rest of this paper will soon return to. But the immediate impulse is the changed world situation after September 11, 2001. As is well known, this has been invoked not only to legitimize the military invasions of Afghanistan and Iraq but a more belligerent international stance generally, partially expressed in terms of U.S. unilateralism in world affairs.

To be sure, unilateralism is certainly not the isolationism some commentators sometimes invoke. And the Bush administration is hardly unconstrained, sometimes alternating between unilateralism when desirable, possible, or feasible, and multilateralism when unavoidable or necessary. Some perceive this as a "hard cop, soft cop" strategy while others see this as necessary to unite the disparate elements supporting the Bush administration.

And the shadowy, if not sinister, rise to influence of the so-called neoconservatives is often cited in this context. Quite understandably, the neocons claim to be political liberals in so far as they espouse a liberal democratic political agenda, at least for the Middle East, and would prefer to dissociate themselves from the patrician conservative patronage of fascists as well as other pro-U.S. despots and reactionaries characteristic of the Reagan and older Bush administrations. But as is also well known, they have not been reluctant to forge alliances with others who will support the Netanyahu wing of the Likud Party in Israel.

Clearly, these are interesting new times, where many old alliances are under stress, and coalitions are being put together or abandoned in response to new developments. Most importantly for our purposes, this new situation has given rise to new justifications for assertion of imperial dominance, whether in the form of direct unilateral occupation (even if by the rarely fully specified "coalition of the willing") or involving some multilateral administration (NATO or UN).

To be sure, justifications for international inequality and dominance have been around for a long time, though there has been a perceptible revival in the last two decades or so of renewed right-wing hegemony in the anglophone West (e.g., with the revival of interest in "social darwinism," "failed states," "vampire states," "rogue states," etc.). And as is now well known, the initially triumphalist "end of history" à la Fukuyama soon gave way to the Bernard Lewis-Samuel Huntington warnings about a "clash of civilizations" between the Judeo-Christian North Atlantic West (a recent invention, if there ever was one) and the rest. The rest, of course, principally referred to the then economically ascendant and ostensibly Confucian East Asia, led by Japan and now China, and Islam, conveniently disowned by its older Abrahamic brethren.

But rather than dwell in the realm of the political and cultural, let me instead urge a return to the economic, to consider whether recent economic globalization has changed international economic relations in ways that either undermine or strengthen international dominance and exploitation. And while there is no automatic and simple relationship between the economic and the political, especially when security considerations seemed to have overwhelmed economic ones, there is good reason to believe that economic imperialism is alive and well, albeit considerably transformed.

To be sure, contemporary economic imperialism predates recent empire talk and is understood here as a consequence of the development and restructuring of capitalism on a world scale since the late nineteenth century. Such a view of capital accumulation recognizes its changing character, not unrelated to developments in technology and social organization. Such a view of imperialism is obviously influenced by the pioneering work of the English liberal John Hobson, which in turn influenced the work of others, including Vladimir Ilyich Lenin.

This view associates imperialism with monopoly capital, or oligopolistic capitalism, but also recognizes how much the processes, mechanisms, and institutions of imperialism have changed over what may be called "the long twentieth century." Hence, imperialism is associated not only with contemporary economic globalization, but also with the earlier period of globalization, from the end of the nineteenth century until World War I. By identifying it with oligopolistic capitalism, this view distinguishes modern imperialism from earlier imperialisms associated with other economic systems. The end of colonialism, the postwar Golden Age, significant changes in international economic specialization, serious efforts at multilaterial institution building, initiatives to reduce international inequalities and promote economic development, as well as the multifarious developments associated with globalization more generally have all transformed the international economic and political relations that characterize contemporary imperialism. As the next part suggests, much of what are called economic globalization and liberalization at the international level has served to consolidate and deepen contemporary imperialism. The earlier period of crises and labor movement led reforms in advanced capitalist economies, while decolonization in Africa and Asia expanded the scope for welfare state and developmental state interventions, which regulated, but never undermined capital accumulation.

Recent work (e.g., by Kozul-Wright and Nayyar) has emphasized that the current phase of economic globalization is far from unprecedented, with some transborder flows (e.g., labor) in the earlier phase from the last third of the nineteenth century—associated with what Hobson and Lenin called imperialism—even exceeding contemporary flows in relative, if not absolute, terms. There are many other important differences between the two periods, but none of these fundamentally undermine the assessment of the current period as one still characterized by what they termed economic imperialism.

IMPERIALISM AND GLOBALIZATION

It seems necessary to begin this quick review of how recent economic globalization has advanced imperialism by noting that globalization means different things to different people. At least five aspects of recent economic globalization have served to enhance external economic domination, including the liberalization of foreign direct investment (FDI), international finance, and international trade. In fact, such economic liberalization has involved re-regulation, rather than deregulation. In two other areas, regulation has been clearly and unambiguously strengthened, namely intellectual property rights and the new institutional economic governance.

FOREIGN DIRECT INVESTMENT

The higher rates of return to foreign direct investment (FDI) are generally considered to be a major aspect of imperialism. These higher returns are usually explained away by neoliberals as including rewards for taking higher risks by investing abroad. Others would suggest that such investments are able to secure higher returns because of the monopolistic powers and political influence usually associated with such investments. FDI is considered to be better able to capture rents, to use the mainstream economic term,[1] or larger surpluses or superprofits, depending on one's terminological preference.

With the postwar demise of the prewar colonial empires and the consequent availability of market access, microeconomic analysis of the firm was extended to consider the international, multinational, or transnational corporation (TNC). The analysis of FDI was thus extended and reconsidered in terms of the interests and dynamics of firm expansion and responses to the changing imperatives of capital accumulation. Such analysis has involved the analysis of competition and competitiveness, in terms of "market power" as well as (mainly production) "cost considerations."

In the economics literature, the debate on the pros and cons of FDI continues without any consensus, though there is little real disagreement that gains from "green-field" FDI are more likely than from other types of FDI, such as mergers and acquisitions as well as reinvestment of profits. However, it has been common to exaggerate the role of FDI in economic development, both historically and more recently. For example, the role of such FDI in the East Asian miracle was modest, accounting for less than 2 percent of gross domestic capital formation during the high-growth periods in Japan, South Korea, and Taiwan compared to the developing country average of 5–6 percent and Malaysia's own double-digit percentage.

In the aftermath of the 1997–98 Southeast Asian economic crises, it is now acknowledged that the region's industrial capabilities had been much weaker because of greater reliance on and domination by FDI. Foreign industrial domination also meant that public policy in the region came to be dominated by financial rentier interests, which contributed to greater financial fragility and vulnerability.[2]

The 1999 UNCTAD *World Investment Report* shows that most FDI in the 1990s has been for mergers and acquisitions (M&As), not "green-field" FDI that would create new productive or economic capacities. In developing countries, M&As have mainly involved acquisitions, particularly during periods of distress, especially after the ever more frequent currency and financial crises of recent times. Such "fire-sale FDI" has reduced the likelihood of superior management emerging due to M&As.

INTERNATIONAL FINANCIAL LIBERALIZATION

Three expected gains touted by advocates of international financial liberalization have simply not materialized. First, there have not been net flows of funds from the capital-rich countries to the capital poor, except to East Asia during the early and mid-1990s until the massive and sudden capital flight of 1997–98. Elsewhere, capital flight from other developing and transitional countries has grown. Second, the expected lower cost of funds has not materialized. While some margins have declined, financial deepening—involving the development of new financial instruments resulting in more layers of financial intermediation—has increased the variety of rentier claims. Third, while financial deepening has undoubtedly reduced some of the old sources of financial volatility and vulnerability, it has also introduced new sources (e.g., hedge funds), resulting in the greater frequency and magnitude of currency and financial crises.

Meanwhile, the policy influence of financial interests has grown, especially with greater central bank independence, resulting in greater deflationary macroeconomic policy bias, whereas the postwar record suggests that moderate inflation has contributed to growth. Financial liberalization has also undermined financial policy instruments to accelerate development, which even the World Bank acknowledged helped promote growth and structural change in East Asia.[3] For example, though "directed credit"—specially discounted and targeted to encourage investments in priority sectors or activities—has been very important in almost all cases of "late industrialization,"[4] many such financial institutions, facilities, and instruments have been undermined and eliminated with financial liberalization to counter "financial repression" and "restraint."

Through its agreement on financial services, the WTO has furthered the IMF and market promotion of international financial liberalization since the 1980s. But the series of international currency and financial crises since the early 1990s have underscored the greater volatility and vulnerability of international finance as a consequence. Even the IMF and the influential *Economist* weekly have come to acknowledge, albeit reluctantly, the minimal gains from and the grave dangers posed by international financial liberalization, especially on the capital account. Kaminsky and Schmukler found that although much of the finance literature claims that deregulation is beneficial for growth, with financial liberalization reducing the cost of capital, the crisis literature suggests that severe volatility in financial markets is at the core of currency crises and that such volatility has been triggered by financial deregulation.[5]

IMF research staff members Prasad et al. note that "the volatility of consumption growth relative to that of income growth has on average increased for the emerging market economies in the 1990s, which was precisely the period of a rapid increase in financial globalization."[6] This clearly contradicts claims by proponents of financial liberalization that "the volatility of consumption relative to that of output should go down as the degree of financial integration increases, since the essence of global financial diversification is that a country is able to offload some of its income risk in world markets." Most damningly, Prasad et al. observe that "an objective reading of the vast research effort to date suggests that there is no strong, robust and uniform support for the theoretical argument that financial globalization per se delivers a higher rate of economic growth."[7]

INTERNATIONAL TRADE

There continues to be an ongoing debate as to whether international trade should be seen as part of economic imperialism (e.g., Gallagher and Robinson; Emmanuel). David Ricardo's theory of comparative advantage is often dishonestly invoked to justify international trade, while even later neoclassical economic elaborations/distortions by Heckscher-Ohlin and Stolper-Samuelson cannot honestly be invoked to explain the injustice of international trade. While this is not the place to critically review international trade theory and justifications for international trade liberalization, there is widespread recognition of what is widely recognized as "unfair trade." Several observed long-run trends have undoubtedly contributed to such unfair trade, which is often linked to patterns and practices of international economic exchange dating to the colonial period as well as the ongoing unequal economic power of trading partners, not unrelated to imperialism:

- Deteriorating terms of trade for primary products compared to manufactures, observed in the middle of the twentieth century by Raul Prebisch[8] and Hans Singer.[9]

• Deteriorating terms of trade for tropical primary products compared to temperate primary products à la W. Arthur Lewis.[10]

• More recent price deflation of "generic manufactures" produced by newly industrializing countries' industries compared to those products with strong intellectual property rights, i.e., technological monopolies, now strengthened by the WTO's TRIPs agreement.

There are probably potential gains from trade due to international specialization, while much existing protection is more burdensome than advantageous to development. However, advocates of trade liberalization ignore "transitional costs" (e.g., employment and income losses due to trade liberalization, including the destruction of existing industries, jobs, etc.) and that there is no guarantee that better new jobs will replace lost jobs as suggested by modeling exercises operating under unrealistic and often optimistic assumptions. As Weisbrot and Baker write, "The removal of all of the rich countries' barriers to the merchandise exports of developing countries—including agriculture, textiles, and other manufactured goods—would result in very little additional income for the exporting countries."[11] They cite World Bank estimates that after such changes are fully implemented by 2015, they would only add 0.6 percent to the GDP of low- and middle-income countries.[12]

The myth that developing countries will be the main beneficiaries of agricultural trade liberalization in the rich countries of the North, particularly in Europe and Japan, has been revived with the World Trade Organization's so-called Doha Development Round in late 2001 after September 11. While many developing economies will gain from easier and greater access to the protected agricultural markets of the North, the main beneficiaries will actually be from rich agricultural exporting countries, the settler colonies of North America and Australasia, rather than from the developing world.[13]

Perhaps most importantly, from the perspective of developing robust national capitalisms that might undermine imperialist hegemony, trade liberalization also undermines the possibility of developing temporarily protected "infant industries." While import substituting industrialization has undoubtedly had a mixed record, the East Asian miracle was undoubtedly principally due to *effective protection conditional on export promotion,* rather than trade liberalization or open economies, as claimed by neoliberal economists. Trade protection has not only been an important tool of development strategy, as suggested by the infant industry argument, but has also been a tool of welfare policy, albeit not necessarily well conceived or particularly efficient, but nonetheless important for the cohesion of modern societies.

Technology

Technological advantage has become increasingly important for corporate economic dominance, especially at the international level. Intellectual property rights and incomes generated from them have largely been a twentieth-century phenomenon, which have only attained their current significance in the last couple of decades. Consequently, strengthened intellectual property rights (IPRs) in recent years have raised the costs of acquiring technology, reduced the likelihood of technology transfers and strengthened transnational corporations' monopoly powers, with adverse consequences for development and industrialization. If IPRs had been similarly asserted in earlier periods, it is very likely that the pace of technological diffusion and learning would have been considerably slowed in the last two centuries.

Western governments, led by the United States, successfully asserted IPRs at the international level from the mid-1980s, i.e., from the second Reagan administration. Then U.S. Secretary of State Shultz successfully got many friendly governments to uphold and enforce IPRs, principally in favor of U.S. transnational corporations. The transactions costs of having and enforcing many bilateral agreements were considerably reduced with the GATT/WTO agreement on Trade-Related Intellectual Property Rights (TRIPs). Thus, TRIPs has reinforced the assertion of monopolistic IPRs in ways not provided for by the World Intellectual Property Organization (WIPO), which has not been very successful in asserting these rights. With the WTO's dispute settlement mechanism, IPRs can now be asserted as equivalent to any other WTO-recognized trade issue, i.e., far more effectively than through the WIPO.

The significance of this development can be seen in the context of income from IPRs now constituting the single largest source of foreign-exchange earnings for the United States. However, to secure developing-country support for a new Doha Round of WTO trade negotiations, the United States promised to substantially reduce pharmaceutical drug prices for the fight against HIV/AIDS, suggesting the possibility of a more comprehensive review and revision of intellectual property rights and the WTO's TRIPs enforcement regime. Developments since the Doha meeting suggest, however, that such expectations were unrealistic and the United States offer was simply bait to get developing countries to agree to the Doha Round, deceptively called a Development Round.

New International Economic Governance

The Bretton Woods institutions—the International Monetary Fund (IMF) and the World Bank—are increasingly seen as obstacles to development because of their roles in dogmatically promoting economic liberalization, especially since the 1980s, despite dubious empirical and theoretical support for the so-called Washington Consensus.[14] They have also been seen as taking advantage of economic distress to push through policy agendas promoting economic liberalization and globalization favoring powerful transnational corporate interests. The U.S. Fed-led deflation and debt crises of the early 1980s provided the thin edge of the wedge for the neoliberal economic subordination of the South, often through the IMF-led stabilization and World Bank–led structural adjustment programs as well as WTO rules and regulations of the last decade.

More recently, the expanded program of the World Trade Organization (WTO) has not only accelerated the trade liberalization agenda for manufactures, but also broadened it to agriculture and services. However, actual progress has been uneven, mainly favoring powerful corporate interests. Among services, for example, there has been little liberalization of construction or shipping services, where developing countries have a significant presence, while financial services, dominated by U.S. and UK interests, have been liberalized on many fronts, including the WTO.

Even more alarmingly, as noted above, the WTO has strengthened transnational corporate monopolies known as intellectual property rights, besides broadening the economic liberalization agenda well beyond trade liberalization to many other spheres as well. One big struggle at the WTO now is over broadening the range of issues considered to be trade related with the developed country governments almost united in their determination to extend so-called trade issues to investment, government procurement, etc.

Admittedly, the World Trade Organization has a more democratic governance structure than the IMF and the World Bank, where one dollar gives one vote, besides the excessive weight of the founders, especially the United States. In recent years, there is evidence that this multilateral approach is being increasingly marginalized by the Bush administration in favor of more unilateralist and potentially unequal bilateral arrangements with partners favored for political, if not economic, reasons. Nevertheless, the WTO is now widely seen as furthering the neoliberal project of the Washington Consensus. It is also far more powerful and biased than its predecessor GATT (General Agreement on Tariffs and Trade) was, and has acquired a record of promoting trade as well as economic liberalization more generally, at the expense of development.

GLOBALIZATION AND U.S. HEGEMONY

The last two decades, associated with globalization and liberalization, have been associated with much lower growth than the quarter century after World War II. The evidence points to increased economic volatility, growing international economic inequalities, reduced aid flows, and other contradictory economic developments favoring transnational corporate—especially financial—ascendance. In an emerging era of unchallenged—and seemingly unchallengeable—U.S. hyperpower, many existing multilateral institutions, including the United Nations system, and even NATO, are being redefined.

As noted earlier, the political developments in the world since the terror attacks in the United States on September 11, 2001, have had rather serious implications for economic globalization. Most importantly, more assertive U.S. "unilateralism"— apparently under the influence of neoconservatives—continues to profoundly transform international relations and institutions, including those involved in international economic governance such as the IMF, WB, and the WTO. While the Zionist and selectively liberal democratic agenda of the neoconservatives is clear, their actual influence in the Bush conservative camp as well as its economic implications are still unclear.

There is now growing acknowledgement of the many false promises associated with economic globalization and international economic liberalization. Total official development assistance (ODA) from the rich countries as a share of GNP continued to decline from 0.49 of 1 percent in 1992 to 0.29 of 1 percent in 2002, instead of rising to the three-decade-old target of 0.7 of 1 percent. Meanwhile, the U.S. contribution had dropped to 0.09 percent in 2001 before U.S. President George W. Bush promised at Monterrey in March 2002 to raise its contribution by half over five years, i.e., to around 0.13 of 1 percent.[15]

Recent developments, especially after the invasion of Iraq, suggest that such disbursements are likely to be even more politicized and conditional than ever. It is well known that Israel has long been the highest recipient of U.S. assistance by far, with Egypt second since Camp David. After the defeat of the Taliban government, the subsequent U.S. budget failed to make any provisions for Afghanistan until a hasty amendment providing $300 million was made on the floor of the U.S. Congress to a country that had been at war since the late 1970s and was bombed extensively after 9/11.

U.S. DOMINANCE AND VULNERABILITY

David Dapice has argued that "No nation can dominate for long when its very economic health, much less its ability to project power, is based on the cooperation of those supposedly dominated."[16] He concludes that without greater economic strength, the future of U.S. hegemony is likely to be either shorter or more nuanced than either the friends or critics of the United States realize. While his observations are important, he seems to ignore the entire economic history of imperialism, which has not always been characterized by the consistent economic strength of hegemons.

He may well have in mind British capital exports, especially to the settler colonies, but this ignores the massive wealth transfers from the rest of the empire.[17]

Right after World War II, export earnings from British Malaya exceeded those of the rest of the empire while Britain itself relied on net capital inflows. While this post-war condition was undoubtedly exceptional, there is growing evidence of massive wealth transfers on both the current and capital accounts from much of its empire, including British India, the West Indies, sub-Saharan Africa, and Southeast Asia, i.e., colonialism was profitable, albeit unevenly so.

Undoubtedly, the U.S. economy remains stronger and more dynamic than its two major economic rivals. Japan has remained moribund after more than a decade of virtual stagnation after its disastrous financial "big bang." Meanwhile, Europe has become increasingly fettered by its Growth and Stability Pact, which is increasingly believed to have deprived Europe of antideflationary monetary policy instruments.

Nevertheless, the emerging view of the United States as a "hyperpower" may not fully take into account the country's economic vulnerabilities. For example, the United States' "twin deficits" on its fiscal and current account balances as well as electoral considerations have compromised U.S. positions on trade liberalization, e.g., its 2002 steel tariffs and agricultural subsidies, which ensured retention of a Republican Congress and Senate. The United States also relies on an average of over $1.3 billion of capital inflows each day to finance its imports and the resulting current account deficit. U.S. foreign-exchange earnings are led by royalties from intellectual property rights, followed by financial services.

With the demise of the gold standard, the U.S. dollar has increasingly become accepted as the universal store of value and medium of exchange. The emergence and consolidation of a de facto "dollar standard" has not been entirely smooth. European skepticism from the late 1960s, especially after the Tet offensive in Vietnam, mounted greater pressure on the greenback, leading to the U.S. dollar devaluation in 1971 with Nixon's unilateral renunciation of U.S. obligations under the Bretton Woods system set up in 1944 in anticipation of a postwar Pax Americana. Later, the September 1985 Plaza Accord dollar devaluation—following Volcker's U.S. Fed high-interest-rate deflationary interventions that precipitated the series of sovereign debt crises of the 1980s—did not succeed in rectifying the large U.S. current account deficit with Japan. Instead, subsequent capital inflows to the United States, including from East Asia, have since financed the subsequent U.S. current account deficits with East Asia.

In recent decades, the strength of the greenback has been increasingly propped up by vast imports of capital from the rest of the world, rather than by the strength of U.S. exports. Ironically, much of these capital inflows have come from East Asia itself, i.e., East Asian exporters have been earning U.S. dollars, which have been used by their governments to buy U.S. Treasury bonds. Almost half of all U.S. Treasury bonds are held as reserves by foreign central banks, principally in East Asia. During the 1990s, many central banks were encouraged to sell down their gold holdings, but only to replace them with even more U.S. Treasury bonds. Most of these foreign central banks are unlikely to sell them for fear of weakening their own currencies.

The Bretton Woods system of fixed exchange rates tied to gold and the U.S. dollar has been replaced by a system of flexible exchange rates since the early 1970s. But the demise of the Bretton Woods system in 1971 did not mean an end to the internationalization of the greenback, the virtual "dollar standard" implicit in pegging the value of the greenback to the price of gold, and buildup of U.S. liabilities abroad. Without the Bretton Woods system's framework, political hegemony and confidence have become all the more important. Globalization in this context and the demise of systemic alternatives (mainly posed by the Soviet system) have also served to strengthen the new arrangements.

U.S. dollar hegemony has meant that economic growth abroad increases demand for dollar assets. As central banks increase money supply, they also want to hold more dollar assets in reserve to support their currencies. With globalization, the disproportionate rise in cross-border transactions requires even more dollars to cover such dealings. Thus, the world economy is increasingly hostage to U.S. monetary policy as the U.S. Federal Reserve determines world liquidity. The generally deflationary stance of the U.S. Fed thus combines with the European Growth and Stability Pact and the Bank of Japan's historically deflationary monetary policy to conspire against more rapid economic growth globally and attendant inflation.

But the evolution of this system has also meant that global liquidity is dependent on acceptance on both sides of foreigners building up increasing claims on U.S. assets. After all, dollar bills or Treasury bonds abroad imply a promise by the U.S. Treasury to eventually pay up. In the meantime, the buildup of such liabilities could eventually undermine confidence in their value. But the irony, of course, is that the world cannot afford to risk the U.S. reversing these trends, without threatening a global liquidity crunch. Not surprisingly, U.S. creditors gain from this de facto dollar standard. Already, over half of all dollar bills in circulation are to be found abroad. We have created a world where the rest of the world exports to America, and must settle for less in return for the "privilege" of securing enough dollars to sustain international liquidity.

UNDERSTANDING IMPERIALISM

This brief essay has argued the continuing relevance of the concept of imperialism. Almost a century ago, Hobson opposed imperialism on the grounds that it reflected the concentration of business interests—inimical to liberal, laissez-faire capitalism—and their influence on public policy, specifically in terms of colonial expansion. Lenin went on to link this with Hilferding's recognition of the then recent dominance of finance capital in the form of a bank-industry nexus, and to argue that the social democratic movements then should oppose national chauvinism in the form of support for their states during World War I, better characterized as an intra-European interimperialist war. Many other writings from that period, including Kautsky's discussion of ultra-imperialism, may well be of much contemporary relevance. However, the Hobson-Lenin view of imperialism did not pay much attention to Marx's insight, later elaborated by Gallagher and Robinson as the "imperialism of free trade."

There have been many other changes in the organization of the world economy that must also be incorporated into an analysis of contemporary economic imperialism. There is now a widespread consensus about the ascendance of finance capital in the last quarter century, partly reflected in the promotion of an Anglo-American norm for capitalist reform. On the other hand, others (e.g., Hardt and Negri[18]) have exaggerated the significance of recent post-Fordism, international subcontracting, and organizational innovations, which they claim is inexorably leading to a decentered network empire where state power hardly matters; hence, Hardt's appeal to ruling classes to recognize that their lot does not lie with U.S. imperialism, which he deems an atavism from the past not in their best interests[19]—not unlike Schumpeter before him.[20]

Recent "empire talk" in the United States initially emerged from public discussion about the ostensible need for U.S. interventions abroad after the Vietnam debacle and the first Gulf War. Not unlike the discourses of the nineteenth century in Europe (see Saada and others in this volume) and the early twentieth century in the United States with the recolonization of the Philippines following the Spanish-American War (see Go in this volume), higher motives—"human rights," "democracy," "good governance" recently—have been invoked once again, even before the "war against terror" began after September 11, 2001.

There is also a strong tendency to contrast Bush's ostensible unilateralism with his predecessor's supposed multilateralism, but it is increasingly clear that while U.S. military power encourages the former, the Washington administration recognizes the greater legitimacy and lower costs of the latter, as long as it does not operate against its interests. The potential for multilateral institutions to constrain the hegemon is the fear in Washington, but the lower costs and greater legitimacy of multilateral endorsement for achieving U.S. objectives are not lost on an administration presiding over ever increasing twin deficits and initiating multilateral projects of its own such as the "coalition of the willing" and Free Trade Area of the Americas. While the United States may have been forced to go to the UN Security Council in 2002 by its British ally to gain legitimacy for its invasion of Iraq, it went to NATO of its own volition in early 2004 as part of a desperate bid for an exit strategy from Iraq as the costs of occupation continue to mount and the November 2004 presidential election loomed large.

Hardt is right to point out that "anti-Americanism" can only lead to a political cul-de-sac.[21] While understandable in the face of U.S. arrogance, militarism, and unilateralism, neither anti-Americanism nor multilateralism amount to an anti-imperialist strategy. The horsemen of the contemporary apocalypse in the South— the Bretton Woods institutions and the WTO—are all multilateral institutions, as is the UN Security Council and countless other institutions that have been successfully used to advance, protect, and legitimize contemporary economic imperialism. The main case for anti-Americanism in international relations today must surely be to try to check the hegemon, considering the failure of the existing multilateral and other institutions to do so. But countries in the South cannot expect a much more sympathetic position from Europe or Japan, judging by their respective stances at the September 2003 Cancun WTO interministerial conference.

But Hardt's appeal to the global elite to oppose U.S. imperialism in favor of a de-centered network empire ("multilateralism squared") clearly does not recognize the contemporary nature of capitalism, imperialism, and state power. This is not to invoke a functionalist view of the imperialist state, but merely to underscore the central role of that state in achieving capitalist reform besides protecting and advancing particular interests, especially internationally, with increased cross-border economic flows in this age of globalization. The current multilateral WTO regime for IPRs has been far less costly and far more effective than the many bilateral arrangements Shultz spent so much time, effort, and resources on. Of course, the WTO's rejection of U.S. steel tariffs embarrassed the Bush administration. And the supposed "failure at Cancun" in September 2003 has encouraged unilateral U.S. "free trade agreements" with willing partners and renewed U.S. efforts to create an FTAA.

But it would be wrong to conclude that the United States has become dogmatically "unilaterist" or even "militarist." Instead, the United States generally prefers multilateralism insofar as it is convenient, but the Bush administration is more ready and willing to fall back on unilateralism when it cannot get its way otherwise: "rule by law," insofar as it is convenient, rather than a serious and consistent commitment to the "rule of law." Or multilateralism where convenient, and unilateralism when necessary! But such debates over the "niceties" of imperialism should not detract us from the very core of the system, namely imperialism as it continues to transform and manifest itself.

Imperialism has never been well understood in functionalist terms, or through cost-benefit analyses or calculus of every state action or intervention. Rather, it has to be understood historically and as full of contradictions, not as a clear, rational, and consistent hegemonic view. In particular, the current interest in political and military dimensions has obscured the transformation and persistence of economic imperialism. The popularity of the ambiguous term "globalization"—referring to all manner of cross-border flows—has led to false debates between its proponents and opponents, not unlike the blind men debating the nature of the proverbial elephant.

Finally, it may be noted that for Hardt, "imperialism is bad for business because it sets up barriers that hinder global flows."[22] Such a claim rests on a nineteenth-century view of imperialism linked exclusively to colonialism, implying that imperialism died with colonialism. As everyone knows, the IMF, World Bank, and the WTO have done precisely what Hardt claims imperialism would oppose, implying that the three "horsemen" are pro-empire, but anti-imperialist! Only gobbledygook semantic convolutions—invoking a notion of empire that is anti-imperialist—can lead to such an analysis and conclusion.

17. MYTHS OF EMPIRE AND STRATEGIES OF HEGEMONY

JACK SNYDER

The United States is far stronger in relative military and economic terms than any previous state in the modern international system, yet it feels itself to be highly vulnerable to external threats in the wake of the September 11 attacks. This paradoxical combination of omnipotence and vulnerability creates a nearly irresistible temptation to use its might to root out these threats at their sources and to organize the world in a way that will make it safe for democracy—or at any rate safe for America.[1] This temptation is magnified by a set of assumptions, which I call "myths of empire," that exaggerate the prospects of success for a strategy of security through military expansion.[2] Because terrorism directed at a democratic occupying power is often effective, a more sustainable strategy would be to establish a system of consensual domination in which America's coercive power is used selectively for purposes that enjoy a broadly accepted legitimacy and are laundered through co-opted local, regional, and multilateral institutions.[3]

In thinking through these strategic options, it may be useful to distinguish between the terms *empire* and *hegemony*. Popular discourse has embraced the word *empire* to characterize America's bid for global assertiveness. Even some proponents like the term, despite the fact that an American "empire" would not be based on formal colonization, as was commonly the case in past European empires.[4] Michael Doyle offers a standard scholarly definition of empire as "a system of interaction between two political entities, one of which, the dominant metropole, exerts political control over the internal and external policy—the effective sovereignty—of the other, the subordinate periphery."[5] *Hegemony,* in contrast, pertains only to the control of the most general patterns of external relations among states. Thus, Robert Keohane and Joseph Nye define hegemony as a situation in which "one state is powerful enough to maintain the essential rules governing interstate relations, and willing to do so."[6] In short, empire implies control of the internal and external arrangements of the dominated political units, whereas hegemony implies the effective laying down of rules governing external relations between units.[7]

REALIST SKEPTICISM ABOUT EMPIRE: THE U-SHAPED COST CURVE FOR EXPANSION

Among the prominent critics of the Bush administration's policy of the preventive use of force against Iraq were self-styled realists, people who pride themselves on accepting the hard reality that the use of force is often necessary in the defense of national interests. Kenneth Waltz, the godfather of contemporary realism, and thirty-two other prominent international-relations scholars, most of them realists, bought an ad in the *New York Times* to make their case against the Bush strategy.[8] Opponents of the Bush strategy even include the most prominent member of the school of thought called "offensive realism," John Mearsheimer, a professor at the University of Chicago. Among international-relations experts, offensive realism is a minority viewpoint, which holds that what I call the myths of empire are in fact often true. That is, they believe that self-defense in the rough-and-tumble of international politics often requires adopting offensive tactics. They see the expansion of powerful states as simply inevitable. Mearsheimer was a prominent advocate of offensive tactics in the first war against Saddam Hussein and correctly predicted that U.S. casualties would be astonishingly low.[9] In debates in the fall of 2002, however, Mearsheimer opposed the strategy of preventive war, challenging the administration's strategic arguments on nearly every point.[10]

The skeptical views of many of these realists are anchored in the logic of Robert Gilpin's influential statement of the dynamic of imperial expansion and hegemonic power contests. Gilpin begins with the truistic assumption that states expand their sphere of control up to the point where they think the benefits of doing so will outweigh the costs.[11] Typically, he says, states seek to exploit the benefits of their distinctive technological or organizational innovations by reaping the profits from them on a wider scale. Within this sphere, they lay down a set of rules that subordinate powers will accept out of a combination of coercion, self-interest, and legitimacy. As the state expands its zone of control, the cost of each additional increment of expansion initially falls, because of the benefits of scale economies in the exploitation of the innovation, which are reinvested in enhanced technologies of power, whether military or economic. As the course of expansion progresses, however, the costs of incremental expansion eventually rise, because conquest is more difficult at a distance, and because the easiest and most lucrative targets (the low-hanging fruit) have already been picked. Equilibrium is reached when rising costs equal declining benefits of further expansion.[12]

This equilibrium is unstable. Typically, the whole cost curve shifts upward over time, so that the most recent, most marginal conquests become a net burden on imperial resources. This happens because organized opponents both inside and outside the empire successfully emulate the innovations that gave the imperial metropole its advantage in the first place. Typically, the *pax imperium* spreads skills and mobilizes populations in ways that break the empire's monopoly on crucial power resources. Social change in the imperial periphery often brings rising literacy and nationalism. Defeated powers typically undergo a postwar economic recovery. For all these reasons, resistance to imperial control increases. The balance of power kicks in, and the costs of imperial policing rise. At this point, the empire faces a choice among three options: retrenchment to maintain an equilibrium between revenues and expenditures, redoubled efforts at repression, or the institutionalization of a sustainable hegemonic order based on consent.

THE STRATEGY OF RETRENCHMENT

Empires are typically loath to retrench. They organize their institutions, ideologies, and domestic political coalitions around scale economies that presuppose a broad imperial scope. Like all successful social arrangements, once established, they tend to lock in. Dramatic change, especially to accommodate a shrinking pie, is a last resort. Instead, the empire typically fights to retain control of its periphery against rising odds and eventually gambles on a hegemonic war against a coalition of rising challengers.[13]

Some of the great powers, however, have pulled back from overstretch and husbanded their power for another day. Democratic great powers, notably Britain and the United States, are prominent among these empires that learned to retrench. At the turn of the twentieth century, Britain saw that its strategy of "splendid isolation," what we would now call unilateralism, was getting it into trouble. The independence struggle of Boer farmers in South Africa drained the imperial coffers. At the same time, the European great powers were challenging Britain's naval mastery and its other colonial positions. Quickly doing the math, the British patched up relations with their secondary rivals, France and Russia, and formed an alliance directed at the main danger, Germany. Likewise, when the United States blundered into a costly, unwinnable war in Vietnam, it retrenched and adopted a more patient strategy for waiting out its less capable Communist opponents.

Like these earlier democratic great powers, contemporary America is capable of learning to anticipate the counterproductive effects of its offensive policies and to moderate them before too much damage is done. The Bush team, guided by wary public opinion, worked through UN resolutions during the fall of 2002 to increase multilateral support for its threats of preventive war against Iraq. Moreover, the administration declined to apply mechanically its preventive war principles when North Korea renounced international controls on its nuclear materials in December 2002. Strikingly, a December 2002 Bush administation strategy document, dealing specifically with the proliferation of weapons of mass destruction, failed to mention the option of preventive attack, which had figured so prominently in the broader strategic study of September 2002.[14] A brief tour through the misguided strategic ideas of previous empires underscores the wisdom of this kind of strategic self-restraint.

THE STRATEGY OF SECURITY THROUGH FURTHER EXPANSION

Rather than retrench, many historical great powers decided to solve their security dilemma through even bolder preventive offensives. None of these efforts have worked. Napoleon and Hitler marched to Moscow and were engulfed in Russian winter. Kaiser Wilhelm's Germany tried to break the allies' encirclement through unrestricted submarine warfare, which brought America's industrial might into the war against it. Imperial Japan, facing a quagmire in China and a U.S. oil embargo, tried to break the encirclement by seizing the Indonesian oil fields and preventively attacking Pearl Harbor. All sought security through expansion, and all ended in imperial collapse.

The strategy of redoubled expansion looks like an attractive option when imperial strategists believe in the myths of empire. Since many of these myths were echoed eerily in the Bush administration's strategic rhetoric on the eve of the Iraq war, it will be worthwhile recalling how those earlier advocates of imperial overstretch tried to make their dubious cases.

Offensive Advantage

The most general of the myths of empire is that the attacker has an inherent advantage. Sometimes this is explained in terms of the advantages of surprise. More often, it relies on the broader notion that seizing the initiative allows the attacker to impose a plan on the passive enemy and to choose a propitious time and circumstance for the fight. Even if the political objective is self-defense, in this view, attacking is still the best strategy. As the Bush strategy document says, "our best defense is a good offense."[15]

Throughout history, strategists who have blundered into imperial overstretch have shared this view. For example, General Alfred von Schlieffen, the author of Germany's misbegotten plan for a quick, decisive offensive in France in 1914, used to say that "if one is too weak to attack the whole" of the other side's army, "one should attack a section."[16] This idea defies elementary military common sense. In war, the weaker side normally remains on the defensive precisely because defending its home ground is typically easier than attacking the other side's strongholds.

The idea of offensive advantage also runs counter to the most typical patterns of deterrence and coercion. Sometimes the purpose of military operations is not to take or hold territory but to influence the adversary by inflicting pain. This is especially true when weapons of mass destruction or suicide terror tactics are used. In that case, war may resemble a competition in the willingness to endure pain. Here, too, the defender normally has the advantage, because the side defending its homeland and the survival of its regime typically cares more about the stakes of the conflict. Whereas it is hard to imagine North Korea using nuclear weapons or mounting a conventional artillery barrage on the South Korean capital of Seoul for purposes of conquest, it is much easier to envision such desperate measures in response to "preventive" attacks on the core power resources of the Communist regime. Because the Bush administration saw such retaliation as feasible and credible, it was deterred from undertaking preventive strikes when the North Koreans unsealed a nuclear reactor in December 2002. Indeed, deterring any country from attacking is almost always easier than compelling it to disarm, surrender territory, or change its regime. Once stated, this point seems utterly obvious, but the logic of the Bush strategy implies the opposite.

One reason that blundering empires were keen on offensive strategies was that they relied on preventive attacks to forestall unfavorable shifts in the balance of power. In both world wars, for example, Germany's leaders sought war with Russia in the short run because they expected the Russian army to gain in relative strength over time.[17] However, this tactic backfired. Preventive aggression not only turned a possible enemy into a certain one, but in the long run it also helped bring other powers into the fight to prevent Germany from gaining hegemony over all of them.

This reflects a fundamental principle of the balance of power. In the international system, states and other powerful actors tend to form alliances against the most expansionist state that threatens them. Attackers provoke fears that drive their potential victims to cooperate with each other.

Astute strategists learn to anticipate this and try to use it to their advantage. For example, one of the most successful diplomats in European history, Otto von Bismarck, achieved the unification of Germany by always putting the other side in the wrong, and whenever possible, maneuvering the opponent into attacking first. As a result, Prussia expanded its control over the German lands without provoking fears or resistance. Pressed by his generals on several occasions to authorize preventive attacks, Bismarck said that "preventive war is like committing suicide from fear of death"; it would "put the full weight of the imponderables . . . on the side of the enemies we have attacked."[18] Instead, he demanded patience: "I have often had to stand for long periods of time in the hunting blind and let myself be covered and stung by insects before the moment came to shoot."[19] Germany fared less well under Bismarck's more reckless successors, who shared his ruthlessness but lacked his understanding of the balance of power.

Because Saddam Hussein attacked Kuwait, the elder Bush enjoyed a diplomatic advantage in the 1991 war. That is why the coalition against Iraq was so large and willing. This advantage is vastly more difficult to achieve in a strategy of preventive attack. Especially when an adverse power shift is merely hypothetical and not imminent, it hardly seems worthwhile to incur the substantial diplomatic disadvantages of a preventive attack.

Nowadays it might be impractical for states to form traditional military alliances to directly resist American hegemony. However, Robert Pape has coined the term "soft balancing" to denote some states' foot-dragging and oblique resistance to what they saw as America's imperial project in Iraq. Likewise, the spontaneous self-defense efforts on the part of several simultaneous targets of American intervention could, even if uncoordinated, amount to a de facto balancing of American power.

PAPER TIGER ENEMIES

Empires also become overstretched when they view their enemies as paper tigers, fiercely threatening if appeased, but easily crumpled by a resolute attack. These images are often not only wrong, but self-contradictory. For example, the Japanese militarists saw the United States as so strong and insatiably aggressive that Japan would have to conquer a huge, self-sufficient empire in order to get the resources to defend itself; yet at the same time, the Japanese regime saw the United States as so vulnerable and irresolute that a sharp rap against Pearl Harbor would cause the United States to quit the fight.

Similarly, the Bush administration's arguments for preventive war against Iraq portrayed Saddam Hussein as completely undeterrable from using weapons of mass destruction, yet Secretary of Defense Donald Rumsfeld said he expected that Iraq would not use them even if attacked because "wise Iraqis will not obey his orders to use WMD."[20] In other words, the Bush administration strategists thought that deterrence would be impossible in situations in which Saddam lacked a motive to use weapons of mass destruction, but they thought deterrence would succeed when a U.S. attack provided Iraq the strongest imaginable motive to use its weapons. The U.S. national strategy paper says "the greater the threat, the greater is the risk of inaction," but this is a rationale for preventive attack only if we accept a self-contradictory paper tiger image of the enemy.[21] The fact that it now appears that Iraq had no weapons of mass destruction and no program to obtain them adds a further twist to this form of strategic mythology.

BANDWAGONS

Another myth of empire is that states tend to jump on the bandwagon with threatening or forceful powers. During the cold war, for example, the Soviet Union thought that forceful action in Berlin, Cuba, and the developing world would demonstrate its political and military strength, encourage so-called progressive forces to ally actively with the Soviets, and thereby shift the balance of forces still further in the favor of the Communist bloc. The Soviets called this the "correlation of forces" theory. In fact, the balance-of-power effect far outweighed and erased the bandwagon effect. The Soviet Union was left far weaker in relative terms as a result of its pressing for unilateral advantage. As Churchill said of the Soviets in the wake of the first Berlin crisis, "Why have they deliberately acted for three long years so as to unite the free world against them?"[22]

During the 1991 war against Iraq, the earlier Bush administration argued that rolling back Saddam Hussein's conquest of Kuwait was essential to discourage Arabs throughout the Middle East from jumping on the Iraqi bandwagon. Now, the current Bush administration hopes that bandwagon dynamics can be made to work in its own favor. Despite the difficulties that the United States had in lining up support for an invasion of Iraq, the Bush administration nonetheless asserts that its strategy of preventive war will lead others to jump on the U.S. bandwagon. Rumsfeld has said that "if our leaders do the right thing, others will follow and support our just cause—just as they have in the global war against terror."[23]

At the same time, the self-styled realists of the current Bush administration also argue that their policy is consistent with the opposite concept of the balance of power, but the rhetoric of the national strategy paper pulls this concept inside out: "Through our willingness to use force in our own defense and in the defense of others, the United States demonstrates its resolve to maintain a balance of power that favors freedom."[24] What this Orwellian statement really means is that preventive war will attract a bandwagon of support that creates an imbalance of power in our favor, a conception that is logically the same as the Soviets' wrong-headed theory of the "correlation of forces." The Bush strategists like to use the terminology of the balance of power, but they understand that concept exactly backwards.

BIG-STICK DIPLOMACY

A closely related myth is the big-stick theory of making friends by threatening them. Before World War I, Germany's leaders found that its rising power and belligerent diplomacy had pushed France, Russia, and Britain into a loose alliance against it. In the backwards reasoning of German diplomacy, they decided to try to break apart this encirclement by trumping up a crisis over claims to Morocco, threatening France with an attack, and proving to France that its allies would not come to its rescue. In fact, Britain did support France, and the noose around Germany grew tighter.

Today, how does the United States seek to win friends abroad? The Bush strategy paper offers some reassuring language about the need to work with allies. Unlike

President Bill Clinton in the Kosovo War, Bush worked hard for a UN resolution to authorize an attack on Iraq. Nonetheless, on the Iraq issue and a series of others, the Bush administration has extorted cooperation primarily by threats to act unilaterally, not gained it by persuasion or concessions. Russia was forced to accept a new strategic arms control regime on take-it-or-leave-it American terms. Europe was similarly compelled to accept an exemption for U.S. officials from prosecution by the International Criminal Court. Germany was snubbed for resisting the war against Iraq. Multilateral initiatives on the environment were rejected. Rumsfeld, in his personal jottings on strategy, raised to the level of principle the dictum that the United States should "avoid trying so hard to persuade others to join a coalition that we compromise on our goals."[25] Either the Bush administration believed allies were dispensable, or a powerful faction within it adhered to the Kaiser Wilhelm theory of diplomacy.

No Tradeoffs

A final myth is that in strategy there are no tradeoffs. Proponents of imperial expansion tend to pile on every argument from the whole list of myths of empire. It is rarely enough to argue that the opponent is a paper tiger, or that dominoes tend to fall, or that big-stick diplomacy will make friends, or that a preventive attack will help to civilize the natives. Rather, proponents of offensive self-defense inhabit a rhetorical world in which *all* of these things are simultaneously true, and thus all considerations point in the same direction.

The Bush administration's strategic rhetoric about Iraq in the fall of 2002 did not disappoint our expectations in this regard. Saddam was portrayed as undeterrable, he would get nuclear weapons unless deposed, he would give them to terrorists, the war against him would be cheap and easy, grumbling allies would jump on our bandwagon, Iraq would become a democracy, and the Arab street would thank the United States for liberating it. In real life, as opposed to the world of imperial rhetoric, it is surprising when every conceivable consideration supports the preferred strategy. As is so often the case with the myths of empire, this piling on of reinforcing claims smacks of ex post facto justification rather than serious strategic assessment. At the outset of the 2000 presidential campaign, Condoleezza Rice wrote that "the first line of defense should be a clear and classical statement of deterrence—if they do acquire WMD, their weapons will be unusable because any attempt to use them will bring national obliteration."[26] Two years later, however, the possibility of deterrence had become unthinkable. Administration dogma left no room for any assessment that did not perfectly reinforce the logic of the prevailing preventive strategy.

CONSENSUAL, INSTITUTIONALIZED HEGEMONY

In addition to the strategies of retrenchment and further expansion, a third strategy for managing the costs of dominance is to try to institutionalize a consensual hegemonic order. Gilpin argues that all hegemonic powers attempt to institutionalize their rule. In a study of the aftermath of major wars, John Ikenberry notes that democracies have generally been better than autocracies at organizing hegemonic systems because they are better at making binding agreements that reassure the lesser powers that benefits will be mutual.[27] The system set up by the United States after World War II is Ikenberry's prime model of this kind of well-institutionalized hegemony.

America's global reach was achieved through what some have called "empire by invitation," acquired in the course of leading successful coalitions balancing against more menacing imperial competitors.[28] When competitors like Nazi Germany and Soviet Russia collapsed, the United States temporarily found itself with a huge, but to some degree temporary, advantage in military and economic resources, as well as a clear field to expand the scope of its informal hegemonic sphere. In 1945, for example, the United States commanded nearly half of the world's economic product, a figure that reverted to its normal position of less than a quarter some two decades later. More than for most empires, which have to win their holdings through piecemeal conquests in normal times, the United States therefore has faced the distinctive problem of how to institutionalize a leadership role won at moments of unusual, fleeting disparity of global power.

A second distinctive feature of American imperial power was its anticolonial nature. Won in the wake of failed imperial grabs by dictators, and picking up the detritus of failed colonial systems, America's sphere of influence was necessarily based on indirect rule through the compliance of (preferably democratic) weaker states to rules of multilateral cooperation, proposed by the United States but adopted with the consent of all. The Bretton Woods system, NATO, and somewhat less successfully the United Nations met the needs of both of these features of American hegemony—that is, the institutionalization of huge but fleeting advantages and the need for a consent-based system of indirect hegemony.[29] Liberal, democratic ideology, plus the continuing geopolitical contest against the Soviet Union, helped to lock in these mutually beneficial arrangements even when U.S. unilateral power began to slip relative to that of its allies after the 1960s.

However, institutions are binding only if they succeed in reorienting interests and attitudes in ways that eliminate incentives to exploit the cooperation of others.[30] Relating this to Gilpin's *problematique*, what keeps former rivals, junior partners, and peripheral powers from rebelling once America's relative power returns to normal levels? During the cold war, the mechanisms that accomplished this included the need for military protection from Russia and other regional threats, the efficiency of cooperative institutions in producing joint gains, the co-optation of local elites who benefited from the system of American hegemony even if the broader population might not have, and the penetration of imperial ideology into at least some key circles. In this way, the diffusion of American innovations could occur without egregiously upsetting the hegemonic system, as it had typically done in the historical cases that Gilpin analyzed.

Will such methods work in the contemporary period? The set of economic, technological, and cultural processes commonly labeled as "globalization" provides a powerful engine for diffusing American innovations abroad. Some competitors and semiperipheries, such as China, may narrow the gap in relative power by emulating and incorporating these successfully, whereas others may lack the institutional or cultural capacity to do so. Even in the latter case, this may not be good news for the stability of the hegemonic order, since failure to plug into the western, secular, liberal model of nation building can lead in two directions, both of them bad. On the one hand, as in the more coherent Islamic states, nation builders may call upon indigenous religious traditions inimical to liberal hegemony in an effort to strengthen their states and mobilize their populations in order to compete successfully in an ever more challenging world.[31] In oil states such as Iran and Iraq, religious nationalists may have extensive resources to devote to this counterhegemonic project. On the other hand, the less coherent states of the periphery may turn repressive, breeding terrorism as in Saudi Arabia and Egypt, or they may collapse entirely under the pressures of international military and economic competition, producing anarchic swamps in which terrorism thrives.[32] To counteract or manage these destabilizing processes, powerful tools of institutionalization and co-optation are needed. The more far-reaching the hegemonic ambitions of the United States, the more effective these institutions will have to be.

INSTITUTIONALIZING EFFICIENT CONTRACTING BETWEEN HEGEMON AND FOLLOWERS

Ikenberry's vision of a stable hegemonic order depends on the achievement of a credible, mutually beneficial security contract between the hegemon and the less powerful states. In a research project on American grand strategy in the twentieth century, David Lake asked under what conditions does it make sense for states to cooperate through alliances between formally equal parties, as opposed to creating a more hierarchical relationship, such as empire. Following a deductive logic, Lake anticipates that the choice between free contracting and hierarchic authority depends on the size of the benefit from producing security jointly, on the severity of the danger that freely contracting parties will act opportunistically toward each other, and on the costs of governing a hierarchical system.[33]

What might this mean in the context of the joint production of security from threats such as terrorism and rogue states wielding weapons of mass destruction? According to conventional wisdom, the benefits of combating terrorists cooperatively are huge. In Lake's terminology, there are substantial scale economies in taking an intensely cooperative approach to seeking out and destroying terrorism, a factor that favors but in itself does not require a hegemonic approach. If information can be fully and reliably shared across states, for example, the chance increases that pieces of the puzzle can be successfully put together. Likewise, division of labor is necessary. Most states are best equipped to operate in their own territory, but a handful of states have specialized comparative advantages, either in military capacity or in cultural access, for some tasks that are jointly beneficial. Finally, combating global terrorism provides what Lake calls "positive externalities." That is, wiping out an al-Qaeda cell makes everyone more secure, not just the people of the country where the cell was based. Such positive externalities may be weaker for terrorists that have strictly local objectives, but since even these often seek cooperative ties based on expediency with terrorist groups elsewhere, the principle should apply even in this case. In other words, combating terrorism is a collective good that must be jointly supplied.

There are similar "joint economies" in producing security from so-called rogue-state threats. Everyone needs to be on board a program of sanctions and embargoes to keep potential proliferators from getting technology needed to build weapons. However, geography means that different states face different degrees of threat from any particular rogue state. As a result, a hegemonic leader may be needed to organize cooperation, either through side payments and/or coercive pressure, if decentralized efforts fail.

The risk of opportunism by the would-be cooperating partners is a factor affecting the attractiveness of hierarchical security arrangements, such as empire. Some states might desire the destruction of terrorist networks or rogue neighbors, but they may find it inexpedient to take forceful steps to accomplish this because some domestic constituencies sympathize ideologically with them or profit from doing business with them. Thus, they may opportunistically try to ride free on the efforts of others. In such a situation, there is an incentive to organize collective efforts by a hegemonic leader if decentralized cooperation breaks down. Lake notes that this hierarchical solution, including the possibility of an imposed one, is more likely when certain assets for countering the threat are irreplaceable, costly, and nonfungible.

American military bases in the Persian Gulf are an example. When this is the case, the United States, which cannot ride free because it has the default responsibility for security provision nearly everywhere, faces a powerful incentive to impose a sufficiently hierarchic arrangement to make sure that what Lake calls "specific assets" are available for use.

Finally, Lake notes that hierarchy is more likely when the governance costs in policing it are fairly low. Since physical coercion is costly to impose over a long period of time, Lake argues that low-cost hierarchies are ones that the subordinate parties join more or less voluntarily, because the dominant parties devise credible guarantees against exploiting their weaker partners and give side payments to offset the costs of contributing to collective imperial projects.

In the analyses of Lake and Ikenberry, like those of Gilpin, there is no particular reason why hierarchical empire is the only alternative when cooperation through decentralized alliances fails to produce effective security cooperation. In principle, multilateral institutions should in most settings be able to organize cooperation that captures joint gains and reduces the risk of opportunism at a lower governance cost than that of empire.

Nonetheless, it should not be assumed that multilateral arrangements will automatically be responsive to the needs of the lesser states in the hegemonic order or succeed in gaining their voluntary consent. It is sobering, for example, to assess the strategies of contemporary multilateral organizations influence in light of the criteria for successful hegemony set out in this volume by Bin Wong and by Matthew Connelly. Wong argues that the Chinese empire endured so long because it ruled in the interests of its weaker, poorer peripheries. Given the recurrent squabbles between the European Union's core states of France and Germany on the one hand and the eastern and southern states of the "new Europe" on the other, it would be hard to contend that multilateralism has automatically made the EU sensitive to its peripheries. Connelly's qualms about empires likewise seem to apply to many contemporary multilateral institutions: they are too often closed systems, refusing to allow disgruntled peripheries to opt out (think of the International Criminal Court and doctrines of universal criminal jurisdiction); that they meddle too forcefully in the domestic politics of peripheral states (think of the conditionality requirements on loans from the International Monetary Fund); and that they are unaccountable to publics (think of the EU's democratic deficit).

Ikenberry may be right that multilateralism organized by powerful democratic states is the best hope for a stable, consensual hegemonic order, but multilateral institutions do not in themselves bring those outcomes. It is also important to consider how institutions interact with the social and culture networks that breathe life and purpose into the institutional forms.

SOCIAL AND CULTURAL NETWORKS OF EMPIRE

Michael Mann's monumental study of the origins of social power examines how power is generated to organize human activity effectively on a larger scale and at a higher level of productivity. The rise of empires is one of the forms of power that he studies. Like Gilpin, Mann begins with the observation that generating a quantum leap in social power depends in part on developing techniques that increase social efficiency. This in turn requires the development of institutional arrangements, which Mann calls "power containers," that lock people into a set of social arrangements through a set of incentives and constraints. He analyzes these in terms of a full range of ideological, economic, military, and political mechanisms for gaining social compliance.[34]

In his multifaceted discussions of the rise and revitalization of powerful historical empires, two elements stand out. First is the importance of networks of people that lie at the margins of existing societies and that cut across the boundaries of political entities and social groups. Mann shows, for example, the centrality of traders and ethnically mixed urban middle classes in the rise of the Christian ideology that revitalized the Roman Empire. Second is the role of new forms of organization and loyalty in overcoming social contradictions that limit the effectiveness of old institutions in generating social power. In a series of examples of the rise of empires, Mann shows how social cleavages, localistic perspectives, or entrenched privileges blocked the development of social cohesion, economic efficiency, or powerful military techniques. Once these contradictions were unblocked by ideological or institutional innovations carried out through networks of marginal and integrative groups, the capacity to generate social power to create or to revitalize empire was unleashed.

The rise of Islam, for example, shows how a new ideology can lay down a pattern of social organization that integrated a vast array of disparate societies. Muhammad's doctrine provided an ideological solution to the collective action dilemmas that had left the Arabian tribes divided and their disenfranchised younger sons discontented amid the growing trading wealth of Mecca. Ties of reciprocity based on belief rather than kinship, welded together by a simple doctrine and intensive ritual, created the morale that was needed for military victories and the openness to conversion that was needed for the network's open-ended growth. However, the extent of the growth followed a pattern that was the opposite of that of Christianity, which expanded only as far as the latent network that Rome had provided for it. Instead, Islam rolled up the areas that lacked any comparable ideology of mass collective action, but came to a halt when it reached the edges of civilizations that had already discovered such power techniques. Thus, Christianity reorganized an existing civilization, whereas Islam created a civilization mainly out of hinterlands.

What might this mean for an assessment of the feasibility of empire or hegemony today? In the contemporary era, international politics is increasingly animated by the projects of ideology-infused transnational networks of the kind that Mann studies.[35] In the wake of the attack on the World Trade Center, the attempt to squelch the al-Qaeda global Islamic terrorist network was the all-absorbing foreign-policy enterprise of the advanced democracies. At the same time, transnational networks, especially non-governmental activist organizations linked in what is styled a "global civil society," have become a central carrier of liberalism's worldwide ideological project of promoting democracy and human rights.

Both of these socially marginal, transnational movements piggyback on networks that are sustained by the varied processes of globalization. Both arguably seek, each in its own way, to resolve the contradictions between the universalistic norms of secular, liberal society and the very different practices of societies that are struggling to adapt successfully to the world that globalization is creating.[36] Both draw on deep ideological and political reserves, including religious nationalism. Although liberalism deploys far stronger military and economic resources, contradictions between the idealist agenda of the transnational activists and the geopolitical agenda of the hegemonic American state limit the synergies that can be gained between material power and democratic ideology. Moreover, the further the United States extends its global reach into terrain where liberal networks are thin, the more it will have to rely on costly, coercive instruments of power. In short, although the dynamics that Mann discusses are present, they point at least in the near term toward the likelihood of a global stalemate rather than a snowballing of American successes leading expeditiously to an easy global hegemony.

CONCLUSION

These perspectives of the opportunities and costs of empire provide insights on the dilemmas that America may confront in a hegemonic effort to reshape world politics. They alert us to the rising costs of expansion, the need for some form of governance to coordinate collective action, the benefits of voluntarily institutionalized cooperation over hierarchical domination, and the catalytic role of culturally creative transnational networks in developing new sources of social power. Overall, these insights suggest that America needs to use its vast resources to organize global politics more successfully, but that a coercive attempt to roll up the system in the name of global liberal democracy will be self-defeating. More promising would be a system of consensual domination in which America's coercive power is used selectively for purposes that enjoy broad legitimacy and are actively supported by local, regional, and multilateral institutions. Empire will not work, but a flexible, scaled-down form of hegemony by invitation just might.

NOTES

Introduction

1. Niall Ferguson, *Empire: The Rise and Demise of the British World Order and the Lessons for Global Power* (New York: Basic Books, 2003), is the exception that proves the rule. The first 355 pages portray the British Empire as swashbuckling, often brutal, stingy, and only rarely interested in reforming conquered societies—and then unable to pay the bills. The last 13 pages make an argument for the British Empire being a model for American foreign policy, as if the history of the British Empire can be boiled down to an essence of rule of law and free-market economics. The contradiction is such that Ferguson had to write another book, *Colossus: The Price of America's Empire* (New York: Penguin, 2004), to make his empire-as-model argument less self-contradictory. For further discussion see Matthew Connelly's chapter in this volume.

2. For summaries of such scholarship, see Dominic Lieven, *Empire: The Russian Empire and Its Rivals* (New Haven: Yale University Press, 2000); Ann Laura Stoler and Frederick Cooper, eds., *Tensions of Empire: Colonial Cultures in a Bourgeois World* (Berkeley: University of California Press, 1997); and Stoler, this volume.

3. Compare (as does Connelly) Ferguson, *Empire*, and Michael Hardt and Antonio Negri, *Empire* (Cambridge, MA: Harvard University Press, 2001). Hardt and Negri describe "empire" as not merely the project of U.S. power, but as a more or less seamless structure of global capitalism for which the United States provides the primary enforcement without itself being the autonomous protagonist. Indeed, in their account empire is so lacking in internal contradictions that it cannot be transformed from within its social formation, though it can be resisted from without by the global "multitude" (a proliferation of different groups and individuals who discover that hyperglobalization gives them much in common without in fact rendering them a unified social force). See also their *Multitude* (New York: Penguin, 2004).

4. This is the problem with Michael Doyle's definition of empire as control of "a subordinated society by an imperial society": societies are not necessarily what does the subordinating; they may be produced in the building and evolution of empires. *Empires* (Ithaca: Cornell University Press, 1986), p. 30.

5. Patrick Geary's argument against pushing backward the notion of nation into earlier periods of European history might be made in regard to more recent periods too, when the national idea was far from dominant. *The Myth of Nations: The Medieval Origins of Europe* (Princeton: Princeton University Press, 2002).

6. Ronald Robinson and John Gallagher, "The Imperialism of Free Trade," *Economic History Review,* 2nd series, 6 (1953), pp. 1–15.

7. The phrase comes from the opinion of Chief Justice John Marshall in *Cherokee Nation v. Georgia,* 30 U.S. (5 Pet.) 1, 17 (1831). It is still in official use. See President Bill Clinton's Executive Order 13175 (November 6, 2000).

8. In addition to Go's chapter, see the analyses of continental empire in Richard White, *The Middle Ground: Indians, Empires, and Republics in the Great Lakes Region, 1650–1815* (Cambridge: Cambridge University Press, 1991); D. W. Meinig, *The Shaping of America: A Geographical Perspective on 500 Years of History* (New Haven: Yale University Press, 1986); and Richard White, *It's Your*

Misfortune and None of My Own: A History of the American West (Norman: University of Oklahoma Press, 1991).

9. A phrase lifted from Sara Berry, "Hegemony on a Shoestring: Indirect Rule and Access to Agricultural Land," *Africa* 62 (1992), pp. 327–55.

10. On air power in colonial situations, see David E. Omissi, *Air Power and Colonial Control: The Royal Air Force, 1919–1939* (Manchester: Manchester University Press, 1990); Sebastian Balfour, *Deadly Embrace: Morocco and the Road to the Spanish Civil War* (Oxford: Oxford University Press, 2002), ch. 5.

11. Rashid Khalidi, *Resurrecting Empire: Western Footprints and America's Perilous Path in the Middle East* (Boston: Beacon, 2004). Christopher Schmidt-Nowara's chapter brings the issue of differential memories of conquest and occupation closer to the United States, pointing out the tensions between Americans and Cubans and Americans and Spanish over the history of American actions in the Spanish-speaking Caribbean since 1898.

12. Benedict Anderson, *Imagined Communities: Reflections on the Origin and Spread of Nationalism* (London: Verso, 1983). Anderson's influential argument could be complemented by analysis of the continuing importance and adaptability of imperial imaginaries in uneasy relationship to the national imaginaries he emphasizes.

13. Linda Colley, *Britons: Forging the National Identity, 1707–1837* (New Haven: Yale University Press, 1994); Emmanuelle Saada, this volume.

14. Jeremy Adelman, *Struggle for Sovereignty: Empire and Revolution in the Iberian Atlantic* (forthcoming).

15. On the importance of contests over citizenship within the space of empire, see both the classic account, C.L.R. James, *The Black Jacobins* (New York: Vintage, 1963; orig. pub. 1938), and the recent work of Laurent Dubois, *A Colony of Citizens: Revolution and Slave Emancipation in the French Caribbean, 1787–1804* (Chapel Hill: University of North Carolina Press, 2004).

16. This line of argument is spelled out in Frederick Cooper, "States, Empires, and Political Imagination," in his *Colonialism in Question: Theory, Knowledge, History* (Berkeley: University of California Press, 2005).

17. Mark Elliott, *The Manchu Way: The Eight Banners and Ethnic Identity in Late Imperial China* (Stanford: Stanford University Press, 2001); Peter Perdue, "Comparing Empires: Manchu Colonialism" and "Boundaries, Maps, and Movement: Chinese, Russian, and Mongolian Empires in Early Modern Central Asia," *International History Review* 20 (1998), pp. 253–86.

18. C.A. Bayly, *Imperial Meridian: The British Empire and the World, 1780–1830* (Harrow, Eng.: Longman, 1989); C.A. Bayly, *Rulers, Townsmen and Bazaars: Northern Indian Society in the Age of British Expansion, 1770–1870* (Cambridge: Cambridge University Press, 1983).

19. William J. Foltz, *From French West Africa to the Mali Federation* (New Haven: Yale University Press, 1965), pp. 75–76.

20. Margaret Keck and Kathryn Sikkink, *Activists beyond Borders: Advocacy Networks in International Politics* (Ithaca: Cornell University Press, 1998).

21. Engseng Ho, "Empire through Diasporic Eyes: A View from the Other Boat," *Comparative Studies in Society and History* 46 (2004), pp. 210–46.

22. Craig Calhoun, "The Class Consciousness of Frequent Travelers: Toward a Critique of Actually Existing Cosmopolitanism," *South Atlantic Quarterly* 101 (2003), pp. 869–97.

23. See Connelly's chapter for criticism of the globality thesis and those of Craig Murphy, Jomo K.S., and Jack Snyder for alternative formulations of international order and economy.

24. See Craig Calhoun, "A World of Emergencies: Fear, Intervention, and the Limits of Cosmopolitan Order," The 2004 Sorokin Lecture, *Canadian Review of Sociology and Anthropology*, forthcoming.

25. On Ottomanism and provincial structures, see Hasan Kayali, *Arabs and Young Turks: Ot-*

tomanism, Arabism, and Islamism in the Ottoman Empire, 1908–1918 (Berkeley: University of California Press, 1997).

26. Rogers Brubaker, *Nationalism Reframed: Nationhood and the National Question in the New Europe* (Cambridge: Cambridge University Press, 1996), pp. 148–69.

1. The New Imperialists

1. Allan Murray, "Political Capital: Manifesto Cautions about the Dangers an Empire Presents," *Wall Street Journal*, July 15, 2003, p. 4.

2. Anne McClintock, *Imperial Leather: Race, Gender, and Sexuality in the Colonial Contest* (New York: Routledge, 1995); Thomas Richards, *The Imperial Archive: Knowledge and the Fantasy of Empire* (New York; London: Verso, 1993); *The Colonial Harem*, trans. Myrna Godzich and Wlad Godzich (Minneapolis: University of Minnesota Press, 1986).

3. Max Boot, *The Savage Wars of Peace: Small Wars and the Rise of American Power* (New York: Basic Books, 2002), p. xv; Niall Ferguson, *Empire: How Britain Made the Modern World* (London: Allen Lane, 2003), pp. 186, 215.

4. Michael Hardt and Antonio Negri, *Empire* (Cambridge, MA: Harvard University Press, 2000), pp. 168, 402, 413.

5. Garrick Utley, "The Shrinking of Foreign News: From Broadcast to Narrowcast," *Foreign Affairs* 76, no. 2 (1997), pp. 2–10.

6. John Gallagher and Ronald Robinson, "The Imperialism of Free Trade, 1815–1914," *Economic History Review* 6, no. 2 (1953), pp. 1–15.

7. *Africa and the Victorians: The Climax of Imperialism in the Dark Continent* (New York: St. Martin's Press, 1961). Gallagher later collaborated with Wm. Roger Louis in applying these concepts to the United States, "The Imperialism of Decolonization," *Journal of Imperial and Commonwealth History* 22, no. 3 (1994), pp. 462–511.

8. See Frank's autobiographical essay, "The Underdevelopment of Development," in *The Underdevelopment of Development*, ed. Sing C. Chew and Robert A. Denemark (London: Sage, 1996), pp. 23–31.

9. Edward Said, *Orientalism* (New York: Pantheon Books, 1978). For a recent rearticulation with particular reference to the U.S; see Said, "A Window on the World," *The Guardian*, August 2, 2003.

10. *The Rise and Fall of the Great Powers: Economic Change and Military Conflict from 1500 to 2000* (New York: Random House, 1987). For a commentary on contemporary parallels see Kennedy, "The Perils of Empire," *Washington Post*, April 20, 2003.

11. David Harvey analyzes the conflict between the "logic of territory" and the "logic of capital" in *The New Imperialism* (New York: Oxford University Press, 2003). Similarly, Charles S. Maier is presently at work on a project highlighting the growing tendency for power and wealth to accrue without territorial control, particularly in the case of the U.S., "An American Empire? The Problems of Frontiers and Peace in Twenty-first-century World Politics," *Harvard Magazine*, November–December 2002, pp. 28–31.

12. Boot, "America's Destiny Is to Police the World," *Financial Times*, February 17, 2003; Ferguson, "America as Empire, Now and in the Future," *In the National Interest*, July 23, 2003, www.inthenationalinterest.com/Articles/Vol2Issue29/Vol2Issue29Ferguson.html (March 9, 2004); Hardt and Negri, *Empire*, p. 181.

13. Hardt and Negri, *Empire*, p. 345.

14. Boot, "Who Says We Never Strike First?" *The New York Times*, October 4, 2002.

15. Boot, *Savage Wars*, pp. 120, 125–26, 341–42.

16. Ibid., pp. xix–xx.

17. Ibid., pp. 38, 347.

18. Robert Beisner, *Twelve Against Empire: The Anti-Imperialists, 1898–1900,* 2d. ed., (Chicago: University of Chicago Press, 1985), p. 233; and see also Walter L. Williams, "United States Indian Policy and the Debate over Philippine Annexation: Implications for the Origins of American Imperialism," *The Journal of American History* 66, no. 4 (1980), pp. 814–17.

19. "The British Empire, Bad or Good?" The Penguin Lectures, Institute of Historical Research, University of London, January 14, 2003.

20. Ferguson, *Empire,* p. 216.

21. Kingsley Davis, *The Population of India and Pakistan* (New York: Russell and Russell, 1951, 1968), pp. 35–36; David Arnold, "Colonial Medicine in Transition: Medical Research in India, 1910–1947," *South Asia Research* 14, no. 1 (1994), p. 18; Ira Klein, "Imperialism, Ecology, and Disease: Cholera in India, 1850–1950," *The Indian Economic and Social History Review* 31, no. 4 (1994), p. 494; "Note on the Problem of Malnutrition in India," circa 1935, British Library, London, India Office Records, L/E/9/265; *Report of the Health Survey and Development Committee, Vol. I: Survey* (New Delhi: Government of India Press, 1946), pp. 45–49.

22. Kenneth Pomeranz and Steven Topik, *The World That Trade Created: Society, Culture, and the World Economy, 1400–the Present* (Armonk, NY: M.E. Sharpe, 1999), p. 72; B.M. Bhatia, *Famines in India, 1850–1945* (Bombay: Konark, 1963), p. 94; Mike Davis, *Late Victorian Holocausts: El Niño Famines and the Making of the Third World* (London; New York: Verso, 2001), pp. 26–27, 111–12; David Hardiman, "Usury, Dearth and Famine in Western India," *Past and Present* 152 (August 1996), pp. 133, 145–46.

23. Sheldon Watts, *Epidemics and History: Disease, Power and Imperialism* (New Haven, CT: Yale University Press, 1997), pp. 201–202; Davis, *Late Victorian Holocausts,* pp. 38–40; Ferguson, *Empire,* p. 188.

24. Sheldon Watts, "British Development Policies and Malaria in India, 1897–c. 1929," *Past and Present* 165 (November 1999), pp.141–44, 170–74; Watts, *Epidemics and History,* p. 205; Leela Visaria and Pravin Visaria, "Population (1757–1947)," in *The Cambridge Economic History of India,* ed. Dharma Kumar (Cambridge: Cambridge University Press, 1983), pp. 480–81; Ira Klein, "Death in India, 1871–1921," *Journal of Asian Studies* 32, no. 4 (1973), pp. 645–46.

25. Watts, *Epidemics and History,* p. 203.

26. *Heart of Darkness,* Norton Critical Edition, 3rd edition, ed. Robert Kimbrough (New York; London: W.W. Norton, 1988), p. 10.

27. "Supremacy by Stealth: Ten Rules for Managing the World," *Atlantic Monthly,* July–August 2003, www.theatlantic.com/issues/2003/07/kaplan.htm (March 9, 2004).

28. Hardt and Negri, *Empire,* pp. 23–24, 213.

29. Ibid., p. 181.

30. The classic text is Robert Keohane, *After Hegemony: Cooperation and Discord in the World Political Economy* (Princeton: Princeton University Press, 1984). For a review of subsequent work and its policy implications, almost all by political scientists, see Keohane, "International Institutions: Can Interdependence Work?" *Foreign Policy* (spring 1998), pp. 82–96. Historians have only recently started to give serious attention to international organizations as actors in themselves rather than as mere fora of great power politics. See especially Akira Iriye, *Global Community: The Role of International Organizations in the Making of the Contemporary World* (Berkeley: University of California Press, 2002).

31. Hardt and Negri, *Empire,* p. 181.

32. Ibid., pp. 211, 399–400, 407. At one point they hint darkly at "gathering together these experiences of resistance and wielding them in concert against the nerve centers of imperial command," (p. 399) but here again the centers are not specified.

33. Ibid., p. 11.

34. Ibid., p. 404.

35. This description is based on research for a book to be published by Harvard University Press. For a review of the literature see Matthew Connelly, "Population Control is History: New Perspectives on the International Campaign to Limit Population Growth," *Comparative Studies in Society and History* 45, no. 1 (2003), pp. 122–47.

36. Michael Ignatieff, *Empire Lite: Nation Building in Bosnia, Kosovo, Afghanistan* (London: Vintage, 2003).

2. The History of Lessons

1. David Ignatius, "Think Strategy, Not Numbers," *The Washington Post,* August 26, 2003.

2. For an analysis of this imitative dimension of empire building, see Sheldon Pollock's "Empire and Imitation," this volume.

3. These were the positions adopted respectively by historian Niall Ferguson and international-relations specialist Robert Kagan in a debate organized by the American Enterprise Institute, titled "The United States Is, and Should Be, an Empire: A New Atlantic Initiative Debate" (July 17, 2003; http://www.aei.org/events/filter.,eventID.428/transcript.asp). I will quote extensively from this exchange because it features most of the central arguments in the debate on the imperial characteristics of U.S. power.

4. Niall Ferguson, "The Empire Slinks Back," *New York Times Magazine,* April 27, 2003.

5. Kagan, "The United States Is, and Should Be, an Empire."

6. Ibid. Kagan continues: "We cannot simply declare that we are an Empire and therefore it flows mechanically. We must all continue to work to make our fellow Americans understand the important role that the United States has to play. And we also have the task of convincing the rest of the world that America's actions are not purely selfish but are in the interest of many others who share its views."

7. "The hypothesis, in other words, is a step in the direction of political globalization, with the United States shifting from informal to formal empire much as late Victorian Britain once did. That is certainly what we should expect if history does indeed repeat itself. Like the United States today, Britain did not set out to rule a quarter of the world's land surface. As we have seen, its empire began as a network of coastal bases and informal spheres of influence, much like the post-1945 American 'empire.' But real and perceived threats to their commercial interests constantly tempted the British to progress from informal to formal imperialism. That was how so much of the Atlas came to be coloured imperial red." Niall Ferguson, *Empire: The Rise and Demise of the British World Order and the Lessons for Global Power* (New York: Basic Books, 2003), p. 368.

8. Ferguson, "The Empire Slinks Back."

9. On the "politics of comparison," see Ann Laura Stoler, "Caveat on Comfort Zones and Comparative Frames," in her *Carnal Knowledge and Imperial Power* (Berkeley: University of California Press, 2003), pp. 205–217. On the ideological uses of the notions of *direct* and *indirect rules* by the British and French colonial administrations, see Véronique Dimier, "Direct or Indirect Rule: Propaganda around a Scientific Controversy," in *Propaganda and Empire in France,* ed. Tony Chafer (London and New York: Macmillan, 2002).

10. In "Empire on a Shoestring" (*Washington Post,* July 20, 2003), Ferguson argues that it is not possible to "run" an empire on the "Wal-Mart principle of 'always low prices.' "

11. On this, see Jacques Marseille, *Empire colonial et capitalisme français: histoire d'un divorce* (Paris: Albin Michel, 1984).

12. Ferguson is also rather inconsistent on this point: both in his book and his popular writing, he argues that the British Empire was a stage for upwardly mobile Scots and Irishmen, and he compares this process to the overrepresentation of African Americans in the U.S. army.

13. Morocco became a protectorate in 1912 and the mandates over Togo, Cameroon, Lebanon, and Syria were granted in 1919 and 1920.

14. On this, see Frederick Cooper and Ann Laura Stoler, eds., *Tensions of Empire: Colonial Cultures in a Bourgeois World* (Berkeley: University of California Press, 1997) and especially their introduction to the volume, *Between Metropole and Colony: Rethinking a Research Agenda,* pp. 1–56.

15. Jules Michelet, *History of France from the Earliest Period to the Present Time,* vol. 1 (New York: Appleton, 1845), p. 182.

16. Ferguson, *Empire,* pp. 358–59.

17. http://www.whitehouse.gov/nsc/nss.pdf

18. Kennedy affirms: "We comprise slightly less than 5 percent of the world population; but we imbibe 27 percent of the world's annual oil production, create and consume nearly 30 percent of its Gross World Product and spend a full 40 percent of ALL [his emphasis] the world's defense expenditures. As I have noted, the Pentagon's budget is nowadays roughly equal to the defense expenditures of the next nine or 10 highest defense spending nations—which has never happened in history." Paul Kennedy, "The Greatest Superpower Ever," *New Perspective Quarterly* 19 (spring 2002).

19. Ferguson, "The U.S. Is, and Should Be, an Empire."

20. The use of these terms can be traced to the work of Joseph Nye in the late 1980s as a counter to those who foresaw the decline of the United States as a great power as a result of "overstretch." *Born to Lead: The Changing Nature of American Power* (New York: Basic Books, 1990). The notion has been more recently revisited by Nye who identifies hard with "command power" and soft with "co-optive power." See B. Keohane and J. Nye, "Power and Independence in the Information Age," *Foreign Affairs* 77, no. 5 (1998), pp. 81–94.

21. Robert Kagan, *Of Paradise and Power: America and Europe in the New World Order* (New York: Knopf, 2003), p. 37.

22. In a surprisingly simplistic analogy in a book which has attracted so much attention, Kagan states: "The differing psychology of power and weakness are easy enough to understand. A man armed only with a knife may decide that a bear prowling the forest is a tolerable danger, inasmuch as the alternative—hunting the bear armed only with a knife—is actually riskier than lying low and hoping the bear never attacks, will likely make a different calculation of what constitutes a tolerable risk. Why should he risk being mauled to death if he doesn't have to? This perfectly normal human psychology has driven a wedge between the United States and Europe" (*Of Paradise,* p. 31).

23. "The United States must act unilaterally, not out of a passion for unilateralism but only because, given a weak Europe that has moved beyond power, the United States has no choice *but* to act unilaterally" (*Of Paradise,* p. 99).

24. Kagan, *Of Paradise,* p. 18. In an article for *Policy Review* on the same topic, this point is even more explicit: "Europe has been militarily weak for a long time, but until fairly recently its weakness had been obscured. World War II all but destroyed European nations as global powers, and their postwar inability to project sufficient force overseas to maintain colonial empires in Asia, Africa, and the Middle East forced them to retreat on a massive scale after more than five centuries of imperial dominance—perhaps the most significant retrenchment of global influence in human history." "Power and Weakness," *Policy Review,* June 2002, p. 113.

25. Kagan, *Of Paradise,* p. 101.

26. For a more elaborate formulation of this idea, see Frederick Cooper's "Modernizing Colonialism and the Limits of Empire," this volume.

27. This confusion is not new. Political theorists of many kinds have criticized the loose use of the notion of "power" within the field of international relations and political science. In the 1960s, Raymond Aron took a critical stance toward the use of the expression "power politics," as prominent then as it is today in the analysis of the U.S. international role. He also warned against the quantification of power so prevalent today: "Being a relationship between men or groups, power does not lend itself to quantification as readily as goods or things: relative, not absolute, power ex-

tends over some men or groups and not others; it controls some behavior, not all." Raymond Aron, "*Macht,* Power, *Puissance:* Democratic Prose or Demoniac Poetry?" in *Politics and History* (New York: The Free Press, 1978 [1964]), pp. 102–121, 108. Hannah Arendt also pleaded for greater clarity and suggested that one should "distinguish among such key words as 'power,' 'strength,' 'force,' 'authority,' and, finally, 'violence.'" Hannah Arendt, *On Violence* (New York: Harcourt, Brace and World, 1969), p. 43. With a radically different philosophical agenda, Michel Foucault also advocated a break from "a metaphysics or an ontology of power" in favor of a "critical investigation into the thematics of power" which would concentrate on analysis of the means of exercise of power. Michel Foucault, "The Subject and Power," in *Michel Foucault: Beyond Structuralism and Hermeneutics,* ed. Hubert L. Dreyfus and Paul Rabinow (Chicago: University of Chicago Press, 1982), pp. 208–226, 217.

28. Kagan, *Of Paradise,* p. 99.

29. On this see Cooper and Stoler, "Beyond Metropole and Colony," in *Tensions of Empire.*

30. Philippe Darriulat, *Les patriotes: la gauche républicaine et la nation, 1830–1870* (Paris: Le Seuil, 2001); and Henri Solus, *Traité de la condition des indigènes en droit privé. Colonies et pays de protectorat et pays sous mandat* (Paris: Recueil Sirey, 1927), pp. 313–21.

31. http://www.whitehouse.gov/nsc/nss.pdf, p. 3.

32. "As of this month, [Afghanistan] has a new constitution, guaranteeing free elections and full participation by women. [. . .] Last January, Iraq's only law was the whim of one brutal man. Today, our coalition is working with the Iraqi Governing council to draft a basic law with a bill of rights. We're working with Iraqis and the United Nations to prepare for a transition to full Iraqi sovereignty by the end of June." President Bush, State of the Union address, January 20, 2004.

33. On this see A. Esmein, *Eléments de droit constitutionnel français et comparé* (Paris: Sirey, 1914), p. 2.

34. John Comaroff, "Colonialism, Culture and the Law: A Foreword," *Law and Social Inquiry* 26 (spring 2001), pp. 305–314, 309.

35. Antony Anghie, "Finding the Peripheries: Sovereignty and Colonialism in Nineteenth-Century International Law," *Harvard International Law Journal* 40, no. 1 (winter 1999), pp. 1–80.

36. Isabelle Merle, "La construction d'un droit foncier colonial. De la propriété collective à la constitution des réserves en Nouvelle-Calédonie," *Enquête, Anthropologie, Histoire, Sociologie* 7 (1998), pp. 97–126.

37. In the capitulation treaty of the Bey of Algiers' 1830, France pledged not to "encroach on the inhabitants' freedom and religion." Bush made the same promise to the Iraqi people shortly after the fall of Baghdad: "We will respect your great religious traditions, whose principles of equality and compassion are essential to Iraq's future." President Bush's message to the Iraqi people, April 10, 2003, http://www.whitehouse.gov/news/releases/2003/04/20030410-2.html.

38. This articulation between civility and citizenship distinguished the French imperial polity from other historical models, such as the late Roman Empire in which *Civita Romana* was only superimposed on local status, or the Ottoman Empire where the community-based legal order prevailed locally while state law prevailed at the imperial level. See Caglar Keyder, "Law and Legitimation on Empire," this volume.

39. Raberh Achi, "La séparation des églises et de l'Etat à l'épreuve de la situation coloniale. Les usages de la dérogation dans l'administration du culte musulman en Algérie (1905–1959)," *Politix. Revue des sciences sociales du politique* 17, no. 66 (2004).

40. See Jean-Paul Charnay, *La Vie musulmane en Algérie d'après la jurisprudence de la première moitié du XXème siècle* (Paris: PUF, 1965).

41. For a more general discussion of this, see Lauren Benton, *Law and Colonial Cultures: Legal Regimes in World History, 1400–1900* (Cambridge: Cambridge University Press, 2002).

42. Noah Feldman, *After Jihad: America and the Struggle for Islamic Democracy* (New York: Farrar, Straus and Giroux, 2003).

43. Isabelle Merle, "Retour sur le régime de l'indigénat: Genèse et contradictions des principes répressifs dans l'Empire français," *French Politics, Culture and Society* 20, no. 2 (summer 2002), pp. 77–97.

44. Nowhere has this tension become more visible than in the case of Zacharias Moussaoui. The administration ascribed two contradictory functions to his trial: it would be a showcase for the American justice system and its respect of formal rules *and also* a showcase of U.S. power to suppress terrorist threats. These distinct goals have produced a deadlock as Moussaoui asserts his rights to a fair trial (specifically, the right to depose witnesses to his alleged crime). The double bind of justice and security will continue to be at the center of the legal controversy surrounding the case.

45. *Hamdi v. Rumsfeld,* 03-6696.

46. On Algeria, see Sylvie Thénault, *Une drôle de Justice. Les magistrats dans la guerre d'Algérie* (Paris: La Découverte, 2001).

47. On this see Maurice Duverger, *Le Concept d'Empire* (Paris: Presses Universitaires de France, 1980).

48. Joseph Nye, "Surpassing Rome," *New Perspectives Quarterly* 19 (winter 2002).

49. Bernard Cohn and Nicholas Dirks, "Beyond the Fringe: The Nation State, Colonialism, and the Technologies of Power," *Journal of Historical Sociology* 1, no. 2 (June 1988), pp. 224–29.

3. Imperial Formations and the Opacities of Rule

1. I want to thank Frederick Cooper, Fernando Coronil, George Steinmetz, and Lawrence Hirschfeld for pressing their questions.

2. Michael Ignatieff, "The American Empire: The Burden," *New York Times Magazine,* January 5, 2003.

3. Immanuel Wallerstein, *The Decline of American Power* (New York: The New Press, 2003).

4. Michael Hardt and Antonio Negri, *Empire* (Cambridge, MA: Harvard University Press, 2000).

5. Dinesh D'Souza, "Colonialism and Reality," *Rhodesian.Net,* May 17, 2002; Niall Ferguson, *Empire: The Rise and Demise of the British World Order and the Lessons for Global Power* (London: Penguin, 2003).

6. Martin Sieff, "Analysis: Arguments against U.S. Empire," *Washington Times,* www.washtimes.com/upi-breaking/200030715-110839-2320.htm.

7. See, for example, the *BoondocksNet.com* sites on "Mark Twain on War and Imperialism" by Jim Zwick, a listing of hundreds of newspaper articles for the 1890s alone by such well-known figures as William James and Jane Addams.

8. W.E.B Du Bois, "The African Roots of War, " *Atlantic Monthly,* May 1915, reprinted in *Monthly Review* 24, no. 11 (1973), pp. 28–40.

9. William Appelman Williams, *Empire As a Way of Life* (Oxford: Oxford University Press, 1980.)

10. Nicholas Dirks, ed., *Culture and Colonialism* (Ann Arbor: University of Michigan Press, 1992), p. 5.

11. Eric Hobsbawm, "Ou va l'Empire americain?" *Le Monde Diplomatique,* June 2003, p. 1.

12. A.G. Hopkins, "Lessons of 'Civilizing Missions' Are Mostly Unlearned," *New York Times,* March 23, 2003, p. 5.

13. Robert Kagan, "The Benevolent Empire," *Foreign Policy,* summer 1998; Robert Cooper, "Why We Still Need Empires," *The Observer,* 7 April 2002; Daniel Vernet, "Postmodern Imperialism," *Le Monde,* 24 April 2003. These are echoed by Niall Ferguson, who approvingly invokes what he calls late-nineteenth-century Britain's most self-consciously authentic imperial politician Joe Chamberlain's favored term—"an imperial preference" (*Empire,* p. 284).

14. Michael Mann, *The Incoherent Empire* (London: Verso, 2003), p. 29.

15. Michael T. Kaufman, "What Does the Pentagon See in 'Battle of Algiers'?" *New York Times,* 7 September 2003, p. 3.

16. J. Hoberman, "Revolution Now (and Then)!" *American Prospect* 15, no. 1 (January 2004), www.prospect.org/print/V15/hoberman-johtml; Rialto Pictures, critics on *The Battle of Algiers,* www.railtopictures.com/eyes; Peter Rainer, "Prescient Tense," www.newyorkmetro.com.

17. George Monbio, "Backyard Terrorism," *The Guardian,* 30 October 2001.

18. What Kaufman reported as a "civilian-led organization" that he was told by a Defense Department official was responsible "for thinking aggressively and creatively" on issues of guerilla war is run by the assistant director of defense. As described in the Special Operations and Combating Terrorism Web site of the Department of Defense, the SOF's members are "versatile," "diplomatic warriors," whose specialty is "unconventional warfare"—low visibility, covert or clandestine operations. The SOF is an "organic staff element" within the Office of the Secretary of Defense. See its Web site: www.dod.gov/policy/solic.

19. Nostalgia for French Algeria has been common fare for some time, but few have shared Benjamin Stora's searing condemnation of the relationship between that memory and anti-Arab racism as it exists in France today. On the former, see Jeannine Verdes-Leroux, *Les Francias d'Algérie de l830 à aujourd'hui: Une page d'histoire dechirée* (Paris: Fayard, 2001). Stora's works include: *Le Transfert d'une Mémoire: de l'Algérie-francaise au racisme anti-arabe* (Paris: Le Découverte, 1999); *La Guerre Invisible: Algérie, années 90* (Paris: Presse de Sciences Po, 2001).

20. James Kurth, "Migration and the Dynamics of Empire," *National Interest* (spring 2003), pp. 5–28.

21. On imperial blueprints, see my "Developing Historical Negatives: Race and the Modernist Visions of a Colonial State," in *From the Margins,* ed. Brian Axel (Durham: Duke University Press, 2002), pp. 156–88.

22. Ignatieff, "American Empire," p. 24.

23. Ibid.

24. Sue Peabody and Tyler Stovall, eds., *The Color of Liberty: Histories of Race in France* (Durham: Duke University Press, 2003).

25. Ignatieff, "American Empire," p. 24.

26. Anatol Lieven, "The Empire Strikes Back," *The Nation,* 27 July 2003, p. 25.

27. Norman Mailer, "Only in America," *New York Review of Books,* 27 March 2003, p. 52.

28. Ann Laura Stoler, "Habits of a Colonial Heart: The Affective Grid of Racial Politics," in *A Companion to Anthropology and Politics,* ed. Joan Vincent and David Nugent (Cambridge: Blackwell, 2004).

29. Brooks Adams, quoted in Neil Smith, *American Empire: Roosevelt's Geographer and the Prelude to Globalization* (Berkeley: University of California Press, 2003), p. 10; Hannah Arendt, *The Origins of Totalitarianism* (New York: Harcourt, Brace, 1979), p. 125.

30. Thongchai Winichakul, *Siam Mapped: A History of the Geo-Body of a Nation* (Honolulu: University of Hawaii Press, 1994), p. 130.

31. Hannah Arendt, *The Origins of Totalitarianism* (New York: Harcourt Brace, 1975), pp. 222–66.

32. I owe this phrase to Carole McGranahan who used it in the context of Nepal in a conference we organized at the School of American Research in Fall 2004, entitled "Empire Beyond Europe."

33. Robert F. Rogers, *Destiny's Landfall: The History of Guam* (Honolulu: University of Hawaii Press, 1995), pp. 225–27; and Penelope B. Hofschneider, *A Campaign for Political Rights on the Island of Guam, 1899–1950* (Northern Mariana Islands Division of Historic Preservation, 2001).

34. Amy Kaplan, *The Anarchy of Empire in the Making of U.S. Culture* (Cambridge, MA: Harvard University Press, 2002), p. 3; Amy Kaplan, "Guantanamo's Limbo Is Too Convenient," *International Herald Tribune,* 24 November 2003.

35. Edward Said, *Orientalism* (New York: Vintage, 2003), p. xxi.

36. Stephen Rosen, professor of national security and military affairs at Harvard's Olin Institute for Strategic Studies, makes a similar point when he argues that "the organizing principle of empire

rests on the existence of an overarching power that creates and enforces the principle of hierarchy, but is not itself bound by such rules," in "An Empire, If You Can Keep It," *National Interest* 71 (spring 2003), p. 53.

37. See Hannah Arendt, who noted "the intimate traditional connection between imperialist politics and rule by 'invisible government' and secret agents," in *The Origins of Totalitarianism,* p. xx.

38. Carl Schmitt, *The Nomos of the Earth,* pp. 281–94.

39. On these enduring networks of those not bound by but far exceeding imperial ties, see Engseng Ho's "Empire through Diasporic Eyes," *Comparative Studies in Society and History* 46 (April 2004), pp. 210–46.

40. Arendt, *The Origins of Totalitarianism,* p. 131.

41. Andrew Hacker, *Two Nations: Black and White, Separate, Hostile and Unequal* (New York: Ballantine, 1992).

42. Samuel Huntington, *Who We Are: The Challenges to America's National Identity* (New York: Simon and Schuster, 2004).

43. Samuel Huntington "The Hispanic Challenge," *Foreign Policy* (March/April 2004), www .foreignpolicy.com/story/cms.php?story_id=2495.

44. Michel Foucault, *"Society Must Be Defended": Lectures at the Collège de France, 1975–1976* (New York: Picador, 2003), esp. pp. 254–56.

45. Louise Cainkar, "Targeting Muslims, at Ashcroft's Discretion," *Middle East Report Online,* March 14, 2003; and the ACLU's Web page on "National Security," www.aclu.org/National Security/National*SecurityMain.cfm.*

46. See Andrew Shryock, "New Images of Arab Detroit: Seeing Otherness and Identity through the Lens of September 11," *American Anthroplogist* 104, no. 3, 2002, pp. 917–22.

47. Arendt, *The Origins of Totalitarianism,* p. 131.

4. Modernizing Colonialism and the Limits of Empire

1. The shift is embodied in the contrasting arguments of two books called *Empire,* one by Michael Hardt and Antonio Negri (Cambridge, MA: Harvard University Press, 2000), which dissolves politics into amorphous but all-powerful global networks, and another by Niall Ferguson (London: Allen Lane, 2002), which concludes with a plea for the United States to take up the mantle of the British Empire, an argument that contradicts his relatively critical, sometimes cynical, view of the empire that actually existed.

2. As Craig Calhoun has argued, the sense of community comes from thinking and debating about constitutions, institutions, and norms—not just from prior sentiments—which makes all the more important an effort to address issues of shared and compromised sovereignty and non-national institutions. "Imagining Solidarity: Cosmopolitanism, Constitutional Patriotism, and the Public Sphere," *Public Culture* 14 (2002), pp. 147–71.

3. The chapters of George Steinmetz and Jack Snyder bring out the distinctions among such modes of intervention by a powerful polity in the affairs of weaker ones: imperial (intervening in another polity without actually governing it), hegemonic (setting the rules of the game which others must follow), and colonial (governing internal affairs of a subordinated polity). These do not in fact exhaust the possibilities, and historically the category of "empire" includes a considerable range of ways in which the incorporation of different population groups and the differentiation of those groups was managed and contested.

4. Donald Hepburn, "Nice War. Here's the Bill," *New York Times,* September 3, 2003, A19. The author is not a liberal academic or development professional, but an oil executive.

5. This article draws on previously published research. For the general argument about the ambiguities of colonial rule, see Ann Stoler and Frederick Cooper, "Between Metropole and Colony: Rethinking a Research Agenda," in Cooper and Stoler, *Tensions of Empire: Colonial Cultures in a*

Bourgeois World (Berkeley: University of California Press, 1997), pp. 1–56; and for the argument about the late—and abortive—episode of colonial modernization, see my *Decolonization and African Society: The Labor Question in French and British Africa* (Cambridge: Cambridge University Press, 1996).

6. Alice Conklin, *A Mission to Civilize: The Republican Idea of Empire in France and West Africa, 1895–1930* (Stanford: Stanford University Press, 1998).

7. Thomas Holt, *The Problem of Freedom: Race, Labor and Politics in Jamaica and Britain, 1832–1938* (Baltimore: Johns Hopkins University Press, 1990); Catherine Hall, *Civilising Subjects: Metropole and Colony in the English Imagination, 1830–1867* (Chicago: University of Chicago Press, 2002).

8. Hence the great concern among the advocates of a new imperialism that it be done right, that its considerable costs be recognized, and that the new imperial power acts in a way that is consistent with the rule of law and international opinion. There is much room for doubt on all these fronts, as acknowledged in Michael Ignatieff, "The American Empire: The Burden," *New York Times Magazine*, January 5, 2003, all the more so over a year after the invasion.

9. Seeley cited in Dominic Lieven, *Empire: The Russian Empire and Its Rivals* (New Haven: Yale University Press, 2001), p. 108. For the argument that Britain was a "wary titan" never willing to make the effort to organize an international order, rather than a "weary titan"—a once hegemonic power that subsequently lost its initiative, see John M. Hobson, "Two Hegemonies or One? A Historical-Sociological Critique of Hegemonic Stability Theory," in *Two Hegemonies: Britain 1846–1914 and the United States 1941–2001*, ed. Patrick Karl O'Brien and Armand Clesse (London: Ashgate, 2003), p. 316.

10. Ferguson, *Empire*. Compare the conclusions, pp. 357–70, with the core of the book. For an argument about the exercise of colonial power through the "decentralized despotisms" of African chiefs under British authority, see Mahmood Mamdani, *Subject and Citizen: Contemporary Africa and the Legacy of Late Colonialism* (Princeton: Princeton University Press, 1996). Mamdani is convincing in demonstrating British intent, especially in the 1920s and 1930s, to rule through "tribal" entities, but does not explore the cross-cutting linkages that Africans developed or the extent to which political mobilization in the 1940s and 1950s developed viable alternatives, at least for a time. On law, see Martin Chanock, *Law, Custom and Social Order: The Colonial Experience in Malawi and Zambia* (Cambridge: Cambridge University Press, 1985).

11. Stephen Constantine, *The Making of British Colonial Development Policy, 1914–1940* (London: Cass, 1984).

12. S. Herbert Frankel, *Capital Investment in Africa: Its Course and Effects* (London: Oxford University Press, 1938). On the ambivalence of French capital regarding colonial investment, see Jacques Marseille, *Empire colonial et capitalisme français: Histoire d'un divorce* (Paris: Albin Michel, 1984).

13. On the limits of capitalist development in rural Africa, see Sara Berry, *No Condition Is Permanent: The Social Dynamics of Agrarian Change in Sub-Saharan Africa* (Madison: University of Wisconsin Press, 1993).

14. On the claim making of military veterans, see Gregory Mann, "Immigrants and Arguments in France and West Africa," *Comparative Studies in Society and History* 45 (2003), pp. 362–85.

15. Pierre-Henri Teitgen, Assemblée Nationale, *Débats*, 20 March 1956, pp. 1,072–73.

16. This point is also made by Wm. Roger Louis and Ronald Robinson, "The Imperialism of Decolonization," *Journal of Imperial and Commonwealth History* 22 (1994), pp. 462–512.

17. An influential series of articles in the Paris press by a conservative journalist led to a public discussion of whether African colonies paid, at a time when the Overseas Ministry was producing ambiguous reports on the results of the development process. In Great Britain, Prime Minister Macmillan, not long after Suez, commissioned a colony-by-colony cost-benefit analysis, with not particularly encouraging results. See Cooper, *Decolonization*, ch. 10.

18. A notorious case of economic growth leading to revolt was the Mau Mau Emergency that broke out among the Kikuyu of Kenya in 1952. It followed not only the intensification of agriculture on

white settler farms—and hence the expulsion of many Kikuyu squatters who had combined labor for whites with their own farming—but also the acceleration of market-oriented agriculture by better-off Kikuyu (following the lifting of racial restrictions on coffee growing), who would not let expelled squatters obtain land in their former villages. Mau Mau was very much a crisis of intensified "development." See John Lonsdale and Bruce Berman, *Unhappy Valley: Conflict in Kenya and Africa*, 2, *Violence and Ethnicity* (London: James Currey, 1992); Tabitha Kanogo, *Squatters and the Roots of Mau Mau, 1905–63* (London: James Currey, 1987).

19. For an interpretation of the Algerian revolution that punctures the myth of victorious armed struggle and emphasizes that international factors shaped the outcome, see Matthew Connelly, *A Diplomatic Revolution: Algeria's Fight for Independence and the Origins of the Post–Cold War Era* (New York: Oxford University Press, 2002). More generally, I have written about the relationship between struggles within empires and struggles against empires in "Mobilization and Accommodation," paper for a Conference at the Institut des Hautes Etudes Internationales, Geneva, March 2003.

20. As John Ikenberry notes, public support for the war in Iraq "plummeted" when the price tag was revealed. G. John Ikenberry, "Illusions of Empire: Defining the New American Order," *Foreign Affairs* 83, no. 2 (2004), pp. 144–54.

21. Niall Ferguson, "The Empire Slinks Back: Why Americans Don't Really Have What It Takes to Rule the World," *New York Times Magazine*, April 27, 2003, pp. 52–57. The phrase "butcher and bolt" comes from *Empire*, p. 179.

22. Deepak Lal makes a tortured argument for an American imperialism that detaches minimalist overrule from a reformist or moralizing agenda. It fails to confront the difficulty of detaching minimalist rule making from the ideological baggage that attaches to legal and administrative institutions. And it misreads the current American administration, which often sounds as if maintaining its Christian fortress is its prime objective and which evinces little interest in submitting itself to any form of accountability except its own. Deepak Lal, "In Defense of Empires," Speech to American Enterprise Institute, October 30, 2002, www.aei.org/news. For more on the conservative embrace of empire, see Matthew Connelly's "The New Imperialists," in this volume.

23. Ferguson's evocation of this overwrought and overused text of Kipling is in *Empire*, p. 369.

5. Learning from Empire

1. This chapter has been a work-in-progress for many years, and parts were published in "The Empire Strikes Out! Imperial Russia, 'National Identity,' and Theories of Empire," in *A State of Nations: Empire and Nation-Making in the Age of Lenin and Stalin*, ed. Ronald Grigor Suny and Terry Martin (New York and Oxford: Oxford University Press, 2001), pp. 23–66. A later version was given as a talk at the conference "Empires in Modern Times," Institut Universitaire de Haute Études Internationales, Geneva, Switzerland, March 20–22, 2003, and the comments and criticisms offered at that meeting and at the meeting of authors of this volume at New York University, September 26–27, 2003, contributed to the further (probably not final) refinement of the argument presented here.

2. John A. Armstrong, *Nations Before Nationalism* (Chapel Hill: University of North Carolina Press, 1982); Michael W. Doyle, *Empires* (Ithaca: Cornell University Press, 1986).

3. Ibid., p. 36.

4. As Alexander J. Motyl argues, the peripheries must be distinct by population—class, ethnicity, religion, or something else—have a distinct territory, and be either a distinct polity or a distinct society. "From Imperial Decay to Imperial Collapse: The Fall of the Soviet Empire in Comparative Perspective," in *Nationalism and Empire: The Habsburg Empire and the Soviet Union*, ed. Richard L. Rudolph and David F. Good (New York: St. Martin's Press, 1992), p. 18.

5. Of course, as an imperial metropole grows weaker and peripheries stronger, as in the Habsburg Empire after 1848, it is forced to negotiate with powerful peripheries, as Vienna did with Budapest,

and in time the empire may become a hybrid empire with various autonomous "kingdoms" and "principalities" that no longer respect the authority of the center as it had in the past.

6. Fatma Müge Göçek, "The Social Construction of an Empire: Ottoman State Under Suleiman the Magnificent," in *Suleiman II and His Time,* ed. Halil Inalcik and Cemal Kafadar (Istanbul: Isis Press, 1993), pp. 93–108.

7. Mark R. Beissinger, "Demise of an Empire-State: Identity, Legitimacy, and the Deconstruction of Soviet Politics," in *The Rising Tide of Cultural Pluralism: The Nation-State at Bay?* ed. Crawford Young (Madison: University of Wisconsin Press, 1993), pp. 98, 99. To Beissinger's shrewd point that imperial relationships are about perceptions, it should be added that the perception of empire is not only about the attitude of peripheries but of metropoles as well. Empire exists even if peripheral populations are convinced that the result of their association with the empire is beneficial rather than exploitative, as long as the two conditions of distinction and subordination obtain. Indeed, much of the "post-colonialism" literature has dealt precisely with the ways in which hegemonic cultures of difference and development have sanctioned imperial relations and mediated resistance.

8. Suny, "The Empire Strikes Out!," p. 28. For similar views on the nation, see Etienne Balibar, "The Nation Form: History and Ideology," in Etienne Balibar and Immanuel Wallerstein, *Race, Nation, Class: Ambiguous Identities* (London: Verso, 1991), pp. 86–106; Benedict Anderson, *Imagined Communities: Reflections on the Origin and Spread of Nationalism* (London: Verso, 1983, 1991).

9. The distinction between ethnic group and nationality/nation need not be territory but rather the discourse in which they operate. The discourse about ethnicity is primarily about culture, cultural rights, and some limited political recognition, while the discourse of the nation is more often about popular sovereignty, state power, and control of a territorial homeland. But this is not necessarily or exclusively so, for one can conceive of nonterritorial nationalisms, like those of the Jews before Zionism, the Armenians in the nineteenth century, and the Gypsies. For another view on the problems of definitions, see Lowell W. Barrington, " 'Nation' and 'Nationalism': The Misuse of Key Concepts in Political Science," *PS: Political Science & Politics* 30, no. 4 (December 1977), pp. 712–16.

10. Rogers Brubaker, *Citizenship and Nationhood in France and Germany* (Cambridge, MA: Harvard University Press), pp. 22, 27.

11. Nation-states and empires can be seen as two poles in a continuum, but rather than fixed and stable, they may flow into one another, transforming over time into the other. A nation-state may appear stable, homogeneous, coherent, and yet with the rise of ethnic, subethnic, or regionalist movements be perceived by subaltern populations as imperial. For those identifying with the dominant population in Belgium, it is a nation-state, perhaps a multinational state, but for a Flemish militant who feels the oppression of the Walloon majority, Belgium is a kind of mini-empire. The term *empire* has been used polemically for small states like Belgium, Georgia, and Estonia, and it may seem anomalous to refer to such nationalizing states as empires. But it is precisely with the assimilating homogenizing, or discriminating practices of the nationalizing state that relationships of difference and subordination—here considered the ingredients of an imperial relationship—are exposed.

12. On the Ottoman case, see Ronald Grigor Suny, "Religion, Ethnicity, and Nationalism: Armenians, Turks, and the End of the Ottoman Empire," in *In God's Name: Genocide and Religion in the Twentieth Century,* ed. Omer Bartov and Phyllis Mack (Berghahn Press, forthcoming).

13. See Frederick Cooper and Randall Packard, "Introduction," in *International Development and the Social Sciences: Essays on the History and Politics of Knowledge,* ed. Cooper and Packard (Berkeley, Los Angeles, and London: University of California Press, 1997), pp. 1–41.

14. Ibid., p. 3.

15. Richard Wortman, *Scenarios of Power: Myth and Ceremony in Russian Monarchy,* vol. 1, *From Peter the Great to the Death of Nicholas I* (Princeton: Princeton University Press, 1995).

16. Ibid., p. 6.

17. James Cracraft, "Empire Versus Nation: Russian Political Theory Under Peter I," *Harvard*

Ukrainian Studies 10, no. 3/4 (December 1986), pp. 524–40; reprinted in *Major Problems in the History of Imperial Russia*, ed. Cracraft (Lexington and Toronto: D. C. Heath, 1994), pp. 224–34. Citations hereafter are from the latter publication.

18. Wortman, *Scenarios of Power*, p. 33.

19. Ibid., p. 38.

20. Ibid., p. 6.

21. Ibid., p. 41.

22. Ibid., p. 44.

23. Ibid., p. 61.

24. Ibid., p. 64.

25. Ibid., p. 81.

26. Ibid.

27. Ibid., p. 82; for a discussion of the state as defender of noble interests, see Ronald Grigor Suny, "Rehabilitating Tsarism: The Imperial State and Its Historians," *Comparative Studies in Society and History* 31, no. 1 (January 1989), pp. 168–79.

28. Wortman, *Scenarios of Power*, pp. 82–83.

29. Ibid., p. 170.

30. Marc Szeftel, "The Form of Government of the Russian Empire Prior to the Constitutional Reforms of 1905–06," in *Essays in Russian and Soviet History in Honor of Geroid Tanquary Robinson*, ed. John Shelton Curtiss (New York: Columbia University Press, 1962), pp. 105–119.

31. In Western Europe after the French Revolution a new image of monarchy, one in which the ruler was less like a God and more like a human with conventional family values, developed. Monarchs "became exemplars of human conduct, of modest virtue, to be admired by their subjects." The idealization of the monarch's family elevated the ruling dynasty as the historical embodiment of the nation." This move toward family lessened the distance between monarch and his people, as now all were part of a common nation. This ideal of bourgeois monarchy took on a distinctive shape in tsarist Russia. Nicholas I identified his dynasty with the historical destinies of the Russian state and people. "His scenario . . . portrayed the emperor as exemplifying the attributes of Western monarchy, but now as a member of his family, as a human being elevated by heredity and his belonging to a ruling family that embodied the highest values of humanity. . . . The private life of the tsar was lavishly staged to portray a Western ideal before the Russian public." Wortman, *Scenarios of Power*, p. 402; see also, George Mosse, *Nationalism and Sexuality: Middle-Class Morality and Sexual Norms in Modern Europe* (Madison: University of Wisconsin Press, 1985), passim.

32. Anderson, *Imagined Communities*, pp. 86–87, 110.

33. Ibid., pp. 109–110.

34. Isabelle Kreindler, "A Neglected Source of Lenin's Nationality Policy," *Slavic Review* 36, no. 1 (March 1977), pp. 86–100; Wayne Dowler, *Classroom and Empire: The Politics of Schooling Russia's Eastern Nationalities, 1860–1917* (Montreal: McGill-Queen's University Press, 2001).

35. Theodore R. Weeks, *Nation and State in Late Imperial Russia: Nationalism and Russification on the Western Frontier, 1863–1914* (De Kalb, IL: Northern Illinois University Press, 1996), pp. 70–91.

36. This conflict between rival views of how to construct a modern Russian political community is worked out in Joshua A. Sanborn, *Drafting the Nation: Military Conscription, Total War, and Mass Politics, 1905–1925* (De Kalb, IL: Northern Illinois University Press, 2003).

37. Weeks, *Nation and State*, pp. 131–92.

38. Mark Beissinger, "The Persisting Ambiguity of Empire," *Post-Soviet Affairs* 11, No. 2 (April–June 1995), p. 2.

39. "Evil empire" is, of course, the famous phrase of President Ronald Reagan; "affirmative action empire" comes from Terry Martin; "empire of nations" is the title of a forthcoming book by Francine Hirsch; and "imperialism as the highest stage of socialism" was employed by Yuri

Slezkine. See Francine Hirsch, "Toward an Empire of Nations: Bordermaking and the Formation of Soviet National Identities," *Russian Review* 59, no. 2 (April 2000), pp. 201–226; and Yuri Slezkine, "Imperialism As the Highest Stage of Socialism," ibid., pp. 227–34.

40. Hirsch, "Toward an Empire of Nations," p. 204, n. 15. Terry Martin distinguishes his affirmative action empire as a "national entity" from ideal types like nation-state, city-state, federation, confederation, or empire. *The Affirmative Action Empire: Nations and Nationalism in the Soviet Union, 1923–1939* (Ithaca and London: Cornell University Press, 2001), pp. 18–20.

41. Terry Martin, "The Soviet Union as Empire: Salvaging a Dubious Analytical Category," *Ab Imperio* 2 (2002), p. 98.

42. Slezkine, "Imperialism As the Highest Stage of Socialism," p. 234.

43. An excellent discussion of economic and ethnic *raionirovanie* is in Martin, *Affirmative Action Empire*, pp. 33–55; see also, Hirsch, "Toward an Empire of Nations," pp. 205–213.

44. Stalin's lieutenant in Georgia, "Sergo" Orjonikidze, told his comrades that expertise was more important than nationality as a criterion for selecting economic officials: "It is necessary to work for the economic renaissance of our country, and for this it is not enough to be a Georgian, one must also know one's business." Ronald Grigor Suny, *The Making of the Georgian Nation* (Bloomington: Indiana University Press, 1988, 1994), p. 230.

45. Rogers Brubaker, "Nationhood and the National Question in the Soviet Union and Post-Soviet Eurasia: An Institutionalist Account," *Theory and Society* 23, no. 1 (February 1994), pp. 47–78.

46. See Ronald Grigor Suny, *The Revenge of the Past: Nationalism, Revolution, and the Collapse of the Soviet Union* (Stanford: Stanford University Press, 1993), on the deep contradictions between nation-making practices and assimilationist tendencies fostered by the central state.

47. Miles Kahler, "Empires, Neo-Empires, and Political Change: The British and French Experience," in *The End of Empire? The Transformation of the USSR in Comparative Perspective*, ed. Karen Dawisha and Bruce Parrott (Armonk, NY: M.E. Sharpe, 1997), p. 288. This delegitimatizing of empires seems to have occurred at several historical conjunctures, not only after the two world wars but, for example, in the second half of the eighteenth century as the French, Spanish, and British empires in the Americas began to break down. See Anthony Pagden, *Lords of All the World: Ideologies of Empire in Spain, Britain, and France, 1500–c. 1800* (New Haven: Yale University Press, 1995).

48. Ibid.

6. Empires of Liberty?

1. Michael W. Doyle, "Liberalism and World Politics," *American Political Science Review* 80, no. 4 (Dec. 1986), pp. 1,151–69; this quote on p. 1,152.

2. William H. Sewell Jr., "Historical Events as Transformations of Structures: Inventing Revolution at the Bastille," *Theory and Society* 25, no. 6 (Dec. 1996), pp. 841–81.

3. MacGregor Knox, "Conquest, Foreign and Domestic, in Fascist Italy and Nazi Germany," *Journal of Modern History* 56, no. 1 (Mar. 1984), pp. 1–57, this quote on p. 8.

4. Schumpeter in Doyle, "Liberalism and World Politics," p. 1,152.

5. Lynn Hunt, David Lansky, and Paul Hanson, "The Failure of the Liberal Republic in France, 1795–1799: The Road to Brumaire," *Journal of Modern History* 51, no. 4 (Dec. 1979), pp. 734–59.

6. Joseph-Marie Moiret, *Mémoires sur l'expedition d'Égypte* (Paris: P. Belfond, 1984), p. 21.

7. Anon., *Bonaparte au Caire* (Paris: Prault, 7 R.), pp. 14–15.

8. Lynn Hunt, *Politics, Culture, and Class in the French Revolution* (Berkeley and Los Angeles: University of California Press, 1986), p. 21.

9. Jean-Gabriel de Niello-Sargy, *Sur l'expédition d'Égypte*, vol. 1, *Mémoires secrets et inédits pour servir à l'histoire contemporaine*, ed. M. Alph. de Beauchamp, 2 vols. (Paris: Vernarel et Tenon, 1825), p. 12.

10. François Bernoyer, *Avec Bonaparte en Égypte et en Syrie, 1798–1800: dix-neuf lettres inédits* (Abbeville: Les Presses françaises, 1976), pp. 19–20.

11. Moiret, *Mémoires sur l'expedition d'Égypte,* pp. 25 ff.

12. Bernoyer, *Avec Bonaparte,* p. 75.

13. Anon., *Bonaparte au Caire,* p. 104.

14. Ibid., p. 142.

15. Napoleon I, *Correspondance de Napoléon Ier; publiée par ordre de l'empereur Napoléon III,* 32 vols. (Paris: H. Plon, J. Dumaine, 1858–70), vol. 4, no. 286.

16. Robespierre in Hunt, *Politics,* p. 46.

17. Anon., *Bonaparte au Caire,* p. 139.

18. Ibid., pp. 166–67.

19. Ibid., p. 91.

20. Sarah C. Maza, *Private Lives and Public Affairs: The Causes Célèbres of Prerevolutionary France* (Berkeley: University of California Press, 1993), pp. 279–80.

21. Bernoyer, *Avec Bonaparte,* pp. 85–86.

22. The following account is documented in Juan R. I. Cole, *Colonialism and Revolution in the Middle East: Social and Cultural Origins of Egypt's `Urabi Movement* (Princeton: Princeton University Press, 1993); see also Alexander Schölch, *Egypt for the Egyptians!: The Socio-Political Crisis in Egypt, 1878–1882* (London: Ithaca, 1981).

23. Juan R. I. Cole, "Of Crowds and Empires: Afro-Asian Riots and European Expansion, 1857–1882," *Comparative Studies in Society and History* 31, no. 1 (Jan. 1989), pp. 106–33.

24. John S. Galbraith and Afaf Lutfi al-Sayyid-Marsot , "The British Occupation of Egypt: Another View," *International Journal of Middle East Studies* 9, no. 4 (Nov. 1978), pp. 471–88.

25. William McGonagall, *Poetic Gems* (Trowbridge, England: Trowbridge and Esher, 1890/1975), pp. 35–6.

26. See Juan Cole, "Review of Bernard Lewis's" *What Went Wrong: Western Impact and Middle Eastern Response, Global Dialogue,* vol. 4, no. 4, Autumn 2002.

27. The following is based on an interview of Deputy Secretary Wolfowitz on National Public Radio, February 19, 2003 (www.washingtonfile.net/2003/Feb/Feb21/EUR509.htm).

28. Juan Cole, "The United States and Shi'ite Religious Factions in Post-Ba'thist Iraq," *Middle East Journal* 57, no. 4 (autumn 2003), pp. 543–66; Juan Cole, "The Iraqi Shiites: On the History of America's Would-be Allies," *Boston Review,* fall 2003; Juan Cole and Shahin Cole, "Shiites are Emerging from Fear," *Los Angeles Times,* December 28, 2003.

29. *Fox Special Report with Brit Hume,* July 18, 2003, transcript #071805cb.254, Lexis Nexis.

7. Law and Legitimation in Empire

1. I am using *millet* somewhat anachronistically here to mean corporate organization based on religion. See Benjamin Braude and Bernard Lewis, eds., "Introduction," *Christians and Jews in the Ottoman Empire: The Functioning of a Plural Society* (New York: Holmes and Meier, 1982), pp. 1–34; and Kemal H. Karpat, "*Millets* and Nationality: The Roots of the Incongruity of Nation and State in the Post-Ottoman Era," pp. 141–69.

2. There has always been speculation as to the different origins of these two forms of law. In the Ottoman case imperial law may have borrowed from Byzantine or Islamic state tradition (itself indebted to Roman law). Community legal traditions were proximately the product of religious traditions. Imperial law reflected the concerns of the instrumental realm of administration.

3. On the Ottoman age of reforms, see Stanford J. Shaw and Ezel K. Shaw, *A History of the Ottoman Empire and Modern Turkey,* vol. 2 (Cambridge: Cambridge University Press, 1977). For the reception of European law, see Gulnihal Bozkurt, *Bati Hukukunun Turkiye'de Benimsenmesi* [The reception of western law in Turkey] (Ankara: Turk Tarih Kurumu, 1996).

4. Constitutionalism establishes a *Rechtsstaat* which seeks to universalize its dealings with differ-

ent groups in the population. It also subjects the powerful to the rule of law. A third element is the restriction of the space of democracy because law begins to regulate fields that used to be open to deliberation. See a recent collection of articles on constitutions in *International Sociology* 18, no. 1 (March 2003), especially Said Amir Arjomand, "Law, Political Reconstruction and Constitutional Politics," pp. 7–32.

5. See S. N. Eisenstadt, *The Political Systems of Empires* (New York: Free Press, 1963), for this concept.

6. The following discussion is based on Max Weber, *Economy and Society* (Berkeley: University of California Press, 1978), especially pp. 809–900.

7. Weber, *Economy and Society,* p. 976.

8. The books reviewed by Sally Merry Engle, and the review article itself, provide an excellent discussions of this issue: "Law and Colonialism," *Law and Society Review* 25, no. 4, 1991, pp. 889–921; also Lauren Benton, *Law and Colonial Cultures: Legal Regimes in World History, 1400–1900* (Cambridge: Cambridge University Press, 2002).

9. See Selim Deringil, *The Well Protected Domains: Ideology and Legitimation of Power in the Ottoman Empire, 1876–1909* (London: I.B. Tauris, 1998); for the attempts at constructing a new ideology for the legitimation of the empire.

10. Shaw and Shaw, *A History of the Ottoman Empire and Modern Turkey,* vol. 2, pp. 181–82 for this first Parliament; p. 278 for the composition of the Parliament in 1908.

11. Cabinet ministers were often Greeks and Armenians. For the Armenian case see Mesrob K. Krikorian, *Armenians in the Service of the Ottoman Empire, 1860–1908* (London: Routledge, Kegan Paul, 1978).

12. D. Quataert, *The Ottoman Empire, 1700–1922* (Cambridge: Cambridge University Press, 2000); Sevket Pamuk, *The Ottoman Empire and European Capitalism, 1820–1913* (Cambridge: Cambridge University Press, 1987).

13. For an illustrative case see Yucel Terzibasoglu, "Landlords, Refugees and Nomads: Struggles for Land around Late Nineteenth-century Ayvalik," *New Perspectives on Turkey* 24 (spring 2001), pp. 51–82. For a general interpretation of the 1858 legislation, see Haim Gerber, *The Social Origins of the Modern Middle East* (Boulder: Lynne Rienner, 1987).

14. Albert Hourani, *Arabic Thought in the Liberal Age, 1798–1938* (Cambridge: Cambridge University Press, 1983), p. 281.

15. The Public Debt Administration was in a curious position of rationalizing tax collection in certain areas where it was ceded this privilege, while it had no responsibility to use the revenue for public good. In fact, the revenue serviced the debt. Nonetheless, since it succeeded in eliminating arbitrary impositions, it seems to have enjoyed some legitimacy. "Modern" welfare institutions came on the agenda only toward the end of the period. See Nadir Ozbek, "The Politics of Poor Relief in the Late Ottoman Empire, 1876–1914," *New Perspectives on Turkey* 21 (fall 1999), pp. 1–33.

16. The free-trade agreement—initially with Britain but later extended to other European powers—dictated that trade prohibitions aiming to ban the export of goods deemed necessary for provisionist purposes and export monopolies granted to particular merchants would be lifted. For the course of exports after the treaty, see Pamuk, *The Ottoman Empire.*

17. Amy Chua, *World on Fire: How Exporting Free Market Democracy Breeds Ethnic Hatred and Global Instability* (New York: Doubleday, 2003).

18. On the Young Turks, Ernest E. Ramsaur, *The Young Turks: Prelude to the Revolution of 1908* (Princeton: Princeton University Press, 1957); and Feroz Ahmad, *The Young Turks: the Committee of Union and Progress in Turkish Politics, 1908–1914* (Oxford: Oxford University Press, 1968).

19. Georges Haupt, Michael Lowy, and Claudie Weill, *Les Marxistes at la Question Nationale, 1848–1914* (Paris: Francois Maspero, 1974), pp. 208–72, for Karl Renner and Otto Bauer; also, Uri Ra'anan, "Nation and State: Order Out of Chaos," in *State and Nation in Multi-ethnic Societies: The Breakup of Multinational States,* ed. Uri Ra'anan et al. (New York: Manchester University Press, 1991), pp. 3–32.

20. Cf. Kemal Karpat, "*Millet*s and Nationality," p. 144.

21. See my article, "The Ottoman Empire," in *After Empire: Multiethnic Societies and Nation-Building*, ed. K. Barkey and M. von Hagen (Boulder: Westview, 1997), pp. 30–44.

22. For a historical analysis of hegemony in the world-systems mode, see Giovanni Arrighi, Beverly Silver, et al., *Chaos and Governance in the Modern World System* (Minneapolis: University of Minnesota Press), 1999.

23. Daniel Bell's *East Meets West: Human Rights and Democracy in Asia* (Princeton: Princeton University Press, 2000) is a remarkable reconstruction of the Asian values debate.

24. The discussion on cosmopolitan democracy, e.g., David Held, *Democracy and the Global Order: From the Modern State to Cosmopolitan Governance* (Palo Alto: Stanford University Press, 1996), on a new role for the UN, and more generally the movements seeking to reform the WTO, or increasing the jurisdiction of human rights courts, and instituting global labor standards, seems to be within this rubric.

25. For example, Thomas M. Franck, *The Empowered Self, Law and Society in the Age of Individualism* (Oxford: Oxford University Press, 1999).

26. Susan Sell, *Private Power, Public Law: the Globalization of Intellectual Property Rights* (Cambridge: Cambridge University Press, 2003).

27. As I was writing this paper, I chanced upon the evening news in Istanbul on one of the popular TV channels. One news item was a reporter interviewing a group of women in a street in Usak, a western province of Turkey, who were waiting in early morning for employment. This was a street-corner labor market for day work, and wages were between $4–$6 a day. One of the women said that there were no jobs for men, not an uncommon situation in Turkey and elsewhere, and that household income depended on women's work. The next news item was an interview with the representative of Sony music in Istanbul who complained that because there was widespread piracy of CDs, music lovers were deprived of seeing artists such as Madonna and Shakira, who would not come to Istanbul to give concerts because they knew that royalties on their recordings would be stolen by pirates. He appealed to the government to better enforce intellectual property rights. Legitimate CDs sell for around $15, and pirated ones for less than $3.

28. Alex Callinicos, "Marxism and Global Governance," in *Governing Globalization*, ed. David Held and A. McGrew (Cambridge: Polity, 2002), pp. 249–66; also Massimo Salvadori, *Karl Kautsky and the Socialist Revolution, 1880–1938* (London: New Left Books, 1979), pp. 181–203.

29. Pierre Bourdieu, "The Force of Law: Toward a Sociology of the Juridical Field," *Hastings Law Journal* 38 (July 1987), pp. 805–53.

30. I am not arguing for a strict autopoietic, self-referential version of global law. There might be individual spheres in which it makes more sense to talk about such self-sufficiency. For purposes here the emphasis is on the logic of multilateralism where unilateral control becomes unlikely once an organization is set up. There are, of course, competing forces vying to determine the prevalent interpretations of law, but these are not dominated by the state actors of the dominant state. See Kanishka Jayasuriya, "Globalization, Law, and the Transformation of Sovereignty: The Emergence of Global Regulatory Governance," *Indiana Journal of Global Legal Studies* 6, no. 2 (1999).

31. While the United States emerges as seeking to establish a unilateral order against the maturing multilateralism of the previous era, "old" Europe is now cast into the position of defending the institutions and juridification of globalization. The confusion this new alignment has led to within the so-called antiglobalization movement is telling.

8. Imperialism or Colonialism?

1. I am grateful to the editors of this volume, especially Fred Cooper, for comments on an earlier draft of this chapter.

2. *New York Times*, Jan. 21, 2004, p. A18, "President's State of the Union Message to Congress and the Nation."

3. Carl Schmitt, "The New *Nomos* of the Earth" (orig. 1955), reprinted in *The Nomos of the Earth in the International Law of the Jus Publicum Europaeum,* trans. G.L. Ulmen (New York: Telos Press, 2003), p. 355.

4. James B. Rule, contribution to symposium "Imperialism and the United States: Responses to Michael Walzer," *Dissent* 5, no. 1 (2004), pp. 96–99.

5. Chalmers Johnson, *The Sorrows of Empire* (New York: Metropolitan Books, 2004), p. 188.

6. For a critical discussion of the geopolitical "declinist" school, see Bruce Cumings, "Still the American Century," *Review of International Studies* 25, no. 2 (1999), pp. 271–82. For examples of geopolitical declinism, see especially Paul Kennedy, *The Rise and Fall of the Great Powers* (New York: Random House, 1987), pp. 514ff.; also Robert O. Keohane, *After Hegemony: Cooperation and Discord in the World Political Economy* (Princeton, NJ: Princeton University Press, 1984); Donald Wallace White, *The American Century: The Rise and Decline of the United States as a World Power* (New Haven: Yale University Press, 1996); and Stanley Hoffman, *World Disorders: Troubled Peace in the Post–Cold War Era* (Lanham, MD: Rowman and Littlefield, 1998). World-system theorists have argued for American economic (and hence geopolitical) decline throughout the entire period since the mid-1980s: see Albert Bergesen and C. Sahoo, "Evidence of the Decline of American Hegemony in World Production," *Review* 8, no. 4, (1985), pp. 595–611; more recently restated forcefully by Immanuel Wallerstein, *The Decline of American Power: The U.S. in a Chaotic World* (New York: The New Press, 2003). An alternative economic-Marxist declinist portrait is given by Robert Brenner, "New Boom or New Bubble," *New Left Review* 25 (Jan.–Feb. 2004), pp. 1–34.

7. Jürgen Habermas, *The Inclusion of the Other: Studies in Political Theory* (Cambridge, MA: MIT Press, 1998), p. 150.

8. Of course at a different level Hardt and Negri's dissolution of Empire into the stateless global economy harkens back to earlier Marxist discussions of imperialism by writers like Lenin and Hilferding, who also downplayed the importance of specifically colonial-statist assaults on indigenous sovereignty. Hardt and Negri's more recent book adheres doggedly to the idea that "the national space . . . is no longer the effective unit of sovereignty" while acknowledging that the United States is the "only remaining superpower"; *Multitude: War and Democracy in the Age of Empire* (New York: Penguin Press, 2004), pp. 4, 8.

9. But see Emmanuel Todd, *After the Empire: The Breakdown of the American Order* (New York: Columbia University Press, 2003), on the Russian reassertion of power.

10. Some counterarguments against the description of U.S. military power as enormous and unprecedented point to its frequent inability to create order (e.g., Michael Mann, *Incoherent Empire* [London, New York: Verso, 2003]). But as Timothy Mitchell points out, this result is not necessarily a failure from the standpoint of American policy; indeed, Mitchell argues, between the late 1970s and the recent past, the United States often tried to *prevent* the resolution of conflicts in the Middle East and to spread chaos and disorder there (most obviously in the case of the Soviet invasion of Afghanistan and the Iran-Iraq war). Tim Mitchell, "McJihad: Islam in the U.S. Global Order," *Social Text* 20:4, no. 73 (winter 2002), pp. 14–16. The ability of the United States in the post-1945 period to prevent most countries in the Western hemisphere (with the major exception of Cuba) from going over to socialism/Communism for more than a fleeting historical moment (Nicaragua under the Sandanistas, Grenada) must be read as sign of America's considerable power. Similarly, the violence and chaos in Iraq at the time of writing should not distract us from the equally salient historical fact of the elimination of the Baathist regime there.

11. The difference, as Carl Schmitt suggested in *The* Nomos *of the Earth,* was that even if Britain was unchallenged militarily on the high seas in the mid-nineteenth century, the center of the global Nomos, or spatial-legal order, was still continental Europe, with its Westphalian system of controlled anarchy and its self-definition against the outside. The human-rights universalism of contemporary American hegemony does not constitute a Nomos, since it has no *spatial* demarcation against an outside, but only a moral demarcation that runs *within* states (including the United States) as well as across them. I am grateful to Andreas Kalyvas and the Nomos reading group for discussions of this thorny issue.

12. For figures comparing U.S. and E.U. population and economic production see Steven K. Weisman, "Europe United is Good, Isn't It?," *New York Times*, National Edition, Sunday, February 20, 2005, section 4, pp. 1, 3; on the *relative* decline of the United States vis-à-vis the rest of the world, especially Europe, between the 1950s and the 1980s, see Bergesen and Sahoo, "Evidence of the Decline."

13. Steven Kinzer, "Revisiting Cold War Coups and Finding them Costly," *New York Times*, Nov. 30, 2003, p. 3.

14. Lawrence Summers, "America: The First Nonimperialist Superpower," *New Perspectives Quarterly* 15 (spring 1998), pp. 34–35. Conservatives agreed with this description, although they derided Clinton's foreign policy as "social work." See Michael Mandelbaum, "Foreign Policy as Social Work," *Foreign Affairs* 75 (Jan./Feb.1996), pp. 16–32. According to Condoleezza Rice, the Clinton administration had replaced the "national interest" with "humanitarian interests or the interests of the international community." See "Promoting the National Interest," *Foreign Affairs* (Jan./Feb. 1999), pp. 45–62.

15. The Gulf War does not represent a counterexample, since it (a) was not a preemptive strike; (2) was not unilateralist, or even cryptounilateralist; (3) did not seek "regime change" in Iraq or even to capture Saddam Hussein; and (4) was justified as a defense of (Kuwait's) state sovereignty.

16. Patrick Tyler, "U.S. Strategy Plan Calls for Insuring No Rivals Develop," *New York Times*, March 7, 1992; idem, "Lone Superpower Plan: Ammunition for Critics," *New York Times*, March 10, 1992; idem, "Senior U.S. Officials Assail Lone-Superpower Policy," *New York Times*, March 11, 1992; and idem, "Pentagon Drops Goal of Blocking New Superpowers," *New York Times*, March 24, 1992; on this episode see also William C. Wohlforth, "The Stability of a Unipolar World," *International Security* 24, no. 1 (1999), pp. 5–41.

17. White House, *The National Security Strategy of the United States of America* (2002); John Gaddis, "A Grand Strategy," *Foreign Policy* (Nov./Dec. 2002), p. 52.

18. See Helmut Schmidt, "Europa braucht keinen Vormund, *Die Zeit* 57 (August 1, 2002), p. 3; Herfried Münkler, *Der neue Golfkrieg* (Berlin: Rowohlt, 2003); Andrew J. Bacevich, *American Empire: The Realities and Consequences of U.S. Diplomacy* (Cambridge, MA: Harvard University Press, 2002); Chalmers A. Johnson, *Blowback: The Costs and Consequences of American Empire* (New York: Metroplitan Books, 2000); Claus Leggewie, "Globalisierung versus Hegemonie: Zur Zukunft der transatlantischen Beziehungen," *Internationale Politik und Gesellschaft* 1 (2003), pp. 87–111.

19. For a theoretical analysis of the simultaneous reassertion of U.S. state power in both the foreign and domestic arenas, see my article "The State of Emergency and the Revival of American Imperialism: Toward an Authoritarian Post-Fordism," *Public Culture* 15, no. 2 (2003), pp. 323–45. Some leftists refuse to acknowledge this historical shift, focusing on continuity throughout the 1990s; see James F. Petras and Morris H. Morley, *Empire or Republic? American Global Power and Domestic Decay* (New York: Routledge, 1995).

20. See Wallerstein, *The Decline of American Power*; and Bergesen and Sahoo, "Evidence of the Decline."

21. See William Rasch, "Human Rights as Geopolitics," *Cultural Critique* 54 (spring 2003), pp. 120–147. Hardt and Negri's *Empire* leaves its own geopolitical conditions of possibility unexplored. But these knowledge-conditions hover symptomatically just below the surface of their text, resurfacing repeatedly in the authors' acknowledgment of continuing U.S. military supremacy throughout the 1990s. The problem of reconciling this nationally defined military dominance with the image of decentralized Empire is never addressed.

22. John Rawls, *The Law of Peoples* (Cambridge, MA: Harvard University Press, 1999); Habermas, "Remarks on Legitimation through Human Rights," in his *The Postnational Constellation*, trans. Max Pensky (Cambridge: MA: MIT Press, 2001), p. 124. See also G.L. Ulmen's introduction to the English translation of Carl Schmitt, *Nomos*.

23. For an overview of the resurgence of the discourse of empire and its conservative rearticulation, see the spring 2003 issue of the *National Interest*.

24. See William Appleman Williams, *The Tragedy of American Diplomacy* (Cleveland: World Pub. Co., 1959), and *The Roots of the Modern American Empire: A Study of the Growth and Shaping of Social Consciousness in a Marketplace Society* (New York: Random House, 1969); R.W. Van Alstyne, *The Rising American Empire* (New York: Oxford University Press, 1960); and Walter LaFeber, *The New Empire: An Interpretation of American Expansionism, 1860–1898* (Ithaca, NY: Cornell, 1963; revised edition, 1998).

25. E.g., Michael Hudson, *Super Imperialism: The Economic Strategy of American Empire* (New York: Holt, Rinehart and Winston, 1972); John M. Swomley, *American Empire: The Political Ethics of Twentieth-Century Conquest* (New York: Macmillan, 1970); Claude Julien, *America's Empire* (New York: Pantheon, 1971); Sidney Lens, *The Forging of the American Empire* (New York: Thomas Y. Cromwell Co, 1971); Raymond Aron, *The Imperial Republic: The United States and the World, 1945–1973*, trans. Frank Jellinek (Cambridge, MA: Winthrop, 1974).

26. William Appleman Williams, *Empire as a Way of Life* (New York: Oxford University Press, 1980), p. viii.

27. Philip Zelikow, "The Transformation of National Security," *National Interest* 71 (spring 2003), pp. 17–28.

28. Michael Ignatieff, *Empire Lite: Nation Building in Bosnia, Kosovo, Afghanistan* (London: Vintage, 2003), p. 2.

29. Arthur Schlesinger Jr., *Cycles of American History* (Boston: Houghton Mifflin, 1986), pp. 141, 162, 161, my emphasis.

30. Raymond Williams, *Keywords*, 2d ed. (New York: Oxford University Press, 1983), pp. 159–160.

31. The literature on this topic is enormous; on the implications of this theoretical shift for the study of the state, see the essays in George Steinmetz, ed., *State/Culture* (Ithaca, NY: Cornell University Press, 1999), which also survey the cultural turn in the social sciences.

32. Williams, *Tragedy*, p. 45 passim.

33. For a discussion of the "looping effects" between theoretical classification schemes and the social objects they reference, see Ian Hacking, "The Looping Effects of Human Kinds," in *Causal Cognition: A Multidisciplinary Debate*, ed. David Premack. et al. (New York: Oxford University Press, 1995), pp. 351–94. Also see Ian Hacking, *The Social Construction of What?* (Cambridge, MA: Harvard University Press, 1999).

34. Chalmers Johnson, *Sorrows*, pp. 111–12, 117; Michael Schneider, "Paranoia und permanenter Krieg," *Freitag: Der Ost-West-Wochenzeitung*, Feb. 21, 2003.

35. Nicolai Ouroussoff, "A Tower of Impregnability, the Sort Politicians Love," *New York Times*, June 30, 2005, p. A21.

36. Anthony Pagden, *Peoples and Empires* (New York: Modern Library, 2003), p. 26.

37. See the papers by Ann Stoler and Sheldon Pollock, this volume.

38. Ann Stoler and Fred Cooper, "Between Metropole and Colony: Rethinking a Research Agenda," in *Tensions of Empire: Colonial Cultures in a Bourgeois World*, eds. Frederick Cooper and Ann Laura Stoler (Berkeley: University of California Press, 1997), p. 1.

39. Relations among different parts of the core constitute a fifth type, similar but not identical to type 2. For example, the German colonizers variously studied, copied, and tried to distinguish themselves from the British, French, Dutch, and Spanish colonizers, while the Americans in U.S. Samoa studied German Samoa next door, and the colonizers who took over Germany's colonies after WWI often copied the inherited German approaches (e.g., the Belgians in Rwanda, the New Zealanders in Samoa). This topic has reemerged in the current U.S. context with calls to emulate the British Empire.

40. Raymond Aron, *The Imperial Republic*, pp. 254, 259.

41. Anthony Pagden, pp. xvi–xxiii, 13, 26.

42. S.N. Eisenstadt, *The Political Systems of Empires* (London [New York]: Free Press of Glencoe, 1963), pp. 50–68. Unlike the Chinese emperor, however, who for centuries was able to make Euro-

peans kowtow to him, Kaiser Wilhelm was unable to elicit much of a response among fellow Europeans or his colonial subjects other than ridicule. The dances performed in German East Africa on the Kaiser's birthday contained elements of political satire; see John Iliffe, *A Modern History of Tanganyika* (Cambridge, New York: Cambridge University Press, 1979), pp. 238–39.

43. Andreas Kalyvas suggested in private conversation that the republican form is particularly suited to imperial expansionism. On the imperial characteristics of the U.S. presidency, see Robin Blackburn, "The Imperial Presidency, the War on Terrorism, and the Revolutions of Modernity," *Constellations* 9, no. 1 (2002), pp. 3–33.

44. Riehl (1854), summarized by David Blackbourn, *The Long Nineteenth Century: A History of Germany, 1780–1918* (New York: Oxford University Press, 1997), p. 286.

45. On Catholics in Germany, see V.R. Berghahn, *Imperial Germany, 1871–1914* (Oxford, New York: Berghahn Books, 1994), p. 97. The official political response to the large Catholic minority during the 1870s and 1880s was the *Kulturkampf* (and legislation against the public speaking of Polish), but Catholic and Polish resistance slowed these assimilationist policies.

46. Michael Stürmer, *Das ruhelose Reich* (Berlin: Severin und Siedler, 1983), p. 58.

47. See John Torpey, "Reparations Politics in Southern Africa," paper prepared for the Annual Meeting of the Social Science History Association, Baltimore, November 2003; and "Reviewing Foreigners' Use of Federal Courts," *New York Times,* Dec. 2, 2003, p. A22.

48. Laura Benton, "Colonial Law and Cultural Difference: Jurisdictional Politics and the Formation of the Colonial State," *Comparative Studies in Society and History* 41:3 (July 1999), pp. 563–88. There were exceptions such as the legal system established by the British at the Cape Colony in the second and third decades of the nineteenth century, which "did not make racial distinctions in assigning different status to litigants, witnesses, or defendants (ibid., p. 581). On the other hand, a detailed study of court cases at the early-nineteenth Cape would be necessary to determine whether there was not, in practice, discrimination against Khoikhoi.

49. As Fred Cooper observes, "Great Britain and France were trapped by the logical and political consequences of their universalism." Notions of development, citizenship, equal pay and equal social benefits, all of which were introduced to reform colonialism, soon began to point beyond it and toward either independence or incorporation into the colonizing nation-state as a noncolonial province or federal state (as with the state of Hawai'i in the U.S. polity). Although French and British colonizers during the mid-twentieth century swung back and forth between "reifying differences and pretending that a little more time and effort" would eliminate those differences, the central point seems to be that whenever the colonizers abandoned the cultural-political Maginot Line between themselves and their subjects for more than a token number of *assimilés,* they were already moving away from the specifically colonial form of rule. Cooper, *Decolonization and African Society* (1996), p. 468, and private comments on an earlier draft of this chapter. I discuss the dualistic legal codes for Chinese and non-Chinese in German Qingdao in my forthcoming book, *The Devil's Handwriting: Precoloniality and the German Colonial State in Qingdao, Samoa, and Southwest Africa* (University of Chicago Press, 2006).

50. I discuss the structural similarities and differences between modern colonial and noncolonial states in more detail in "Precoloniality and Colonial Subjectivity: Ethnographic Discourse and Native Policy in German Overseas Imperialism, 1780s–1914," *Political Power and Social Theory* 15 (2002), pp.135–228, and in chapter 1 of *The Devil's Handwriting: Precoloniality and Native Policy in German Overseas Rule* (Duke University Press, forthcoming).

51. The German colonial strategy in Samoa of protecting the Samoans from settlers' demands to turn them into wage labor, for example, was driven by concerns of stabilization, not economic development; see my article " 'The Devil's Handwriting': Precolonial Discourse, Ethnographic Acuity and Cross-Identification in German Colonialism," *Comparative Studies in Society and History* 45, no. 1 (2003), pp. 41–95. The German genocide against the Ovaherero in 1904, which was also triggered by (hallucinatory) "security" concerns, deprived the colonial economy of its main labor force; see Jan-Bart Gewald, *Herero Heroes: A Socio-Political History of the Herero of Namibia,*

1890–1923 (Athens, OH: Ohio University Press, 1998). The German shift to a more conciliatory native policy in Qingdao after 1904 was related to a growing emphasis within the Foreign Official on cultivating China as an ally as world war with Britain, France, and Russia became increasingly inevitable; see Hans-Christian Stichler, *Das Gouvernement Jiaozhou und die deutsche Kolonialpolitik in Shandong 1897–1909* (Ph.D. diss., Humboldt University, 1989).

52. There are always exceptions, but these are usually marginal. Despite the alleged nonracialism of Portuguese colonialism, for instance, less than 1 percent of the Africans in Angola were considered "assimilated" under Portuguese (pre-1961) law. Gerald J. Bender, *Angola under the Portuguese* (Berkeley: University of California Press, 1978), p. xxiii.

53. Todorov, *The Conquest of America: The Question of the Other,* trans. Richard Howard (New York: Harper and Row, 1984).

54. Sexual liaisons and marriages between European men and indigenous women were also common in the *precolonies* of nineteenth-century Samoa and Southwest Africa, suggesting again that colonialism was a necessary ingredient in the hardening of intimate racial boundaries in this period. On the shift against intermarriage in Dutch Indonesia, see the work of Ann Stoler, most recently *Carnal Knowledge: Race and the Intimate in Colonial Rule* (Berkeley: University of California Press, 2002). On the relaxed attitude of the Portuguese toward cultural syncretism and mixed marriage in Goa and Macao, see Urs Bitterli, *Cultures in Conflict: Encounters between European and Non-European Cultures, 1492–1800,* trans. Ritchie Robertson (Stanford, CA: Stanford University Press, 1989), ch. 2. Racial and cultural *métissage* at the early modern Cape is evidenced by the existence in the nineteenth century of a sizable population of so-called Basters, who were descendents of Khoikhoi and Boers (or other Europeans); see Maximilian Bayer, *The Rehebother Baster Nation of Namibia* (Basel: Basler Afrika Bibliographien, 1984 [1906]); and Steinmetz, *The Devil's Handwriting,* ch. 5. On precolonial liaisons and marriages in Samoa, see Damon Ieremia Salesa, " 'Troublesome Half-Castes': Tales of a Samoan Borderland" (M.S. Thesis, University of Auckland, 1997).

55. Both texts reflected conditions of well-established colonialism: Gerstäcker's novel was written four decades after the French annexation of Tahiti in 1842, while Maugham's story was written toward the end of New Zealand colonial rule in (western) Samoa.

56. Clearly much hinges on definitions here, and these are inherently political. According to my definition, Hawai'i would probably not be counted as a U.S. colony today (although it might well be one kind of postcolony), since ethnic Hawai'ians have the same rights as other U.S. citizens. The residents of Washington D.C. do not have electoral representation in the U.S. Congress, but because they are not the territory's indigenous inhabitants it seems arbitrary to call them "colonized." American Samoa or Guam exist in a kind of political limbo—neither fully independent nor colonized. But these are exceptional statuses. The vast majority of states—most of Africa and East Asia, for example—are unambiguously non- or postcolonial. Most formerly independent territories that have been incorporated into other states (like Hanover in Prussia/Germany, Languedoc in France, and Wales in England/Britain) cannot be called colonized.

57. Tariq Ali, *Bush in Babylon: The Recolonisation of Iraq* (London, New York: Verso, 2003).

58. General Wesley Clark, "America's Virtual Empire," *Washington Monthly* (Nov. 2003), p. 24. Clark equates "classical empire" with colonialism.

59. As Carl Schmitt pointed out, stability *within* the Nomos of the *jus publicum Europaeum* was predicated on the chaos outside its boundaries. Similarly, U.S. imperialism seems to be willing to accept chaos in parts of Africa and Oceania.

60. See Jürgen Osterhammel, *Colonialism: A Theoretical Overview* (Princeton: Markus Wiener Publications, 1997), pp. 51–52; on the question of variations of sovereignty see also Ann Stoler's contribution here.

61. Osterhammel, *Colonialism,* pp. 21–22.

62. Carl Schmitt, *Nomos,* pp. 281–83, 355; also James Chase, "Imperial America and the Common Interest," *World Policy Journal* 19, no. 1 (2002), pp. 1–9.

63. See *Le monde diplomatique,* June 2003, for a map of U.S. and British bases, military facilities,

and ongoing military interventions. The number of countries in which the United States has over-seas bases is given as 59 in "U.S. Military Bases and Empire," *Monthly Review* (March 2002); the to-tal number of countries with installations of any sort is given by Ellen Meiksins Wood as 140 (in *Empire of Capital* [London: Verso, 2003], p. 1). Chalmers Johnson, *Sorrows*, finds 153 countries in which the United States was deploying military personnel in 2001, 33–38 countries with bases em-ploying at least 100 active-duty military personnel, and a total of 725 miltary bases worldwide. But as Johnson points out, counting bases is extremely difficult both due to the existence of "officially nonexistent sites" and the difference between the number of nominally and physically distinct bases (pp. 4, 153–155, 195). For earlier accountings see George Marion, *Bases and Empire: A Chart of U.S. Expansion*, 3d ed. (New York: Fairplay, 1949); and Joseph Gerson and Bruce Birchard, eds., *The Sun Never Sets: Confronting the Network of Foreign U.S. Military Bases* (Boston, MA: South End Press, 1991); for charts of all U.S. overseas interventions, see Williams, *Empire as a Way of Life* (1980). Brief histories of noncovert U.S. interventions from midcentury are provided by James Dobbins et al., *America's Role in Nation-Building from Germany to Iraq* (Santa Monica, CA: Rand Corporation, 2003).

64. John Villiers, "The Estato da India in Southeast Asia," in *The First Portuguese Colonial Empire*, ed. Malyn Newitt (Exeter: University of Exeter, 1986), pp. 40–41, 44–45, 50; Philippe Pons, *Macao*, trans. Sarah Adams (London: Reaktion Books, 2002 [1999]).

65. M.D.D. Newitt, *Portuguese Settlement on the Zambezi* (New York: Africana Pub. Co. 1973), p. 49.

66. Robin Blackburn, *The Making of New World Slavery: From the Baroqueto the Modern 1492–1800* (Verso, 1997), chs. 2 and 4.

67. Bitterli, *Cultures in Conflict*, p. 59.

68. Allen F. Isaacman, *Mozambique: The Africanization of a European Institution: The Zambezi Pra-zos, 1750–1902* (Madison: University of Wisconsin Press, 1972), pp. 24, 28, 30, 35–36, 59–62; 159. The prazos officially belonged to the Portuguese crown and the lessees had to pay taxes and pro-vide military and other services (ibid., ch. 7; see also Malyn Newitt, *Portuguese Settlement of the Zambezi*, [Harlow: Longman, 1973]), pp. 58–64).

69. Isaacman, *Mozambique*, p. 162; Allen F. Isaacman and Barbara Isaacman, *The Tradition of Re-sistance in Mozambique* (Berkeley: University of California Press, 1976).

70. Gerald J. Bender, op. cit., and Lawrence W. Henderson, *Angola: Five Centuries of Conflict* (Ithaca: Cornell University Press, 1979), pp. 68, 105.

71. Chandra Richard De Silva, *The Portuguese in Ceylon, 1617–1638* (Colombo: H. W. Cave and Co., 1972). The Portuguese also claimed Timor as part of their *Estado da India* after 1681, and be-gan to set up a systematic administration of the islands in 1702, but they had little power outside their fortresses until the nineteenth century; see Villiers, "The Estato," pp. 57–60.

72. For the most systematic statement of this thesis, see Albert Bergesen and Ronald Schoenberg, "Long Waves of Colonial Expansion and Contraction," in *Studies of the Modern World-System*, ed. Albert Bergesen (New York: Academic Press, 1980), pp. 231–77.

73. The treaty ports were not really colonies, even if they infringed on Chinese sovereignty, since they did not subject Chinese citizens to their rule. See John King Fairbank, *Trade and Diplomacy on the China Coast* (Cambridge, MA: Harvard University Press, 1953).

74. Jürgen Kloosterhuis, *Friedliche Imperialisten: Deutsche Auslandsvereine und auswärtige Kultur-politik, 1906–1918* (FrankfurtiM.: Peter Lang Verlag, 1994).

75. This paragraph is based on chapters 8 and 9 of Steinmetz, *The Devil's Handwriting*.

76. Elisabeth von Heyking, diary entry, in *Tagebücher aus vier Weltteilen, 1886–1904*, ed. Grete Litzmann (Leipzig: Koehler and Amelang, 1926), p. 205.

77. German Federal Archives, Records of the German Legation in China (R 9208), vol. 1259, p. 35 (Truppel to German Minister Rex, Sept. 1, 1908).

78. Ibid., vol. 1258, p. 215 (Kiaochow Government [Truppel] to German Envoy Rex, Aug. 18, 1908).

79. This paragraph is based on chapters 3 and 4 of Steinmetz, *The Devil's Handwriting*.

80. See Malama Meleisea, *The Making of Modern Samoa: Traditional Authority and Colonial Administration in the History of Western Samoa* (Suva, Fiji: Institute of Pacific Studies of the University of the South Pacific, 1987); Captain J.A.C. Gray, *Amerika Samoa* (Annapolis: United States Naval Institute, 1960), and my article "Discours racial précolonial, posture ethnographique, et tensions dans l'administration coloniale allemande," *Politix Revue des sciences sociales du politique*, no. 66 (2004), pp. 49–80.

81. See Carl Cananagh Hodge, "Botching the Balkans: German's Recognition of Slovenia and Croatia," *Ethics and International Affairs* 12 (1998). West Germany assimilated the former GDR after 1990, but this can hardly be considered indicative of broader territorial ambitions, and is certainly not colonial—despite the widespread use of that language by former inhabitants of East Germany.

82. John King Fairbank, *Trade and Diplomacy*, p. 212.

83. Rather than extending all the way to latitude 54°40' N, the Oregon country as defined in the 1846 treaty reached only to 49° N, and the British retained navigation rights along the Columbia River.

84. Of these, 74,796 were military and 32,927 were Department of Defense civilians. Figures from http://web1.whs.osd.mil/MMID/M05/m05sep03.pdf. Japan is the country with the second largest number of U.S. troops. The numbers for Sept. 2003 include forces deployed in Iraq but based in these countries.

85. See William Roger Louis and Ronald Robinson, "The Imperialism of Decolonization," *Journal of Imperial and Commonwealth History* 22, no. 3 (1993), pp. 462–511. The question is whether American hegemony today is qualitatively different from British hegemony in the nineteenth century, as Schmitt suggested, or is basically the same, as "international relations" and "world-systems" theorists argue. I tend to think that hegemony and American *Großraum* practices coincide today, whereas the overlapping and parceling out of international sovereignties was much more complex in the nineteenth century: British global hegemony underwrote European and international rules of behavior in places like Shanghai and Canton; a nomos based on the Westphalian system governed international behavior within continental Europe; and the Western Hemisphere was increasingly under the influence of an emerging American claim.

86. See Benedict Anderson, *The Spectre of Comparisons: Nationalism, Southeast Asia, and the World* (London: Verso, 1998), introduction.

87. August Kubizek, *The Young Hitler I Knew*, trans. E.V. Anderson (Boston: Houghton Mifflin, 1955), pp. 64–66; also Albert Speer, *Spandauer Tagebücher* (Frankfurt [M.]: Propyläen, 1994 [1975]), p. 136. Ian Kershaw, *Hitler, 1889–1936: Hubris* (London: Allen Lane, 1998), p. 610, note 128, dismisses the Rienzi viewing episode as a pure invention of Kubizek's. The more important point, however, is that the story of Hitler's love of Rienzi was repeated, and that it formed part of his larger fascination with Rome and antiquity more generally. See Peter Cohen's film *The Architecture of Doom* (*Undergångens arkitektur*; 1989/91).

88. Dr. Henry Picker, *Tischgespräche im Führerhauptquartier, 1941–42* (Stuttgart: Seewald Verlag, 1963 [1951]), pp. 53, 98.

89. Anthony Pagden, *Peoples and Empires*, p. 19. See also Niall Ferguson, *Colossus* (New York: Penguin, 2004).

90. See my article "The Devil's Handwriting."

91. On images of Africa in German literature that were generated from a non-German colonial setting, see Julia Hell, "Wilhelm Raabes *Stopfkuchen*: Der ungleichzeitige Bürger," in *Jahrbuch der Raabe-Gesellschaft* (1992); on early modern German images of Native Americans, see Susanne Zantop, *Colonial Fantasies: Conquest, Family, and Nation in Precolonial Germany, 1770–1870* (Durham, NC: Duke University Press, 1997).

92. For a comparative analysis of neoliberal politics see Monica Prasad, *The Politics of Free Markets: The Rise of Neoliberal Economic Policy in Britain, France, and the United States* (Ph.D. diss.,

University of Chicago, 2000); on flexible specialization, see Ash Amin, ed., *Post-Fordism: A Reader* (Oxford, Cambridge, MA: Blackwell, 1994); and Ulrich Brand and Werner Raza, eds., *Fit für den Postfordismus?* (Münster: Verlag Westfälisches Dampfboot, 2003). Recent discussions have entertained the possibility of thinking of post-Fordism as a mode of societal regulation whose reach is spatially much wider than the nation-state. This raises the question of the relationship between the theoretical category of "regulation" and Carl Schmitt's concept of Nomos. Both concepts (along with Foucault's category of *discipline* and Laclau and Mouffe's *articulation*) are attempting to grasp something similar: the ordering of signifying systems and practices in ways that make them congeal, at least temporarily, in an orderly way; see Nancy Fraser, "From Discipline to Flexibilization? Rereading Foucault in the Shadow of Globalization," *Constellations* 10, no. 2 (June 2003), pp. 160–71. Regulation theorists have not addressed the applicability of their concepts to geopolitical analysis. But clearly, the dynamics and motives of sociopolitical stabilization and capital accumulation at the core of regulation theoretical analysis are central to imperialism. Without concerns of profitability there would be no modern empire, even if the connections between capitalism and indivdual foreign interventions are not always direct.

93. Max Boot, "The New American Way of War," *Foreign Affairs* 82 (July/August 2003); Peter J. Boyer, "The New War Machine," *The New Yorker* (June 30, 2003), pp. 55–71.

94. Christopher Layne, "America as European Hegemon," *National Interest* 72 (summer), pp. 17–29, p. 25.

95. See Tim Mitchell, "McJihad"; also his lecture "On Petro-Knowledge: The Iraq War and the Techno-Social Life of Oil," October 30, 2003, University of Michigan. On the link between financialization and post-Fordism, see David Harvey, *The Condition of Postmodernity: An Enquiry into the Origins of Cultural Change* (Cambridge, MA: Blackwell, 1989), and *The New Imperialism* (Oxford, New York: Oxford University Press, 2003), pp. 62–74. I am grateful to Robin Blackburn for asking me to consider this question at the SSRC conference on "Lessons of Empire."

96. Peter W. Singer "Beyond the Law," *The Guardian,* May 3, 2004. See especially the important work of Deborah Avant, including her forthcoming book *The Market for Force: Private Security and Political Change* (2005). A summary of some of her arguments is presented in "Privatizing Military Training," *Foreign Policy in Focus* 5, no. 17 (June 2000). See also Peter W. Singer, "Corporate Warriors," *International Security* 26, no. 3 (winter 2001/02), pp. 186–220 and Johnson, *Sorrows,* ch. 5. Thanks to Deborah Avant for permitting me to read her unpublished chapters.

97. Johnson, *Sorrows,* p. 143.

98. There have also been tentative moves in the direction of a new protectionism, as with the March 2002 steel tariffs, and even some partial tendencies away from privatization of state functions, as in the creation of the Transportation Security Administration. But this is not to suggest that protectionism has become dominant. Free trade and "openness" are still central goals in the 2002 *National Security Strategy* paper, and the administration lifted the steel tariffs in December 2003 in an effort to win the automaking vote in the 2004 election. CAFTA continues this "free trade" trend.

99. Johnson, *Sorrows,* p. 122.

100. For a pessimistic reading of the U.S. economy, see Robert Brenner, "New Boom or New Bubble?" *New Left Review* 25 (Jan.–Feb. 2004).

101. Johnson, *Sorrows,* pp. 35–36; Fairbank, *Trade and Diplomacy.*

102. Niall Ferguson, *Empire: The Rise and Demise of the British World Order and Its Lessons for Global Power* (New York: Basic Books, 2002), p. 368.

103. On the idea of an "explanatory critique" as "an explanation that criticizes what it explains, not *in addition to* but *by virtue of* the explanation," see Andrew Collier, "Critical Realism," in *The Politics of Method in the Human Sciences: Positivism and Its Epistemological Others,* ed. George Steinmetz (Duke University Press, 2005); and Roy Bhaskar, *The Possibility of Naturalism: A Philosophical Critique of the Contemporary Human Sciences* (Brighton, Sussex: Harvester Press, 1979).

104. I am thinking here of the subtitle of Ferguson's book *Empire,* which includes the phrase

"lessons for global power." More recently, see Anna Bernasek, "Lessons for the American Empire," *The New York Times,* National Edition, Sunday, January 30, 2005, Business section, p. 4.

105. For further discussion, see my article "The Uncontrollable Afterlives of Ethnography: Lessons from German 'Salvage Colonialism' for a New Age of Empire," *Ethnography* 5, no. 3 (2004), pp. 274–78.

9. Who Counts?

1. On capital and the British Empire, see Eric Hobsbawm, *The Age of Empire, 1875–1914* (New York: Vintage Books, 1987). On the United States after World War II, see G. John Ikenberry, *After Victory: Institutions, Strategic Restraint, and the Rebuilding of Order After Major Wars* (Princeton: Princeton University Press, 2001).

2. On Rome and India, see Bernard S. Cohn, *Colonialism and Its Forms of Knowledge* (Princeton: Princeton University Press, 1996). On Wolfe as a Roman, and the rise of public monuments comparing Britons and Romans in the wake of Pitt's elegy for Wolfe in 1759, see Douglas Fordham, "Imperial London and the Creation of a British School of Art, 1745–1776," (Ph.D. diss., Yale University, 2003).

3. The scholarship on Rome in European and American political imagery is wide ranging, from Marx to Auerbach to Benjamin to Pocock, and cannot be addressed adequately here. Martha Kaplan and I are currently finishing a book, *Laws Like Bullets,* on British governors who imagine themselves akin to Roman lawgivers, especially in the Pacific and in India, and the aftermath as recipients respond to their gifts of law.

4. The questions about British and French self-comparison to Roman imperials and republicans might raise, genealogically, the question why their Iberian predecessors did not surround themselves with Roman parallels, and declare themselves the successors of Rome. It could not be ignorance of things ancient and classical, in the southern Europe of renaissance. Since the rebirth was of civilization in the singular, the measure for most would be measuring up, not measuring against. But even if many Iberians were not so committed to Rome's singular superiority in history, the religious situation was, I suspect, key to the comparative method available. Henry VIII enabled the British to not always already be in the continuation of the Roman Empire; for the Roman Catholics, the Pope's imperium already filled the space of Rome succession. Rome was succeeded by Rome. After all, Pope Alexander VI's line, dividing the globe into Spanish and Portuguese halves, set the first legal framework for European colonizing.

5. Whorf, *Language, Thought and Reality* (Cambridge, MA: MIT Press, 1956). For Shakespeare on the measure phrase, accounting, and contracts, recall the pound of flesh in *The Merchant of Venice.*

6. Fukuyama, "The End of History?" *National Interest* (summer 1989), pp. 3–18.

7. Literary critic Marc Shell has documented the gradual rise of various, connected economic tropes, and resistance to them, in western letters: see Marc Shell, *The Economy of Literature* (Baltimore: Johns Hopkins University Press, 1993); and Shell, *Money, Language and Thought: Literary and Philosophical Economies from the Medieval to the Modern Era* (Baltimore: Johns Hopkins University Press, 1994).

8. I have been collecting possible explanations for the relative evanescence of the joint-stock companies in the new world (and also Africa): (1) inverse relationship between settler enterprises and joint-stock companies (cf., for example, the failure of the New Zealand Company); (2) emergence of mortgage-bank financing, more successful than company financing especially for the Caribbean, with slaves a particularly fungible, reliable collateral, mitigating the risks of unseen real estate collateral; (3) differing geographies of monopoly, failures of new world commercial-geographical knowledge for early companies there (n.b. the South Seas Company and Mississippi Company bubbles in 1720); (4) Iberian predecessors made a difference somehow; or, perhaps the best; (5) much better developed commodity markets in "old world" colonies made trading company business possible in Asia, while the "new world" colonies required commodity production for pursuit of profit, something the seventeenth and eighteenth century companies were not ready to manage

efficiently and reliably enough (but note that the Caribbean planters pulled it off and became the biggest moneymakers in the European empires). The exception proves the rule: the Hudson Bay Company made its profits trading, for fur.

9. Thomas Babington Macaulay, Government of India, A Speech Delivered in the House of Commons, July 10, 1833. Reprinted pp. 146–93 of *The Miscellaneous Works,* vol. 19 of *The Complete Works of Lord Macaulay* (Philadelphia: The University Library Association, 1910). Quotations are from pp.152–54 and 162–63. Discussion of the strangeness of company rule did not begin with Macaulay, of course. It was a vexing question in the trial of Hastings (governor of Bengal, accused of corruption and arbitrary rule, tried in the House of Lords in 1787–95). Adam Smith's *Inquiry into the Nature and Causes of the Wealth of Nations,* also published in 1776, was in its own way an attack on the company's hegemony, though largely on grounds of alleged economic inadequacy rather than political immorality.

10. A little more from Macaulay's observations, on the point that sovereign power was part of the premise of chartered, joint-stock companies from the outset of European colonization: "It is a mistake to suppose that the Company was a merely commercial body till the middle of the last century. Commerce was its chief object; but in order to enable it to pursue that object, it had been, like the other Companies which were its rivals—like the Dutch Indian Company, like the French India Company—invested from a very early period with political functions. More than a hundred and twenty years ago the Company was in miniature precisely what it now is. It was intrusted with the very highest prerogatives of sovereignty. It has its forts, and its white captains, and its black sepoys; it had its civil and criminal tribunals; it was authorized to proclaim martial law; it sent ambassadors to the native governments, and concluded treaties with them; it was Zemindar [Lord, landlord] of several districts, and within those districts, like other Zemindars of the first class, it exercised the powers of a sovereign, even to the infliction of capital punishment on the Hindoos within its jurisdiction. It is incorrect, therefore, to say that the Company was at first a mere trader, and has since become a sovereign" (ibid., 150–51). Mintz has argued that plantations in the new world were an industrial mode of production scandalously prior to "the industrial revolution" in Europe. Similarly, the joint-stock companies, which began almost entirely as colonial and maritime enterprises, come far too early and become leviathans far too early for most theories of the firm as an organic outgrowth of industrial necessities or market situations (for example economist Ronald Coase's recently revived explanation of "the firm"). The intertwining of joint-stock companies with sovereignty is vital to the grasp of their institutional dynamics. Here, and on these grounds, the return to Veblen is also a turn away from the newer institutional economics, which seeks to find generic economic explanations for social and economic institutions. Instead with Veblen I return to some of the thematics of the older American institutional economics, including both the importance of historical context (as one finds better articulated in Max Weber's sociology) and also the irreducibility of political structure to economic relationships, reversing the privilege to general economic models and restoring the political intrinsic to political economy. Coase's models of transaction costs and firm and market efficiencies attend little to real historical metrics—efficient for whom, towards what end, costs to whom, reckoned how—and to the politics intrinsic to all institutional structures, whose efficiencies in the management of cost obviously include, as Veblen showed long ago, the redistribution as well as the avoidance of risks and costs. The actual history of joint-stock enterprise fits ill with Coase's chronotope, suggesting that we need better descriptions of the history and politics of the firm, not merely a general theory of its "nature." And, ironically, the colonial joint-stock companies are similarly scandalous in the real history of governmentality: against Foucault's modernism, we find objectification of populations, and the undertaking of their management, born in the wrong places and times, and for the "wrong" reason, more piratical than Apollonian.

11. Thorstein Veblen, *The Vested Interests and the Common Man ("The Modern Point of View and the New Order")* (New York: Augustus M. Kelly, 1964 [1919]). See also Thorstein Veblen, *Absentee Ownership* (New Brunswick: Transaction, 1997 [1923]).

12. Assessment of the history of accounting in relation to the history of taxation and reportage

might begin with Braudel's critique of Weber's theory of rational accounting (Fernand Braudel, *Civilization and Capitalism, 15–18th Century, vol. 2, The Wheels of Commerce* [New York: Harper and Row, 1983]). There are many excellent studies in the complex history of measurement, including recent and nuanced studies of the struggles to measure space and time (Ken Alder, *Measure of All Things* [New York: Simon and Shuster, 2002]; Peter Galison, *Einstein's Clocks, Poincare's Maps: Empires of Time* [New York: Norton, 2003]; David Landes, *Revolution in Time*, rev. ed. [Cambridge, MA: Harvard University Press, 2000]). But the most valuable discussion still might be E.P. Thompson's remarkable, influential study connecting time measurement, work organization, and changes in industry (Thompson, "Time, Work-Discipline, and Industrial Capitalism," *Past and Present* 38, pp. 56–97 [1967]).

13. Anderson has argued that "nations dream of being free," transporting a twentieth-century, Truman Doctrine premise down into the roots of nationalisms (see p. 7 of *Imagined Communities* [London and New York: Verso, 1991]). Max Weber defined nations more inclusively, as groups that seek and exercise political power. From the center of British arts and letters of the nineteenth century, John Stuart Mill provides an example of a vision of nations cognizant of deep asymmetries and centering nationalism on "privileges of citizenship" much closer to shareholderdom than a "dream of being free": "Experience proves, that it is possible for one nationality to merge and be absorbed in another: and when it was originally an inferior and more backward portion of the human race, the absorption is greatly to its advantage. Nobody can suppose that it is not more beneficial to a Breton, or a Basque of French Navarre, to be brought into the current of the ideas and feelings of a highly civilized and cultivated people—to be a member of the French nationality, admitted on equal terms to all the privileges of French citizenship, sharing the advantages of French protection, and the dignity and prestige of French power—than to sulk upon his own rocks, the half-savage relic of past times, revolving in his own little mental orbit, without participation or interest in the general movement of the world" (p. 431 of "Considerations on Representative Government," *On Liberty and Other Essays* [Oxford: Oxford University Press, 1991 (1861)]).

14. As K.N. Chaudhuri has observed, the kinds and intensities of obligations, forces, and pressures that built up especially in the eighteenth-century East India Company seemed to catch all participants by surprise: "The East India Company's decision-makers learnt early on that the principle of joint-stock capital and the separation of ownership from the management of commercial affairs had a plain meaning. To trade with other people's money created new responsibilities and the non-mercantile investors had little understanding or patience with the detailed explanations of events that had caused the Company's fortunes to go wrong. The Court of Directors was held constitutionally responsible and this responsibility was collective. There is no question that in the economic conditions of the seventeenth and eighteenth centuries this was a profound innovation. The king's ministers in all countries and in all times were accountable for their acts. But there was no legal or business tradition that obliged merchants to trade profitably under any circumstances. The medieval institution of commenda contracts clearly stipulated the conditions under which an active younger merchant raised capital from a senior non-traveling partner, and beyond the enforcement of ordinary commercial debts the mercantile community, whether in Europe or Asia, was not burdened with non-contractual moral obligations toward maintaining a certain level of performance and efficiency. The English East India Company however operated with this precise brief and the principle today underlies all corporate business management. The economists might wonder but they are not able to provide any rational explanation why salaried executives should want to provide yet higher rates of return to capital which they themselves do not own" (pp. 99–100 of K.N. Chaudhuri, "The English East India Company and its Decision-Making" in *East India Company Studies: Papers Presented to Professor Sir Cyril Philips*, eds. Kenneth Ballhatchet and John Harrison [Hong Kong: Asian Research Service, 1986]).

15. This policy shift might be a missing piece in scholarly debates about the mid-nineteenth-century gap in the pattern to the history of British colonization, the debate started by Robinson and Gallagher. The first test of the new policy was also the fiasco that closed the alleged first period of British colonization, the British government's rush to preempt a maverick "New Zealand Company"

with an intention to privately and "scientifically" colonize New Zealand on the Wakefield plan in the late 1830s, with the flim-flam Treaty of Waitangi. The failure of both the New Zealand Company and the government's modified version of Wakefield's scientific plan cast a long shadow in the reckoning of the profits for new colonial enterprises. See my essay "The Other Leviathans: Corporate Investment and the Construction of a Sugar Colony," *White and Deadly: Sugar and Colonialism,* eds. Pal Ahluwalia, Bill Ashcroft, and Roger Knight (Commack, NY: Nova Science Publishers, 1999).

16. The word *nation-state* has an important history, as Martha Kaplan and I have discussed in detail elsewhere (Kelly and Kaplan, *Represented Communities: Fiji and World Decolonization* [Chicago: University of Chicago Press, 2001]). It does not arrive into any major dictionary of the English language until after World War II, and it is present in all of them by 1970: we argue that it is fundamentally a creature of the era of decolonization, and the changing grammar for political possibility under discussion here. Its first attestations connect, precisely, to Wilson and Versailles, though Wilson himself never used the word.

17. The essays were later published. See Veblen, "Suggestions Touching the Working Program of an Inquiry into the Prospective Terms of Peace," and "Outline of a Policy for the Control of the 'Economic Penetration' of Backward Countries and of Foreign Investments," *Essays in Our Changing Order* (New Brunswick: Transaction, 1991). Note the shift of "development" from a count to a mass noun: one can speak of developments in physics and biology but not developments in Brazil and Burma, or to put it differently, one might compare religious developments in Brazil and Burma, but when talking capitalist economics one is comparing development in Brazil and Burma. Development in the capitalist economic sense becomes, in the twentieth century, something open-endedly progressive, but also quantifiable and comparable in principle, much like what management owes shareholders in the world of joint-stock enterprise. Once open-ended development is the goal, colonial governments are obviously ill-suited to the management process, given intrinsic conflicts of interest within their reporting structure. (Civilization meanwhile shifted from mass to count, also undermining logics of colonial sovereignty.)

18. This dynamic Veblen understood far more clearly than many current observers attempting to measure the implications of a knowledge-based economy, for example Michael Hardt and Antonio Negri, authors of *Empire* (Cambridge, MA: Harvard University Press, 2000).

19. Much else could be said about Iraq in particular: the 9/11 sabotage had the mark of the anarchic violence intrinsic to what Mark Duffield has called the "new wars," rather than the style of warfare anticipated for nation-states. But Iraq itself was clearly not a site of anarchy or Duffieldian new war before the United States reopened hostilities. Nor was the 1991 Gulf War a new war. Rather, Saddam Hussein's Iraq was an extreme, classic, example of another of the unintended consequences of actual decolonization, the obligatory reorganization of world sovereignty into a patchwork of nation-states. Iraq was a classic case of the rise of what Kees Koonings and Dirk Kruijt have called the "political army," a state dominated by a military apparatus that positions itself as intrinsically rather than democratically the living will of the people, creator and sustainer of the nation's independence. Koonings and Kruijt argue that in actual decolonization, states dominated by political armies (e.g., from Indonesia and Burma to most of the Americas) might be the most common outcome rather than the exception. In Iraq, the United States may be repairing its own pride. The United States may succeed only in replacing a political army with an unsolvable anarchy, directly albeit inadvertently sponsoring the constitution of new war. But its fashion of occupying the landscape—all the Americans sleeping behind barbed wire, plans to move the Americans out of the cities entirely, no surrender of an "adverse party" nor recognition of existing, continuing civil institutions—resembles cowboys-and-indians logic (come in, build the fort, protect your own precarious supply lines, secure and dominate the coveted resources, and eventually, shepherd the superseded peoples onto reservations) more closely than actual Asian colonizations past. Suggestions, for example, of "reconquering" recalcitrant regions are symptomatic of the fact that this "conquest" amounted to the self-dispersion of Iraq's political army accompanied by a vast military parade in some ways kindred to showing of the instruments of torture. But despite U.S. reluctance

to actually devolve authority onto its appointed local government, to declare this Iraq episode less than a redecolonization because the appointed government is less than the freely chosen representatives of the people would imply that the original decolonizations were authentic self-expressions of actual, constitutive national wills, which would miss the point entirely. As a colonization or imperial exercise the U.S. military action in Iraq is a fraud. As a replay of decolonization, though, it is right on the actual tracks. The media constantly reminds us; it is all about exit strategy. On "new wars," see Mark Duffield, *Global Governance and the New Wars: The Merging of Development and Security* (London and New York: Zed, 2001). On "political armies" see Kees Koonings, Dirk Kruijt, eds., *Political Armies: The Military and Nation Building in the Age of Democracy* (London: Zed, 2002). On 9/11 and U.S. power see also my essay "U.S. Power, after 9/11 and before It: If Not an Empire, Then What?" *Public Culture* 15, pp. 347–369 (2003).

20. Prasenjit Duara, *Rescuing History from the Nation: Questioning Narratives of Modern China* (Chicago: University of Chicago Press, 1995).

10. Empire and Imitation

1. I am grateful to Dipesh Chakrabarty and Sudipta Kaviraj as well as to the participants in the SSRC workshop for their criticisms on an earlier draft of this essay.

2. And historians seem ready to take advantage. "Historians now have an opportunity to connect their knowledge to far-reaching policy recommendations," A.G. Hopkins, ed., *Globalization in World History* (New York: Norton, 2002), p. ix.

3. Not that none of the scholars just cited never thought of this. See for example Hayden White, "Afterword," in V.E. Bonnell and L. Hunt, *Beyond the Cultural Turn* (Berkeley: University of California Press, 1999).

4. *Oxford English Dictionary,* s.v. See S.N. Eisenstadt, *The Political Systems of Empires* (London, New York: Free Press of Glencoe, 1963), and ed., *The Decline of Empires* (Englewood Cliffs, NJ: Prentice-Hall, 1967); M. Duverger, ed., *Le Concept d'empire* (Paris: Presses universitaires de France, 1980); S. Alcock et al., eds., *Empires* (Cambridge: Cambridge University Press, 2001). For the general problem of defining empire, see Duverger, *Le Concept d'empire,* pp. 5–23; Morrison in Alcock et al., *Empires,* pp. 1–9.

5. When one scholar writes "Rome was more than simply a typical early empire: in some senses it was an archetypal one," he captures at once the scholarly problem of taxonomy and the historical dimension of imitation addressed below (G. Woolf in Alcock et al., eds., *Empires,* pp. 311ff.).

6. This section is adapted from "Axialism and Empire," in *Axial Civilizations and World History,* ed. J. Arnason et al. (Leiden: Brill).

7. I found imperial imitation noted first by Duverger, *Le Concept d'empire,* 2005, p. 21. On competition and emulation among peer polities, see C. Renfrew and J. Cherry, eds., *Peer Polity Interaction and Socio-political Change* (Cambridge: Cambridge University Press, 1986).

8. J.-P. Sartre, *Search for a Method* (New York: Knopf, 1963), pp. 45ff. The sociological theory referred to (for which I am indebted to conversation with Craig Calhoun) is P.J. DiMaggio and W. Powell, "The Iron Cage Revisited: Institutional Isomorphism and Collective Rationality in Organizational Fields," *American Sociological Review* 48 (1983), pp. 147–60; on Durkheim and Tarde, see R.A. Jones, *Emile Durkheim: An Introduction to Four Major Works* (Beverly Hills: Sage, 1986), pp. 82ff.

9. A. Padgen, *Lords of All the World: Ideologies of Empire in Spain, Britain and France, c. 1500–c.1800* (New Haven: Yale University Press, 1995), pp. 5, 17.

10. M. Alam and S. Subrahmanyam, *The Mughal State, 1526–1750* (Delhi: Oxford University Press, 1998), p. 23 (the British abandoned their Mughal ways after the 1857 Rebellion; see below); S. Bose, this volume. The southwest Asian ancestry of the Mongals' belief in Tengri, the supreme sky god of the steppe, who conferred the right to rule on a single clan, may be an earlier instance of such fusion. Sanping Chen, "Son of Heaven and Son of God," *Journal of the Royal Asiatic Society,*

3rd series, vol. 12, no. 3 (2002), pp. 289–325, cited in M. Biran, "Eurasian Transformations 10th–13th Centuries: The Mongol Case," in *Medieval Encounters* (forthcoming).

11. S.N. Eisenstadt, *The Origins and Diversity of Axial Age Civilizations* (Albany: State University of New York Press, 1986), p. 8; so already implicitly M. Weber, *Economy and Society* (Berkeley: University of California Press, 1978), vol. 1, p. 418.

12. M. van Creveld, *The Rise and Decline of the State* (Cambridge: Cambridge University Press, 1999), pp. 35–52.

13. P. Briant, "Ethno-class dominante et populations soumises dans l'empire achéménide: le cas d'Egypte," in *Achaemenid History, III: Method and Theory*, ed. A. Kuhrt and H. Sancisi-Weerdenburg (Leiden: Netherlands Institute for the Near East, 1988.)

14. Pliny, *Natural History* (iii.39), cited in G. Woolf, *Becoming Roman: The Origins of Provincial Civilization in Gaul* (Cambridge: Cambridge University Press, 1998), p. 57. See my "Cosmopolitan and Vernacular in History," in *Cosmopolitanism*, ed. C. Breckenridge et al. (Durham: Duke University Press, 2002), and "India in the Vernacular Millennium," *Daedalus* 127, no. 3 (1998), pp. 41–74.

15. *Brihaspatisutra* 3.64ff. (probably twelfth or thirteenth century).

16. O. Wolters, "Khmer 'Hinduism' in the Seventh Century," *Early South East Asia: Essays in Archaeology, History and Historical Geography*, ed. R.B. Smith and W. Watson (New York, Kuala Lumpur: Oxford University Press, 1979), p. 438.

17. The social role of the cult is discussed in J.E. Lendon, *Empire of Honor: The Art of Government in the Roman World* (Oxford: Clarendon Press, 1997), pp. 160–72.

18. B. Stein, *Vijayanagara* (Cambridge: Cambridge University Press, 1989); on the Mughals, see works by S. Bose; also M. Alam, *Languages of India's Political Islam* (Chicago: University of Chicago Press, 2004), especially ch. 2 on "social balance." The quotations from Badayuni and Aurangzeb are found in Alam and Subrahmanyam, *The Mughal State*, p. 1.

19. These important observations are owing to Frederick Cooper.

20. On the Habsburgs, see S. Subrahmanyam (this volume).

21. C. Maier, "An American Empire? The Problems of Frontiers and Peace in Twenty-first-century World Politics," *Harvard Magazine*, Nov.–Dec. 2002, pp. 28–31; M. Walker, "America's Virtual Empire," *World Policy Journal* 19, no. 2 (2002), pp. 13–21. More candor and realism are available in T. Ali, "Re-Colonizing Iraq," *New Left Review* 21 (2003), pp. 5–19.

22. V.D. Hanson, "A Funny Sort of Empire," *National Review Online*, Nov. 27, 2002.

23. More than two-thirds of all U.S. citizens believe in the existence of the devil, nearly half accept creationism and think the Antichrist is now on earth; even more hold that the events prophesied in Revelation are going to come true (M. McAlister, "An Empire of their Own," *The Nation*, Sept. 22, 2003).

24. Where non-English persists as form, its content is increasingly Americanized. Last year, German publishers bought translation rights to 3,782 American books; American publishers bought rights for 150 German books. The figures for other European countries are comparable. "A main reason for it is simply that America dominates the world, whether in film or literature or politics" (*New York Times*, July 26, 2003).

25. S. Kurtz, "Democratic Imperialism: A Blueprint. Lessons from the British in India," *Policy Review* 118 (April–May 2003); cited also in the next paragraph. For a critique of "democratic fundamentalism" (the phrase is Gabriel García Marquez's), see Luciano Canfora, *L'Imposture démocratique: du Procès de Socrate à l'Élection de G. W. Bush* (Paris: Flammarion, 2003; original Italian ed. 2002), especially pp. 25–29. Readers should also dust off their copies of Edward S. Herman and Frank Brodhead's *Demonstration Elections: U.S.-Staged Elections in the Dominican Republic, Vietnam, and El Salvador* (Boston: South End Press, 1984).

26. See J. Majeed, "Comparativism and References to Rome in British Imperial Attitudes to India," in *Roman Presences: Receptions of Rome in European Culture, 1789–1945*, ed. C. Edwards (Cambridge University Press, 1999), pp. 88–109. Various parallels in actual practices could easily be ad-

duced. With respect to communication and culture, for example, a clear analog to Pliny the Elder is Lord Macaulay in his *Minute*: "Of all foreign tongues, the English tongue is that which would be the most useful to our native subjects."

27. A point raised in conversation with Sudipta Kaviraj.

28. Its recent actions in Gujarat give substance to what might otherwise seem a cheap slur. See M. Nussbaum, "Genocide in Gujarat: The International Community Looks Away," *Dissent*, summer 2003.

29. P. Wolfe, "History and Imperialism: A Century of Theory, from Marx to Postcolonialism," *American Historical Review* 102, no. 2 (1997), pp. 388–420.

30. T. Negri and M. Hardt, for instance, can rightly be faulted for their strange (and strangely emphatic) position on U.S. empire (*"The United States does not, and indeed no nation-state can today, form the center of an imperialist project. Imperialism is over"*) and for their idealization of U.S. constitutionalism and of Rome itself (*Empire* [Cambridge: Harvard University Press, 2000]; the quote is on p. xiv). Their present thinking is little changed, see "Adventures of the Multitude: Response of the Authors," *Rethinking Marxism* 13, no. 3/4 (2001), especially p. 239.

31. Joseph Conrad, "Heart of Darkness," in *Longman Anthology of World Literature,* vol. F: The Twentieth Century, ed. D. Damrosch et al. (New York: Longman, 2004), pp. 63–64.

11. China's Agrarian Empire

*Thanks to Mark Elliott for his thoughtful comments, to the editors for their helpful suggestions, and to other conference participants for their distinctive perspectives on empire.

1. For an overview of the early period, see Nicola Di Cosmo, *Ancient China and Its Enemies: The Rise of Nomadic Power in East Asian History* (Cambridge: Cambridge University Press, 2002); for a more general overview, see Thomas Barfield, *The Perilous Frontier: Nomadic Empires and China* (New York: Basil Blackwell, 1989).

2. See Warren Cohen, *East Asia at the Center: Four Thousand Years of Engagement with the World* (New York: Columbia University Press, 2000); Martina Deuchler, *The Confucian Transformation of Korea* (Cambridge, MA: Harvard University Press, 1992); Gregory Smits, *Visions of Ryukyu: Identity and Ideology in Early-modern Thought and Politics* (Honolulu: University of Hawai'i Press, 1999); Alexander Woodside, *Vietnam and the Chinese Model* (Cambridge, MA: Harvard University Press, 1971).

3. For an extended discussion see R. Bin Wong, *China Transformed: Historical Change and the Limits of European Experience* (Ithaca, NY: Cornell University Press, 1997), pp. 9–52, 127–49.

4. R. Bin Wong,"Formal and Informal Mechanisms of Rule and Economic Development: The Qing Empire in Comparative Perspective," *Journal of Early Modern History* 5, no. 4 (2001), pp. 387–408.

5. A good example of the process of official management of gods is in James Watson, "Standardizing the Gods: The Promotion of T'ien Hou ('Empress of Heaven') Along the South China Coast, 960–1960," in *Popular Culture in Late Imperial China,* ed. David Johnson, Andrew J. Nathan, and Evelyn S. Rawski (Berkeley: University of California Press, 1985), pp. 292–324.

6. For examples of activity by an especially activist official, see William Rowe, *Saving the World: Chen Hongmou and Elite Consciousness in Eighteenth-Century China* (Palo Alto: Stanford University Press, 2001). For examples of the documents showing official efforts to order society see Helen Dunstan, *Conflicting Counsels to Confuse the Age: A Documentary Study of Political Economy in Qing China, 1644–1840* (Ann Arbor, MI: University of Michigan Press, 1996). For a systematic review of one major set of activities regarding food supplies, see Pierre-Etienne Will and R. Bin Wong, *Nourish the People: The State Civilian Granary System in China, 1650–1850* (Ann Arbor, Mich.: University of MI: Press,1991).

7. See Joseph Fletcher, "Ch'ing Inner Asia," in *The Cambridge History of China*, ed. John K. Fairbank (Cambridge: Cambridge University Press, 1978), vol. 10, pp. 35–106; and Joseph Fletcher,

"The Heyday of the Ch'ing Order in Mongolia, Sinkiang, and Tibet," in *The Cambridge History of China*, ed. John K. Fairbank (Cambridge: Cambridge University Press, 1978), vol. 10, pp. 351–408.

8. Fusaaki Maehira, "Jūkyū seki no higashi Ajia kokusai kankei to Ryūkyū mondai," in *Shūen kara no rekishi (Ajia kara kangaeru 3)*, ed. Mizoguchi Yūzō, Hamashita Takeshi, Hiraishi Naoaki, and Miyajima Hiroshi (Tokyo: University of Tokyo Press, 1994), pp. 243–71.

9. R. Bin Wong, "Two Kinds of Nation, What Kind of State," in *Nation Work*, ed. Timothy Brook and Andre Schmid (Ann Arbor, MI: University of Michigan Press, 2000).

10. For political economy examples, see R. Bin Wong, "The Political Economy of Agrarian Empire and its Modern Legacy," in *China and Historical Capitalism: Genealogies of Sinological Knowledge*, ed. Timothy Brook and Gregory Blue (Cambridge: Cambridge University Press, 1999).

12. Imperial Power and Its Limits

1. I would like to thank the organizers and participants of the Lessons of Empire conference for guidance, encouragement, and suggestions on this chapter.

2. "Capitalism and democracy," writes Niall Ferguson, "are not naturally occurring, but require strong institutional foundations of law and order. The proper role of an imperial America is to establish these institutions where they are lacking, if necessary . . . by military force" (*New York Times Magazine*, April 27, 2003, p. 52).

3. Max Boot as quoted in the *Boston Sunday Globe*, March 23, 2002, p. H1.

4. Michael Ignatieff in the *New York Times Magazine*, January 5, 2003, p. 22.

5. Woodrow Wilson, "What Ought We to Do?" in *The Papers of Woodrow Wilson*, vol. 10, ed. Arthur S. Link (Princeton: Princeton University Press), pp. 574–75.

6. Walter Williams, "United States Indian Policy and the Debate Over Philippine Annexation: Implications for the Origins of American Imperialism," *Journal of American History* 66 (1980), pp. 810–31.

7. Quote from William T. Hagan, p. 61 of "United States Indian Policies, 1860–1900," in *History of Indian-White Relations*, ed. Wilcomb E. Wasburn (Washington: Smithsonian Institution, 1988), pp. 51–65. Fittingly, middle-class reformers who had founded the Friends of the Indian Society, a foremost proponent of federal policies aimed at "assimilating" Native Americans, later changed their name to take into account overseas colonial subjects. The group renamed itself the Friends of the Indian and Other Dependent Peoples. For more such connections see Roger Bresnahan, "'Our Little Proteges': Models of American Colonial Rule," *Phillippine Social Science and Humanities Review* 43 (1979), pp. 161–71.

8. See Hagan, "United States Indian Policies, 1860–1900," and Jack Erickson Eben, *The First and Second United States Empires* (Pittsburgh: University of Pittsburgh Press, 1968), p. 3.

9. Quoted in Whitney T. Perkins, *Denial of Empire: The United States and Its Dependencies* (Leyden: A.W. Sythoff, 1962), p. 14.

10. On "incorporated" vs. "unincorporated," see Christina Duffy Burnett and Burke Marshall, *Foreign in a Domestic Sense: Puerto Rico, American Expansion, and the Constitution* (Durham: Duke University Press, 2001).

11. Quoted in ibid., p. 12.

12. D.K. Fieldhouse and Rupert Emerson, "Colonialism," p. 1 in *International Encyclopedia of the Social Sciences*, ed. David L. Sills (New York: Macmillan, 1968), pp. 1–12.

13. Quoted in James Edward Kerr, *The Insular Cases: The Role of the Judiciary in American Expansionism* (Port Washington, NY: Kennikat Press, 1982), p. 3.

14. William F. Willoughby, *Territories and Dependencies of the United States* (New York: The Century Co., 1905), pp. 7-8.

15. The essays by Cooper, Steinmetz, Suny, and Wong in this volume all show the intricacies of the term *empire*. In referring to a formal colonial empire, I am drawing from basic definitions of mod-

ern colonial empires laid out by D.K. Fieldhouse and Rupert Emerson, "Colonialism," in Sills, *International Encyclopedia of the Social Sciences,* pp. 1–12.

16. Ibid., p. 7.

17. Roosevelt quoted on p. 58 of Paul Kramer, "Empires, Exceptions, and Anglo-Saxons: Race and Rule between the British and U.S. Empires, 1880–1910," in *The American Colonial State in the Philippines: Global Perspectives,* ed. Julian Go and Anne Foster (Durham: Duke University Press, 2003), pp. 43–91.

18. Bernard Moses, "Control of Dependencies Inhabited by the Less Developed Races," *University of California Chronicle* 7 (1905), pp. 3–18.

19. Woodrow Wilson, "Democracy and Efficiency," *Atlantic Monthly* 97, 1901.

20. Franklin H. Giddings, "Imperialism?" *Political Science Quarterly* 13, no. 4 (1898), p. 601.

21. Burgess quoted in Julius Pratt, *Expansionists of 1898: The Acquisition of Hawaii and the Spanish Islands* (Baltimore: Johns Hopkins University Press, 1936), p. 8.

22. See Niall Ferguson, *Empire: The Rise and Demise of the British World Order and the Lessons for Global Power* (New York: Basic Books, 2003).

23. Root as quoted in Frank Schumacher, "The American Way of Empire: National Tradition and Translantic Adaptation in America's Search for Imperial Identity, 1898–1910," *GHI Bulletin* 31 (fall 2002), p. 40.

24. Donna Amoroso, "Inheriting the 'Moro Problem': Muslim Authority and Colonial Rule in British Malaya and the Philippines," p. 118 in Go and Foster, *The American Colonial State in the Philippines,* pp. 118–47.

25. See Franklin Ng, "Knowledge for Empire: Academics and Universities in the Service of Imperialism," in *On Cultural Ground: Essays in International History,* ed. Robert David Johnson (Chicago: Imprint Publications, 1994), pp. 123–46.

26. Moses, "Control of Dependencies," p. 7.

27. Wilson, "Democracy and Efficiency," pp. 297–98.

28. Moses, "Control of Dependencies," p. 18.

29. "Report of the Secretary of War," in *Annual Report of the United States War Department* (Washington: Government Printing Office, 1899), p. 24.

30. Ibid, p. 27.

31. William F. Willoughby, "The Problem of Political Education in Porto Rico," in Report of the Twenty-Seventh Annual Meeting of the Lake Mohonk Conference of Friends of the Indian and Other Dependent Peoples, October 20th, 21st and 22nd, 1909, p. 166, ed. Charles F. Meserve (Lake Mohonk: Lake Mohonk Conference of Friends of the Indian and Other Dependent Peoples, 1909).

32. "Report of the Military Governor of Porto Rico," in *Annual Report of the United States War Department* (Washington: Government Printing Office, 1899), I, p. 342.

33. Willoughby, *Territories and Dependencies,* p. 15.

34. Taft in United States Congress, *Hearings before the Committee on Insular Affairs* (Washington: Government Printing Office, 1906), part 3.

35. Mrs. Campbell Dauncy, *An Englishwoman in the Philippines* (London: John Murray, 1906), pp. 134–35.

36. William H. Taft, Special Report of Wm. H. Taft Secretary of War to the President on the Philippines (Washington, D.C.: Government Printing Office, 1908).

37. Quoted from p. 246 of Oscar Alfonso, "Taft's Views on 'The Phillippines for the Filipinos,'" *Asian Studies* 6 (1968), pp. 237–47.

38. This is the view presented in Stanley Karnow's Pulitzer Prize–winning book, *In Our Image: America's Empire in the Phillippines* (New York: Random House, 1989). I offer an extended critique of the exceptionalism view in my introduction to Go and Foster, eds., *The American Colonial State in the Philippines.*

39. U.S. Navy Department, *Annual Reports of the Navy Department for the Year 1901,* part 1 (Washington: Government Printing Office, 1901), pp. 85–86.

40. I discuss Guam and Samoa in further detail in J. Go, " 'Racism' and Colonialism: Meanings of Difference and Ruling Practices in America's Pacific Empire," forthcoming in *Qualitative Sociology* 27 (2004), pp. 35–58.

41. Anne Perez Hattori, "Righting Civil Wrongs: The Guam Congress Walkout of 1949," *ISLA: A Journal of Micronesian Studies* 3 (1995), pp. 1–27, p. 4.

42. Quoted in Philip Jessup, *Elihu Root,* vol. 1 (New York: Dodd, Mead & Company, 1938), p. 349.

43. *Annual Report of the Governor of Guam,* 1901, p. 14 (unpublished ms., USNA, Office of the Secretary of the Navy, Record Group 80, microfilm no. 181).

44. "Annual Report of Brig. Gen. W.A. Kobbe," in *Annual Reports of the War Department,* 1900, vol. 3, p. 269.

45. Patricio Abinales, "Progressive Machine Conflict in Early Twentieth-Century U.S. Politics and Colonial State Building in the Phillippines," in Go and Foster, eds., *The American Colonial State in the Philippines,* pp. 148–81.

46. Quoted in Donna Amoroso, "Inheriting the 'Moro Problem': Muslim Authority and Colonial Rule in British Malaya and the Philippines," p. 136 in Go and Foster, eds., *The American Colonial State in the Philippines.*

47. "Report of the Governor of the Moro Province," in *Report of the Philippine Commission* (Washington: Government Printing Office, 1909), pp. 3–4.

48. I borrow the term "imperial archipelago" from Thompson's illuminating piece on cultural representations of America's colonial subjects. See Lanny Thompson, "Representation and Rule in the Imperial Archipelago," *American Studies Asia* 1 (2002), pp. 3–39.

49. Williams Jennings Bryan, "What Next?" *New York Journal,* Feb. 12, 1899.

50. Reynaldo C. Ileto, "Orators and the Crowd: Philippine Independence Politics, 1910–1914," in *Reappraising an Empire: New Perspectives on Philippine-American History,* ed. Peter Stanley (Cambridge: Harvard University Press, 1984), pp. 85–113.

51. J. Go, "Chains of Empire, Projects of State: Political Education and U.S. Colonial Rule in Puerto Rico and the Phillipines," *Comparative Studies in Society and History* 42, no. 2 (2000), pp. 333–62.

52. Benedict Anderson, "Cacique Democracy in the Philippines," in *Discrepant Histories: Translocal Essays on Filipino Cultures,* ed. Vicente L. Rafael (Philadelphia: Temple University Press, 1995), pp. 3–47. For an excellent critique of existing scholarship on Filipino "caciques," see Reynaldo C. Ileto, *Knowing America's Colony: A Hundred Years from the Philippine War,* Philippine Studies Occasional Paper Series No. 13 (Manoa: Center for Philippine Studies, 1999).

53. I discuss in greater detail in J. Go, *Transcultured States: Elite Political Culture and U.S. Colonialism in Puerto Rico and the Philippines* (Ph.D. dissertation, University of Chicago, 2000); for the same translation issues in the Philippines, see J. Go, "Colonial Reception and Cultural Reproduction: Filipino Elite Response to U.S. Colonial Rule," *Journal of Historical Sociology* 12, no. 4 (1999), pp. 337–68.

54. See Fred Cooper's essay in this volume, as well as the essays in Frederick Cooper and Ann Laura Stoler, *Tensions of Empire: Colonial Cultures in a Bourgeois World* (Berkeley: University of California Press, 1997).

13. Imperial and Colonial Encounters

1. Anthony Pagden, *Peoples and Empires: Europeans and the Rest of the World, from Antiquity to the Present* (London: Weidenfeld and Nicolson, 2001).

2. Susan E. Alcock et al., eds., *Empires* (Cambridge: Cambridge University Press, 2001).

3. Pagden, *Peoples and Empires,* p. 10.

4. Ibid.

5. Ibid., p. 11.

6. Alcock et al., *Empires*, p. xix.

7. The passage from Joseph A. Schumpeter, *Imperialism and Social Classes,* trans. Heinz Norden (Fairfield, NJ: A.M. Kelley, 1989 [1919]), is taken from http://www.fordham.edu/halsall/mod/1918schumpeter1.html.

8. http://www.wordorigins.org/wordord.htm

9. Halil Inalcik and Donald Quataert, *An Economic and Social History of the Ottoman Empire,* 2 vols. (Cambridge: Cambridge University Press, 1994), p. xlii.

10. Serge Gruzinski, *The Conquest of Mexico* (Cambridge: Basil Blackwell, 1993).

11. P.J. Cain and A.G. Hopkins, *British Imperialism,* 2 vols. (London: Longmans, 1993).

12. C.A. Bayly, *Imperial Meridian* (London: Longmans, 1989), p. 193.

13. Vincent Harlow, *The Founding of the Second British Empire, 1763–1793,* 2 vols. (London: Longmans, 1952–64).

14. Bayly, *Imperial Meridian,* p. 253.

14. Ways of Remembering the *Maine*

1. My thanks to the editors of this volume for their invitation to particpate and for their helpful suggestions during revisions. Thanks also to Anne Watters, Héctor Lindo-Fuentes, and colleagues at the Fordham history department workshop for their many thoughtful and provocative observations. I hope I can respond to them all one day.

2. Anthony Lane, "Ruling the Waves," *New Yorker,* November 17, 2003, p. 173 (emphasis in the original). A.O. Scott, "Master of the Sea (and the French)," *New York Times,* November 14, 2003, p. E13.

3. Niall Ferguson, *Empire: The Rise and Demise of the British World Order and the Lessons for Global Power* (New York: Basic Books, 2002); Fareed Zakaria, "'A History of Britain': The Previous Superpower," *New York Times Book Review,* July 27, 2003.

4. National *Maine* Monument. Photograph by the author. The figure atop is Columbia Triumphant. For a description of the monument and the history of its construction, see Donald Martin Reynolds, *Monuments and Masterpieces: Histories and Views of Public Sculptures in New York City* (New York: Thames and Hudson, 1997), pp. 347–54.

5. Taft quoted in Reynolds, *Monuments and Masterpieces,* p. 350. See also Reynolds, pp. 347–54. On this previous passing of the imperial mantle, see Paul Kramer, "Empires, Exceptions, and Anglo-Saxons: Race and Rule between the British and United States Empires, 1880–1910," *Journal of American History* 88 (2002), pp. 1, 319–53. National *Maine* Monument. Photograph by author.

6. Elisabeth Bumiller, "Bush Promises Cuban-Americans to Keep up Pressure on Castro," *New York Times,* 11 October 2003, p. A5.

7. See Manuel Moreno Fraginals, *The Sugarmill,* trans. Cedric Belfrage (New York: Monthly Review Press, 1978); and Rebecca J. Scott, *Slave Emancipation in Cuba,* 2nd ed. (Pittsburgh: University of Pittsburgh Press, 2001).

8. Louis A. Pérez Jr., *The War of 1898: The United States and Cuba in History and Historiography* (Chapel Hill: University of North Carolina Press, 1998). On midcentury filibustering, see Robert E. May, *The Southern Dream of a Caribbean Empire, 1854–1861* (Athens: University of Georgia Press, 1989).

9. "El gat y la rata [Cat and Mouse]," *La Campana de Gracia* (Barcelona), 5 February 1898.

10. This thesis has made a comeback—in the United States. Its most recent advocate is none other than Samuel Huntington himself. See his essay "The Hispanic Challenge," *Foreign Policy* (March/April 2004). In response to Mexican American and other Latino pundits who posit an "Americano dream," Huntington, troubled by the possibility of a bilingual national culture and institutions, caustically concludes: "There is no Americano dream. There is only the American dream created by an Anglo-Protestant society. Mexican Americans will share in that dream and in that society only

if they dream in English." Similarly, the historian David Kennedy, in contemplating a Mexican "Reconquista," comments that "the possibility looms that in the next generation or so we will see a kind of Chicano Quebec take shape in the American Southwest." See "Can We Still Afford to Be a Nation of Immigrants?" *Atlantic Monthly* 278 (November 1996), p. 68.

11. Luis María Pastor, "Sobre reformas colonials," *Gaceta Economista* (April 1862), p. 281; and Eduardo Asquerino, "Nuestro pensamiento," *La América* (Madrid), 24 March 1857, n.p. See also Christopher Schmidt-Nowara, *Empire and Antislavery: Spain, Cuba, and Puerto Rico, 1833–1874* (Pittsburgh: University of Pittsburgh Press, 1999), ch. 5.

12. José Martí, "Our America [1891]," in *Our America by José Martí: Writings on Latin America and the Struggle for Cuban Independence,* ed. Philip S. Foner, trans. Elinor Randall with Juan de Onís and Roslyn Held Foner (New York: Monthly Review Press, 1977), p. 84. Note: Juan de Castellanos was a sixteenth-century Spanish poet who wrote about the conquests in the Caribbean. On Cuban nationalism in the later nineteenth century, see Ada Ferrer, *Insurgent Cuba: Race, Nation, and Revolution, 1868–1898* (Chapel Hill: University of North Carolina Press, 1999).

13. On the events leading to the U.S. intervention, see John Offner, *An Unwanted War: The Diplomacy of the United States and Spain over Cuba, 1895–1898* (Chapel Hill: University of North Carolina Press, 1992).

14. "Liberty Outraged," *La Campana de Gracia* (Barcelona), 23 April 1898.

15. Raymond Carr, *Spain, 1808–1975,* 2nd ed. (Oxford: Clarendon Press, 1982); and Jordi Nadal, *El fracaso de la revolución industrial en España, 1814–1913* (Barcelona: Ariel, 1975).

16. See the discussion in Christopher Schmidt-Nowara, "After 'Spain': A Dialogue with Josep M. Fradera on Spanish Colonial Historiography," in *After the Imperial Turn: Thinking with and through the Nation,* ed. Antoinette Burton (Durham: Duke University Press, 2003), pp. 157–69.

17. For a good discussion of the Spanish state and the commemorations in 1992, see Stephen J. Summerhill and John Alexander Williams, *Sinking Columbus: Contested History, Cultural Politics, and Mythmaking during the Quincentenary* (Gainesville: University Press of Florida, 2001).

18. See Joseph Smith, *The Spanish-American War: Conflict in the Caribbean and the Pacific, 1895–1902* (New York: Longman, 1994). On the experience of warfare in Morocco, see Sebastian Balfour, *Deadly Embrace: Morocco and the Road to the Spanish Civil War* (Oxford: Oxford University Press, 2002).

19. Germán Ojeda, "La cuestión cubana," *El País* (Madrid), 30 July 1996.

20. Leonard Wood quoted in Louis A. Pérez Jr., *Cuba under the Platt Amendment, 1902–1934* (Pittsburgh: University of Pittsburgh Press, 1986), p. 40.

21. Beveridge quoted in ibid., p. 50.

22. Emilio Roig de Leuchsenring, *Cuba no debe su independencia a los Estados Unidos* (Havana: Sociedad Cubana de Estudios Históricos e Internacionales, 1950).

23. Fidel Castro quoted in Pérez, *The War of 1898,* pp. 126–27; in the same work, see pages 108–33 on the relative stasis of both U.S. and Cuban interpretations of 1898 since 1959.

24. David Brooks, "Al Qaeda's Wish List," *New York Times,* 16 March 2004, p. A27; Edward N. Luttwak, "Rewarding Terror in Spain," ibid.

25. Also crucial in shaping the Spanish electorate's decision were the attempts of the PP to place blame for the bombing on the Basque separatist group, ETA, rather than on Al-Qaeda. Azuar's cynical and heavy-handed efforts to distract attention from his government's role in the Iraq war reactivated memories of the Franco regime's manipulations of information and public life. Given his party's origins in the Franco regime, many Spaniards voted for Zapatero and the PSOE as a protest of the PP's apparently dubious commitment to democracy and openness. See the lucid discussion in Antonio Feros, "Civil War Still Haunts Spanish Politics," *New York Times,* 20 March 2004.

15. Agriculture, Industry, Empire, and America

* I am grateful to Christopher Candland, Andre Gunder Frank, V. Spike Peterson, Kathryn Sikkink, and Rorden Wilkinson for comments on earlier versions of the same arguments.

1. Jonathan Schell, *The Unconquerable World: Power, Nonviolence, and the Will of the People* (New York: Metropolitan Books, 2003), pp. 339–45.

2. Compare James N. Rosenau, "International Relations," in *The Oxford Companion to the Politics of the World,* ed. Joel Krieger, 2nd ed. (New York: Oxford University Press, 2001), pp. 424–27.

3. See Claudio Cioffi-Revilla, "Origins and Evolution of War and Politics," *International Studies Quarterly* 40, no. 1 (1996), pp. 1–22; and Barry and Richard Little, *International Systems in World History: Remaking the Study of International Relations* (Oxford: Oxford University Press, 2000).

4. Robert P. Clark, *The Global Imperative: An Interpretive History of the Spread of Humankind* (Boulder, CO: Westview Press, 1997); compare James L. Newman, *The Peopling of Africa: A Geographic Interpretation* (New Haven: Yale University Press, 1995).

5. Hans J. Morgenthau, *Politics among Nations: The Struggle for Power and Peace* (New York: Alfred A. Knopf, 1948), p. 17.

6. Andrew Schmookler, *The Parable of the Tribes* (Berkeley: University of California Press, 1984). J.R. McNeill and William H. McNeill argue that, in Eurasia, the simultaneous rise of settled agricultural cities and of pastoral societies along their frontiers, gave us the regular pattern of raiding horsemen from the steppes and the "enhanced role of military leadership," the militarization of the agricultural cities, *The Human Web: A Bird's Eye View of World History* (New York: W. W. Norton & Company, 2003), pp. 48–50.

7. S.E. Finer, *The History of Government, vol. 1, Ancient Monarchies and Empires* (Oxford: Oxford University Press, 1997).

8. Finer, *The History of Government,* pp. 57–58.

9. Massimo Livi-Bacci, *A Concise History of World Population,* 2nd ed., Carl Ipsen, translator (Oxford: Blackwell Publishers, 1997), pp. 24–34.

10. Karl Marx, "What the Machine Is," in *Readings in Industrial Society: A Study of the Structure and Functioning of Modern Economic Organization,* ed. Leon Carroll Marshall (Chicago: University of Chicago Press, 1918 [1867]), pp. 426–28.

11. John A. Hobson, *The Evolution of Modern Capitalism* (London: Walter Scott, 1894), p. 74.

12. Quoted in Hobson, p. 74.

13. Karl Polanyi, *The Great Transformation: The Political and Economic Origins of Our Time,* trans. R.M. MacIver. (Boston: Beacon Press, 1957 [1944]), p. 49.

14. Quoted in Joan V. Bondurant, *Conquest of Violence: The Gandhian Philosophy of Conflict* (Princeton: Princeton University Press, 1958), p. 157; and see J. Ann Tickner, *Self Reliance versus Power Politics: The American and Indian Experience in Building Nation States* (New York: Columbia University Press, 1987), pp. 146–59.

15. Adam Smith, *An Inquiry into the Nature and Causes of the Wealth of Nations,* vol. 1 (Oxford: Oxford University Press, 1976 [1776]), p. 30.

16. Craig N. Murphy, *Global Institutions, Marginalization, and Development* (London: Routledge, 2004), ch. 5.

17. Robert O. Keohane and Craig N. Murphy, "International Institutions," in *Routledge Encyclopedia of Government and Politics,* ed. Maurice Kogan and Mary Hawkesworth, 2nd ed. (London: Routledge, 2004), pp. 920–22.

18. Karl Deutsch et al., *Political Community and the North Atlantic Area: International Organization in the Light of Historical Experience* (Princeton, NJ: Princeton University Press, 1957).

19. Craig N. Murphy, *International Organization and Industrial Change: Global Governance since 1850* (Cambridge and New York: Polity Press and Oxford University Press, 1994).

20. Jawaharlal Nehru, *The Discovery of India* (Delhi: Oxford University Press, 1985 [1946]), pp. 418, 481–82.

21. Patrick Chabal, *Amílcar Cabral: Revolutionary Leadership and People's War* (Cambridge: Cambridge University Press, 1983), pp. 46–47.

22. Pat Gowan, Leo Panitch, and Martin Shaw, "The State, Globalisation, and the New Imperialism: A Roundtable Discussion," *Historical Materialism: Research in Critical Marxist Theory* 9 (autumn 2001). Found on the Internet at http://www.theglobalsite.ac.uk/press/201gowan.htm on March 10, 2004.

23. William Robinson and Jerry Harris, "Towards a Global Ruling Class? Globalization and the Transnational Capitalist Class," *Science and Society* 64, no. 1 (2000), pp. 11–54.

24. See Michael Lind, *Made in Texas: George W. Bush and the Southern Takeover of American Politics* (New York: New America Books, 2003).

25. John A. Hobson, "The Economic Taproot of Imperialism," in *Imperialism* (Ann Arbor: University of Michigan Press, 1965 [1905]), pp. 71–93.

26. Mary Parker Follett, *The New State: Group Organization, the Solution of Popular Government* (University Park: Pennsylvania State University Press, 1998 [1918]). The forewords to the book by political theorists Benjamin R. Barber and Jane Mansbridge explain some of the relevance of Follett's kind of ideas to the problem of resolving the fundamental conflicts associated with the industrial system; and see Joan C. Tonn, *Mary P. Follett: Creating Democracy, Transforming Management* (New Haven: Yale University Press, 2003).

27. Ashis Nandy, "The Beautiful, Expanding Future of Poverty: Popular Economics as a Psychological Defense," *International Studies Review* 4, no. 2 (2002), pp. 107–21.

16. Imperialism Is Alive and Well

1. Mushtaq H. Khan and Jomo K. S., eds., *Rents, Rent-seeking and Economic Development: Theory and Evidence in Asia* (Cambridge: Cambridge University Press, 2000).

2. Jomo K. S., ed., *Tigers in Trouble* (London: Zed Books, 1998).

3. World Bank, *The East Asian Miracle* (New York: Oxford University Press, for World Bank, 1993).

4. Ibid.

5. Graciela Kaminsky and Sergio Schmukler, "Short-Run Pain, Long-Run Gain: The Effects of Financial Liberalization," IMF Working Paper No. 03/34 (1 February 2003) (Washington, DC: International Monetary Fund).

6. Eswar Prasad, Kenneth Rogoff, Shang-jin Wei, and M. Ayhan Kose, "The Effects of Financial Globalization on Developing Countries: Some Empirical Evidence," Occasional Paper (17 March), p. 9 (Washington, DC: International Monetary Fund, 2003).

7. Ibid., p. 8.

8. Raúl Prebisch, *The Economic Development of Latin America and Its Principal Problems* (New York: United Nations, 1950). Reprinted in *Economic Bulletin for Latin America* 7 (1962).

9. Hans W. Singer, "The Distribution of Gains Between Investing and Borrowing Countries," *American Economic Review* 40. Reprinted in David Greenaway and C.W. Morgan, eds., *The Economics of Commodity Markets* (Cheltenham, UK: Edward Elgar, 1999).

10. Arthur W. Lewis, *The Evolution of the International Economic Order* (Princeton, NJ: Princeton University Press, 1977).

11. Mark Weisbrot and Dean Baker, *The Relative Impact of Trade Liberalization on Developing Countries*, CEPR briefing paper (Washington, DC: Center for Economic and Policy Research, 2002).

12. Ibid., table 6.1.

13 Kym Anderson, "Agricultural Trade and Rural Poverty Reduction: Market Access," paper at Fourth Asia Development Forum on Trade and Poverty Reduction, Seoul, 4–5 November 2002.

14. J. E. Stiglitz, *Globalization and Its Discontents* (New York: Norton, 2002).

15. With Israel and Egypt at the top of the U.S. recipients' list by far, one should not be surprised that it was left to Japan to pay the bills for the last Gulf War or for the rebuilding of Cambodia a decade ago, or to others to pay for rebuilding Afghanistan after the regime change in Kabul.

16. David Dapice, "Does the 'Hyper-Power' Have Feet of Clay?" *YaleGlobal*, 3 March 2003.

17. Jomo K. S., ed., *The Long Twentieth Century: Oligopoly, Globalization and Economic Dominance* (Delhi: Oxford University Press, 2004).

18. Michael Hardt and Antonio Negri, *Empire* (Cambridge, MA: Harvard University Press, 2000).

19. Michael Hardt, "Folly of Our Masters of the Universe: Global Elites Must Realise That US Imperialism Isn't in Their Interest," *The Guardian*, December 18, 2002.

20. Joseph A. Schumpeter, *Imperialism and Social Classes*, trans. Heinz Norden (Fairfield, NJ: A.M. Kelley, 1989 [1919]).

21. Michael Hardt, "A Trap Set for Protesters," *The Guardian*, February 21, 2003.

22. Hardt, "Folly of Our Masters."

17. Myths of Empire and Strategies of Hegemony

1. Office of the President, *National Security Strategy of the United States,* September 2002, at www.whitehouse.gov/nsc/nss.html; Robert Jervis, "The Compulsive Empire," *Foreign Policy* 137 (July/August 2003), pp. 82–87.

2. Jack Snyder, "Imperial Temptations," *National Interest,* 71 (spring 2003), pp. 29–40; and Snyder, *Myths of Empire: Domestic Politics and International Ambition* (Ithaca: Cornell University Press, 1991).

3. On the effectiveness of suicide terrorism against democratic occupation powers, see Robert Pape, "The Strategic Logic of Suicide Terrorism," *American Political Science Review* 97, no. 3 (August 2003), pp. 343–62.

4. E.g., Michael Ignatieff, "The Burden," *New York Times Magazine,* January 5, 2003.

5. Michael Doyle, *Empires* (Ithaca: Cornell University Press, 1986), p. 12. Empires may sometimes take the initiative in organizing administrative units of subject peoples, not simply take over existing units.

6. Robert Keohane and Joseph Nye, *Power and Interdependence* (Boston: Little, Brown, 1977), p. 44.

7. In some of my previous writings, I used the term *empire* in a looser sense to refer to any "powerful state that uses force to expand its influence abroad beyond the point at which the costs of expansion begin to rise sharply," but here I will stick to Doyle's usage. See Snyder, "Imperial Temptations," p. 31, note 3; and Snyder, *Myths of Empire*, p. 6.

8. *New York Times,* September 26, 2002.

9. John J. Mearsheimer, "A War the U.S. Can Win—Decisively," *Chicago Tribune,* January 15, 1991.

10. John J. Mearsheimer, "Hearts and Minds," *National Interest* 69 (fall 2002), p. 15; for other realists, see Nicholas Lemann, "The War on What?" *New Yorker,* September 16, 2002, p. 11 of the Web version.

11. Robert Gilpin, *War and Change in World Politics* (Cambridge: Cambridge University Press, 1981).

12. Gilpin, *War and Change,* chapters 2 and 3.

13. Gilpin, *War and Change,* chapters 4 and 5.

14. Office of the President, *National Strategy to Combat Weapons of Mass Destruction,* December 2002, at http://www.whitehouse.gov/news/releases/2002/12/WMDStrategy.pdf.

15. *National Security Strategy of the United States,* p. 6.

16. Jack Snyder, *Ideology of the Offensive: Military Decision Making and the Disasters of 1914* (Ithaca: Cornell, 1984), p. 113.

17. Dale C. Copeland, *The Origins of Major War* (Ithaca, NY: Cornell University Press, 2000).

18. Jack Levy and Joseph Gochal, "Democracy and Preventive War: Israel and the 1956 Sinai Campaign," *Security Studies* 11, no. 2 (winter 2001–2), p. 11; Snyder, *Ideology of the Offensive*, p. 128.

19. Snyder, *Myths of Empire*, p. 83.

20. Testimony before House Armed Services Committee, September 18–19, 2002.

21. *National Security Strategy of the United States*, p. 15.

22. Snyder, *Myths of Empire*, p. 213.

23. Testimony before House Armed Services Committee, September 18–19, 2002.

24. *National Security Strategy of the United States*, p. 29.

25. "In Rumsfeld's Words: Guidelines for Committing Forces," *New York Times*, October 4, 2002, p. A9.

26. Condoleezza Rice, "Promoting the National Interest," *Foreign Affairs* 79, no.1 (January/February 2000), p. 61.

27. G. John Ikenberry, *After Victory: Institutions, Strategic Restraint, and the Rebuilding of Order after Major Wars* (Princeton: Princeton University Press, 2001), chapters 1, 2, 7, and 8.

28. John Lewis Gaddis, *We Now Know: Rethinking Cold War History* (New York: Oxford, 1997), p. 285.

29. Robert Keohane, *After Hegemony* (Princeton: Princeton University Press, 1984); and Stephen Krasner, ed., *International Regimes* (Ithaca: Cornell University Press, 1983).

30. John Mearsheimer, "The False Promise of International Institutions," *International Security* 19, no. 3 (winter 1994/95), pp. 5–49; Robert Jervis, "Institutionalized Disagreement," *International Security* 27, no. 1 (summer 2002), pp. 174–77.

31. Mark Juergensmeyer, *The New Cold War? Religious Nationalism Confronts the Secular State* (Berkeley: University of California Press, 1993).

32. Barnett Rubin, *The Fragmentation of Afghanistan: State Formation and Collapse in the International System* (New Haven: Yale University Press, 1995).

33. David Lake, *Entangling Relations: American Foreign Policy in Its Century* (Princeton: Princeton University Press, 1999), chapter 3.

34. Michael Mann, *The Sources of Social Power*, volumes 1 and 2 (Cambridge: Cambridge University Press, 1986 and 1993).

35. Jack Snyder, "Networks and Ideologies: The Fusion of 'Is' and 'Ought' as a Means to Social Power," in *The Anatomy of Power*, ed. John Hall, forthcoming.

36. Michael Mousseau, "Market Civilization and Its Clash with Terror," *International Security* 27, no. 3 (winter 2002/03), pp. 5–29.

CONTRIBUTORS

Craig Calhoun is president of the Social Science Research Council and University Professor of the Social Sciences at New York University.

Juan Cole is professor of Modern Middle East and South Asian History at the University of Michigan.

Matthew Connelly is an associate professor of history at Columbia University.

Frederick Cooper is a professor of history at New York University.

Julian Go is an assistant professor of sociology at Boston University.

John D. Kelly is a professor of anthropology at the University of Chicago.

Caglar Keyder is a professor of sociology at Binghamton University.

Jomo K. S. is Assistant Secretary-General for Economic Development at the United Nations.

Kevin W. Moore is associate dean for research, College of Arts and Sciences, University of North Carolina, Greensboro.

Craig N. Murphy is an historian of the UN Development Programme and M. Margaret Ball Professor of International Relations at Wellesley College.

Sheldon Pollock is George V. Bobrinskoy Professor of Sanskrit and Indic Studies at the University of Chicago.

Emmanuelle Saada is a professor and researcher at the Ecole des Hautes Etudes en Science Sociales.

Christopher Schmidt-Nowara is an assistant professor of history and director of the Latin American and Latino Studies program at Fordham University.

Jack Snyder is the Robert and Renée Belfer Professor of International Relations in the Political Science Department and Institute of War and Peace Studies at Columbia University.

George Steinmetz is a professor of sociology and German studies at the University of Michigan.

Ann Laura Stoler is Distinguished University Professor of Anthropology at New School University's Graduate Faculty of Political and Social Science, and chair of its Department of Anthropology.

Sanjay Subrahmanyam holds the Navin and Pratima Doshi Chair in Indian History at UCLA and the Chair in Indian History and Culture at the University of Oxford.

Ronald Grigor Suny is a professor of political science and history at the University of Chicago.

R. Bin Wong is a professor of history at UCLA and director of its Asia Institute.

INDEX

violence (con't)
imitation, 187, 188; and imperial formations and opacities of rule, 49, 51, 52, 59; legitimate, 75; and lesson of empires, 5; and lessons of 1898 in Spain and Cuba, 237, 241; and lessons of empire, 49, 51, 52, 59; and lessons of history, 6, 7, 45, 51; and power, 45; and public order, 45; and Soviet Union, 87, 89; and Subrahmanyam's comparative reflections, 222; and U.S. shift from imperialism to empire, 49; and who counts, 165, 170
Volcker, Paul, 264

Wallerstein, Immanuel, 48, 148, 149
Waltz, Kenneth, 270
War Department, U.S., 205
war on terror. See terrorism
wars: benefits of, 25–26; Bush's justifications for, 92; costs of, 96–97; and differentiation between nation-states and empires, 7; and imperial formations as states of exception, 58; just, 58; justifications for, 95–96, 156; and lessons of history, 7; "objectless," 96; provocation for, 25; and retrenchment strategy, 271; rhetoric about, 95–96; "small," 25; U.S. tradition of launching undeclared, 25; yield curve for, 25
Washington Consensus, 262
Watts, Sheldon, 28
Weber, Max, 40, 118, 119, 126, 159, 162, 311n13
Weisbrot, Mark, 260
welfare, 121, 124, 260
welfare state, 127, 256
Wells, H. W., 168
Westphalian system, 6, 7, 13, 151
what-if scenarios, 28
White, Hayden, 175–76
"white man's burden," 40, 53, 201
Whorf, Benjamin Lee, 160–61

Williams, Raymond, 138
Williams, William Appleman, 49, 138, 139
Willoughby, William, 203–4, 207
Wilson, Woodrow, 6, 22, 87, 163, 167–68, 169, 202, 204–5, 206, 214, 312n16
Winichakul, Thongchai, 54
Wolfowitz, Paul, 106, 107, 108, 112, 136
Wolseley, Garnet, 105
women, 44, 81, 96
Wood, Ellen Meiksins, 306n63
Wood, Leonard, 238–39
Woolf, G., 313n5
World Bank, 11, 31, 32, 33, 258, 260, 261–62, 268
World Health Organization, 31, 32
world order: and America's colonial empire, 205; and comparison of Germany and America, 151–52; and empire versus humanitarian republic, 52; evolution of, 131; and industry, 250–52; and lessons of 1898 in Spain and Cuba, 241; "new," 22, 169, 205; theories about, 22–23; of Wilson, 169, 205
World Trade Organization (WTO), 125, 127, 128, 129, 259, 260, 261, 262, 263, 267, 268
World War I, 7, 49, 167–68, 266; and British in Egypt, 113; and comparison of Germany and America, 153; and corporate structures, 168; and Iraq, 5; and Ottoman Empire, 117, 130; and security through expansion strategy, 272–74
World War II, 45, 113, 247
Wortman, Richard S., 80, 81, 296n31

xenophobia, 227–28

Young Turks, 78, 123, 124

Zapatero, José Luis Rodríguez, 240
Zionism, 186